EXPOSITORY DISCOURSES ON GENESIS

ANDREW FULLER
Author of *A Heart for Missions* and *The Backslider*

SOLID GROUND CHRISTIAN BOOKS
BIRMINGHAM, ALABAMA USA

OTHER SOLID GROUND TITLES

We recently celebrated our eighth anniversary of uncovering buried treasu to the glory of God. During these eight years we have produced over 2: volumes. A sample is listed below:

Biblical & Theological Studies: *Addresses to Commemorate the 100th Anniversary of Princeton Theological Seminary in 1912* by Allis, Machen, Wilson Vos, Warfield and many more.

Notes on Galatians by J. Gresham Machen

The Origin of Paul's Religion by J. Gresham Machen

A Scientific Investigation of the Old Testament by R.D. Wilson

Theology on Fire: *Sermons from Joseph A. Alexander*

Evangelical Truth: *Sermons for the Family* by Archibald Alexander

A Shepherd's Heart: *Pastoral Sermons of James W. Alexander*

Grace & Glory: *Sermons from Princeton Chapel* by Geerhardus Vos

The Lord of Glory by Benjamin B. Warfield

The Person & Work of the Holy Spirit by Benjamin B. Warfield

The Power of God unto Salvation by Benjamin B. Warfield

Calvin Memorial Addresses by Warfield, Johnson, Orr, Webb…

The Five Points of Calvinism by Robert Lewis Dabney

Annals of the American Presbyterian Pulpit by W.B. Sprague

The Word & Prayer: *Classic Devotions from the Pen of John Calvin*

A Body of Divinity: *Sum and Substance of Christian Doctrine* by Ussher

The Complete Works of Thomas Manton (in 22 volumes)

A Puritan New Testament Commentary by John Trapp

Exposition of the Epistle to the Hebrews by William Gouge

Exposition of the Epistle of Jude by William Jenkyn

Lectures on the Book of Esther by Thomas M'Crie

Lectures on the Book of Acts by John Dick

To order any of our titles please contact us in one of three ways:

Call us at **1-866-789-7423**
Email us at **sgcb@charter.net**
Visit our website at **www.solid-ground-books.com**

EXPOSITORY DISCOURSES

ON

THE BOOK OF

GENESIS,

INTERSPERSED WITH

PRACTICAL REFLECTIONS.

BY ANDREW FULLER.

VOL. I.

Printed by J. W. Morris, Dunstable,
FOR J. BURDITT, 60, PATERNOSTER-ROW,
London:
SOLD ALSO BY W. BUTTON, 24, PATERNOSTER-ROW; WILLIAMS AND SMITH, STATIONERS' COURT; AND T. GARDINER, PRINCES STREET.

1806.

Solid Ground Christian Books
PO Box 660132
Vestavia Hills AL 35266
205-443-0311
sgcb@charter.net
solid-ground-books.com

Expository Discourses on the Book of Genesis
by Andrew Fuller (1754 – 1815)

First Solid Ground Paperback Edition June 2009

Taken from the 1806 edition published by
J. Burditt, London

Cover design by Borgo Design, Tuscaloosa, AL

Cover image is entitled *The Trial of Abraham's Faith*, which is taken from "The Dore Bible Illustrations"

ISBN: 978-159925-213-1

TO THE

BAPTIST CHURCH OF CHRIST

AT

KETTERING.

My dear brethren,

It is now upwards of twenty-two years since I first took the oversight of you in the Lord. During the last fifteen years, it has, as you know, been my practice to expound amongst you on a Lord's-day morning some part of the holy Scriptures, commonly a chapter. From all that I have felt in my own mind, and heard from you, I have reason to hope these exercises have not been in vain. They have enabled us to take a more connected view of the scriptures than could be obtained merely by sermons on particular passages ; and I acknowledge that as I have proceeded, the work of exposition has become more and more interesting to my heart.

I have not been in the habit of writing Dedications to what I have published; but in this instance I feel inclined to deviate from my usual practice. Considering my time of life, and the numerous avocations on my hands, I may not be able to publish any thing more of the kind; and if not, permit me to request that this Family book may be preserved as a Memorial of our mutual affection, and of the pleasures we have enjoyed together in exploring the treasures of the lively oracles.

You will consider these discourses as the result of having *once* gone over that part of the scriptures to which they relate. Were we to go over it again, and again, such is the fulness of God's word, that we should still find interesting and important matter, which had never occurred in reading it before; and this should encourage us not to rest in any exposition, but to be constantly perusing the scriptures themselves, and digging at the precious ore.

As the Exposition was delivered in public worship, it was not my wish to dwell upon particular words, so much as to convey the general scope and design of the scriptures. Whether I have in any considerable degree caught the *spirit* which runs through them, is too much for me to decide: but this I can say, that such has been my aim. I know by experience, that, with respect to this, when I have been the most spiritually minded, I have succeeded the best; and therefore conclude, that if I had lived nearer to God, the work had been better executed. But such as it is, I commend it to the blessing of God, and your candid acceptance;

And remain,

Your affectionate Pastor,

THE AUTHOR.

KETTERING,
October 29. 1805.

CONTENTS.

VOL. I.

DISCOURSE I.
Chap. i. 1—4.

Page.
On the book in general, and the first day's creation   1

DISCOURSE II.
Chap. i. 6—31.
On the five last days' creation - - - - - -   7

DISCOURSE III.
Chap. ii.
Creation reviewed - - - - - - - - - - 14

DISCOURSE IV.
Chap. iii. 1—7.
The fall of man - - - - - - - - - - 26

DISCOURSE V.
Chap. iii. 8—14.
The trial of the transgressors - - - - - - - 32

CONTENTS.

DISCOURSE VI.
Chap. iii. 15—24.
The curse of Satan including a blessing to man—Effects of the fall - - - - - - - - - - 40

DISCOURSE VII.
Chap. iv. 1—8.
The offerings of Cain and Abel - - - - - - 51

DISCOURSE VIII.
Chap. iv. 9—24.
Cain's punishment and posterity - - - - - - 58

DISCOURSE IX.
Chap. iv. 25, 26. and chap. v.
The generations of Adam - - - - - - - - 66

DISCOURSE X.
Chap. vi. 1—7.
The cause of the deluge - - - - - - - - 73

DISCOURSE XI.
Chap. vi. 8—22.
Noah finds favour with God, and is directed to build the ark - - - - - - - - - - - - - 80

DISCOURSE XII.
Chap. vii.
The Flood - - - - - - - - - - - - 93

DISCOURSE XIII.
Chap. viii.
The Flood (continued) - - - - - - - - 100

CONTENTS.

DISCOURSE XIV.
Chap. ix. 1—24.
God's covenant with Noah - - - - - - - 109

DISCOURSE XV.
Chap. ix. 25—27.
Noah's prophecy - - - - - - - - - - 118

DISCOURSE XVI.
Chap. x.
The generations of Noah - - - - - - - 125

DISCOURSE XVII.
Chap. xi. 1—9.
The confusion of tongues - - - - - - - 132

DISCOURSE XVIII.
Chap. xi. 10—32. xii. 1—4.
The generations of Shem, and the call of Abram - 145

DISCOURSE XIX.
Chap. xii. 6—20.
Abram dwelling in Canaan, and removing to Egypt on account of the famine - - - - - - - 155

DISCOURSE XX.
Chap. xiii.
The separation of Abram and Lot - - - - - 159

DISCOURSE XXI.
Chap. xiv.
Abram's slaughter of the kings - - - - - - 167

CONTENTS.

DISCOURSE XXII.
Chap. xv. 1—6.
Abram justified by faith - - - - - - 180

DISCOURSE XXIII.
Chap. xv. 7—21.
Renewal of promises to Abram - - - - - 183

DISCOURSE XXIV.
Chap. xvi.
Sarai's crooked policy for the accomplishment of the promise - - - - - - - - - - 194

DISCOURSE XXV.
Chap. xvii.
God's covenant with Abram and his seed - - - 202

DISCOURSE XXVI.
Chap. xviii.
Abraham entertaining angels, and interceding for Sodom - - - - - - - - - - - 216

DISCOURSE XXVII.
Chap. xix.
The destruction of Sodom and Gomorrha - - - 226

DISCOURSE XXVIII.
Chap. xx.
Abraham and Abimelech - - - - - - - 238

DISCOURSE XXIX.
Chap. xxi.
The birth of Isaac, &c. - - - - - - - 245

DISCOURSE XXX.
Chap. xxii.
Abraham tempted to offer up his son Isaac - - 257

DISCOURSE XXXI.
Chap. xxiii.
The death and burial of Sarah - - - - - - 268

DISCOURSE XXXII.
Chap. xxiv. 1—28.
Abraham sending his servant to obtain a wife for Isaac - - - - - - - - - - - - - 273

DISCOURSE XXXIII.
Chap. xxiv. 29—67.
Abraham sending his servant to obtain a wife for Isaac (continued) - - - - - - - - - 283

DISCOURSE XXXIV.
Chap. xxv.
Abraham's marriage with Keturah, and death; Ishmael's posterity, and death; with the birth and characters of Esau and Jacob - - - - - - 295

DISCOURSE XXXV.
Chap. xxvi.
Isaac and Abimelech - - - - - - - - - 310

ERRATA.
P. 29. l. 22. for impolite, read *unpolite*.
53. l. 12. for that was, read that *which* was.

EXPOSITORY DISCOURSES,

&c.

DISCOURSE I.

ON THE BOOK IN GENERAL, AND THE FIRST DAY's CREATION.

GENESIS i. 1——4.

IT is common for the writers of other histories to go back in their researches as far as possible; but Moses traces his from "the beginning." The whole book is upon *the origin of things*, even of all things that had a beginning. The visible creation, the generations of man, moral evil among men, the spiritual kingdom of the Messiah, the new world, the church in the family of Abraham, the various nations and tribes of man; every thing, in short, now going on in the world may be traced hither as to its spring head. Without this history the world would be in total darkness, not knowing whence it came, nor whither it goeth. In the first page of this sacred book a child may learn more in an hour than all the philosophers in the world learned without it in thousands of years.

There is a majestic sublimity in the introduction. No apology, preamble, or account of the writer: you are introduced at once into the very heart of things. No vain conjectures about what was before time, nor *why* things were done thus and thus: but simply so it was.

In this account of the creation nothing is said on the *being of God:* this great truth is taken for granted. May not this apparent omission be designed to teach us, that those who deny the existence of a Deity are rather to be rebuked than reasoned with? All reasoning and instruction must proceed upon some principle or principles, and what can be more proper than this? Those writers who have gone about to prove it, have, in my opinion, done but little, if any good; and in many instances have only set men a doubting upon a subject which is so manifest from every thing around them, as to render the very heathens *without excuse.**

The foundation of this vast fabric is laid in an adequate cause—ELOHIM, *The Almighty.* No-

* Rom. i. 20.

thing else would bear it. Man, if he attempt to find an adequate cause for what is, to the overlooking of God, shall but weary himself with very vanity.

The writer makes use of the plural term *Elohim*, which yet is joined to singular verbs. This has been generally thought to intimate the doctrine of a plurality in the unity of the Godhead. It is certain, the scriptures speak of the Son, and holy Spirit, as concerned in creation, as well as the Father.* Nor can I on any other supposition affix a consistent meaning to such language as that which afterwards occurs: " Let *us* make man in *our* image, after *our* likeness—Behold, the man is become like *one of us*."

The account given by Moses relates not to the *whole creation*, but merely to what immediately concerns us to know. God made angels; but nothing is said of them. The moon is called one of the *greater* lights, not as to what it is in itself, but what it is *to us*. The scriptures are written not to gratify curiosity, but to nourish faith. They do not stop to tell you *how*, nor to answer a number of questions which might be asked; but tell you so much as is necessary, and no more.

* John i. 1. Gen. i. 2.

Ver. 1, 2. The first act of creations seem to have been *general*, and the foundation of all that followed. What the *heavens* were when first produced, previous to the creation of the sun, moon, and stars, did not greatly concern us to know, and therefore we are not told. What the *earth* was, we are informed in ver. 2. It was a chaos, " without form, and void;" a confused mass of earth and water, covered with darkness, and void of all those fruits which afterwards covered the face of it. As regeneration is called a *creation*, this may fitly represent the state of the soul while under the dominion of sin.—" The Spirit of God *moved* upon the face of the waters." The word signifies as much as brooded; and so is expressive of " an active, effectual energy, agitating the vast abyss, and infusing into it a powerful vital principle." Hence those lines of Milton:

> " And chiefly thou, oh SPIRIT———
> ————That with mighty wings outspread,
> Dove like, satt'st *brooding* on the vast abyss,
> And mad'st it pregnant."

Thus also God hath wrought upon the moral world, which, under sin, was without form, and void; and thus he operates upon every individual mind, causing it to bring forth fruit unto himself.

Gen. 1.] FIRST DAY'S CREATION. 5

Ver. 3. From a general account of the creation, the sacred writer proceeds to particulars; and the first thing mentioned is the production of *light*. The manner in which this is related has been considered as an example of the sublime. It expresses a great event in a few simple words, and exhibits the almighty God perfectly in character: *He speaks, and it is done; he commands, and it stands fast.* The work of the holy Spirit upon the dark soul of man is fitly set forth in allusion to this great act of creation: *God, who commanded the light to shine out of darkness, hath shined into our hearts, to give the light of the knowledge of the glory of God, in the face of Jesus Christ.** As soon might chaos have emerged from its native darkness, as our benighted world, or benighted souls, have found the light of life of their own accord. Nor was it sufficient to have furnished us with a revelation from heaven: the same almighty power that was necessary to give the one a being in the world, was necessary to give the other a being in the heart.

The *light* here mentioned was not that of the sun, which was created afterwards. From hence a late infidel writer has raised an objection against the scriptures, that they speak of *light*, and even

* 2 Cor. iv. 6.

of *night* and *day*, which are well known to arise from the situation of the earth towards the sun, before the sun was made. But he might as well have objected, that they speak of the *earth* in ver. 1, 2; and yet afterwards tell us of the dry land, as separated from the waters, constituting the earth. (ver. 9, 10.) The truth seems to be, that what the chaos was to the earth, that the light was to the sun: the former denotes the general principles of which the latter was afterwards composed. A flood of light was produced on the first day of creation; and on the fourth it was collected and formed into distinct bodies. And though these bodies when made, were to rule day and night; yet prior to this, day and night were ruled by the Creator's so disposing of the light and darkness as to *divide* them. (ver. 4.) That which was afterwards done ordinarily by the sun, was now done extraordinarily by the division of darkness and light.

Ver. 4. "God saw the light that it was good." Light is a wonderful creature, full of goodness to us. This is sensibly felt by those who have been deprived of it, either by the loss of sight, or by confinement in dungeons or mines. How pathetically does our blind poet lament the loss of it:

> "Seasons return; but not to me returns
> Day, or the sweet approach of ev'n or morn,
> Or sight of vernal bloom, or summer's rose,
> Or flocks, or herds, or human face divine:
> But cloud instead, and ever-during dark
> Surrounds me! From the cheerful ways of men
> Cut off; and for the book of knowledge fair,
> Presented with a universal blank
> Of nature's works, to me expunged and rased,
> And wisdom at one entrance quite shut out!"

If such be the value of material light, how much more of that which is mental and spiritual; and how much are we indebted to the holy Spirit of God for inditing the scriptures, and opening our benighted minds to understand them!

DISCOURSE II.

ON THE FIVE LAST DAY's CREATION.

GENESIS i. 6——31.

VER. 6—8. We here enter upon the second day, which was employed in making a *firmament* or *expanse*. It includes the atmosphere, and all that is visible, from the position of the sun, moon, and stars, down to the surface of the globe. ver. 14, 15, 20.

The *use* of it was to "divide the waters from the waters:" that is, the waters on the earth from the waters in the clouds, which are well known to be supported by the buoyant atmosphere. The "division" here spoken of is that of *distribution*. God having made the substance of all things, goes on to distribute them. By means of this the earth is watered by the rain of heaven, without which it would be unfruitful, and all its inhabitants perish. God makes nothing in vain. There is a grandeur in the firmament to the eye; but this is not all: usefulness is combined with beauty. Nor is it useful only with respect to animal subsistence: it is a mirror, conspicuous to all, displaying the glory of its Creator, and shewing his handy works.* The clouds also, by emptying themselves upon the earth, set us an example of generosity; and reprove those who, *full* of this world's good, yet keep it principally to themselves.†

Ver. 9—13. God having divided the heavens and the earth, he now on the third day proceeds to subdivide the earth, or chaos, into land and water. The globe became terraqueous; partly earth, and partly sea.

It is easy to perceive the goodness of God in this distribution. Important as earth and water

---

* Psal. xix. 1.   † Eccles. xi. 1—3.

both are, yet while mixed together they afford no abode for creatures: but separated, they are each a beautiful habitation, and each subserves the other. By means of this distribution the waters are ever in motion, which preserves them and almost every thing else from stagnancy and putrefaction. That which the circulation of the blood is to the animal frame, that the waters are to the world: were they to stop, all would stagnate and die.*—See how careful our heavenly Father was to build us a habitation before he gave us a being. Nor is this the only instance of the kind: our Redeemer has acted on the same principle, in going before to *prepare a place for us.*

Having fitted the earth for fruitfulness, God proceeds to clothe it with grass, and herbs, and trees of every kind. There seems to be an emphasis laid on every herb and tree "having its seed in itself." We here see the prudent foresight, if I may so speak, of the great Creator, in providing for futurity. It is a character that runs through all his works, that having communicated the first principles of things, they should go on to multiply and encrease; not independent of him, but as blessed by his con-

* Eccles. i. 7.

servative goodness. It is thus that true religion is begun and carried on in the mind, and in the world.

Ver. 14—19. After dividing this lower world, and furnishing it with the principles of vegetation, the Creator proceeded, on the fourth day, to the producing of the heavenly bodies. First, they are described in general as the " lights of heaven;" (ver. 14, 15.) and then more particularly, as the sun, moon, and stars. ver. 16—19.

The *use* of these bodies is said to be not only for dividing the day from the night, but " for signs and seasons, and days and years." They ordinarily afford *signs* of weather to the husbandman;* and prior to the discovery of the use of the loadstone, were of great importance to the mariner.† They appear also on some extraordinary occasions to have been premonitory to the world. Previous to the destruction of Jerusalem, our Lord foretold that there should be " great earthquakes in divers places, and famines, and pestilences, and fearful sights, and great *signs* from heaven.‡ And it is said by Josephus, that a comet like a flaming sword was seen for a long time over that devoted city,

* Matt. xvi. 3. † Acts xxvii. 20. ‡ Luke xxi. 11.

a little before its destruction by the Romans. Heathen astrologers made gods of these creatures, and filled the minds of men with chimerical fears concerning them. Against these God warns his people; saying, " Be ye not dismayed at the signs of heaven."* This however does not prove but that he may sometimes make use of them. Modern astronomers, by accounting for various phenomena, would deny their being signs of any thing: but to avoid the superstitions of heathenism, there is no necessity for our running into atheism.

The heavenly bodies are also said to be for *seasons*, as winter and summer, day and night. We have no other standard for the measuring of time. The grateful vicissitudes also which attend them are expressive of the *goodness* of God. If it were always day or night, summer or winter, our enjoyments would be unspeakably diminished. Well is it said at every pause, " And God saw that it was *good!*"

David improved this subject to a religious purpose.† He considered " day unto day as uttering speech, and night unto night as shewing knowledge." Every night we retire we are

* Jer. x. 2.   † Psal. xix.

reminded of death, and every morning we arise of the resurrection. In beholding the sun also, " which as a bridegroom cometh out of his chamber, and rejoiceth as a strong man to run his race," we see every day a glorious example of the steady and progressive " path of the just, which shineth more, and more unto the perfect day."

Ver. 20—25. We are next led to review the animal creation; a species of being less resplendant, but not less useful than some of greater note. In one view, the smallest animal has a property belonging to it which renders it superior to the sun. It has life, and some degree of knowledge. It is worthy of notice too, that the creation begins with things without life, and proceeds to things possessing vegetative life, then to those which have animal life, and after that to man, who is the subject of rational life. This shews that life is of great account in the Creator's estimation, who thus causes the subject to rise upon us as we proceed.

Ver. 26—31. We are now come to the sixth and last day's work of creation, and which is of greater account to us than any which have gone before, as the subject of it is *man.*—We may observe,

1. That the creation of man is introduced differently from that of all other beings. It is described as though it were the result of a special counsel, and as though there were a peculiar importance attached to it: "God said, let us make man." Man was to be the lord of this lower world, under the great Supreme. On him would depend its future well-being. Man was to be a distinguished link in the chain of being; uniting the animal with the spiritual world, the frailty of the dust of the ground with the breath of the Almighty; and possessing that consciousness of right and wrong which should render him a proper subject of moral government.

2. Man was honoured in being made after his Creator's *image*. This is repeated with emphasis: "God created man in his own image; in the image of God created he him." The image of God is partly natural, and partly moral; and man was made after both. The former consisted in *reason,* by which he was fitted for dominion[*] over the creatures: the latter in *righteousness and true holiness,* by which he was fitted for communion with his Creator. The figure of his body, by which he was distinguished from all other creatures, was an emblem of his mind:

[*] James iii. 9.

"God made man upright." I remember once, on seeing certain animals which approached near to the human form, feeling a kind of jealousy, shall I call it, for the honour of my species. What a condescension then, thought I, must it be for the eternal God to stamp *his image* upon man!

"God made man upright." He knew and loved his Creator, living in fellowship with him, and the holy angels. Oh, how fallen! How is the gold become dim, and the most fine gold changed!

DISCOURSE III.

CREATION REVIEWED.

GENESIS ii.

This chapter contains a review of the creation, with the addition of some particulars; such as the institution of the sabbath, the place provided for man, the law given him, and the manner of the creation of woman.

Ver. 1. There is something impressive in this review: "*Thus* the heavens and the earth were finished, and all the host of them"—wisely, mightily, kindly, gradually, but perfectly. Man's work, especially when great, is commonly a work of ages. One lays the foundation, and another the top-stone; or what is worse, one pulls down what another had reared: but God finishes his work. "He is a rock, and his work is perfect."

Ver. 2, 3. The conclusion of so divine a work required to be celebrated, as well as the Creator adored, in all future ages: hence arose the institution of the sabbath. We are not to imagine that God was weary, or that he was unable to have made the whole in one day; but this was done for our example.

The keeping of a sabbath sacred for divine worship, has been a topic of much dispute. Some have questioned whether it was kept by the patriarchs, or before the departure of Israel from Egypt; supposing that Moses, who wrote the book of Genesis about that time, might be led to introduce God's resting from his works on the seventh day as a motive to enforce what was then enjoined upon them. But if there were social worship before the flood, and during the patriarchal ages, one should think there must be a time for it. We expressly read of time being divided into *weeks* during these ages:*

* Gen. xxix. 27, 28.

and as early as the flood, when Noah sent out the dove once and again from the ark, the term of "seven days" is noticed as the space between the times of sending her.* Add to this, the division of time into weeks is said to have been very common in heathen nations in all ages; so that though they ceased to worship God, yet they retained what was a witness against them, the time of its celebration.

The sabbath was not only appointed for God, but to be *a day of rest for man*, particularly for the poor. It was enjoined on Israel for this reason, " That thy man servant and thy maid servant may rest as well as thou: and remember that thou wast a servant in the land of Egypt."† Those who would set it aside are no less the enemies of the poor, than of God and religion: they consult only their worldly interest. If such sordid characters could so order it, their servants would be always in the yoke. Nor would their being so in the least tend to increase their wages: every day's work would be worth a little less than it is now, and the week's work amount to much the same. To those who fear God it is also a rest to the *mind;* a time of refreshing, after the toils of worldly care and labour.‡

* Gen. viii. 10, 12.   † Deut. v. 14, 15.   ‡ Exod. xxxi. 17.

The *reason* for keeping the sabbath was drawn not only from God's having rested, but from the rest which Israel felt from the yoke of Egypt.* And we have since that time another reason; namely, " Christ having rested from his works, as God did from his."† Hence, according to the practice of the primitive christians, the day was altered:‡ and by how much more interesting the work of redemption is than that of creation, by so much is this reason greater than the other.

Finally: It is a jewish tradition, and seems to have generally prevailed, that as there is a harmony of times in the works of God, this seventh day of rest is prefigurative of the seven thousandth year of the world being a rest to the church. We know that years were divided into sevens, and seven times sevens. Every seventh year the land was to have its sabbath, and every fiftieth year its jubilee: and thus it may be with the world. If so, we are not at a great distance from it; and this will be the period when a great number of prophecies of the universal spread of the gospel shall be fulfilled.

Ver. 4—7. After reviewing the whole in general, and noticing the day of rest, the

---

* Deut. v. 14, 15. † Heb. iv. 4—10. ‡ Acts xx. 7.

sacred writer takes a special review of the vegetable creation, with an intent to mark the difference of its first production, and ordinary propagation. Plants are now ordinarily produced by rain upon the earth, and human tillage: but the first plants were made before there was any rain, or any human hand to till the ground. *After this*, a mist or vapour arose, which engendered rain, and watered the earth. (ver. 6.) So also *after this*, God formed man to till the ground. (ver. 7.) It is God's immediate work to communicate the first principles of things; but their growth is promoted by the instrumentality of man. And now, having made mention of man, he tells us of what he was made. His body was formed " of the dust of the ground." Humbling thought; and which was afterwards alleged in his doom.* His soul proceeded from the inspiration of the Almighty. What a wonderful compound is man! There seems to be something in the additional phrase: " And man became a living soul." God is said to breathe the breath of life into all animals; and we sometimes read of the *soul* of every living thing: but they are never said to *be* living souls, as men are. God hath stamped rationality and immortality upon men's souls, so as to render

* Gen. iii. 19.

them capable of a separate state of being, even when their bodies are dead. Hence the soul of a beast, when it dies, is said to go downward; but the soul of man upward.*

Ver. 8. Next we have an account of the *place* provided for man: not only the world at large, but a pleasant part of it. It was situated in the country of Eden, in Asia; probably among the mountains of the East. It was near the origin of several rivers, which always proceed from mountainous parts of the country. It is spoken of as rich and fruitful in a high degree, so as even to become proverbial.†

Ver. 9. Things were also adapted to *accommodate* man: trees and fruits for pleasure and use, are ready to his hand. Amongst the trees of Eden there were two in particular which appear to have been *symbolical*, or designed by the Creator to give instruction, in the manner which is done by our positive institutions. One was " the tree of life," to which he had free access. This was designed as a symbol to him of that life which stood connected with his obedience; and therefore when he sinned, he was debarred from eating it, by the flaming

---
* Eccles. xii. 7.   † Gen. xiii. 10. Isai. li. 3.

sword and cherubim, which stood every way to guard it. The other was "the tree of knowledge of good and evil," and which was the only tree of the fruit of which he was forbidden to eat. As the name of the first of these trees is given it from the effect which should follow obedience, so that of the last seems to have been from the effect which should follow on disobedience. Man on the day he should eat thereof should know good in a way of loss, and evil in a way of sufferance.

Ver. 10—14. Besides this, it was a well-watered garden. A river rose among the mountains of the country of Eden, which directed its course through it; and afterwards divided into four heads, or branches. Two of them are elsewhere mentioned in scripture; viz. the Hiddikel or Tigris, and the Euphrates, both rivers of Asia. With the others we are less acquainted.

Ver. 15. Among the provisions for man's happiness was *employment*. Even in innocence he was to *dress the garden, and keep it*. Man was not made to be idle. All things are full of labour: it is a stupid notion, that happiness consists in slothful ease, or in having nothing to do. Those who are so now, whether the very rich or the very poor, are commonly among the most worthless and miserable of mankind.

Ver. 16, 17. The trial of man by a special prohibition was singularly adapted to the end. To have conformed to his Creator's will, he must always have been contented with implicit obedience, or satisfied in abstaining from a thing on the mere ground of its being forbidden of God, without perceiving the *reason* of his being required to do so. In truth, it was a test of his continuing in the spirit of a little child, that should have no will of its own; and this is still the spirit of true religion.—The consequences attached to a breach of this positive law teach us also not to trifle with the will of God in his ordinances, but implicitly to obey it.

More particularly: Observe, (1.) The *fulness* of the grant. Here was enough for man's happiness, without the forbidden fruit; and so there is now in the world, without transgressing the boundaries of heaven.—(2.) The *positiveness* of the prohibition: "Thou shalt not eat of it." So long as this was kept in mind, it was well; and it appears to have been deeply impressed, from the first answer of the woman to the serpent.* It was this impression which he aimed to deface by his devilish question, "Yea, hath God said it?" And when once she began to doubt of this, all was over. Let us learn to keep God's words in our minds, and hide them in our hearts, that we may not sin against him. It was with thus and thus " it is written" that our Lord repelled all his temptations.—(3.) The *penalty* annexed: "thou shalt die," or "dying thou shalt die." Some think this means corporeal death, and that only; and that if the threatening had been executed, man must have been immediately struck out of existence. But the death here threatened, whatever it was, is said to have "passed upon all men," which implies the existence of all men, and which would have been prevented if Adam had at that time been reduced to a state of non-existence. The original constitution of things provided for the existence of every individual that has since been born into the world, and that whether man should stand or fall. The death here threatened doubtless included that of the body, and which God might execute at pleasure—the day he should eat, he would be dead in law. But it also included the loss of the divine favour, and an exposedness to his wrath. If it were not so,

* Gen. iii. 3.

the redemption of Christ would not be properly opposed to it, which it frequently is.* Nor is Adam to be considered as merely a private individual: he was the public head of all his posterity, so that his transgression involved their being transgressors from the womb, and alike exposed to death with himself. Such has been the character of all mankind; and such is the account of things given in the scriptures. If men now find fault with this part of the divine government, it is what they will not be able to stand to at the last day. The judge of all the earth will in that day appear to have done right, whatever may be thought of him at present.—
(4.) The *promise* of life implied by it. There is every reason to believe that if man had obeyed his Creator's will, he would of his own boundless goodness have crowned him with everlasting bliss. It is his delight to impart his own infinite blessedness as the reward of righteousness: if Adam, therefore, had abode in the truth, he and all his posterity should have enjoyed what was symbolically promised him by the tree of life. Nor is there any reason to suppose but that it would have been the same *for substance* as that which believers now enjoy through a Mediator: for the scriptures speak of that which the law

* Rom. v. 12—21. Heb. ix. 27, 28.

could not do, in that it was weak *through the flesh,* that is, through the corruption of human nature, as being accomplished by Christ.*

Ver. 18—25. The subject closes with a more particular account of the creation of woman. We had a general one before :† but now we are led to see the reasons of it.—Observe, (1.) It was not only for the propagation of the human race, but a most distinguished provision for human happiness. The woman was made " for the man :" not merely for the gratification of his appetites, but of his rational and social nature. It was not good that man should be alone ; and therefore a helper that should be " meet," or suitable, was given him. The place assigned to the woman in heathen and mahometan countries has been highly degrading ; and the place assigned her by modern infidels is not much better. Christianity is the only religion that conforms to the original design, that confines men to one wife, and that teaches them to treat her with propriety. Go you among the enemies of the gospel, and you shall see the woman either reduced to abject slavery, or basely flattered for the vilest of purposes : but in christian families you may see her treated with honour

---

* Rom. viii. 3, 4. † Gen. i. 27.

and respect; treated as a friend, as naturally an equal, a soother of man's cares, a softener of his griefs, and a partner of his joys.—(2.) She was made after the other creatures were named; and consequently, after Adam, having seen and observed all the animals, had found none of them a fit companion for himself, and thus felt the want of one. The blessings both of nature and grace are greatly endeared to us by our being suffered to feel the want of them before we have them.—(3.) She was made *out of man*, which should lead men to consider their wives as a part of themselves, and to love them as their own flesh. The woman was not taken, it is true, from the head; neither was she taken from the feet; but from somewhere near the heart!—(4.) That which was now done would be a standing law of nature. Man would "leave father and mother, and cleave to his wife, and they should be one flesh."—Finally: It is added, "They were both naked and were not ashamed." There was no guilt, and therefore no shame: shame is one of the fruits of sin.

DISCOURSE IV.

THE FALL OF MAN.

GENESIS iii. 1———7.

We have hitherto seen man as God created him, upright and happy. But here we behold a sad reverse; the introduction of moral evil into our world, the source of all our misery.

There can be no doubt but that the serpent was used as an instrument of Satan, who from hence is called "that *old serpent*, the devil." The subtilty of this creature might answer his purposes. The account of the serpent *speaking* to the woman might lead us to a number of curious questions, on which after all we might be unable to obtain satisfaction. Whether we are to understand this, or the temptations of our Lord in the wilderness, as spoken in an audible voice, or not, I shall not take upon me to decide. Whatever may be said of either case, it is certain from the whole tenor of scripture, that evil spirits have, by the divine permission, access to human minds: not so indeed as to be able to impel us to sin without our consent; but it may be in some such manner as men influence each others minds to evil. Such seems to be the proper idea of a tempter. We are conscious of *what we choose;* but are scarcely at all acquainted with the things that *induce* choice. We are exposed to innumerable influences; and have therefore reason to pray, " Lead us not into temptation, but deliver us from evil!"

With respect to the temptation itself, it begins by calling in question the *truth* of God ' Is it true, that God has prohibited any tree? Can it be? For what was it created?' Such are the enquiries of wicked men to this day. ' For what are the objects of pleasure made, (say they) but to be enjoyed? Why did God create meats and drinks, and dogs and horses?' What are appetites for, but to be indulged?' We might answer, among other things, to try them who dwell on the earth.

It seems also to contain an insinuation, that if man must not eat of " *every* tree," he might as well have eaten of none. And thus discontent continues to overlook the good, and pores upon the one thing wanting. "All this avails me nothing, so long as Mordecai is at the gate."

Ver. 2, 3. The answer of Eve seems to be very good at the outset. She very properly repels the insinuation against the goodness of

God, as though, because he had withheld one tree, he had withheld or might as well have withheld all. 'No, (says she) we may eat of the fruit of the trees of the garden; there is only one withheld.' She also, with equal propriety and decision, repelled the doubt which the tempter had raised respecting the prohibition of that one. The terms by which she expresses it shew how clearly she understood the mind of God, and what an impression his command had made upon her mind: "Of the fruit of this tree, God hath said, ye shall not eat of it; neither shall ye touch it, lest ye die!" We do not read that they were forbidden to *touch* it: but she understood a prohibition of eating to contain a prohibition of *touching*. And this exposition of the woman while upright affords a good rule to us. If we would shun evil, we must shun the *appearance* of it, and all the avenues which lead to it. To parley with temptation is to play with fire. In all this Eve sinned not, nor charged God foolishly.

Ver. 4, 5. The wily serpent now proceeds to a second attack. Mark the progress of the temptation. At the outset he only suggested his doubts; but now deals in positive assertion. In this manner the most important errors creep into the mind. He who sets off with apparently modest doubts, will often be seen to end in downright infidelity.

The positivity of the tempter might be designed to oppose that of the woman. She is peremptory; he also is peremptory, opposing assertion to assertion. This artifice of Satan is often seen in his ministers. Nothing is more common than for the most false and pernicious doctrines to be advanced with a boldness that stuns the minds of the simple, and induces a doubt: 'Surely I must be in the wrong, and they in the right, or they could not be so confident.'

Yet the tempter, it is observable, does not positively deny that God might have said so and so; for this would have been calling in question the veracity of Eve, or denying what she knew to be true, which must have defeated his end. But he insinuates, that whatever God might have said, which he would not now dispute, *it would not in the end prove so.* Satan will not be so impolite as to call in question either the honour or the understanding of Eve, but scruples not to make God a liar: yea, and has the impudence to say that *God knew* that instead of proving an evil, it would be a benefit. Alas, how often has man been flattered by the ministers of Satan at God's expense! Surely we need not be at a loss in judging whence those doctrines proceed which invalidate the divine threatenings, and teach sinners, going on still in their trespasses, " Ye shall not surely die." Nor those which lead men to consider the divine prohibitions as aimed to diminish their happiness, or, which is the same thing, to think them rigid or hard, that we should be obliged to comply with them. And those doctrines which flatter our pride, or provoke a vain curiosity to pry into things unseen, proceed from the same quarter. By aspiring to be a god, man became too much like a devil; and where human reason takes upon itself to set aside revelation, the effects will continue to be much the same.

Ver. 6. This poison had effect .... the woman paused .... looked at the fruit .... it began to appear desirable .... she felt a wish to be *wise* .... in short, she took of the fruit .... and did eat! But was she not alarmed when she had eaten? It seems not; but, feeling no such consequences follow as she perhaps expected, ventured even to persuade her husband to do as she had done; and with her persuasion he complied. The connexion between sin and misery is *certain*, but not always *immediate*: its immediate effect is deception, and stupefaction, which commonly induce the party to draw others into the same condition.

It does not appear that Adam was deceived; but the woman only.* He seems to have sinned with his eyes open; and perhaps from love to his wife. It was the first time, but not the last, in which Satan has made use of the nearest and tenderest parts of ourselves to draw our hearts from God. Lawful affection may become a snare. If the nearest relation or friend tempt us to depart from God, we must not hearken. When the woman had sinned against God, it was the duty of her husband to have disowned her for ever, and to have left it to his Creator to provide for his social comfort: but a fond attachment to the creature overcame him. He "hearkened to her voice," and plunged headlong into her sin.

Ver. 7. And now, having both sinned, they begin to be sensible of its effects. Conscious innocence has forsaken them. Conscious guilt, remorse, and shame possess them. Their " eyes are now opened" indeed, as the tempter had said they would be; but it is to "sights of woe." Their naked bodies, for the first time, excite

* 1 Tim. ii. 14.

shame; and are emblems of their souls, which, stripped of their original righteousness, are also stripped of their honour, security, and happiness.

To hide their outward nakedness, they betake themselves to the " leaves of the garden." This, as a great writer observes, was " to cover, not to cure." And to what else is all the labour of sinners directed? Is it not to *conceal* the bad, and to *appear* what they are not, that they are continually studying and contriving? And being enabled to impose upon one another, they with little difficulty impose upon themselves, " trusting in themselves that they are righteous, and despising others." But all is mere shew; and when God comes to summon them to his bar, will prove of no account.

DISCOURSE V.

THE TRIAL OF THE TRANSGRESSORS.

GENESIS iii. 8----14.

Ver. 8. We have seen the original transgression of our first parents; and now we see them called to account, and judged. The Lord God is represented as " walking in the garden in the *cool* of the day," that is in the evening.

This seems to denote the ordinary and intimate communion which man enjoyed with his Maker, while he kept his first estate. We may be at a loss in forming an idea how God could *walk* in the garden, and how he *spake;* but he was not at a loss how to hold communion with them that loved him. To accommodate it to our weak capacities, it is represented under the form of the owner of a garden taking his evening walk in it, to see, as we should say, " how the vine flourished, and the pomegranate budded;" to see and converse with those whom he had placed over it.

"The cool of the day," which to God was the season for visiting his creatures, may, as it respects man, denote a season of *reflection*. We may sin in the day time; but God will call us to account at night. Many a one has done that in the *heat* and bustle of the day, which has afforded bitter reflection in the *cool* of the evening; and such in many instances has proved the evening of life.

The *voice* of God was heard, it seems, before any thing was seen: and as he appears to have acted towards man in his usual way, and as though he knew of nothing that had taken place till he had it from his own mouth, we may consider this as the voice of kindness, such, whatever it was, as he had used to hear beforetime, and on the first sound of which he and his companion had been used to draw near, as sheep at the voice of the shepherd, or as children at the voice of a father. The voice of one whom we love conveys life to our hearts: but alas, it is not so now! Not only does conscious guilt make them afraid, but contrariety of heart to a holy God renders them averse to drawing near to him. The kindest language to one who is become an enemy will work in a wrong way. " Let favour be shewed to the wicked, yet will he not learn righteousness: in the land of uprightness will he deal unjustly, and will not behold the majesty of the Lord."* Instead of coming at his call as usual, they " hide themselves from his presence among the trees of the garden." Great is the *cowardice* which attaches to guilt. It flies from God, and from all approaches to him in prayer or praise; yea, from the very thoughts of him, and of death and judgment when they must appear before him.— But wherefore flee to the trees of the garden? Can they screen them from the eyes of Him with whom they have to do? Alas, they could not hide themselves and their nakedness from

* Isai. xxvi. 10.

their own eyes; how then should they elude discovery before an omniscient God! But we see here to what a stupid and besotted state of mind sin had already reduced them.

Ver. 9. God's general voice of kindness receiving no answer, he is more particular; calling Adam *by name*, and enquiring, "Where art thou?" In vain does the sinner hide himself: the Almighty will find him out! If he answer not to the voice of God in his word, he shall have a special summons served upon him before it be long! Observe what the summons was: *Where art thou?* It seems to be the language of injured friendship. As if he should say, 'How is it that I do not meet thee as heretofore? What have I done unto thee; and wherein have I wearied thee? Have I been a barren wilderness, or a land of drought? How is it that thou hailest not my approach as on former occasions?' It was also language adapted to lead him to reflection. *Where art thou?* Ah, where indeed! God is thus interrogating sinful men. Sinner, where art thou? What is thy condition? In what way art thou walking, and whither will it lead thee?

Ver. 10. To this trying question man is compelled to answer. See with what ease God can bring the offender to his bar. He has only to speak, and it is done. "He shall call to the heavens and the earth, that he may judge his people." But what answer can be made to him? "I heard thy voice in the garden." Did you? Then you cannot plead ignorance. No, but something worse! "I was afraid, because I was naked, and I hid myself." Take notice, he says nothing about his *sin*, but merely speaks of its *effects;* such as fear, and conscious nakedness, or guilt. The language of a contrite spirit would have been, *I have sinned!* But this is the language of *impenitent misery.* It is of the same nature as that of Cain: "My punishment is heavier than I can bear!" This spirit is often apparent in persons under first convictions, or when brought low by adversity, or drawing near to death; all intent on bewailing their misery, but insensible to the evil of their sin. To what a condition has sin reduced us! Stripped naked to our shame, we are afraid to meet the kindest and best of Beings! Oh reader! We must now be clothed with a better righteousness than our own, or how shall we stand before him?

Ver. 11. Adam began, as I have said, with the *effects* of his sin; but God directed him to its *cause.* 'Naked! q. d. How came such a thought into thy mind? The nakedness of thy body, with which I created thee, was no nakedness: neither fear nor shame attached to that. What meanest thou by being naked?' Still there is no confession. The truth will not come out without a direct enquiry on the subject. Here then it follows—" Hast thou eaten of the tree whereof I commanded thee that thou shouldst not eat?" Thus the sinner stands convicted. Now we might suppose he would have fallen at the feet of his Maker, and have pleaded guilty: ' Yes, Lord; yes! This is the cause!' But oh, the hardening nature of sin!

Ver. 12. Here is, it is true, a confession of his sin. It comes out at last, *I did eat;* but with what a circuitous, extenuating preamble, a preamble which makes bad worse. The first word is, "The woman," aye the woman; it was not my fault, but her's. The woman whom "thou gavest to be with me"—It was not ~~me~~; it was *thou thyself!* If thou hadst not given me this woman to be with me, I should have continued obedient. Nay, and as if he suspected that the Almighty did not notice his plea sufficiently, he repeats it emphatically: "*She* gave me, and I did eat!" Such a confession was infinitely worse than none. Yet such is the spirit of fallen man to this day. It was not ~~me~~.... it was my wife, or my husband, or my acquaintance, that persuaded me; or it was my situation in life, in which *thou* didst place me! Thus " the foolishness of man perverteth his way, and his heart fretteth against the Lord."*

It is worthy of notice that God makes *no answer* to these perverse excuses. They were unworthy of an answer. The Lord proceeds, like an aggrieved friend who would not multiply words: ' I see, (q. d.) how it is: stand aside!'

Ver. 13. Next the woman is called, and examined. *What is this that thou hast done?* The question implies that it was no trifling thing; and the effects which have followed, and will follow, confirm it. But let us hear the woman's answer. Did she plead guilty? The circumstance of her being first in the transgression, and the tempter of her husband, one should have thought, would have shut her mouth at least; and being also of the weaker sex, it might have been expected that she would not have gone on to provoke the vengeance of her Creator. But lo, she also shifts the blame—*The serpent beguiled me, and I did eat.* ' I was deceived. I did not mean evil; but was drawn into it through the wiles of an evil being.' Such is the excuse which

* Prov. xix. 3.

multitudes make to this day, when they can find no better; 'the devil tempted me to it!' Still God continues his forbearance, makes no answer; but orders her, as it were, to stand aside.

Ver. 14. And now the serpent is addressed: but mark the difference. Here is no question put to him, but merely a doom pronounced. Wherefore? Because no mercy was designed to be shewn him. He is treated as an avowed and sworn enemy. There was no doubt *wherefore* he had done it, and therefore no *reason* is asked of his conduct.

The workings of conviction in the minds of men are called the " strivings of the Spirit," and afford a hope of mercy. Though they are no certain sign of grace received, (as there was nothing good at present in our first parents) yet they are the workings of a merciful God, and prove that he has not given over the sinner to hopeless ruin. But the serpent has nothing to expect but a fearful looking for of judgment.

The form under which Satan is cursed is that of *the serpent*. To a superficial reader it might appear that the vengeance of heaven was directed against the animal, distinguishing him from all cattle, subjecting him to a most abject life, condemning him to creep upon his belly, and of course to have his food besmeared with dust. But was God angry with the serpent? No: but as under that form Satan had tempted the woman, so that shall be the form under which he shall receive his doom. The spirit of the sentence appears to be this—' Cursed art thou above all creatures, and above every being that God hath made. Miserable shalt thou be to an endless duration!' Some have thought, and the passage gives some countenance to the idea, that the state of fallen angels was not hopeless till now. If it had, the curse could only have added a greater degree of misery.

DISCOURSE VI.

THE CURSE OF SATAN INCLUDING A BLESSING TO MAN— EFFECTS OF THE FALL.

GENESIS iii. 15——24.

VER. 15. By all that had hitherto been said and done, God appears to have concealed from man who was his tempter; and for this reason among others, to have pronounced the doom on Satan under the form of a curse upon the serpent. By this we may learn, that it is of no account as to the criminality of sin, whence it comes, or by whom or what we are tempted to it. If we choose it, it is *ours;* and we must be accountable for it.

But mark the wisdom and goodness of God: as under the form of cursing the serpent, he had pronounced a most tremendous doom on the tempter, so under the form of this doom is covertly intimated a design of mercy the most transcendent to the tempted! If man had been in a suitable state of mind, the promise might have been *direct,* and addressed to him: but he was not; for his heart, whatever it might be afterwards, was as yet hardened against God. It was fit therefore, that whatever designs of mercy were entertained concerning him, or his posterity, they should not be given in the form of a promise to *him,* but of threatening to Satan. The situation of Adam and Eve at this time was like that of sinners under the preaching of the gospel. The intimation concerning the Woman's Seed would indeed imply that she and her husband should live in the world, that she should bring forth children, and that God would carry on an opposition to the cause of evil; but it does not ascertain *their salvation:* and if there appear nothing more in their favour in the following part of the history than what has hitherto appeared, we shall have no good ground to conclude that either of them are gone to heaven. The Messiah might come as the Saviour of sinners, and might descend from them after the flesh; and yet they might have no portion in him.

But let us view this famous passage more particularly, and that in the light in which it is here represented, as *a threatening to the serpent.* This threatening does not so much respect the *person* of the grand adversary of God and man, as his *cause* and *kingdom* in this world. He will be punished in his person at the time appointed; but this respects the manifestation of the Son of God to destroy his *works.*—There are four things here intimated which are each worthy of notice.—(1.) The ruin of Satan's cause was to be accomplished by *one in human nature.* This must have been not a little mortifying to his pride. If he must fall, and could have had his choice as to the mode, he might rather have wished to have been crushed by the immediate hand of God: for however terrible that hand might be, it would be less humiliating than to be subdued by one of a nature inferior to his own. The human nature especially appears to have become odious in his eyes. It is possible that the rejoicings of eternal wisdom over man was known in heaven, and first excited his envy; and that his attempt to ruin the human race was an act of revenge. If so, there was a peculiar fitness that from *man* should proceed his overthrow.—(2.) It was to be accomplished by the seed of the *woman*. This would be more humiliating still. Satan had made use of her to accomplish his purposes, and God would defeat his schemes through the same medium: and by how much he had despised and abused her, in making her the instrument of drawing her husband aside, by so much would he be mortified in being overcome by one of her descendents.—(3.) The victory should be obtained not only by the Messiah himself, but by all his adherents. The seed of the woman, though it primarily referred to him, yet being opposed to "the seed of the serpent," includes all that believe in him. And there is little or no doubt that the account in Rev. xii. 17 has allusion to this passage—"And the dragon was wroth with the woman, and went to make war with the remnant of her seed, who keep the commandments of God, and the faith of Jesus." Now if it were mortifying for Satan to be overcome by the Messiah himself, considered as the seed of the woman, how much more when in addition to this every individual believer shall be made to come near, and as it were set his feet upon the neck of his enemy?—Finally: though it should be a long war, and the cause of the serpent would often be successful, yet in the end it should be utterly ruined. The "head" is the *seat of life,* which the "heel" is not: by this language therefore is intimated that the life of Christ's cause should not be affected by any part of Satan's opposition; but that the life of Satan's cause should by that of Christ. For this purpose is he manifested in human nature, that he may *destroy* the works of the devil: and he will never desist till he have utterly crushed his power.

Now as the threatenings against Babylon conveyed good news to the church, so this threatening against the old serpent is full of mercy to men. But for this enmity which God would put into the woman's seed against him, he would have had every thing his own way, and every child of man would have had his portion with him and his angels.

From the whole, we see that Christ is the foundation and substance of all true religion since the fall of man; and therefore, that the only way of salvation is by faith in him. We see also the importance of a decided attachment to him, and his interest. There are two great armies in the world, Michael, and his angels, warring against the dragon, and his angels; and according to the side we take, such will be our end.

Ver. 16—19. The sentence of the woman and of the man which follows, like the rest, is under a veil. Nothing but temporal evils are mentioned: but these are not the whole. Paul teaches us that by the offence of one, judgment came upon all men to *condemnation;* and such a condemnation as stands opposed to *justification of life.** The woman's load in this life was *sorrow in bearing children,* and *subjection to her husband.* The command to be fruitful and multiply might originally, for ought I know, include some degree of pain; but now it should be *greatly multiplied:* and there was doubtless a natural subordination in innocency; but through sin woman becomes comparatively a slave. This is especially the case where sin reigns uncontrolled, as in heathen and mahometan countries. Christianity however, so far as it operates, counteracts it; restoring woman to her original state, that of a friend and companion. (See on ch. ii. 18—25.) The sentence on *man* points out to him wherein consisted his sin; viz. in hearkening to the voice

---

* Rom. v. 18. See the note on ch. iv. 11, 12.

of his wife, rather than God. What a solemn lesson does this teach us against loving the creature more than the Creator, and hearkening to any counsel to the rejection of his. And with respect to his punishment, it is worthy of notice that as that of Eve was common to her daughters, so that of Adam extends to the whole human race. The *ground* is cursed for his sake, cursed with barrenness. God would, as it were, take no delight in blessing it; as well he might not, for all would be perverted to, and become the food of rebellion. The more he should bless the earth, the more wicked would be its inhabitants. He also himself is doomed to wretchedness upon it: he should drag on the few years that he might live in sorrow and misery, of which the *thorns and thistles,* which it should spontaneously produce, were but emblems. God had given him before to eat of *the fruit of the trees of the garden;* but now he must be expelled from thence, and take his portion with the brutes, and live upon *the herb of the field.* He was allowed *bread;* but it should be by the *sweat of his face:* and this is the lot of the great body of mankind. The end of this miserable state of existence was, that he should *return to* his native *dust.* Here the sentence leaves him. A veil is at present drawn over a future world: but we elsewhere learn that at what time " the flesh returns to dust, the spirit returns to God who gave it;" and that the same sentence which appointed man "once to die," added, "but after this the judgment."*

It is painful to trace the different parts of this melancholy sentence, and their fulfilment in the world to this day: yet there is a bright side even to this dark cloud. Through the promised Messiah a great many things pertaining to the curse are not only counteracted, but become blessings. Under his glorious reign, " the earth shall yield its increase, and God, our own God, delight in blessing us." And while its fruitfulness is withheld, it has a merciful tendency to stop the progress of sin: for if the whole earth were like the plains of Sodom in fruitfulness, which are compared to the garden of God, its inhabitants would be as Sodom and Gomorrha in wickedness. The necessity of hard labour too in obtaining a subsistence, which is the lot of the far greater part of mankind, tends more than a little, by separating men from each other, and depressing their spirits, to restrain them from the excesses of evil. All the afflictions of the present life contain in them a motive to look upwards for a better portion: and death itself is

* Heb. ix. 27.

a monitor to warn them to prepare to meet their God. These are things suited to a *sinful* world: and where they are sanctified, as they are to believers in Christ, they become real blessings. To them they are light afflictions, and last but for a moment; and while they do last, "work for them a far more exceeding and eternal weight of glory." To them, in short, death itself is introductory to everlasting life.

Ver. 20. Adam's wife seems hitherto to have been known only by the name of *woman;* but now he calls her *Eve,* i. e. *life, living,* or *the mother of all living.* He might possibly have understood from the beginning that the sentence of death would not prevent the existence of the human race; or if not, what had been said of the woman's seed would at least satisfy him on this subject. But it is generally supposed, and there seems to be ground for the supposition, that in calling his wife *life,* or *living,* he intended more than that she would be the mother of all mankind; that it is expressive of his faith in the promise of her victorious Seed destroying what Satan had accomplished in introducing *death,* and that thus she should be the means of immortal *life* to all who should live in him. If such were his meaning, we may consider this

EFFECTS OF THE FALL.

as the first evidence in favour of his being renewed in the spirit of his mind.

Ver. 21. By the coats of skins wherewith the Lord God clothed them, it seems to be implied that animals were slain; and as they were not at that time slain for food, it is highly probable they were slain for sacrifice; especially as this practice is mentioned in the life of Abel. Sacrifices therefore appear to have been ordained of God to teach man his desert, and the way in which he must be saved. It is remarkable that the clothing of Adam and Eve is ascribed to *the Lord God*, and that it appears to have succeeded the slender covering wherewith they had attempted to cover themselves. Is it not natural to conclude, that God only can hide our moral nakedness, and that the way in which he doth it is by covering us with the righteousness of our atoning sacrifice?

Ver. 22. This ironical reflexion is expressive of both indignation and pity. 'Man is become wonderfully wise! Unhappy creature! He has for ever forfeited my favour, which is life; and having lost the thing signified, let him have no access to the sign. He has broken my covenant: let neither him nor his posterity from henceforward expect to regain it by any obedience of theirs.'*

Ver. 23, 24. God is determined that man shall not so much as dwell in the garden where the tree of life grows; but be turned out, as into the wide world. He shall no longer live upon the delicious fruits of Eden, but be driven to seek his food among the beasts of the field: and to shew the impossibility of his ever regaining that life which he had lost, *cherubim and a flaming sword* are placed to guard it. Let this suffice to impress us with that important truth: " by the deeds of the law shall no flesh living be justified," and to direct us to a tree of life which has no flaming sword to prevent our access! Yet even in this, as in the other threatenings, we may perceive a mixture of mercy. Man had rendered his days *evil*, and God determines they shall be but *few*. It is well for us that a life of sin and sorrow is not immortal.

* See on ch. ii. 9.

DISCOURSE VII.

THE OFFERINGS OF CAIN AND ABEL.

GENESIS iv. 1——8.

Having seen the origin of sin in our world, we have now the origin and progress of things as they at present are amongst mankind, or of the world as it now is.

Ver. 1. Adam has a son by his wife, who is called Cain; viz. *a possession,* or *acquisition:* for said Eve, *I have gotten a man from the Lord!* Many learned men have rendered it, *a man, the Lord;* and it is not very improbable that she should understand *the seed of the woman,* of her immediate offspring: but if so, she was sadly mistaken! However it expresses what we have not seen before, i. e. Eve's *faith* in the promise. Even though she should have had no reference to the Messiah, yet it shews that she eyed God's hand in what was given her; and viewed it as a great blessing, especially considering what a part she had acted. In this she sets an example to parents, to reckon their children *an heritage* *from the Lord.* But she also affords an example of the uncertainty of human hopes. Cain, so far from being a comfort to his parents, proved a wicked man; yea, a pattern of wickedness, held up like Jeroboam, the son of Nebat, as a warning to others—*Not as Cain, who was of that wicked one, and slew his brother!** The joys attending the birth of a child require to be mixed with trembling; for who knoweth whether he shall be a wise man, or a fool?

Ver. 2. Eve bears Adam another son, who was called *Abel,* or *Hebel.* In these names we probably see the partiality of parents to their first-born children. Abel signifies *vanity,* or *a vanishing vapour.* Probably he was not so goodly a child in appearance as Cain, and did not seem likely to live long. The heart and hopes of the parents did not seem to centre in him, but in his brother. But God seeth not as man seeth. In bestowing his blessing he has often crossed hands, as Jacob did in blessing Ephraim and Manasseh. He chooseth the base things of the world, that no flesh should glory in his presence.—These two brothers were of different occupations; one a husbandman, and the other a shepherd: both primitive employments, and both very proper.

---

* 1 John iii. 12.

Gen. 4.] CAIN AND ABEL. 53

Ver. 3—5. In process of time the two brothers each present his offering to God: this speaks something in favour of their parents who had brought them up in the nurture and admonition of the Lord. Ainsworth renders it, " at the end of the days," and understands it at the end of the year, which was then in Autumn, the time of the gathering in of the harvest and the vintage. The institution of a solemn feast among the Israelites on this occasion, (Exod. xxiii. 16.) seems therefore to have borne a near resemblance to that was practised from the beginning.

In the offerings of these two first-born sons of man, we see the essential difference between spiritual worship and that which is merely formal. As to the *matter* of which their offerings were composed, it may be thought there was nothing particularly defective; each brought what he had. There is indeed no mention made of Cain's being of the *best* of the kind, which is noticed of Abel's. And if he neglected this, it was a sign that his heart was not much in it. He might also no doubt have obtained a lamb out of his brother's flock for an expiatory sacrifice. But the chief difference, is that which is noticed by the apostle: " *By faith* Abel offered a more excellent sacrifice than Cain." (Heb.

xi. 4.) Cain's offering was just what a self-righteous heart would offer: it proceeded on the principle that there was no breach between him and his Creator, so as to require any confession of sin, or respect to an atonement. Such offerings abound amongst us; but they are *without faith*, and therefore it is impossible they should please God. The offering of Abel I need not describe: suffice it to say, It was the reverse of that presented by Cain. It was the best of the kind; and included an expiatory sacrifice.

The result was, *the Lord had respect to Abel and to his offering: but unto Cain and his offering he had not respect*. The one was probably consumed by fire from heaven: the other not so. This we know was afterwards a common token of the divine acceptance. (Lev. ix. 24. Psal. xx. 3, margin.) The *order* of things is worthy of notice. God first accepted Abel, and then his offering. If he had been justified on the ground of his good deeds, the order should have been reversed: but believing in the Messiah, he was accepted for his sake; and being so, his works were well-pleasing in the sight of God. And as Abel was accepted as a believer; so Cain was rejected as an unbeliever. Being such, the Lord had no respect to him: he was under the curse, and all he did was abhorred in his eyes.

CAIN AND ABEL.

The rejection of Cain and his offering operated upon him very powerfully. If the love of God had been in him, he would have fallen before him, as Joshua and his brethren did when Israel was driven back; and have pleaded, " Shew me wherefore thou contendest with me?" But he *was wroth, and his countenance fell.* This is just what might be expected from a self-righteous, proud spirit, who thought so highly of his offering as to imagine that God must needs be pleased with it, and with him on account of it. He was "*very* wroth"—so Ainsworth; and that no doubt against God himself, as well as against his brother. He went in high spirits, like the pharisee to the temple; but came away dejected, and full of all foul passions, of which his "fallen countenance" was but the index.

Ver. 6, 7. Cain having returned home, the Lord, perhaps in a dream or vision of the night, expostulated with him. *Why art thou wroth?* What cause is there for this enmity against thy Maker, and envy against thy brother? Doubtless he thought that he had a cause; but when interrogated of God, he found none. *If thou doest well, shalt thou not be accepted? And unto thee shall be his desire, and thou shalt rule over him.* By *doing well* he means doing as Abel did, offering in faith, which is the only well-doing among sinful creatures. If Cain had believed in the Messiah, there was forgiveness for him no less than for his brother; and he should also have had the excellency attached to the first-born, which he reckoned he had a right to, and the loss of which galled him. *If thou doest not well, sin lieth at the door;* * unforgiven, to go down with thee to the grave, and to rise with thee, and appear against thee in judgment.

Observe how things are ordered in the dealings of God with men. Abel was not accepted of God *for* his well-doing; neither faith nor obedience was that on account of which he was justified; but the righteousness of him in whom he believed. Yet it was *in* well-doing that he obtained eternal life. (Rom. ii. 7.) Though faith was not the *cause* of the Lord's having respect to him, nor his having offered in faith, of his having respect to his works; yet each was a necessary concomitant. And this, while it secures the interests of righteousness in the righteous, serves to silence the wicked, and make them feel the justice of their condemnation. Thus at the last judgment, though every one who is

---

* This clause, which is in the middle of ver. 7, I suppose should be in a parenthesis. I have therefore placed the first and last in connexion, and introduced this after them, by which the sense is clear.

saved will be saved by grace only, yet all will be judged according to their works. Things will be so ordered that the righteous will have nothing to boast of, and the wicked nothing to complain of, inasmuch as the decision in both cases will proceed according to character.

But though Cain was silenced by the Almighty, yet his malice was not subdued, but rather inflamed. If the life of God had been within his reach, he would have killed him: but this he could not do. From that time therefore his dark soul meditated revenge upon Abel, as being God's favourite, his own rival, and the only object within his power. This is the first instance of the enmity of the Seed of the Serpent breaking out against the Seed of the Woman: but not the last! Observe the subtlety and treachery with which it was accomplished: *Cain talked with Abel his brother.* He talked with him, probably upon business, and in a very familiar manner, as though he had quite forgotten the affair which had lately hurt his mind; and when they were engaged in conversation, persuaded him to take a walk with him into his field; and having got him away from the family, he murdered him! Oh, Adam, thou didst murder an unborn world; and now thou shalt see some of the fruits of it in thine own family! Thou hast never before witnessed a human death: go, see the first victim of the king of terrors in the mangled corps of Abel thy son!—Poor Abel! Shall we pity him? In one view we must; but in others he is an object of envy. He was the first of the noble army of martyrs, the first of human kind who entered the abodes of the blessed, and the first instance of death being rendered subservient to Christ. When the serpent had drawn man into sin, and exposed him to its threatened penalty, he seemed to have obtained *the power of death:* and had man been left under the ruins of the fall, he would have been continually walking through the earth, arm in arm, as it were, with the monster, the one taking the bodies and the other the souls of men. But the Woman's Seed is destined to overcome him. " By death he destroyed him who had the power of death, and delivered them who must otherwise, through fear of death, have been all their life time subject to bondage." Heb. ii. 14, 15.

DISCOURSE VIII.

CAIN's PUNISHMENT AND POSTERITY.

GENESIS iv. 9——24.

VER. 9. We have seen the tragical end of righteous Abel; but what becomes of the murderer? Probably he had hid the dead body of his brother, to elude detection: but God will find him out. Jehovah said unto Cain, *Where is Abel, thy brother?* What a cutting question! The words *thy brother* would remind him of the tender ties of flesh and blood which he had broken; and if he had any feeling of conscience left in him, must pierce him to the quick. But oh, how black, how hardened is the state of his mind! Mark his answer. First, the falsehood of it—*I know not.* We feel astonished that a man can dare to lie in the presence of his Maker: yet how many lies are uttered before him by formalists and hypocrites! Secondly, the insolence of it—*Am I my brother's keeper?* This man had no fear of God before his eyes: and where this is wanting, regard to man will be wanting also.* Even natural affection will be swallowed up in selfishness. Supposing he had not known where his brother was, it did not follow that he had no interest in his preservation: but he did know, and instead of being his keeper, had been his murderer!

Ver. 10. *And he said, What hast thou done?* Ah, what indeed! This was the question put to Eve: this question will be put to every sinner sooner or later, and conscience must answer to it too! But Cain refuses to speak. Be it so; there needs no confession to substantiate his

* Luke xviii.

guilt. His *brother's blood* had already done this! *Blood* has a voice that will speak; yea, that will *cry to heaven from the ground* for vengeance on him who sheds it; and a *brother's* blood especially.—What a scene will open to view at the last judgment, when the earth shall disclose her blood, and shall no more cover her slain! And if such was the cry of Abel's blood, what must have been that of the blood which was shed on Calvary? We should have thought that blood must have called for vengeance seven-fold; and in one view it did so: but in another it speaks *better things than that of Abel.*

Ver. 11, 12. But let us notice the doom of Cain. He was cursed from the earth; it should in future refuse to yield him its wonted fruits, and he should be a fugitive and a vagabond in it. Three things are here observable:—First: By the sovereign will of the Lord of All, his life was spared. Afterwards a positive law was made by the same authority, that *whosoever should shed man's blood, by man should his blood be shed.* But at present, for reasons of state in the breast of the King of kings,* the murderer shall be

---

* If he had died by the hand of man, it must have been either by an act of private revenge, which would have encreased bloodshed; or Adam himself must have been the executioner of his son, from which trial of "quenching the coal that was left," God might graciously exempt him.

reprieved.—Secondly: The curse which attached to his life, like that of our first parents, is confined to the present state. There is no reason in the world to suppose that the punishment of such a crime would actually be so, any more than others, nor others any more than this; but a future life was at that time sparingly revealed, and almost every thing concealed under the veil of temporal good and evil.—Thirdly: It contains a special addition to that which was denounced on Adam. The earth was cursed to him; but Cain was *cursed from the earth.* It had been his brother's friend, by affording a kind of sanctuary for his blood which he had pursued; but to him it should be an enemy, not only refusing its wonted fruits, but even a place whereon to rest his foot, or in which to hide his guilty head!

Ver. 13, 14. This tremendous sentence draws forth an answer from the murderer. There is a great change since he spoke last, but not for the better. All the difference is, instead of his high tone of insolence, we perceive him sinking into the last stage of depravity, sullen desperation. Behold here a finished picture of impenitent misery. What a contrast to the fifty-first psalm! There the evil dwelt upon and pathetically lamented is sin; but here it is only punishment. See how he expatiates upon it.... Driven from the face of the earth.... deprived of God's favour and blessing, and in a sort, of the means of hope*.... a wanderer and an outcast from men .... to all which his fears add, 'Wherever I am, by night or by day, my life will be in perpetual danger!' Truly it was a terrible doom, a kind of hell upon earth. It is a fearful thing to fall into the hands of the living God!

Ver. 15. From the last part of what his fears foreboded, however, God was pleased to exempt him; yet not in mercy, but in judgment. He shall not die, but live, a monument of divine justice. If he had died, his example might soon have been forgotten: but mankind shall see and fear. *Slay them not, lest my people forget: scatter them by thy power, and bring them down, oh Lord!* (Psal. lix. 11.) God is not obliged to send a sinner to the place of the damned, in order to punish him: he can call his name Magormissabib, and render him a terror to himself and to all about him! (Jer. xx. 3, 4.) What the *mark* was which was set upon Cain, we know not, nor does it behove us to enquire: whatever it was, it amounted to a safe passage through the world,

---

* See verse 16.

so far as respected a punishment from man for his present crime.

Ver. 16. And now having obtained a reprieve, he retires in the true spirit of a reprobate, and tries to forget his misery. It shocked him at first to be driven out from God's face, by which perhaps he meant, from all connexion with the people and worship of God, from the means of grace, and so from the hope of mercy: but in a little time the sensation subsides, and he resolves to enjoy the present world as well as he can. He goes out *from the presence of the Lord*, takes a final leave of God and his worship, and his people, and cares no more about them. If this be the meaning of the words, (and I know of no other so probable) it wears a very favourable appearance with respect to the state of things in Adam's family. It shews that the worship of God was there carried on, and that God was with them. Indeed, if it were not carried on there, it appears to have had no existence in the world, which there is no reason to believe was ever the case when once it had begun. With respect to Cain, the country whither he went is called *Nod*, or *Naid*, which signifies *a vagabond*. It was not so called before, but on his account; as who should say, *the land of the vagabond*.

Ver. 17. He was married before this, though we are not told to whom. Doubtless it was to one of Adam's daughters, mentioned in chap. v. 4, which near affinity, though since forbidden, was then absolutely necessary. Of her, in the land of the vagabond, he had a son whom he called Enoch; not him who *walked with God*, but one of the same name. It signifies *taught*, or *dedicated:* it is rather difficult to account for his calling the child by this name, after what had taken place. Possibly it might be one of those effects of education which are often seen in the ungodly children of religious parents. When he himself was born, he was, as we have seen, accounted *an acquisition*, and was doubtless *dedicated*, and as he grew up *taught* by his parents. Of this it is likely he had made great account, priding himself in it, as many graceless characters do in being the children of the righteous: and now having a child of his own might wish to stamp upon him this mark of honour, though it was merely nominal.—After this, Cain built, or was building, a city: a very small one no doubt, as need required. He began what his family, as they encreased, perfected, and called after the name of his son. Thus he amused himself as well as he could. The divine forbearance probably hardened him in his security, as it commonly does the ungodly. *Because sentence against an evil work is not executed speedily, therefore the hearts of the sons of men are fully set in them to do evil.* Eccles. viii. 11.

Ver. 18—24. Next follow the generations of Cain, which present a few general observations.—(1.) Nothing good is said of any one of them; but heathen like, they appear to have lost all fear of God, and regard to man.—(2.) Two or three of them become famous for arts: one was a shepherd, another a musician, and another a smith; all very well in themselves, but things in which the worst of men may excel. Some have supposed that we are indebted to revelation for all this kind of knowledge. Had it been said, we are indebted to our Creator for it, it had been true; for to his instruction the discretion of the husbandman is ascribed. (Isai. xxviii. 26.) But revelation was given for greater and better objects; namely, to furnish not the man, but *the man of God.*—(3.) One of them was infamous for his wickedness, namely Lamech. He was the first who violated the law of marriage; a man giving loose to his appetites, and who lived a kind of lawless life. Among other evils he followed the example of his ancestor, Cain. It is not said who he slew; but he himself says it was *a young man.* This is the first instance, but not the last, in which sensuality and murder are connected. Nor did he barely follow Cain's example; but seems to have taken encouragement from the divine forbearance towards him, and to have presumed that God would be still more forbearing towards him. Thus one sinner takes liberty to sin from the suspension of judgment towards another.

Here ends the account of cursed Cain. We hear no more of his posterity, unless it be as tempters to *the sons of God,* till they were all swept away by the deluge!

DISCOURSE IX.

THE GENERATIONS OF ADAM.

GENESIS iv. 25, 26. AND CHAP. V.

We have of late met with little else than the operations of sin and misery: here I hope we shall find something that will afford us pleasure. Adam had lived to see grievous things in his family. At length, about 130 years after the creation, Eve bare him another son. Him his mother called *Seth;* i. e. set or appointed; *for God,* said she, *hath appointed me another seed instead of Abel, whom Cain slew.* The manner in which the mother of mankind speaks on this occasion is much in favour of her personal religion. The language implies, that though at first she had doted upon Cain, yet as they grew up, and discovered their dispositions, Abel was preferred. He was the child in whom all the hopes of the family seem to have concentrated; and therefore when he fell a sacrifice to his brother's cruelty, it was considered as a very heavy loss. She was not without a son before Seth was born, for Cain was yet alive: but he was considered as none, or as worse than none; and therefore when Seth was born, she hopes to find in him a successor to Abel: and so it proved; for this appears to have been the family in which the true religion was preserved in those times. At the birth of Enos, which was 105 years after that of his father Seth, it is remarked with emphasis by the sacred historian, THEN BEGAN MEN TO CALL UPON THE NAME OF THE LORD. This cheering information doubtless refers to the families in connexion with which it is spoken, and denotes, not that there had been no calling upon the Lord till that time, but that from thence the true religion assumed a more *visible* form; the Seed of the Woman, afterwards called *the sons of God*, assembling together to worship him, while the seed of the serpent might very probably be employed in deriding them.

From the genealogy in chapter v. I shall barely offer the following remarks:—

1. It is a very honourable one. Not only did patriarchs and prophets, and the church of God for many ages, descend from it, but the Son of God himself according to the flesh; and to shew the fulfilment of the promises and prophecies concerning him, is the principal reason of the genealogy having been recorded.

2. Neither Cain nor Abel have any place in it. Abel was slain before he had any children, and *could not;* and Cain by his sin had covered his name with infamy, and *should not.* Adam's posterity therefore, after a lapse of 130 years, must begin anew.

3. The honour done to Seth and his posterity was of grace; for he is said to have been born *in Adam's likeness, and after his image;* a phrase which, I believe, is always used to express the qualities of the mind, rather than the shape of the body. Man was made *after the image of God;* but this being lost, they are born corrupt, the children of a corrupt father. What is true of all mankind is here noted of Seth, because he was reckoned as Adam's first-born. He therefore, like all others, was by nature a child of wrath; and what he, or any of his posterity were different from this, they were by grace.

4. The extraordinary length of human life at that period was wisely ordered; not only for the peopling of the world, but for the supplying of the defect of a written revelation. From the death of Adam to the call of Abram, a period of about eleven hundred years, there were living either Enoch, Lamech, Noah, or Shem; besides other godly persons who were their cotemporaries, and who would feelingly relate to those about them the great events of the creation, the fall, and recovery of man.

5. Notwithstanding the longevity of the antediluvians, it is recorded of them all in their turn that they *died*. Though the stroke of death was slow in its approach, yet it was sure. If a man could live to a thousand years, yet he must die; and if he die in sin, he will be accursed.

6. Though many of the names in this genealogy are passed over without any thing being said of their piety, yet we are not from hence to infer that they were impious. Many might be included among them who *called upon the name of the Lord*, and who are denominated *the sons of God*, though nothing is personally related of them.

7. Two of them are distinguished for eminent godliness; or, as it is here called, *walking*

with God; namely, Enoch and Noah. Both these holy men are enrolled in the list of worthies in the eleventh chapter of the epistle to the Hebrews.

Let us look a little intensely at the life of the first of these worthies, the shortest of all the lives, but surely the sweetest: *Enoch walked with God after he begat Methuselah, three hundred years—He walked with God, and was not; for God took him.* This is one of those brief impressive descriptions of true religion with which the scriptures abound. Its holy and progressive nature is here most admirably marked. *Enoch walked with God*—He must then have been in a state of *reconciliation* with God; for two cannot walk together except they be agreed. He was, what Paul infers from another consideration, *a believer.* Where this is not the case, whatever may be his outward conduct, the sinner walks contrary to God, and God to him. What an idea does it convey also of his setting God always before him, seeking to glorify him in every duty, and studying to shew himself approved of him, whatever might be thought of his conduct by sinful men. Finally: What an idea does it convey of the communion which he habitually enjoyed with God! His conversation was in heaven, while dwelling on the earth. God dwelt in him, and he in God!

Enoch walked with God, after he begat Methuselah, three hundred years, and perhaps some time before that event. Religion with him then, was not a transient feeling, but an habitual and abiding principle. In reviewing such a character, what christian can forbear exclaiming, in the words of our christian poet:*

> "Oh for a closer walk with God, a calm and heavenly frame;
> A light to shine upon the road, that leads me to the Lamb!"

Just so much as we have of this, so much we possess of true religion, and no more.

Enoch walked with God, *and he was not, for God took him;* i. e. as Paul explains it, *He was translated, that he should not see death.* This singular favour conferred on Enoch, like the resurrection of Christ, might be designed to afford a sensible proof of a blessed immortality, which for the want of a written revelation might then be peculiarly necessary. He had warned the wicked of his day, that *the Lord would come with ten thousand of his holy ones, to execute judgment;* (Jude 14.) and now, however offensive his doctrine might have been to *them,* God will bear testimony that he hath *pleased him,* not only to the mind of Enoch, but to the world, by exempting him from the common lot of men.

* Cowper.

It is possible also that the translation of this holy man might be conferred in order to shew what should have been common to all, had man persisted in his obedience; a translation from the earthly to the heavenly paradise.

With respect to Noah, we shall have an account of his righteous life in the following chapters: at present we are only told of the circumstances of his birth. (ver. 28—32.) His father Lamech speaks on this occasion like a good man, and a prophet. He called his son *Noah*, which signifies *rest;* for *this same,* saith he, *shall comfort us concerning our work, and the toil of our hands, because of the ground which the Lord hath cursed.* Noah, by building the ark, saved a remnant from the flood; and by offering an acceptable sacrifice, obtained the promise that the ground should no more be cursed for man's sake. (Chap. viii. 21.) As Lamech could have known this only by revelation, we may infer from thence the sweet rest which divine truth affords to the believing mind from the toils and troubles of the present life; and if the birth of this child afforded comfort in that he would save the world, and remove the curse; how much more HIS who would be a greater Saviour, and remove a greater curse, by being HIMSELF an ark of salvation, and by offering HIMSELF *a sacrifice to God, for a sweet-smelling savour!*

DISCOURSE X.

THE CAUSE OF THE DELUGE.

GENESIS vi. 1——7.

Ver. 1—3. When we read of men beginning to *call upon the name of the Lord*, we entertained a hope of good times, and of comfort as Lamech said, after toil and sorrow: but alas, what a sad reverse! A general corruption overspreads the earth, and brings on a tremendous deluge that sweeps them all, one family only excepted, into oblivion.

In the first place, we may remark the *occasion* of this general corruption, which was the encrease of population. *When men began to multiply* they became more and more depraved: yet an encrease of population is considered as a blessing to a country, and such it is in itself; but through man's depravity it often proves a curse. When men are collected in great numbers they whet one another up to evil, which is the reason why sin commonly grows rankest in populous places. We were made to be helpers; but by sin we are become tempters of one another, drawing and being drawn into innumerable evils.

Secondly: Observe the *first step towards degeneracy*, which was, *the uniting of the world and the church by mixed marriages:* —The sons of God, and the daughters of men; the descendents of Seth, and those of Cain; the seed of the Woman, and the seed of the Serpent. The great end of marriage in a good man should not be to gratify his fancy, or indulge his natural inclinations, but to obtain a helper; and the same in a woman. We need to be helped on in our way to heaven, instead of being hindered and corrupted. Hence it was that marriages with idolaters were forbidden in the law;* and hence christian marriages were limited to those *in the Lord*.† The examples which we have seen of the contrary have, by their effects, justified these injunctions. I would earnestly entreat serious young people, of both sexes, as they regard God's honour, their own spiritual welfare, and the welfare of the church of God, to avoid being unequally yoked together with unbelievers.

Thirdly: Observe the *great offence* that God took at this conduct, and the consequences which grew out of it: *The Lord said, my Spirit shall not always strive with man, &c.* Had the sons of God kept themselves to themselves, and preserved their purity, God would have spared

---

* Deut. vii. 3, 4.   † 1 Cor. vii. 39.

the world for their sakes; but they mingled together, and became in effect one people. The old folks were in their account too bigotted, and it seemed much better for them to give in to a more liberal way of thinking and acting. But this in the sight of God was worse than almost any thing that had gone before it. He was more offended with the religious than with the irreligious part of them. Seeing they had become one people, he calls them all by one name, and that is *man*, without any distinction: and in giving the reason why his Spirit should not always strive with man, special reference is had to their having become degenerate—It was for that *he also,* or *these also were flesh;* that is, those who had been considered as the sons of God were become corrupt. God's holy Spirit in his prophets* had long strove or contended with the world; and while the sons of God made a stand against their wickedness, God was with them, and the contest was kept up: but they having, like false allies, made a kind of separate peace, or rather gone over to the enemy, God will give up the war; let sin have a free course, and let them take the consequences! *Bread-corn is bruised, because he will not ever be threshing it.* Isai. xxviii. 28.

* See Neh. ix. 30. 1 Pet. iii. 19, 20.

Fourthly: Observe the long-suffering of God amidst his displeasure—*His days shall be a hundred and twenty years.* This refers to the period of time which should elapse before the drowning of the world, *when,* as an apostle expresses it, *the long-suffering of God waited in the days of Noah, while the ark was preparing.* (1 Pet. iii. 20.) All this time God *did* strive, or contend with them; but it seems without effect.

Ver. 4. Amongst various other evils which at that time prevailed, a spirit of ambition was predominant; a thirst of conquest and dominion; and of course a flood of injuries, outrages, and oppressions. The case seems to have been this: Previous to the unhappy junction between the families of Cain and Seth, there were among the former, *giants,* or men of great stature, who, tempted by their superior strength, set up for champions and heroes, and bore down all before them.* Nor was the mischief confined to them: for *also after that,* when the two families had become one, as the children that were born unto them grew up, they emulated, as might be expected, not the virtues of their

---

* They are denominated נפלים, from נפל *to fall;* which in this connexion has been thought to mean, that they were a kind of *fellers,* causing men to fall before them like trees by the axe.

fathers, but the vices of their mothers; and particularly those of the gigantic and fierce heroes among their relations. Hence there sprang up a number of characters famous, or rather infamous, for their plunders and depredations. Such in after times was Nimrod, that *mighty hunter before the Lord.*

Ver. 5. The church being thus corrupted, and in a manner lost in the world, there is nothing left to resist the torrent of depravity. *Man* appears now in his true character. The picture which is here drawn of him, though very affecting, is no more than just. If it had been drawn by the pen of a prejudiced erring mortal, it might be supposed to exceed the truth; but that which is written was taken from the perfect and impartial survey of God. Hear ye who pretend that man is naturally virtuous! That the wickedness of man has in all ages, though at some periods more than others, been *great upon the earth,* can scarcely be called in question: but that *every imagination of the thoughts of his heart should be only evil, and that continually,* is more than men in general will allow. Yet such is the account here given.—Mark the affecting gradation. *Evil:* evil *without mixture;* " only evil "—evil *without cessation ;* " continually "— evil from the very *fountain head of action;* " the imagination of the thoughts of the heart"—nor is it a description of certain vicious characters only, but of "man," as left to himself—and all this "God saw," who sees things as they are. This doctrine is fundamental to the gospel: the whole system of redemption rests upon it; and I suspect that every false scheme of religion which has been at any time advanced in the world, might be proved to have originated in the denial of it.

Ver. 6. The effect of this divine survey is described in language, taken it is true from the feelings of men, but unusually impressive. *It repented the Lord that he had made man on the earth, and it grieved him at his heart!* We are not to attribute to an immutable mind the fickleness of man, nor to suppose that the omniscient Jehovah was really disappointed: but thus much we learn, that the wickedness of man is such as to mar all the works of God over which he is placed, and to render them worse than if there were none; so that if He had not counteracted it by the death of Christ, there had better have been no world. In short, that any one but himself, on seeing his work thus marred and perverted, would have really repented and wished from his heart that he had never made them! The words express with an energy and impressiveness which it is probable nothing purely literal could have conveyed, the exceeding sinfulness, and provoking nature of sin.

Ver. 7. From this cause proceeded the divine resolution, to *destroy man from the face of the earth;* and to shew the greatness of his sin, it is represented as extinguishing the paternal kindness of God as his Creator. "The Lord said, I will destroy man, *whom I have created,* from the face of the earth." "He that *made them* would not have mercy on them, and he that *formed them* would shew them no favour!"* And further, to shew his displeasure against man, the creatures which were subject to him should be destroyed with him. Thus when Achan had transgressed, to render his punishment more impressive upon Israel, "his sons and daughters, and oxen and asses, and sheep, and tent, and all that he had, were brought forth, and with himself stoned with stones, and burnt with fire."† However lightly man may make of sin during the time of God's forbearance, it will prove to be an evil and bitter thing in the end.

---

* Isai. xxvii. 11.   † Josh. vii. 24, 25.

DISCOURSE XI.

NOAH FINDS FAVOUR WITH GOD, AND IS DIRECTED TO BUILD THE ARK.

GENESIS vi. 8——22.

By the foregoing account it would seem as if the whole earth had become corrupt. In the worst of times however, God has had a remnant that have walked with him; and over them he has in the most sore calamities directed a watchful eye. When God said, "I will destroy man whom I have created, from the face of the earth," it seemed as if he would make an end of the human race. *But Noah found grace in the eyes of the Lord.*—Observe, (1.) It is painful to find but one family, nay, it would seem but one person, out of all the professed sons of God, who stood firmly in this evil day. Some were dead, and others, by mingling with the wicked, had apostatised.—(2.) It is pleasant to find one upright man in a generation of the ungodly: a lily among thorns, whose lovely conduct would shine the brighter when contrasted with that of the world about him. It is a great matter to be faithful among the faithless. With all our helps from the society of good men, we find it enough to keep on our way: but for an individual to set his face against the whole current of public opinion and custom, requires and implies great grace. Yet that is the only true religion which walks as in the sight of God, irrespective of what is thought or done by others. Such was the resolution of Joshua when the whole nation seemed to be turning aside from God: *As for me and my house, we will serve the Lord.*—(3.) It is encouraging to find that one upright man was singled out from the rest when the world was to be destroyed. If he had been destroyed with the world, God could have taken him to himself, and all would have been well with him; but then there had been no public expression of what he loved, as well as of what he hated.

Ver. 9. As Noah was to be the father of the new world, we have here a particular account of him. His *generations* mean an account of him and his family; of what he was, and of the things which befel him.*—The first thing said of him, as being the greatest, is, " He was a *just,* or *righteous* man, and perfect in his generations, walking with God." Character is of

---
* See chap. xxxvii. 2.

greater importance than pedigree. But notice particularly,

1. He was *just*. He was the first man who was so called, though not the first who was so. In a legal sense a just man is one that doeth good, and sinneth not; but since the fall, no such man has existed upon earth, save the man Christ Jesus. If any of us be denominated just, it must be in some other sense; and what this is the scriptures inform us when they represent *the just as living by faith.* Such was the life of Noah, and therefore he is reckoned among the believing worthies.* And the faith by which he was justified before God, operated in a way of righteousness, which rendered him just before men. He is called *a preacher of righteousness,* and he lived according to his doctrine.†

2. He was *perfect* in his generations. The term in this connexion is not to be taken absolutely, but as expressive not only of sincerity of heart, but of a *decidedness* for God, like that of Caleb, who followed the Lord *fully.* It does not merely distinguish good men from bad men, but good men from one another. It is said of Solomon, that his heart was not *perfect* with the Lord his God, as was the heart of David his

* Heb. xi. 7.   † 2 Pet. ii. 5.

father."* Alas, how much of this half-hearted religion there is amongst us! Instead of serving the Lord with a perfect heart, and a willing mind, we halt as it were between two, the love of God, and the love of the world.

3. He *walked* with God. This is the same as was said of Enoch.† It not only implies his being reconciled to God, and denotes his acknowledging him in all his ways, and enjoying communion with him in the discharge of duties; but is also expressive of the *continuity*, and *progressive tendency* of true religion. Whatever he did, or wherever he went, God was before his eyes; nor did he ever think of leaving off till he should have finished his course.

Ver. 10. From Noah's character the sacred writer proceeds to his descendents. He had three sons, Shem, Ham, and Japheth. These afterwards became the patriarchs of the world, and between whose posterity the three great divisions of Asia, Africa, and Europe have been principally divided. Thus much at present for the favoured family.

Ver. 11. Here we have the charge against the old world repeated, as the ground of what

* 1 Kings xi. 4. † See on chap. v. 23, 24.

should follow. If succeeding generations enquire, Wherefore hath the Lord done thus unto the work of his hands? What meaneth the heat of this great anger? Be it known that it was not for a small matter: *The earth was corrupt before God, and the earth was filled with violence.* Here are two words used to express the wickedness of the world, *corruption* and *violence*, both which are repeated, and dwelt upon in verses 12, 13.—The *former* refers, I conceive, to their having debased and depraved the true religion. This was the natural consequence of the junction between the sons of God and the daughters of men. Whenever the church is become one with the world, the corruption of true religion has invariably followed: for if wicked men have a religion, it must needs be such as to accord with their inclinations. Hence arose all the heresies of the early ages of christianity; hence the grand Romish apostasy; and in short every corruption of the true religion in past or present times.—The *latter* of these terms is expressive of their conduct towards one another. The fear of God, and the regard of man are closely connected; and where the one is given up, the other will soon follow. Indeed it appears to be the decree of the eternal God, that when men have cast off his fear, they shall not continue long in amity one with another. And he has only to let the laws of nature take their course in order to effect it; for when men depart from God, the principle of union is lost, and self-love governs every thing: and being LOVERS OF THEIR OWNSELVES, they will be *covetous, boasters, proud, blasphemers, disobedient to parents, unthankful, unholy, without natural affection, truce breakers, false accusers, incontinent, fierce, despisers of those that are good, traitors, heady, highminded, lovers of pleasure more than lovers of God.* Such a flood of wickedness is at any time sufficient to deluge a world with misery. If these things did not then break forth in national wars as they do with us, it was merely because the world was not as yet divided into nations: the springs of domestic and social life were poisoned, the tender ties of blood and affinity violated, and quarrels, intrigues, oppressions, robberies, and murders pervaded the abodes of man.

From the influence of corruption in producing violence, and bringing on the deluge, we may see the importance of pure religion, and those who adhere to it, to the well-being of society. They are the preserving principle, the salt of the earth; and when they are banished, or in any way become extinct, the consequences will be soon felt. While the sons of God were kept together, and continued faithful, God would not destroy the world for their sakes; but when reduced to a single family, he would, as in the case of Lot, take that away, and destroy the rest. The late convulsions in a neighbouring nation may, I apprehend, be easily traced to this cause: all their violence originated in the corruption of the true religion. About one hundred and thirty years ago the law which protected the reformation in that country was repealed; and almost all the religious people were either murdered or banished. The consequence was, as might have been expected, the great body of the nation, princes, priests and people, sunk into infidelity. The protestant religion, while it continued, was the salt of the state; but when banished, and superstition had nothing left to counteract it, things soon hastened to their crisis. Popery, aided by a despotic civil government, brought forth infidelity, and the child as soon as it grew up to maturity murdered its parents. If the principal part of religious people in this or any other country were driven away, the rest would soon become infidels, and practical atheists; and what every order and degree of men would have to expect from the prevalence of these principles, there is no want of examples to inform them.

Ver. 12, 13. The corruption and violence which overspread the earth attracted the notice of heaven. God knows at all times what is doing in our world; but his *looking* upon the earth denotes a special observance of it, as though he had instituted an enquiry into its affairs. Thus he is represented as "going down to Sodom, to see whether they had done altogether according to the cry of it, which was come up unto him." (chap. xviii. 21.) Such seasons of enquiry are the "days of inquisition for blood," and are so many days of judgment in miniature.

The enquiry being instituted, sentence is passed, and Noah is informed of it. *God said unto Noah, The end of all flesh is come before me ..... behold, I will destroy them, with the earth.* In cases where individuals only, or even a majority, are wicked, and there is yet a great number of righteous characters, God often inflicts only a partial punishment: but where a whole people are become corrupt, he has more than once made a full end of them. Witness the cities of Sodom and Gomorrha, and the seven nations of Canaan; and thus it will be with the world when the righteous shall be gathered out of it.

Ver. 14—16. As it was the design of God to make an exception in favour of his faithful servant Noah, he is directed to the use of an extraordinary mean, namely, the building of the ark; a kind of ship which, though not in the shape of ours, as not being intended for a voyage, should float on the surface of the waters, and preserve him and his family alive in the midst of death. It is possible that this was the first floating fabric that was ever built. Its dimensions were amasing. Reckoning the cubit at only a foot and a half, which is supposed to be somewhat less than the truth, it was a hundred and fifty yards long, twenty-five yards wide, and fifteen yards deep; containing three stories, or as we should call them, decks, each five yards in depth. It had a window also, it should seem, from end to end, a foot and a-half deep, for light, and perhaps for air.*

Ver. 17. When Joseph was called to interpret the dream of Pharaoh, he observed concerning its being *doubled*, that it was "because the thing was established by God, and God would shortly bring it to pass." (chap. xli. 32.) And thus we may consider the repetition which is here given of the sentence: *Behold I, even I, do bring a flood of waters upon the earth, to destroy all flesh wherein is the breath of life from under heaven.*

---

* Noah's ark is said to have been equal to forty of our largest men of war!

Ver. 18—22. But though it was the purpose of God to make an end of the world that then was, yet he did not mean that the generations of men should here be terminated. A new world shall succeed, of which his servant Noah shall be the father. Thus when Israel had offended at Horeb, the Lord said unto Moses, "Let me alone, that I may destroy them, and I will make of thee a great nation." Hence pairs of every living creature were to go with him into the ark, to provide for futurity.

The terms in which this gracious design is intimated are worthy of special notice: *With thee will I establish my covenant.* Observe three things in particular.—(1.) The leading ideas suggested by a covenant are those of *peace and goodwill* between the parties, and if differences have subsisted, forgiveness of the past, and security for the future. Such were the friendly alliances between Abram and Abimelech, Isaac and another of the same name, and between Jacob and Laban.* God was highly displeased with the world, and would therefore destroy that generation by a flood: but when he should have done this, he would return in loving-kindness and tender mercies, and would look upon the earth with a propitious eye. Nor should they be kept

* Gen. xxi. 27—32. xxvi. 28—31. xxxi. 44.

in fearful expectation of being so destroyed again; for he would pledge his word, no more to be wroth with them in such a way, nor to rebuke them for ever.—(2.) In covenants wherein one or both the parties had been offended, it was usual to *offer sacrifices*, in which a kind of atonement was made for past offences, and a perfect reconciliation followed. Such were the covenants before referred to; and such, as we shall see at the close of the eighth chapter, was the covenant in question. "Noah offered sacrifices, and the Lord smelled a sweet savour, and promised to curse the ground no more for man's sake."—(3.) In covenants which include a blessing on MANY, and they *unworthy*, it is God's ordinary method to bestow it *in reward*, or *for the sake of* ONE who was dear to him. God loves men, but he also loves righteousness: hence he delights to bestow his blessings in such a way as manifest his true character. If there had been any dependence on Noah's posterity, that they would all have walked in his steps, the covenant might have been *established with them* as well as him; but they would soon degenerate into idolatry, and all manner of wickedness. If therefore he will bestow favour on them in such a way as to express his love of righteousness, it must be for their father Noah's sake, and in reward of his righteousness. To say, *With* THEE *will I establish my covenant*, was saying in effect, 'I will not treat with thy ungodly posterity: whatever favour I shew them, it shall be for thy sake.'

It was on this principle that God made a covenant with Abram,* in which he promised great blessings to his posterity. "As for me, (saith he) behold, my covenant is with *thee*, and thou shalt be a father of many nations." Hence, in a great number of instances wherein mercy was shewn to the rebellious Israelites, they were reminded that it was not for *their sakes*, but on account of *the covenant made with their father Abraham, and renewed with Isaac and Jacob.*† It was upon this principle also that God made a covenant with David, promising that his seed should sit upon his throne for ever. And this is expressed in much the same language as that of Noah and Abraham: "My covenant shall *stand fast with him*—Once have I sworn by my holiness, that I will not lie *unto David*. His seed shall endure for ever, and his throne as the sun before him."‡ The Lord often reminded them that the favours which they enjoyed were not for their sakes, but for his own Name sake, and

---

* Gen. xvii. 4.

† Lev. xxvi. 42.   Deut. ix. 5.   Psal. cv. 42.   cvi. 45. Mic. vii. 19, 20.   ‡ Psal. lxxxix. 28, 35, 36.

for the covenant which he had made with David his servant.* Solomon pleaded this at the dedication of the temple: Hezekiah also derived advantage from it; and when the seed of David corrupted their way, the Lord reminded them that the favours which they enjoyed were not for their own sakes, but for his Name sake, and for the covenant which he had made with David his servant.†

After these remarks, I scarcely need say, that by these proceedings, God, even at this early period, was preparing the way for the redemption of his Son by rendering the great principle on which it should proceed, familiar to mankind. A very small acquaintance with the scriptures will enable us to perceive the charming analogy between the language used in the covenants with Noah, Abram, David, &c., and that which respects the Messiah. "I will give THEE for a covenant of the people, to establish the earth, to cause to inherit the desolate heritages—It is a light thing that thou shouldst be my servant to raise up the tribes of Jacob, and to restore the preserved of Israel: I will also give thee for a light to the Gentiles, that thou

---

* 1 Kings xi. 12.
† Psal. cxxxii. 10. 2 Chron. vi. 42. Isai. xxxvii. 35.
1 Kings xi. 12, 13, 32, 34.

Gen. 6.] COVENANT WITH NOAH. 93

mayest be my salvation to the ends of the earth—Ask of me, and I will give THEE the heathen for thine inheritance, and the uttermost parts of the earth for thy possession—HE shall see of the travail of his soul, and shall be satisfied."* In these, as in the former instances, God's covenant stands fast with one, and many are blessed for his sake: their salvation is his reward.

DISCOURSE XII.

THE FLOOD.

GENESIS vii.

WE have seen the preparation of the ark, the warnings of God by it, and his long-suffering for a hundred and twenty years. Now we see it finished: now the end of all flesh is come before him.—Observe, (1.) God gave special notice to Noah, saying, *Come thou and all thy house into the ark; for thee have I seen righteous.* He who in well-doing commits himself into the hands of a faithful Creator, needs not fear being overtaken by surprize. What have we to fear, when he whom we serve hath the keys of hell and of death? This is not the only instance in which, when impending ills have been ready to

* Isai. xlix. 6, 8. liii. 11. Psal. ii. 8.

burst upon the world, God hath in effect said to his servants, "Come my people, enter thou into thy chambers, and shut thy doors about thee: hide thyself as it were for a little moment, until the indignation be overpast."—(2.) God gave him all his household with him. We are not informed whether any of Noah's family at present followed his example: it is certain that all did not; yet all entered with him into the ark for his sake. This indeed was but a specimen of the mercy which was to be exercised towards his distant posterity on behalf of him, as we have seen in the former chapter. But it is of importance to observe, that though temporal blessings may be given to the ungodly children of a godly parent, yet without walking in his steps they will not be partakers with him in those which are spiritual and eternal.—(3.) It is an affecting thought, that there should be *no more* than Noah and his family to enter into the ark. Peter speaks of them as *few;* and few they were, considering the vast numbers that were left behind. Noah had long been a preacher of righteousness; and what, is there not one sinner brought to repentance by his preaching? It should seem not one: or if there were any, they were taken away from the evil to come. Not one that we know of was found at the time, who had received his warnings, and was desirous of casting in his lot with him. We are ready to think our ministry has but little success; but his, so far as appears, was without any: yet, like Enoch, he pleased God.—(4.) The righteousness of Noah is repeated, as the reason of the difference put between him and the world. This does not imply that the favour shewn to him is to be ascribed to his own merit; for whatever he was, he was by grace; and all his righteousness was rewardable only out of respect to Him in whom he believed: but being accepted for his sake, his works also were accepted and honoured. And while the *mercy* of God was manifested towards him, the distinction between him and the world being made according to character, would render his *justice* apparent. Thus at the last day, though the righteous will have nothing to boast of, yet every man being judged according to his works, the world will be constrained to acknowledge the equity of the divine proceedings.

Ver. 2, 3. Of the animals which were to enter into the ark with Noah, those that were clean, that is, those which were fit for human food, and for sacrifice to God, were to go in by sevens; and those which were unclean, only by two of a kind. It would seem as if this direction differed from that in chapter vi. 19, 20, which mentions only two of every sort: but the meaning there may be, that whatever number entered in they should be in *pairs*, i. e. male and female, to preserve them alive; whereas here the direction is more particular, appointing the number of pairs that should be admitted, according as they were clean or unclean. This order is expressive of the goodness of God in providing food for man, and of his regard for his own worship.

Ver. 4—9. Just one week was allowed for Noah to embark. What a week was this! What feelings must it excite! His neighbours had seen him busily employed for the last hundred and twenty years in rearing the massy fabric; and doubtless had had many a laugh at the old man's folly and credulity; and now behold, he is going to remove all his family into it; with birds, and beasts, and creeping things, and provisions for their accommodation! 'Well, let him go: a week longer, and we shall see what will become of his dreams!' Meanwhile they eat and drink, and buy and sell, and marry, and are given in marriage.—As for Noah, he must have felt much in contemplating the destruction of his whole species, to whom he had preached righteousness in vain. But it is not for him to linger; but to " do according to all that the Lord commanded him." He had borne his testimony: he could do no more. He, his sons, his wife, and his sons' wives, therefore, with all the inferior creatures, which probably were caused to assemble before him by the same power which brought them to Adam to be named, enter into the ark. The same thing which is said of him in ver. 7, is repeated in ver. 13. He doubtless would have to enter, and re-enter many times, in the course of the week; but the last describes his final entrance, when he should return no more.

Ver. 10—16. From the account taken together, it appears that though God suffered long with the world during the ministry of Noah, yet the flood came upon them at last very suddenly. The words, "*after* seven days," in ver. 10, seem to mean *on* the seventh day;* for that was the day when Noah made his final entrance into the ark; namely, the seventeenth day of the second month, answering to our October or November, in the six hundredth year of his life; and *on that same day were all the fountains of the great deep broken up, and the windows of heaven opened.* What a scene of consternation and dismay must that day have exhibited on the part of those who were left behind! The manner in which the

---

* Such a mode of speaking is usual in the scriptures. Compare ver. 6. with ver. 11, and chap. xl. 18, 20.

rains set in would leave little or no hope of their being soon over. It was not a common rain: it came in torrents, or as we should say, in a manner as though heaven and earth were come together. The waters of the subterraneous cavities from beneath, and of the clouds from above, all met together at God's command, to execute his wrath upon guilty men.*—There is one sentence concerning Noah which is worthy of special notice: when he and all pertaining to him had entered into the ark, it is said, *And the Lord shut him in.* The door of such a stupendous building may be supposed to be too large for human hands to fasten, especially so few as they were, and all within side it. It is possible too there might be by this time numbers crowding round it for admittance: for those who trifle with death at a distance are often the most ter-

---

* The *great deep* seems to mean that vast confluence of waters which are said to have been gathered together on the third day of the creation into one place, and were called seas. (ch. i. 9, 10.) These waters not only extended over a great part of the surface of the earth, but probably flow, as through a number of arteries and veins, to its most interior recesses, and occupy its centre. This body of waters, which was ordained, as I may say, unto life, was turned, in just displeasure against man's sin, into an engine of destruction. Bursting forth in tremendous floods, multitudes were hereby swept away; while from above, the clouds poured forth their torrents, as though heaven itself were a reservoir of waters, and God had opened its windows.

rified when it approaches. But lo, all is over! That act which shut Noah and his family in, shut them for ever out! And let it be considered, that something very nearly resembling this will ere long be acted over again. As it was in the days of Noah, so shall it be at the coming of the Son of Man: not only shall the world, as then, be full of dissipation, but the concluding scene is described nearly in the same words—*And they that were ready went in, and the door was shut!*

Ver. 17—24. We hear no more of the inhabitants of the world, except that "all flesh died that moved upon the earth, both of fowl and of cattle, and of beast, and of every creeping thing that creepeth upon the earth, *and every man:* all in whose nostrils was the breath of life, of all that was in the dry land, died." We are informed, however, of the progress of the flood. For six weeks, within two days, it continued to rain incessantly; during which period it was of sufficient depth to bear up the ark from the earth, which after this floated upon the surface of the waters like a ship on the sea. For some time however, there were mountains and high hills which were out of water. Hither therefore, we may naturally suppose, the inhabitants of the earth would repair as to their last refuge:

but by the end of the forty days, these also were covered; the waters rising above seven yards higher than the highest of them. Thus every creature was swept away, and buried in one watery grave, Noah and his family only excepted.

The waters prevailed upon the earth a hundred and fifty days; that is, about five months, before they began to abate. This might seem to us unnecessary, seeing every living creature would be drowned within the first six weeks; but it would serve to exercise the faith and patience of Noah, and to impress his posterity with the greatness of the divine displeasure against man's sin. As the land of Israel should have its sabbaths during the captivity, so the whole earth, for a time, shall be relieved from its load, and fully purified, as it were, from its uncleanness.

DISCOURSE XIII.

THE FLOOD (CONTINUED.)

GENESIS viii.

THE close of the last chapter brought us to the crisis of the flood, or to the period in which it had arrived at its greatest height: from hence it began to abate. Observe the form in which it is expressed: *God remembered Noah, and those that were with him in the ark.* A common historian would only have narrated the event: but the sacred writers ascribe every thing to God, and often to the omitting of second causes. The term is figurative; for strictly speaking, God never forgot them: but it is one of those modes of speaking which convey a great fulness of meaning. It is expressive of tender mercy, of covenant mercy, and of mercy after a strong expression of displeasure. These are things which frequently occur in the divine proceedings. From hence, a wind passes over the earth, and the waters begin to assuage.

Ver. 2—4. The causes of the deluge being removed, the effects gradually subside; and the waters having performed their work, return into their wonted channels. The ark, which had hitherto floated on the waters, now finds land, and rests upon the top of one of the Armenian mountains; and this just five months after the entrance into it. For a ship in the sea to have struck upon a rock or land, would have been extremely dangerous; but at this stage of the flood we may suppose the heavens were clear, and calm, and the waters still. Noah did not steer the ark: it was therefore God's doing, and was in mercy to him and his companions. Their voyage was now at an end. They put in as at the first possible port. The rest which they enjoy is a prelude to a more perfect one approaching. Thus God places believers upon high ground, on which they are already safe, and may anticipate a better country, even a heavenly one.

Ver. 5—13. The first objects that greet their eyes, after having been nearly eight months a-board, are the tops of the mountains. They had felt one of them before; but now the waters are sufficiently abated to see several of them. If we had been a long and dangerous voyage at sea, we should be better able to conceive of the joy which this sight must have occasioned, than we possibly can be without it. Often has a ship's company been called on deck to see a distant object, which promised to be land. Often too have christians in their voyage been cheered by the signs of approaching blessedness, and the happy foretastes bestowed upon them.—After the lapse of forty days more, the window of the ark was opened, and a raven sent forth for the purpose of experiment, that they might see whether it could subsist of itself or not; and the event was, that it could subsist, for it returned no more. This was encouraging.—Seven days after this, Noah tries a more delicate bird, the dove, which could not live unless the ground was at least in some places dry: but she from necessity returned. A proof this, that the waters as yet were on the face of the whole earth. Tarrying yet other seven days, Noah sends out a second time his faithful messenger, the dove, which again returned to him in the evening; but lo, a sign is in her mouth which gladdens all their hearts. It is *an olive-leaf plucked off!* An olive-leaf might have floated upon the surface of the waters; but it was observable of this that the dove had plucked it off the tree: a proof that the tops of the trees in some places were out of water. I imagine it is from this event that the olive-branch has ever since been considered as the emblem of peace.—After seven days more, Noah sends forth the dove again; which, returning no more, he knew the earth must in some places be dry. The repeated mention of "seven days" seems to imply, that from the beginning, time had been divided into weeks; and which can no otherwise be accounted for, that I know of, than by admitting that from the beginning, those who feared God remembered the sabbath day to keep it holy.—About a month after this, the waters are dried up from off the earth, and the covering of the ark is removed. Now they have the pleasure to look around them, and to see the dry land in every direction; but still it is not habitable. And as Noah came into the ark by God's command, so he must wait his time ere he attempts to go out, and which will be nearly two months longer.

Ver. 14—19. At length the set time to favour this little company is come. On the 27th day of the second month, that is, just a year and ten days after their entrance into the ark, they are commanded to go forth of it, with all that pertained to them, and to begin, not the world, as we should say, again, but a new world. Obedient to the heavenly vision, they take leave of the friendly vessel which through many a storm had preserved them, and landed them in safety.

Ver. 20—22. The first object of attention with a worldly man, might have been a day of rejoicing, or the beginning to build a house: but Noah begins by building *an altar to Jehovah*, on which he offered "burnt offerings of every clean beast, and of every clean fowl." I think this is the first time we read of a *burnt offering*. It was so called, as Moses says, "because of the burning upon the altar all night unto the morning."* It was a substitutional sacrifice for the purpose of atonement: the process is described

* Lev. vi. 9.

in Lev. i. 2—9. The sinner confessed his sin upon its head—the animal was killed, or treated as if it were the transgressor, and as if the sin had been actually transferred to it—the blood of the creature being shed, was sprinkled round about upon the altar—and to shew the divine acceptance of it on behalf of the offerer, to make atonement for him, it was consumed by fire, either descending immediately from heaven, as was the case on some occasions, or kindled by the priest from the sacred fire kept for the purpose.*—Finally: The sacrifice being sprinkled with salt, and perhaps with odours, ascended up in a sweet savour; and God was propitious to the offerer.

The burnt offerings of Noah, according to this, must have been designed for an atonement in behalf of the remnant that was left; and as Hezekiah said, after the carrying away of the ten tribes, "for the making of a covenant with the Lord."† This his offering was graciously accepted: *The Lord smelled a sweet savour*, and bestowed upon him and those who were with him a covenant promise, not to curse the ground any more for man's sake. The reason given for this is singular: *for the imagination of man's heart is evil from his youth*. If God had dealt with

---

* Lev. ix. 24. Psal. xx. 4. margin. † 2 Chron. xxix.

man according to law and justice, this should have been a reason for destroying rather than sparing him; and was the reason why the flood was brought upon the earth.* But here he is represented as dealing with him through a substitute; (for the promise follows the acceptance of the burnt offering) and in this view the wickedness of man, however offensive, should not determine his conduct. He would, as it were, look off from him, and rest his future conduct towards him on another ground. He would in short, knowing what he was, deal with him on a footing of mercy, and forbearance.

Surely I need not say, that this sacrifice of Noah was one of those which bore a peculiar aspect to the offering of the body of Jesus once for all. It is not improbable that the apostle has a direct allusion to it when he says, "Christ hath loved us, and given himself for us, an offering and a sacrifice to God, *for a sweet-smelling savour.*" Ephes. v. 2.

In reviewing the destruction of the world by a flood, and the preservation of Noah and his family, we are furnished with three important reflexions:—

* Chap. vi. 5—7.

1. It is a solid proof of the truth of divine revelation. "We are acquainted (says a late perspicuous and forcible writer) with no ancient people who were without traditions of this great event. From Josephus we learn that Berosus, a Chaldean historian, whose works are now lost, related the same things as Moses of the deluge, and the preservation of Noah in an ark. Eusebius informs us that the history of the flood was contained in the works of Abydenus, an Assyrian writer. Lucian, the Greek writer, says, that the present is not the original race of men; but is descended from Deucalion, who was preserved in an ark from the universal deluge which destroyed men for their wickedness. Varro, the Roman writer, divided time into three periods, the first from the origin of men to the deluge. The Hindoo puranas contain the history of the deluge, and of Noah under the name of Satyavrata. They relate that Satyavrata was miraculously preserved in an ark from a deluge which destroyed all mankind."* The same writer adds, "That the whole of our globe has been sub-

* *Letters on the Evidences of the Christian Religion:* by an Enquirer. First printed in the Oriental Star at Calcutta, reprinted at Serampore in 1802, and lately reprinted in England, with additions and corrections by the author.

"merged by the ocean, is proved, not by tra-
"dition only, but by its mineralogical and fos-
"sil history. On the summits of high moun-
"tains, and in the centres of continents, vast
"beds of shells and other marine productions
"are to be found. Petrified fishes and sea weed
"exist in the heart of quarries. The vegetable
"and animal productions of the torrid zone
"have been dug up in the coldest regions, as
"Siberia; and, vice versa, the productions of
"the polar regions have been found in warm
"climates. These facts are unanswerable proofs
"of a deluge."

2. It is intimated by the apostle Peter, that the salvation of Noah and his family in the ark, was a figure of our salvation by the resurrection of Jesus Christ. It was for a time buried, as it were, in the floods of divine wrath from above and from beneath. It rose however, and weathered the storm, safely landing those on dry ground who had been committed to its care. I need not make the application. A *like figure* of the same thing is christian baptism, in which believers are said to be baptised into the death of Christ: "Buried with him into death, that like as he was raised up from the dead by the glory of the Father, so they also should walk in newness of life."

3. We are directed to consider the destruction of the world by water as a presage and premonition of its being destroyed in the end by fire. "The heavens and the earth, which now are, are kept in store, reserved unto fire against the day of judgment, and perdition of ungodly men." 2 Pet. iii. 5—7.

DISCOURSE XIV.

GOD's COVENANT WITH NOAH.

GENESIS ix.

Ver. 1, 2. We have now the beginning of a new world, and various directions given to those who are to people it. In several respects it resembles its first beginning; particularly in the command to be fruitful and multiply, and in the subjection of the creatures to man. But there is one great difference: all now must rest upon *a gracious covenant*. Man by sin had forfeited, not his existence indeed, for that was given him to hold on no conditional tenure; but the blessing of God, and his dominion over the creatures. Nevertheless, he shall be reinstated in it. God will, as it were, make a covenant for him with the beasts of the field, and they shall be at peace with him, or at least shall be awed by his authority. All this is out of respect to the mediation of Christ, and for the accomplishing of the designs of mercy through him.

Ver. 3, 4. Here is also a special grant which does not appear to have been given before: not only the herbs of the field, but the animals are given to man for food. It is however accompanied with a special exception with regard to *blood*, which is the life. This being forbidden to Noah, appears also to have been forbidden to all mankind: nor ought this prohibition to be treated as belonging to the ceremonies of the jewish dispensation. It was not only enjoined before that dispensation existed, but was enforced upon the gentile christians by the decrees of the apostles.* To allege, as some do, our Lord's words, that "it is not that which goeth into a man which defileth him," would equally justify the practice of cannibals in eating human flesh. The *reason* of this prohibition might be in part the prevention of *cruelty:* the eating of blood implies and cherishes a ferocious disposition. None but the most ferocious of animals will eat it in one another; and one would think none

---

* Acts xv. 20.

Gen. 9.] COVENANT WITH NOAH. 111

but the most ferocious of mankind can endure it. But there may be a higher reason. Blood is the *life*, and God seems to claim it as sacred to himself. Hence in all the sacrifices, the blood was poured out before the Lord: and in the sacrifice of Christ, he shed his blood, or poured out his soul unto death.

Ver. 5, 6. As God was tender of animal blood, in not suffering man to eat it, so on the other hand, he would be especially tender of human blood. If any animal slew a man, let him be slain on that account: or if any man slew himself, God would require it: or if any man slew another man, he should be put to death by man. This also appears to be a new law, as we read of no executions for murder among the antediluvians. The reason for this law is not taken from the well being of man, but man's being made in the *image* of God. The image of God is of two kinds, natural and moral. The latter was lost by sin; but the former continues with man in every state, and renders it peculiarly criminal to abuse him. To deface the king's image is a sort of treason among men, implying a hatred against him, and that if he himself were within reach, he would be served in the same manner: how much more treasonable must it be to destroy, curse, oppress, or in any way abuse the image of the King of kings! James iii. 9.*

Ver. 7. The command to multiply is repeated, and contains permission, not of promiscuous intercourse like the brutes, but of honourable marriage. The same law which forbad the eating of blood, under the gospel, forbad *fornication*, which was common among the heathen; and alas, too common among those who call themselves christians!

---

* In defending the principles of civil and religious liberty against persecution for conscience sake, it has often been alleged, that civil government has no right to restrain or punish men, but on account of their injuring their fellow-men. That whatever is punishable by man *is* injurious to man, is true; because all sin in some way or other is so: but to make this *the sole ground,* or *reason* of punishment, is selfish and atheistical. It is making ourselves the chief end; whereas this is what God claims to himself at the hand of every man, and body of men. The cognizance of the civil magistrate ought indeed to be confined to what is civil and moral; but in punishing men for immorality, he ought not merely to regard his own safety, nor even that of the community, but the honour of God; and if he be a good man, he will do so. If he regard merely his own safety, punishing crimes only in so far as they endanger it, the people will soon perceive that he is a selfish tyrant, and cares not for the general good: and if he regard only the public safety, punishing crimes merely on account of their being injurious to men, it is still a spirit of selfishness, only a little more extended, and God will disapprove of this, as the people do of the other.

Ver. 8—17. Having given the foregoing precepts, God graciously proceeds to enter into a solemn *covenant* with Noah and his posterity, and every living creature that was with them, no more to destroy them by water, and of which *the bow in the cloud* was to be the token. This covenant is an amplification of what was said at the altar, where the Lord smelled a sweet savour; and indeed the first seventeen verses of this chapter are a continuation of that subject.— We see here, (1.) The mercy and goodness of God, in proceeding with us in a way of covenant. He might have exempted the world from this calamity, and yet not have told them he would do so. The remembrance of the flood might have been a sword hanging over their heads in terrorem. But he will set their minds at rest on this score, and therefore promises, and that with an oath, that the waters of Noah should no more go over the earth.* Thus also he deals with us in his Son. Being willing that the heirs of promise should have strong consolation, he confirms his word by an oath.†—(2.) The importance of living under the light of revelation. Noah's posterity by degrees sunk into idolatry, and became "strangers to the covenants of promise." Such were our fathers for many ages, and such are great numbers to this

---

* Isai. liv. 9.   † Heb. vi. 17, 18.

day. So far as respects them, God might as well have made no promise: to them all is lost.—(3.) The importance of being believers. Without this, it will be worse for us than if we had never been favoured with a revelation.—Finally: We see here the kind of life which it was God's design to encourage; *a life of faith.* "The just shall live by faith." If he had made no revelation of himself, no covenants, and no promises, there would be no ground for faith; and we must have gone through life feeling after him, without being able to find him: but having made known his mind, there is light in all our dwellings, and a sure ground for believing not only in our exemption from another flood, but in things of far greater importance.

With respect to the sign or token of this covenant, *the bow in the cloud,* as it seems to be the effect of causes which existed from the beginning, it is probable that that also existed; but it was not till now a *token* of God's covenant with the world. Such a token was extremely suitable on account of its conspicuousness, and its appearance *in the cloud,* or at a time when the fears of man would be apt to rise, lest they should be overwhelmed with another flood. This being a sign of peace, the King of Zion is described as having " a rain-bow about his throne." Rev. iv. 3.

COVENANT WITH NOAH.

Ver. 18, 19. God having thus saved, counselled, and covenanted with this little company, Moses proceeds to narrate their history. In general, we are informed that the fathers of the new world were Noah's three sons, Shem, and Ham, and Japheth, from whom the earth was peopled. And having mentioned Ham, he says, " He was the father of Canaan." This remark of Moses was doubtless made with a special design: for living as he did, when the Israelites who descended from Shem, were about to take possession of the land of Canaan, it was of peculiar importance that they should be informed that the people whose country the Lord their God had given them to possess, were under a curse from the days of their first father. The particulars of this affair will appear in the sequel.

Ver. 20—23. Noah, as soon as he could get settled, betook himself to the employment of husbandry; and the first thing he did in this way was to plant a vineyard. So far all was right: man, as we have seen, was formed originally for an active, and not an idle life. Adam was ordered to keep the garden, and to dress it; and when fallen, to till the ground from whence he was taken, which now required much labour. Perhaps there is no occupation more free from snares. But in the most lawful employments and enjoyments, we must not reckon ourselves out of danger. It was very lawful for Noah to partake of the fruits of his labour; but Noah sinned in drinking to excess. He might not be aware of the strength of the wine, or his age might render him sooner influenced by it: at any rate we have reason to conclude from his general character that it was a fault in which he was *overtaken*. But let us not think lightly of the sin of drunkenness. " Who hath woe; who hath redness of eyes? They that *tarry* long at the wine." Times of festivity require a double guard. Neither age nor character are any security in the hour of temptation. Who would have thought, that a man who had walked with God, perhaps more than five hundred years, and who had withstood the temptations of a world, should fall alone? This was like a ship which had gone round the world, being overset in sailing into port. What need for watchfulness and prayer! One heedless hour may stain the fairest life, and undo much of the good which we have been doing for a course of years! Drunkenness is a sin which involves in it the breach of the whole law, which requires love to God, our neighbour, and ourselves. The first as abusing his mercies; the second as depriving those who are in want of them of necessary support, as well as setting an ill example; and the last as depriving ourselves of reason, self-government, and common decency. It also commonly leads on to other evils. It has been said, and justly, that the name of this sin is Gad—*a troop cometh!*

But sinful as it was for Noah thus to expose himself, it was still more so for *Ham*, on perceiving his situation, to go out and report it with malignant pleasure to his brethren. None but a fool will make a mock at sin in any one: but for children to expose and flout at the sin of their parents, is wickedness of the most aggravated kind. It indicates a heart thoroughly depraved. The conduct of Shem and Japheth on this unhappy occasion, was as commendable as the other was censurable; and as worthy of our imitation as that is of our abhorrence.

Ver. 24. When Noah came to himself, he knew what had been done by his younger son. Nothing is said of his grief for his own sin. I hope his anger did not turn merely against that of his son. Nor are we to consider what follows as an ebullition of personal resentment, but as a prophecy, which was meant to apply, and has been ever since applying to his posterity, and which it was not possible for human resentment to dictate. But as this prophecy is very comprehensive, and will lead us to take notice of some of the great principles of revelation, I shall reserve it for a future discourse.

DISCOURSE XV.

NOAH's PROPHECY.

GENESIS ix. 25----27.

It was common among the patriarchs when about to die, to pronounce a prophetic sentence on their children, and which frequently bore a relation to what had been their conduct, and extended to their remote posterity. This prophecy however, though not immediately after the flood, was probably many years before the death of Noah.—I shall first attempt to ascertain its meaning, and agreement with the great outlines of historic fact, and then endeavour to justify the ways of providence in such dispensations.

The prophecy is introduced with a curse upon the posterity of one of Noah's sons, and concludes with a blessing upon the other two, each corresponding with his conduct on the late unhappy occasion.

Cursed be Canaan: a servant of servants, that is, the meanest of servants, *shall he be unto his brethren*—But why is the name of Ham omitted, and the curse confined to his son Canaan? Some suppose that Canaan must have been in some way partaker in the crime: but this is uncertain. It is thought by several able critics, that instead of Canaan we should read, as it is in ver. 22, *Ham the father of Canaan;** and which seems very plausible, as otherwise there is nothing said of Ham, except in the person of his son; and what is still more, the curse of servitude actually came, though at a remote period, upon other branches of the posterity of Ham, as well as Canaan. It is manifest however, that it was directed *principally* against him in the line of Canaan, and intended by Moses for the encouragement of Israel in going up against his descendents, the Canaanites. Canaan is under a curse of servitude to both Shem and Japheth: the former was fulfilled in the conquest of the seven nations of Israel; and the latter in the subjugation of the Tyrians and Carthaginians, who were the remainder of the old Canaanites, by the Greeks and Romans.

So far as the curse had reference to the other descendents of Ham, it was a long time, as I

---

* *Ainsworth* says, "By Canaan may be understood or implied Canaan's father, as the greek translation hath Ham, and as elsewhere in scripture, Goliath is named for Goliath's father. 2 Sam. xxi. 19, compared with 1 Chron. xx. 5. See also *Bishop Newton* on the prophecies. Disser. I.

have said, ere it came upon them. In the early ages of the world they flourished. They were the first who set up for empire; and so far from being subject to the descendents of Shem or Japheth, the latter were often invaded, and driven into corners by them. It was Nimrod, a descendent of Ham, who founded the imperial city of Babylon; and Mizraim, another of his descendents, who first established the kingdom of Egypt. These, it is well known, were for many ages two of the greatest empires in the world. About the time of the captivity however, God began to cut short their power. Both Egypt and Babylon within a century sunk into a state of subjection, first to the Persians who descended from Shem, and afterwards to the Greeks and Romans, who were the children of Japheth. Nor have they ever been able to recover themselves: for to the dominion of the Romans succeeded that of the Saracens, and to theirs that of the Turks, under which they with a great part of Africa, which is peopled by the children of Ham, have lived and still live in the most degraded state of subjection. To all this may be added, that the inhabitants of Africa seem to be marked out as objects of slavery by the European nations. Though these things are far from excusing the conduct of their oppressors, yet they establish the fact, and prove the fulfilment of prophecy.

Blessed be Jehovah, God of Shem!—The form of this blessing is worthy of notice. It may not seem to be pronounced on him, but on his God. But such a mode of speaking implies his blessedness, no less than if it had been expressly spoken of him; for it is a principle well known in religion, that "blessed is that people whose God is Jehovah." They are blessed in his blessedness. It is in this form that Moses describes the blessedness of Israel: "There is none like unto the God of Jeshurun, who rideth upon the heaven in thy help, and in his excellency on the sky."* Shem was the ancestor of Abram, and so of Israel, who, while the descendents of both Ham and Japheth were lost in idolatry, knew and worshipped Jehovah, the only true God; and of whom as concerning the flesh, Christ came, who is over all, God blessed for ever. It has been remarked too, that Shem is the first person who had the honour of having the Lord styled *his* God; and that this expression denotes his being a God *in covenant* with him, as when he is called the God of Abram, of Isaac, and of Jacob. Noah, foreseeing by a spirit of prophecy that God would enter into a special covenant with the posterity of Shem, taking them to be his peculiar people, and binding himself to be their God, was affected at the consideration of

* Deut. xxxiii. 26.

so great a privilege, and breaks out into an ascription of praise to God on this account.

God shall enlarge Japheth, and he shall dwell in the tents of Shem.—If this part of the prophecy have respect to temporal dominion, it seems to refer to the posterity of Japheth being formerly *straitened*, but in the later ages of the world enabled to extend their conquests, which exactly corresponds with history. For more than two thousand years the empire of the civilized world has in a manner been in the hands of the posterity of Japheth. First the Greeks, after them the Romans, and since the declension of their empire, the different powers of Europe, have entered into the richest possessions of Asia, inhabited by the children of Shem. Add to this, their borders have lately been enlarged beyond the Atlantic, and bid fair to extend over the continent of America.

But as Japheth united with Shem in the act of filial respect to his father, it would seem as if the dwelling of the one in the tents of the other must be friendly, and not hostile; and as the blessing of Shem had a peculiar reference to *the church of God* among his descendents, it may be considered as prophetic of the accession of the gentiles to it, under the gospel. It is a fact, that christianity has principally prevailed amongst the posterity of Japheth. The Lord God of Shem is there known, and honoured. The lively oracles given to the fathers of the one, are possessed and prized by the other: they laboured, and we have entered into their labours. This interpretation is favoured by the marginal reading, and which the very learned Ainsworth says the original word properly signifies: " God shall *persuade* Japheth, and he shall dwell in the tents of Shem."

Let us proceed, in the next place, to offer a remark or two on the *justice* of the divine proceeding in denouncing a curse upon children, even to remote periods, for the iniquity of their parents.—It is worthy of notice that the God of Israel thought it no dishonour to his character to declare, that he would " visit the iniquity of the fathers upon the children, in those that hated him," any more than that he would " shew mercy to those that loved him," which he did in an eminent degree to the posterity of Abram. And should any object to this, and to the bible on this account, we might appeal to universal fact. None can deny that children are the better or the worse for the conduct of their parents. If any man insist that neither good nor evil shall befal him, but what is the immediate consequence of his own conduct, he must go out of the world; for no such state of existence is known in it.

There is however an important difference between *the sin of a parent being the* OCCASION *of the prediction of a curse upon his posterity, who were considered by Him who knew the end from the beginning as walking in his steps, and its being the formal* CAUSE *of their punishment.* The sin of Ham was the *occasion* of the prediction against the Canaanites, and the *antecedent* to the evil predicted; but it was not the *cause* of it. Its formal procuring cause may be seen in the eighteenth chapter of Leviticus. To Ham, and perhaps to Canaan, the prediction of the servitude of their descendents was a punishment: but the fulfilment of that prediction on the parties was no farther such, than as it was connected with their own sin.

There is also an important difference between *the providential dispensations of God towards families and nations in the present world, and the administration of distributive justice towards individuals with respect to the world to come.* In the last judgment, "every one shall give an account of himself to God, and be judged according to the deeds done in the body:" but while we are in this world we stand in various relations, in which it is impossible that we should be dealt with merely as individuals. God deals with families and nations *as such;* and in the course of his providence visits them with good and evil, not according to the conduct of individuals, but, as far as conduct is concerned, that of the general body. To insist that we should in all cases be treated as individuals, is to renounce the social character.

We are informed at the close of the chapter, that Noah lived after the flood three hundred and fifty years, and died at the age of nine hundred and fifty. How long this was after the foregoing prophecy, we are not informed; but he lived to see in the descendents of Shem, Eber, and Nahor, and Terah the father of Abram.

DISCOURSE XVI.

THE GENERATIONS OF NOAH.

GENESIS X.

Without this genealogy we should not have been able to ascertain the fulfilment of Noah's prophecy: but after what has been said on that subject, I need not be particular here. The chapter contains the origin of the various nations of antiquity; and the more it is examined, and compared with universal history, the more credible it will appear. All the researches of the Asiatic Society, into the ancient Hindoo records, go to confirm it. But it does not comport with the object of these discourses to enter minutely into such subjects: I shall therefore pass over it with only a few remarks.

1. Concerning the posterity of *Japheth*, ver. 2—5. His family was the largest, and almost every one of his sons became the father of a nation. In them, amongst others, we trace the names of *Madia*, the father of the Medes;—of *Javan*, and his two sons, *Kittim* and *Dodanim*, the fathers of the Ionians or Greeks, and of the Romans. It was from Japheth that all the nations of Europe appear to have been peopled; and who seem at this early period to have obtained the name of Gentiles; viz. *peoples*, or *nations*. (ver. 5.) This name was given in the apostles' times to all who were not Jews; but in earlier ages it seems to have been chiefly, if not entirely, applied to the Europeans. Such at least is the meaning of "the isles of the gentiles," in which, by a synecdoche, those places which were the nearest to the situation of the sacred writer are put for all the countries beyond them. And the scriptures foreseeing that Europe would from

the first embrace the gospel, and for many ages be the principal seat of its operations, the Messiah himself is introduced by Isaiah as addressing himself to its inhabitants—"Listen, *oh isles*, unto me; and hearken ye people from afar! Jehovah hath called me from the womb, and hath said unto me, It is a light thing that thou shouldst be my servant to raise up the tribes of Jacob—I will also give thee for a light to the *gentiles*, that thou shouldst be my salvation to the end of the earth."* Here we see, not only the first peopling of our native country, but the kind remembrance of us in a way of mercy, and this though far removed from the means of salvation. What a call is this to us who occupy what is denominated *the end of the earth*, to be thankful for the gospel, and to listen to the sweet accents of the Saviour's voice!

2. Concerning the posterity of *Ham*, ver. 6—20. In them, amongst others, we trace the names of *Cush*, the father of the Ethiopians; of *Misraim*, the father of the Egyptians; and of Canaan, the father of the Canaanites.

Particular notice is taken of *Nimrod*, the son of Cush, as the first who set up for empire. He might, for ought I know, be fond of hunt-

* Isai. xlix. 1—6.

ing beasts; but the connexion of this character with a "kingdom," induces me to think that *men* were the principal objects of his pursuit, and that it is in reference to this that he is called *a mighty hunter*, a very proper name for what modern historians would have called a hero. Thus we see from the beginning, that things which are highly esteemed amongst men are held in abomination with God. This perfectly accords with the language of the prophets, in which the great conquerors of the earth are described as so many *wild beasts*, pushing at one another, and whose object it is to seize and tear the prey.—Nimrod was a mighty hunter *before the Lord.* This may denote his daring spirit, doing what he did in the face of heaven, or in defiance of the divine authority. Thus the Sodomites are said to be "wicked, and sinners *before the Lord,* exceedingly." Nimrod's fame was so great that his name became proverbial. When any one in after times was a daring plunderer in defiance of heaven, he was likened to him, just as the wicked kings of Israel were likened to Jeroboam the son of Nebat, who made Israel to sin. In short, he became the type, pattern, or father of usurpers and martial plunderers. Till his time, government had been patriarchal; but his ambition led him to found a royal city, even that which was afterwards called Babel or Babylon; and to add to it (for the ambition of conquerors has no bounds) "Erech, and Accad, and Calneh, in the land of Shinar." Nor was this all. Either he drove Ashur, the son of Shem, from the land of Shinar, who, taking up his residence in Assyria, built Nineveh, and other places; or else, as Ainsworth, and the margin of our own bibles, render it, *He* (Nimrod) *went forth out of that land to Ashur, or Assyria, and builded Nineveh.* This last is very probably the true meaning, as the sacred writer is not here describing what was done by the posterity of Shem, which he introduces afterwards, but by those of Ham; and it perfectly accords with Nimrod's character, to go hunting from land to land, for the purpose of increasing his dominion.

From *Misraim*, the father of the Egyptians, descended also the Philistines. Their situation was near to that of the Canaanites; but not being of them, their country was not given to Israel. This accounts for their not attempting to take it, though in after times there were frequent wars between them.

Finally: Moses was very particular with regard to the Canaanites, describing not only what nations they were, but what were their boundaries, that Israel might know and be content with what the Lord their God had given them. Under this head we see much of what pertains to this world, but that is all. We may learn from it, that men may be under the divine curse, and yet be very successful for a time in schemes of aggrandizement. But if this be their all, woe unto them! There are instances however of individuals, even from amongst Ham's posterity, who obtained mercy. Of them were Rahab the harlot, Uriah the Hittite, Obed-edom, and Ittai, and his brethren the Gittites, and the Syrophenician woman who applied to Christ. The door of mercy is open to faith, without distinction of nations; nor was there ever a time in which the God of Israel refused even a Canaanite who repented and embraced his word.

3. Concerning the posterity of *Shem*, ver. 21—32. The account of this patriarch is introduced in rather a singular manner: it is mentioned as an appendage to his name, a kind of title of honour that was to go along with it, that he was "father of all the children of Eber, and brother of Japheth the elder." Shem had other sons as well as these, and another brother as well as Japheth; but no such special mention is made of them. When Moses would describe *the line of the curse*, he calls Ham "the father

of Canaan;" (ch. ix. 18.) and when *the line of promise*, he calls Shem "the father of all the children of Eber." And as Japheth had been the brother of Shem in an act of filial duty, his posterity shall be grafted in among them, and become fellow-heirs of the same promise; yet, as in divers other instances, the younger goes before the elder.

Among Shem's other descendents we find the names of *Elam* and *Ashur*, fathers of the Persians and Assyrians, two great Asiatic nations. But these not being of the church of God, are but little noticed in the sacred history, except as they come in contact with it.

Eber is said to have had two sons, one of whom is called Peleg, *division;* because in his days the earth was *divided*. This event took place subsequent to the confusion of tongues, which is yet to be related. It seems to refer to an allotment of different countries to different families, as Canaan was divided amongst the Israelites by Joshua. This division of the earth is elsewhere ascribed to the Most High.* Probably it was by lot, which was of his disposing; or if by the fathers of the different families, all was subject to the direction of His providence

* Deut. xxxii. 8.

who fixes and bounds our habitation. It is intimated in the same passage, that at the time of this division, God marked out the holy land as Israel's lot; so that the Canaanites were to possess it only during his minority, and that by sufferance. It was rather lent than given them from the first.

DISCOURSE XVII.

THE CONFUSION OF TONGUES.

GENESIS xi. 1——9.

It has been before noticed, that this story is thrown farther on, on account of finishing the former. The event took place before the division of the earth in the time of Peleg; for every family is there repeatedly said to be divided "after their tongues;"* which implies that at that time they spake various languages, and that this was one of the rules by which they were distinguished as nations.

Prior to the flood, and down to this period, "the whole earth was of one language." We are not told what this was. Whether it was the same which continued in the family of Eber, or

* Chap. x. 5, 20, 31.

whether from this time it was lost, is a matter of small account to us. But it seemed good in the sight of God from hence to divide mankind into different nations, and to this end to give them each a different tongue. The occasion of this great event will appear from the following story.

The posterity of Noah, beginning to encrease, found it necessary to extend their habitations. A company of them, journeying from the east, pitched upon a certain plain in the land of Shinar, by the river Euphrates. Judging it to be an eligible spot, they consulted, and determined here to build a city. There was no stone it seems near at hand; but there was a kind of earth very suitable for bricks, and a bituminous substance which is said to ooze from certain springs in that plain, like tar or pitch, and this they used for cement. Of these materials were afterwards built the famous walls of Babylon.

Having found a good material, they propose to build "a city and a tower" of great eminence, by which they should obtain "a name," and avoid the evil of which they thought themselves in danger, of being scattered upon the face of the whole earth. But here they were interrupted by a divine interposition: the Lord came down and confounded their language, so that they could not understand one another's speech.

To perceive the *reason* of this extraordinary proceeding, it is necessary to enquire into the *object* or *design* of the builders. If this can be ascertained, the whole passage may be easily understood. It could not be, as some have supposed, to provide against a future flood; for this would have needed no divine interposition to prevent its having effect. God knew his own intention never to drown the world any more: and if it had been otherwise, or they from a disbelief of his promise had been disposed to provide against it, they would not have been so foolish as to build for this purpose a tower upon a *plain*, which when raised to the greatest possible height, would be far below the tops of the mountains. It could not have been said of such a scheme, *This they have begun to do: and now nothing will be restrained from them, which they have imagined to do:* for it would have defeated itself.

Neither does it appear to have been designed, as others have supposed, for an *idol's temple*. There is nothing in the story, however, which leads to such a conclusion. It was not for the name of a god, but for their *own name*, that they proposed to build; and that not the *tower* only, but *a city and a tower*. Nor was the confounding of their language any way adapted, that I can perceive, to defeat such a design as this. Idolatry prevailed in the world, for ought appears, as much under a variety of languages as it would under one.

Some have imagined that it was intended merely as a monument of architectural ambition, like the pyramids of Egypt. This supposition might in a measure agree with the idea of doing it for *a name:* but it is far from harmonizing with other parts of the story. It contains no such deep-laid scheme as is intimated in the sixth verse, and given as the reason of the divine interference: nor is it supposable that God should interpose in so extraordinary a manner, by working a miracle which should remain throughout every age of the world, or which at least has remained to this day, merely for the purpose of counteracting a momentary freak of human vanity.

There are four characters by which this design, whatever it was, is described.—(1.) It was founded in *ambition;* for they said, " Let us make us *a name.*"—(2.) It required *union;* for which purpose they proposed to build *a city*, that they might live together, and concentrate their strength and counsels. This is noticed by the Lord himself: " Behold, the people (saith he) *are one*, and have all one language:" and his confounding their language was for the express purpose of destroying this oneness, by *scattering them abroad upon the face of the earth.*—(3.) It required that they should be furnished with the means of *defence;* for which they proposed to add a *tower* to the city, to which the citizens might repair in times of danger; and of such a height as to bid defiance to any who should attempt to annoy them with arrows, or other missive weapons.—(4.) The scheme was *wisely laid;* so much so, that if God had not interposed to frustrate it, it would have succeeded: *And this they have begun to do; and now nothing will be restrained from them, which they have imagined to do.*

The only object which appears to accord with all these general characters, and with the whole account taken together, is that of AN UNIVERSAL MONARCHY, *by which all the families of the earth, in all future ages, might be held in subjection.*—A very little reflexion will convince us that such a scheme must of necessity be founded in *ambition;* that it required *union*, and of course a *city*, to carry it into execution; that a *tower*, or citadel, was also necessary to repel those who might be disposed to dispute their claims; and that if these measures were once carried into effect, there was nothing in the nature of things to *prevent the accomplishment of their design.*

If there were no other reasons in favour of the supposition in question, its agreement with all these circumstances of the history might be thought sufficient to establish it: but to this, other things may be added by way of corroboration.

The *time* when the confusion of tongues took place, renders it highly probable that the scheme which it was intended to subvert was of *Nimrod's* forming, or that he had a principal concern in it. It must have been a little before *the division of the earth* amongst the sons of Shem, Ham, and Japheth, *after their* TONGUES, *in their countries, and in their nations;** being that which rendered such division necessary. Now this was about the time of the birth of Peleg, who was named from that event; and this, by reckoning the genealogies mentioned in chap. xi. 10—16, will appear to have been about a hundred years after the flood. At this time, Nimrod, who was

* Chap. x. 5, 20, 31.

the grandson of Ham, must have been alive, and in his prime. And as he was the first person who aspired to dominion over his brethren, and as it is expressly said of him, that *the beginning of his kingdom was Babel,* nothing is more natural than to suppose that he was the leader in this famous enterprize; and that the whole was a scheme of his, by which to make himself master of the world.

It was also natural for an ambitious people, headed by an ambitious leader, to set up for *universal monarchy.* Such has been the object of almost all the great nations and conquerors of the earth in later periods. Babylon, though checked for the present, by this divine interference, yet afterwards resumed the pursuit of her favourite object; and in the time of Nebuchadnezzer, seemed almost to have gained it. The style used by that monarch in his proclamations comported with the spirit of this idea: "To you it is commanded, oh people, nations, and tongues!"* Now if such has been the ambition of all Nimrod's successors, in every age, it is nothing surprising that it should have struck the mind of Nimrod himself, and his adherents. They would also have a sort of claim to which their successors could not pretend; namely, that

* Dan. iii. 2.

of being the *first*, or *parent* kingdom; and the weight which men are apt to attach to this claim, may be seen by the later pretensions of Papal Rome, (another Babylon) which, under the character of a *mother church*, headed by a *pope*, or pretended holy *father*, has subjected all christendom to her dominion.

To this may be added, That the means used to counteract these builders, were exactly suited to defeat the above design; namely, that of *dividing* and *scattering* them, by confounding their language. And it is worthy of notice, that though several empires have extended their territories over people of different languages, yet language has been a very common boundary of nations ever since. There is scarcely a great nation in the world, but what has its own language. The dividing of languages was therefore, in effect, the dividing of nations; and so a bar to the whole world being ruled by one government. Thus a perpetual miracle was wrought to be an antidote to a perpetual disease.

But why, it may be asked, should it be the will of God to prevent a universal monarchy; and to divide the inhabitants of the world into a number of independent nations?—This question opens a wide field for investigation. Suffice it to say at present, such a state of things contains much mercy, both to the world and to the church.

With respect to the *world*, If the whole earth had continued under one government, that government would of course, considering what human nature is, have been exceedingly despotic and oppressive. We know that in every state of society, where power or wealth, or commerce, is monopolized by an individual, or confined to a few, whose interests may unite them to one another, there is the greatest possible scope for injustice and oppression; and where there is the greatest scope for these evils, human nature being what it is, there they will most abound. Different nations and interests in the world serve as a balance one to the other. They are that to the world which a number of rival merchants, or lesser tradesmen, are to society; serving as a check upon each other's rapacity. Union, when cemented by *good-will to men*, is exceedingly desirable: but when self-interest and ambition are at the bottom, it is exceedingly dangerous. Union in such cases is nothing better than a combination against the general good.

It might be thought that if the whole world were under one government, a great number of *wars* might be prevented, which, as things now are, would be certain to take place. And it is true, that one stable government *to a certain extent*, is on this account preferable to a great number of lesser ones, which are always at variance. But this principle, if carried beyond certain limits, becomes inimical to human happiness. So far as different people can really become one, and drop all local distinctions and interests, it is well: but if the good of the country governed be lost sight of, and every thing is done to aggrandize the city, or country governing, it is otherwise. And where power is thus exercised, which it certainly would be in case of a universal monarchy, it would produce as many wars as now exist, with only this difference, that instead of their being carried on between independent nations, they would consist of the risings of different parts of the empire against the government in a way of rebellion: and by how much wars of this kind are accompanied with less mutual respect, less quarter given and taken, and consequently more cruelty than the other, by so much would the state of the world have been more miserable than it is at present.

The division of the world into independent nations has also been a great check on *persecu-*

tion, and so has operated in a way of mercy towards the *church*.—If the whole world had been one despotic government, Israel, the people of God, must in all ages have been in the condition which they were reduced to from the times of the captivity, as a punishment for their sins, a mere province of another power, which might have crushed them, and hindered them, as was the case from the times of Cyrus to those of Darius.* And since the coming of Christ, the only way in which he permits his followers to avoid the malice of the world which rages against them for his sake, is this: "If they persecute you in one city, flee to another." Of this liberty millions have availed themselves, from the earliest to the latest periods of the christian church: but if the whole world had been under one government, and that government inimical to the gospel, there had been no place of refuge left upon earth for the faithful.

The necessary watch also that governments which have been the most disposed to persecute, have been obliged to keep on each other, has filled their hands, so as to leave them but little time to think of religious people. Saul, when pursuing David, was withdrawn from his purpose by intelligence being brought him, that *the*

* Ezra iv. 23, 24.

Philistines had invaded the land: and thus in innumerable instances, the fallings out of bad men have been advantageous to the righteous.

The division of power serves likewise to check the spirit of persecution, not only as finding employment for persecutors to watch their rivals, but as causing them to be watched, and their conduct exposed by them. While the power of papal Rome extended over christendom, persecution raged abundantly more than it has done since the Reformation, even in popish countries. Since that period, the popish powers, both ecclesiastical and civil, have felt themselves narrowly watched by protestants, and have been almost shamed out of their former cruelties. What has been done of late years has been principally confined to the secret recesses of the Inquisition. It is by communities as it is by individuals: they are restrained from innumerable excesses by the consideration of being under the eye of each other. Thus it is, that liberty of conscience being granted in one or two nations, and becoming honourable, has insensibly made its way into the councils of many others.

From the whole we may infer two things.— (1.) The harmony of divine revelation with all that we know of fact. If any object to the probability of the foregoing account, and imagine that the various languages spoken in the world must have been of human contrivance, let them point us to a page in any history, ancient or modern, which gives an account of the first making of a language, dead or living. If all that man can be proved to have done towards the formation of any language be confined to changing, combining, improving, and reducing it to grammatical form, there is the greatest probability, independent of the authority of revelation, that languages themselves were originally the work of God, as was that of the first man and woman.—(2.) The desirableness of the universal spread of Christ's kingdom. We may see in the *reasons* which render a universal government among men incompatible with the liberty and safety of the world, abundant cause to pray for this, and for the *union* of all his subjects under him. Here there is no danger of tyranny or oppression, nor any need of those low motives of rivalship to induce him to seek the well-being of his subjects. A union with Christ and one another, embraces the best interests of mankind.

DISCOURSE XVIII.

THE GENERATIONS OF SHEM, AND THE CALL OF ABRAM.

GENESIS xi. 10——32. xii. 1——4.

The sacred historian having given an account of the re-peopling of the earth, here takes leave of the children of men, and confines himself to the history of the sons of God. We shall find him all along adhering to this principle. When any of the posterity of the righteous turn their backs on God, he presently takes leave of them, and follows the true church and true religion wherever they go.

Ver. 10—26. The principal use of the genealogy of Shem to Terah, the father of Abram, may be to prove the fulfilment of all the promises in the Messiah. To this purpose it is applied in the new testament.

Ver. 27—29. Terah, after he was seventy years of age, had three sons; Abram, Nahor, and Haran. But the order in which they here stand, does not appear to be that of seniority, any more than that of Shem, and Ham, and

Japheth: for if Abram had been born when Terah was *seventy* years old, he must have been *a hundred and thirty-five* at the time of his father's death; whereas he is said to have been but *seventy-five*, when, after that event, he set out for Canaan. Haran therefore appears to have been the eldest of the three sons. He died in Ur of the Chaldees; but left behind him a son and two daughters; Lot, and Milcah, and Iscah. The two surviving sons, Abram and Nahor, took them wives: the name of Abram's wife was Sarai, of whose descent we are not here told; but by what he said of her in chap. xx. 12, it would seem that she was his half-sister, or his father's daughter by another wife. In those early ages nearer degrees of consanguinity were admitted, than were afterwards allowed by the divine law. Nahor married his brother Haran's eldest daughter Milcah.

Ver. 31. It is said of Terah, that he took Abram his son, and Lot the son of Haran, his grandson, and Sarai his daughter-in-law, his son Abram's wife, and that they went from Ur of the Chaldees to go into the land of Canaan. But here is something supposed which the historian reserves till he comes to the story of Abram, who next to God, was the first mover in the undertaking, and the principal character in the story. In chap. xii. 1. we are told that "the Lord *had* said unto Abram, get thee out of thy country, and from thy kindred, and from thy father's house, unto a land that I will shew thee." Taking the whole together, it appears that God revealed himself to Abram, and called him to depart from that idolatrous and wicked country, whether any of his relations would go with him or not; that Abram told it to his father Terah, and to all the family, and invited them to accompany him; that Terah consented, as did also his grandson Lot; that Nahor and his wife Milcah were unwilling to go, and did not go at present; that seeing they refused, the venerable Terah left them, and being the head of the family he is said to have *taken* Abram, and Sarai, and Lot, though not the first mover in the affair, and journeyed towards Canaan; that stopping within the country of Mesopotamia, he called the place where he pitched his tent, Haran, in memory of his son who died in Ur of the Chaldees; finally, that during his residence in this place he died, being two hundred and five years old.

But though Nahor and Milcah, as it should seem, refused to accompany the family at the time, yet as we find them, in the course of the history, settled at Haran, and Abram and Isaac sending to them for wives, to the rejection of the idolaters among whom they lived, we may conclude that they afterwards repented and went. And thus the whole of Terah's family, though they do not go to Canaan, yet are rescued from Chaldean idolatry; and, settling in Haran, maintain for a considerable time the worship of the true God.

Chap. xii. 1—3. But Abram must not stop at Haran. Jehovah, by whom he was called to depart from Ur, has another country in reserve for him; and he being the great patriarch of Israel, and of the church of God, we have here a more particular account of his call. It was fit that this should be clearly and fully stated, for that it went to lay the foundation of a new order of things in the world. It was therefore like the spring of a great river; or rather, like the hole of a quarry whence the first stone was taken, of which a city was built. It is this which is referred to for the encouragement of the church when in a low condition, and likely to become extinct. God "called Abram alone, and blessed him, and encreased him." Hence the faithful are directed to "look to the rock whence they were hewn, and to the hole of the pit whence they were digged;" and to depend upon his promise, who assured them that he would comfort the waste places of Zion. Isai. li.

Gen. 12.] CALL OF ABRAM. 149

How long Abram continued at Haran, we are not told; but about nine years after his departure from it, we read of his having three hundred and eighteen trained servants, who were "born in his house:* he must therefore have kept house between twenty and thirty years, at least, before that time, and which must have been in Haran, or in both Ur and Haran.

In the call of Abram, we may observe,—(1.) The *grace* of it. There appears no reason to conclude that he was better than his neighbours. He did not choose the Lord, but the Lord him, and brought him out from amongst the idolaters.†—(2.) Its *peremptory tone:* "get thee out." The language very much resembles that of Lot to his sons-in-law, and indicates the great danger of his present situation, and the immediate necessity of escaping, as it were, for his life. Such is the condition of every unconverted sinner, and such the necessity of fleeing from the wrath to come, to the hope set before us in the gospel.—(3.) The *self-denial* required by it. He was called to leave his country, his kindred, and even his father's house, if they refused to go with him; and no doubt his mind was made up to do so. Such things are easier to read concerning others, than to practise ourselves: yet

* Chap. xiv. 14.   † Neh. ix. 7.

he that hateth not father and mother, and wife and children, and brethren and sisters, yea and his own life also, in comparison of Christ, cannot be his disciple. We may not be called upon to part with them; but our minds must be made up to do so, if they stand between us and Christ.—(4.) The *implicit faith* which a compliance with it would call for. Abram was to leave all, and to go .... he knew not whither .... "unto a land that God would shew him." If he had been told it was a land flowing with milk and honey, and that he should be put in possession of it, there had been some food for sense to feed upon: but to go out, "not knowing whither he went," must have been not a little trying to flesh and blood. Nor was this all: that which was promised was not only in general terms, but very *distant*. God did not tell him he would *give* him the land, but merely *shew* him it. Nor did he in his life-time obtain the possession of it: he was only a sojourner in it, without so much as a place to set his foot upon. He obtained a spot, it is true, to lay his bones in; but that was all. In this manner were things ordered on purpose to try his faith; and his obedience to God under such circumstances was among the things which rendered him an example to future generations, even "the father of all them that believe."

Ver. 2. The promise had reference to things which could be but of small account to an eye of sense; but faith would find enough in it to satisfy the most enlarged desires. The objects, though distant, were worth waiting for. He should be the father of *a great nation;* and what was of greater account, and which was doubtless understood, that nation should be the Lord's. God himself would *bless him;* and this would be more than the whole world without it. He would also *make his name great;* not in the records of worldly fame, but in the history of the church: and being himself full of the blessing of the Lord, it should be his to impart blessedness to the world. "I will bless thee, and *thou shalt be a blessing.*" The great names among the heathen would very commonly arise from their being curses and plagues to mankind; but he should have the honour and happiness of being great in goodness, great in communicating light and life to his species.

This promise has been fulfilling ever since. All the true blessedness which the world is now, or shall hereafter be possessed of, is owing to Abram and his posterity. Through them we have a bible, a Saviour, and a gospel. They are the stock on which the christian church is grafted. Their very dispersions and punishments have proved the riches of the world. What then shall be their recovery, but life from the dead! It would seem as if the conversion of the jews, whenever it shall take place, will be a kind of resurrection to mankind. Such was the hope of this calling. And what could the friends of God and man desire more? Yet, as if all this were not enough, it is added—

Ver. 3. "I will bless them that bless thee, and curse him that curseth thee." This is language never used but of an object of special favour. It is declaring that he should not only be blessed himself, but that all others should be blessed or cursed, as they respected or injured him. Of this the histories of Abimelech, Laban, Potiphar, both the Pharaohs, Balak and Balaam furnish examples.

Finally: Lest what had been said of his being *made a blessing* should not be sufficiently explicit, it is added, "and in thee shall all the families of the earth be blessed." This was saying that a blessing was in reserve for all nations, and that it should be bestowed through him and his posterity, as the medium. Paul applies this to Christ, and the believing gentiles being blessed in him: he calls it "the gospel which was preached before unto Abraham." (Gal. iii. 7—16.)

Peter also makes use of it in his address to those who had killed the Prince of life, to induce them to repent and believe in him. "Ye are the children of the prophets, (says he) and of the covenants which God made with our fathers, saying unto Abram, *and in thy seed shall all the kindreds of the earth be blessed.* Unto you *first*, God having raised up his Son Jesus, sent him to bless you, in turning away every one of you from his iniquities."* As if he had said, 'You are descended from one whose posterity were to be blessed above all nations, and made a blessing. And the time to favour the nations being now at hand, God sent his Son *first* to you, to bless you, and to prepare you for blessing them; as though it were yours to be a nation of ministers, or missionaries to the world. But how, if instead of blessing others, you should continue accursed yourselves? You must first be blessed, ere you can, as the true children of Abram, bless the kindreds of the earth, and that by every one of you being turned from his iniquities.'

Ver. 4. The faith of Abram operated in a way of prompt and implicit obedience. First it induced him to leave Ur of the Chaldees, and now he must leave Haran. Haran was become the place of his father's sepulchre, yet he must

* Acts iii. 25, 26.

not stop there, but press forwards to the land which the Lord would shew him. On this occasion young Lot, his nephew, seems to have felt a cleaving to him, like that of Ruth to Naomi, and must needs go with him; encouraged no doubt by his uncle in some such such manner as Moses afterwards encouraged Hobab: Go with me, and I will do thee good; for the Lord hath spoken good concerning Abram.

Ver. 5. We now see Abram, being seventy-five years old, and Sarai, and Lot, with all they are and have, taking a long farewell of Haran, as they had done before of Ur. " The souls that they had gotten in Haran" could not refer to children, but perhaps to some godly servants who cast in their lot with them. Abram had a religious household, who were under his government, as we afterwards read; one of whom went to seek a wife for Isaac. We also read of one " Eliezer of Damascus,"* who seems to have been not only his household steward, but the only man he could think of, if he died childless, to be his heir. With these he set off for the land of Canaan, which by this time he knew to be the country that the Lord would shew him, and to the land of Canaan he came.

* Gen. xv. 2.

DISCOURSE XIX.

ABRAM DWELLING IN CANAAN, AND REMOVING TO EGYPT ON ACCOUNT OF THE FAMINE.

GENESIS xii. 6——20.

VER. 6. Abram and his company having entered into the country, on its north-eastern quarter, penetrate as far southward as *Sichem*, where, meeting with a spacious plain, the plain of Moreh, they pitched their tents. This place was afterwards much accounted of. Jacob came thither on his return from Haran, and bought of the Shechemites a parcel of a field.* It might be the same spot where Abram dwelt, and perhaps on that account. After this it seems to have been taken from him by the Amorites, the descendents of Hamor, of whom he had bought it; and he was obliged to recover it by the sword and by the bow. This was the portion which he gave to his son Joseph.† There seems to be something in the history of this place very much resembling that of the country in general. In the grand division of the earth, this whole land was assigned to the posterity of Shem: but the

---

* Gen. xxxiii. 19. † Chap. xlviii. 22.

Canaanites had seized on it, and as is here noticed, "dwelt in the land." As soon therefore as the rightful owners are in a capacity to make use of the sword and the bow, they must be dispossessed of it.*

Ver. 7. Abram having pitched his tent at Sichem, the Lord renews to him the promise of the whole land, or rather to his seed after him; for with respect to himself, he was never given to expect any higher character than that of a sojourner. But considering the great ends to be answered by his seed possessing it, he is well satisfied, and rears an altar to Jehovah. One sees here the difference between the conduct of the men of this world, and that of the Lord's servants. The former no sooner find a fruitful plain, than they fall to building a city, and a tower, to perpetuate their fame. The first concern of the latter is to raise an altar to God. It was thus that the new world was consecrated by Noah, and now the land of promise by Abram. The rearing of an altar in the land was like taking possession of it, in right, for Jehovah.

Ver. 8, 9. The patriarchs seldom continued long at a place, for they were sojourners. Abram removes from the plain of Moreh to a mountain

---

* See on chap. x. 25, p. 130.

on the east of what was afterwards called Bethel; and here he built an altar, and called upon the name of the Lord. This place was also much accounted of in after times. It was not far from hence that Jacob slept and dreamed, and anointed the pillar.* We may on various occasions change places, provided we carry the true religion with us: in this we must never change.

Ver. 10—20. Abram was under the necessity of removing again, and that on account of a grievous famine in the land. He must now leave Canaan for awhile, and journey into Egypt, where corn, it seems, was generally plentiful, even when it was scarce in other countries, because that country was watered not so much by rain as by the waters of the Nile. Hither therefore the patriarch repaired with his little company. Here we see new trials for his faith. Observe,

1. The famine itself being in *the land of promise*, must be a trial to him. Had he been of the spirit of the unbelieving spies in the times of Moses, he would have said, 'Would God we had staid at Haran, if not at Ur! Surely this is a land that eateth up the inhabitants.' But thus far Abram sinned not.

* Gen. xxviii. 19.

2. The beauty of Sarai was another trial to him; and here he fell into the sin of dissimulation, or at least of equivocation. She was half-sister to him, it seems;* but not in such a sense as he meant to convey. This was one of the first faults in Abram's life; and the worst of it is, it was repeated, as we shall see hereafter. It is remarkable, that there is only one faultless character on record; and more so, that in several instances of persons who have been distinguished for some one excellency, their principal failure has been in that particular. Thus Peter, the bold, sins through fear; Solomon, the wise, by folly; Moses, the meek, by speaking unadvisedly with his lips; and Abram, the faithful, by a kind of dissimulation arising from timid distrust. Such things would almost seem designed of God to stain the pride of all flesh, and to check all dependence upon the most eminent or confirmed habits of godliness.

3. Yet from these trials, and from the difficulties into which he brought himself by his own misconduct, the Lord mercifully delivered him. He feared they would kill him for his wife's sake; but God, by introducing plagues amongst them, inspired them with fear, and induced them to send him and his wife away in

* See on Gen. xi. 27—29. pp.

safety. It was thus that he rebuked kings for their sakes, and suffered no man to hurt them. In how many instances has God, by his kind providence, extricated us from situations into which our own sin and folly had plunged us!

DISCOURSE XX.

THE SEPARATION OF ABRAM AND LOT.

GENESIS xiii.

VER. 1—4. We have heard nothing of Lot, till now, since he left Haran; but he appears to have been one of Abram's family, and to have gone with him whithersoever he went. Here we find him returning with him from Egypt, first to the south of Canaan, and afterwards to Bethel, the place of his second residence, where he had before built an altar. The manner in which "the place of the altar" is mentioned, seems to intimate that he chose to go thither, in preference to another place, on this account. It is very natural that he should do so; for the places where we have called upon the name of the Lord, and enjoyed communion with him, are, by association, endeared to us above all others. There Abram again called on the name of the Lord; and the present exercises of grace, we may suppose, were aided by the remembrance of the past. It is an important rule in choosing our habitations, to have an eye to the place of the altar. If Lot had acted upon this principle, he would not have done as is here related of him.

Ver. 5, 6. We find by the second verse, that Abram was very rich; and here we see that Lot also had "flocks, and herds, and tents;" so that "the land was not able to bear them, that they should dwell together." It is pleasing to see how the blessing of the Lord attends these two sojourners: but it is painful to find that prosperity should become the occasion of their separation. It is pity that those whom grace unites, and who are fellow-heirs of eternal life, should be parted by the lumber of this world. Yet so it is. A clash of worldly interests has often separated chief friends, and been the occasion of a much greater loss than the greatest earthly fulness has been able to compensate. It is not thus with the riches of grace, or of glory: the more we have of them, the closer it unites us.

Ver. 7. The first inconvenience which arose from the wealth of these two good men, appeared in strifes between their herdmen. It was better to be so, than if the masters had fallen out; but even this is far from pleasant. Those of each would tell their tale to their masters, and try to persuade them that the others had used them ill; and the best of men, having such tales frequently repeated, would begin to suspect that all was not fair. What can be done? " The Canaanite and the Perizzite also dwelt in the land." Now Abram and Lot, having never joined in the idolatries and other wickednesses of the country, must needs have been marked as a singular kind of men, and passed as worshippers of the invisible God. If therefore they fall out about worldly matters, what will be thought and said of their religion? 'See how these religious people love one another!'

Ver. 8, 9. Abram's conduct in this unpleasant business was greatly to his honour. To form a just judgment of any character, we must follow him through a number of different situations, and circumstances, and observe how he acts in times of trial. We have seen Abram in his first conversion from idolatry; we have noticed the strength of his faith, and the promptness of his obedience to the heavenly call; we have admired his godly and consistent conduct in every place where he has sojourned, one instance only excepted: but we have not yet seen how he would act in a case of approaching difference with a friend, a brother. Here then we have it.—Observe,

1. He foresees *the danger there is of a falling out between himself and Lot.* It is likely he perceived his countenance was not towards him as heretofore, and that he discovered an uneasiness of mind. This would excite a becoming apprehension, lest that which begun with the servants should end with the masters, and be productive of great evil to them both.

2. He *deprecates it in the frankest, most pacific, and most affectionate manner.* "Let there be no strife between me and thee, and between my herdmen and thy herdmen, for we are brethren"—yes, brethren not only in the flesh, but in the Lord.

3. He *makes a most wise and generous proposal.* "The whole land is before us: separate thyself, I pray thee, from me. If thou wilt go to the left hand, I will go to the right; or if thou wilt go to the right hand, then I will go to the left." As the elder man, Abram might have insisted upon the right of choosing his part of the country first, especially as he was the principal, and Lot only accompanied him: he might have told him that if he was not con-

tented to live with him, he might go whither he would: but thus did not Abram. No, he would rather forego his civil rights than invade religious peace. What a number of bitter animosities in families, in churches, and I may say, in nations, might be prevented, if the parties could be brought to act towards one another in this open, pacific, disinterested and generous manner. There are cases in which it becomes necessary for very worthy and dear friends to separate: it were better to part, than live together at variance. Many may be good neighbours who could not live happy in the same family. Abram and Lot could love and pray for one another when there was nothing to ruffle their feelings: and Saul and Barnabas could both serve the cause of Christ, though unhappily, through a third person, they cannot act in close concert. In all such cases, if there be only an upright, pacific, and disinterested disposition, things will be so adjusted as to do no material injury to the cause of Christ. In many instances it may serve to promote it. In a world where there is plenty of room to serve the Lord, and plenty of work to be done, if those who cannot continue together be disposed to improve their advantages, the issue may be such as shall cause the parties to unite in a song of praise.

Ver. 10, 11. But how does young Lot conduct himself on this occasion? He did not, nor could he object to the pacific and generous proposal that was made to him; nor did he choose Abram's situation, which though lovely in the one to offer, would have been very unlovely in the other to have accepted; and I hope, though nothing is said of his making any reply, it was not from a spirit of sullen reserve. But in the choice he made, he appears to have *regarded temporal advantages only, and entirely to have overlooked the danger of his situation with regard to religion.* " He lifted up his eyes, and beheld a well-watered plain;" and on this he fixed his choice, though it led him to take up his abode in Sodom. He viewed it, as we should say, merely with a grazier's eye. He had better have been in a wilderness than there. Yet many professors of religion, in choosing situations for themselves, and for their children, continue to follow his example. We shall perceive in the sequel of the story, what kind of a harvest his well-watered plain produced him!

Ver. 12, 13. It is possible, after all, that his principal fault lay in pitching his tent in the place he did. If he could have lived on the plain, and preserved a sufficient distance from that infamous place, there might have been nothing the matter: but perhaps he did not like to live alone, and therefore " dwelt *in the cities* of the plain, and pitched his tent *toward Sodom.*" The love of society, like all other natural principles, may prove a blessing or a curse: and we may see by this example, the danger of leaving religious connexions; for as man feels it not good to be alone, if he forego these, he will be in a manner impelled by his inclinations to take up with others of a contrary description. It is an awful character which is here given of Lot's new neighbours. All men are sinners; but they were " wicked, and sinners before the Lord, exceedingly." When Abram went to a new place, it was usual for him to rear an altar to the Lord: but there is no mention of any thing like this, when Lot settled in or near to Sodom. But to return to Abram—

Ver. 14—17. From the call of this great man to the command to offer up his son, a period of about fifty years, he was often tried, and the promise was often renewed. It was the will of God that he should live by faith. Its being renewed at this time, seems to have been on occasion of Lot's departure from him, and the disinterested spirit which he had manifested on that occasion. Lot had " lifted up *his* eyes, and beheld the plain of Jordan;" and being gone to take possession of it, God saith to Abram, "Lift up now *thine* eyes, and look northward, and southward, and eastward, and westward; for all the land which thou seest, to *thee* will I give it, and to thy seed for ever." Thus he who sought this world, lost it; and he who was willing to give up any thing for the honour of God and religion, found it.

Ver. 18. After this, Abram removed to "the plain of Mamre, which is Hebron," where he continued many years. It was here, a long time after, that Sarai died.* It lay about two-and-twenty miles south of Jerusalem. This removal might possibly arise from a regard to Lot, that he might be nearer to him than he would have been at Bethel, though not so near as to interfere with his temporal concerns. Of this we are certain, he was able from a place whereabouts he lived, to descry the plains of Sodom; and when the city was destroyed, saw the smoke ascend like that of a furnace.† Here, as usual, Abram built an altar unto Jehovah.

---

* Gen. xxiii. 2.   † Chap. xix. 28.

DISCOURSE XXI.

ABRAM's SLAUGHTER OF THE KINGS.

GENESIS xiv.

IT has been already observed, that to form a just judgment of character we must view men in divers situations: we should not have expected however, to find Abram in the character of a warrior. Yet so it is: for once in his life, though a man of peace, he is constrained to take the sword. We have seen in him the friend of God, and the friend of a good man: now we shall see in him the *friend of his country*, though at present only a sojourner in it. The case appears to have been as follows.

Ver. 1—7. *Elam* and *Shinar*, i. e. Persia and Babylon, and the country about them, being that part of the world where the sons of Noah began to settle, after they went out of the ark, it was there that population, and the art of war, would first arrive at a sufficient maturity to induce them to attempt the subjugation of their neighbours. Nimrod began this business in about a century after the flood; and his successors were no less ambitious to keep it up. The rest of the world emigrating from those countries, would be considered as colonies, which ought to be subject to the parent states. Such, it seems, were the ideas of *Chedorlaomer*, who was at this time king of Elam or Persia. About three or four years before Abram left Chaldea, he had invaded Palestine; and the country being divided into little kingdoms, almost every city having its king, and having made but little progress in the art of war in comparison of the parent nations, fell an easy prey to his rapacity. In this humiliating condition they continued twelve years: but being by that time weary of the yoke, five of these lesser kings, understanding one another, thought they might venture to throw it off. Accordingly, the next year they refused to pay him tribute, or to be subject to the authority under which he had placed them.

Chedorlaomer hearing of this, calls together his friends and allies among the first and greatest nations, who consent to join their forces, and go with him to reduce these petty states to obedience. Four kings and their armies engage in this expedition. If each one brought only five-hundred men with him, they would form a great host for that early age of the world, and capable of doing a great deal of mischief. This it

Gen. 14.] SLAUGHTER OF THE KINGS. 169

did: for not content with marching peaceably through the country till they arrived at the cities which had rebelled, they laid all places waste which they came at, smiting in their way, first the *Rephaims*, the *Zurims*, and the *Emims;* then the *Horites* of Mount Seir; and after them the *Amalekites*, and the *Amorites*.

Ver. 8—10. By this time Abram's neighbours, the kings of *Sodom*, *Admah*, *Zeboim*, and *Bela*, must have been not a little alarmed. They and their people however determine to fight, and fight they did. The field of action was *the vale of Siddim*. Unhappily, the ground was full of slime pits, or pits of bitumen, much like those on the plain of Shinar; and their soldiers being but little skilled in the art of war, could not keep their ranks, and so were foiled, routed, and beaten by the superior discipline of the invaders. Many were slain in the pits; and those that escaped fled to a neighbouring mountain, which being probably covered with wood, afforded them a shelter in which to hide themselves.

Ver. 11, 12. The conquerors, without delay, betake themselves to the spoil. They take all the goods of Sodom and Gomorrah, and all the victuals; and what few people are left, they take for slaves. Among these was Lot, Abram's brother's son, his friend, and the companion of his travels, with all his family, and all his goods! And this notwithstanding he was only a sojourner, but lately come amongst them, and seems to have taken no part in the war. Oh Lot, these are the fruits of taking up thy residence in Sodom; or rather, the first fruits of it: the harvest is yet to come!

Ver. 13. Among those who fled from the drawn sword, and the fearfulness of war, there was one who reached the plain of Mamre, and told the sad tale to Abram. He feels much: but what can he do? Can he raise an army, wherewith to spoil the spoilers, and deliver the captives? He will try. Yes, from his regard to Lot, whose late faults would be now forgotten, and his former love recur to mind: and if he succeed, he will not only deliver him, but many others. The cause is a just one; and God has promised to *bless Abram, and make him a blessing.* Who can tell, but he may prove in this instance a blessing to the whole country, by delivering it from the power of a cruel foreign oppressor?

Now we shall see how the Lord hath blessed Abram. Who would have though tit? He is able to raise three hundred and eighteen men in his own family; men well instructed too, possessing skill, principle, and courage. Moreover, Abram was so well respected by his neighbours, *Mamre, Eschol,* and *Aner,* that they had already formed a league of confederacy with him, to defend themselves, perhaps, against this blustering invader, whose coming had been talked of for more than a year ago: and they, with all the forces they could muster, consent to join with Abram in the pursuit.

Ver. 15, 16. By prompt movements, Abram and his troop soon come up with the enemy. It was in the dead of night. The conquerors, it is likely, were off their guard, thinking no doubt that the country was subdued, and that scarcely a dog was left in it that dare move his tongue against them. But when haughty men say, Peace, peace; lo, sudden destruction cometh! Attacked after so many victories, they are surprised and confounded: and it being in the night, they could not tell but their assailants might be ten times more numerous than they were. So they flee in confusion, and were pursued from Dan even to Hobah in Syria, a distance, it is said, of fourscore miles. In this battle, Chedorlaomer, and the kings who were with him, were all slain. Abram's object, however, was the recovery of Lot and his family; and having accomplished this, he is satisfied. It is surprising that amidst all this confusion and slaughter, their lives should be preserved; yet so it was: and he with his property, and family, and all the other captives taken with him, are brought safe back again. It was ill for Lot to be found among the Sodomites; but it was well for the Sodomites that he was so, else they had been ruined before they were.

Ver. 17—24. This expedition of Abram and his friends, excited great attention among the Canaanites. At the very time when all must have been given up for lost, lo, they are, without any effort of their own, recovered, and the spoilers spoiled! The little victorious band, now returning in peace, are hailed by every one that meets them.... nay, the kings of the different cities go forth to congratulate them, and thank them as the deliverers of the country. If Abram had been of the disposition of those marauders whom he had defeated, he would have followed up his victory, and made himself master of the whole country, which he might probably have done with ease in their present enfeebled and scattered condition. But thus did not Abram, because of the fear of God.

In the valley of *Shaveh*, not far from Jerusalem, he was met and congratulated by the king of Sodom, who by some means had escaped in the day of battle, when so many of his people were slain. He was also met in the same place, and at the same time, by another king, of high character in the scriptures, though but rarely mentioned; viz. *Melchisedek, king of Salem.* He came not only to congratulate the conquerors, but brought forth *bread and wine* to refresh them after their long fatigues....

The sacred historian having here met with what I may call a lily among thorns, stops, as it were, to describe it. Let us stop with him, and observe the description.—Mention is made of this singular man only in three places; viz. here, in the 110th Psalm, and in the seventh chapter of the epistle to the Hebrews. He is held up in the two latter places as an eminent type of the Messiah. Three things may be remarked concerning him:—(1.) He was doubtless a very holy man; and if a Canaanite by descent, it furnishes a proof among many others, that the curse on Canaan did not shut the door of faith upon his individual descendents. There never was an age or country in which he that feared God, and worked righteousness, was not accepted.—(2.) He was a personage in whom was united the kingly and priestly offices, and as such was a type of the Messiah, and greater than Abram himself. Under the former of these characters, he was by interpretation "king of righteousness, and king of peace;" and under the latter was distinguished as the "priest of the most high God." This singular dignity conferred upon a descendent of Canaan shews that God delights, on various occasions, to put more abundant honour upon the part that lacketh.—(3.) He was what he was, considered as a priest, *not by inheritance,* but *by an immediate divine constitution.* Though as a man he was born like other men, yet as a priest he was "without father, without mother, without descent, having neither beginning of days, nor end of life; but made like unto the Son of God, abiding a priest continually." That is, neither his father, nor his mother, were of a sacerdotal family: he derived his office from no predecessor, and delivered it up to no successor, but was himself an order of priesthood. It is in this respect that he was "made like unto the Son of God;" who also was a priest, not after the manner of the sons of Aaron, by descent from their predecessors; for he descended from Judah, of which tribe Moses said nothing concerning priesthood; but after the similitude of Melchisedek, that is, by an immediate divine constitution, or as the new-testament writer expresses it, "by the word of the oath;" and "continuing ever, hath an unchangeable priesthood."

Ver. 19, 20. Melchisedek being "priest of the most high God," he in that character blessed Abram. It belonged to the priests by divine appointment to bless the people. In this view the blessing of Melchisedek would contain more than a personal well-wishing: it would be prophetic. In pronouncing it, he would set his official seal to what God had done before him. It is not unlikely that he might know Abram previous to this, and be well acquainted with his being the favourite of heaven, in whom all the nations of the earth were to be blessed, and to whose posterity God had promised the land of the Canaanites: and if so, his blessing him in so solemn a manner implies his acquiescence in the divine will, even though it would be at the expense of his ungodly countrymen. His speaking of the most high God as *possessor of heaven and earth*, would seem to intimate as much as this, as it recognizes the *principle* on which the right of Abram's posterity to possess themselves of Canaan depended. There is much heart in the blessing. We see the good man, as well as the priest of the most high God in it: from blessing Abram, it rises to the blessing of

Abram's God for all the goodness conferred upon him.

In return for this solemn blessing, Abram "gave him tithes of all." This was treating him in character, and in fact presenting the tenth of his spoils as an offering to God.

Ver. 21. All this time the king of Sodom stood by, and heard what passed; but it seems without feeling any interest in it. What passed between these two great characters appears to have made no impression upon him. He thought of nothing, and cared for nothing, but what respected himself. He could not possibly claim any right to what was recovered, either of persons or things: yet he asks for the former, and speaks in a manner as if he would be thought not a little generous in relinquishing the latter.

Ver. 22, 23. Abram knew the man, and his communications; and perceiving his affected generosity, gave him to understand that he had already decided, and had even sworn in the presence of the most high God, what he would do in respect of that part of the spoils which had previously belonged to him. Abram knew full well that the man who affected generosity in relinquishing what was not his own, would go on to boast of it, and to reflect on him as though he shone in borrowed plumes. No, says the patriarch, "I will not take, from a thread even to a shoe-latchet, that which was thine, save that which the young men have eaten, and the portion of Aner, Eschol, and Mamre," his allies.

In this answer of Abram we may observe, besides the above, several particulars:—

1. *The character* under which he had sworn to God: "JEHOVAH, the most high God, the possessor of heaven and earth." The first of these names was that by which God was made known to Abram, and still more to his posterity.* The last was that which had been just given to him by Melchisedek, and which appears to have made a strong impression on Abram's

---

* What Moses says in Exod. vi. 3, that God appeared to Abram, Isaac, and Jacob by the name of *God almighty;* but that by his name JEHOVAH he was not known to them, cannot be understood absolutely. It does not appear however to have been used among the patriarchs in so peculiar a sense, as it was after the times of Moses among the Israelites. From thence, it seems very generally to denote the specific name of the God and King of Israel. In this view we perceive the force and propriety of such language as the following: "JEHOVAH is our judge, Jehovah is our lawgiver, Jehovah is our king—Oh JEHOVAH, our Lord, how excellent is thy name in all the earth!" Isai. xxxiii. 22. Psal. viii. 1, 9.

mind. By uniting them together, he in a manner acknowledged Melchisedek's God to be his God; and, while reproving the king of Sodom, expressed his love to him as to a brother.

2. His having decided the matter *before* the king of Sodom met him, as it seems he had, implies something highly dishonourable in the character of that prince. He must have been well known to Abram as a vain, boasting, unprincipled man, or he would not have resolved in so solemn a manner to preserve himself clear from the very shadow of an obligation to him. And considering the polite and respectful manner in which it was common for this patriarch to conduct himself towards his neighbours, there must have been something highly offensive in this case to draw from him so cutting and dismaying an intimation. It is not unlikely that he had thrown out some malignant insinuations against Lot, and his old wealthy uncle, on the score of their religion. If so, Abram would feel happy in an opportunity of doing good against evil, and thus of heaping coals of fire upon his head.

The reason why he would not be under the shadow of an obligation, or any thing which might be construed an obligation to him, was not so much a regard to his own honour, but the honour of HIM *in whose name he had sworn.* Abram's God has blessed him, and promised to bless him more, and make him a blessing. Let it not be said by his enemies, that with all his blessedness, it is of our substance that he is what he is. No, Abram can trust in " the Possessor of heaven and earth" to provide for him, without being beholden to the king of Sodom.

3. His excepting the portion of the young men who were in league with him, shews a just sense of propriety. In giving up our own right, we are not at liberty to give away that which pertains to others connected with us.

Upon the whole, this singular undertaking would raise Abram much in the estimation of the Canaanites, and might possibly procure a little more respect to Lot. It had been better in the latter, however, if he had taken this opportunity to have changed his dwelling place.

DISCOURSE XXII.

ABRAM JUSTIFIED BY FAITH.

GENESIS XV. 1——6.

ABRAM was the father of the faithful, the example or pattern of all after believers; and perhaps no man, upon the whole, had greater faith. It seems to have been the design of God, in almost all his dealings with him, to put his faith to the trial. In most instances it appeared unto praise, though in some it seemed to fail him.

Ver. 1. Several years had elapsed, perhaps eight or nine, since God had first made promise to him concerning his *seed;* and now he is about eighty years old, and Sarai is seventy, and he has no child. He must yet live upon assurances and promises, without any earthly prospects.— He is indulged with a vision, in which God appears to him, saying, " Fear not, Abram: I am thy shield, and thy exceeding great reward." This is certainly very full, and very encouraging. If after having engaged the kings, he had any "fears" of the war being renewed, this would allay them. Who shall harm those to whom Jehovah is a "shield?" Or if, on having no child, he had fears at times lest all should prove a blank, this would meet them. What can be wanting to those who have God for their "exceeding great reward?" Abram had not availed himself of his late victory to procure in Canaan so much as a place to set his foot on: but he shall lose nothing by it. God has something greater in reserve for him: God himself will be his reward, not only as he is of all believers, but in a sense peculiar to himself: he shall be the father of the church, and the "heir of the world."

Ver. 2, 3. Who would have thought, amidst these exceeding great and precious promises, that Abram's faith should seem to fail him? Yet so it is. The promise, to be sure, is great and full; but he has heard much the same things before, and there are no signs of its accomplishment. This works within him in a way of secret anguish, which he presumes to express before the Lord almost in the language of objection: "Lord God, what wilt thou *give* me?" Thou speakest of *giving* thy servant this and that .... but I shall soon be past receiving it .... I go childless. This Eliezer of Damascus is a good and faithful servant; but that is all .... Must I make him my heir; and are the promises to be fulfilled at last in an adopted son?

Ver. 4—6. God in mercy to the patriarch condescends to remove his doubts on this subject, assuring him that his heir should descend from his own body; yet he must continue to live upon *promises*. These promises, however, are confirmed by a sign. He is led abroad from his tent in the night-time, and shewn the stars of heaven; which when he had seen, the Lord assured him, "So shall thy seed be." And now his doubts are removed. He is no longer weak, but strong in faith: he staggers not through unbelief, but is fully persuaded that what God has promised, he is able to perform. And therefore, *it was imputed to him for righteousness.**

Much is made of this passage by the apostle Paul, in establishing the doctrine of justification by faith; and much has been said by others, as to the meaning of both him and Moses. One set of expositors, considering it as extremely evident that by faith is here meant *the act of believing*, contend for this as our justifying righteousness. Faith, in their account, seems to be imputed to us for righteousness by a kind of gracious compromise, in which God accepts of

* Rom. iv. 19—22.

an imperfect, instead of a perfect obedience. Another set of expositors, jealous for the honour of free grace, and of the righteousness of Christ, contend that the faith of Abram is here to be taken *objectively*, for the righteousness of Christ believed in. To me it appears that both these expositions are forced. To establish the doctrine of justification by the righteousness of Christ, it is not necessary to maintain that the faith of Abram means Christ in whom he believed. Nor can this be maintained: for it is manifestly the same thing, in the account of the apostle Paul, as *believing*,* which is very distinct from the object believed in. The truth appears to be this: It is faith, or believing, that is counted for righteousness; not however as a righteous act, or on account of any inherent virtue contained in it, but *in respect of Christ, on whose righteousness it terminates.*†

That we may form a clear idea, both of the text and the doctrine, let the following particulars be considered.

1. Though Abram believed God when he left Ur of the Chaldees,‡ yet his faith in that instance is not mentioned *in connexion with his justification;* nor does the apostle, either in his

* Rom. iv. 5. † Calvin's Inst. Bk. iii. ch. xi. §7. ‡ Heb. xi. 8.

epistle to the Romans, or in that to the Galations, argue that doctrine from it, or hold it up as an example of justifying faith. I do not mean to suggest, that Abram was then in an unjustified state; but that the instance of his faith which was thought proper by the holy Spirit to be selected as the model for believing for justification, was not this, nor any other of the kind; but those only in which there was an *immediate respect had to the person of the Messiah.* The examples of faith referred to in both these epistles, are taken from his believing the promises relative to his *seed;* in which seed, as the apostle observes, *Christ* was included.* Though christians may believe in God with respect to the common concerns of this life, and such faith may ascertain their being in a justified state; yet this is not, strictly speaking, the faith by which they are justified, which invariably *has respect to the person and work of Christ.* Abram believed in God as *promising* Christ: they believe in him as having *raised him from the dead.* "By him, all that believe, (that is, *in him,*) are justified from all things, from which they could not be justified by the law of Moses."—It is through *faith in his blood* that they obtain remission of sins—He is just, and the justifier of him that *believeth in Jesus.*†

* Rom. iv. 11. Gal. iii. 16.
† Rom. iv. 24. Acts xiii. 39. Rom. iii. 25, 26.

2. This distinction, so clearly perceivable both in the old and new testament, sufficiently decides in what sense faith is considered as justifying. Whatever other properties the magnet may possess, it is as pointing invariably to the north that it guides the mariner: so whatever other properties faith may possess, it is as *pointing to Christ*, and bringing us into union *with him*, that it justifies.* It is not that *for the sake of which* we are accepted of God: for if it were, justification by faith could not be opposed to justification by works, nor would boasting be excluded; neither would there be any meaning in its being said to be by faith, *that it might be of grace:* but believing in Christ, we are considered by the Lawgiver of the world as one with him, and so are forgiven and accepted *for his sake*. Hence it is, that to be justified by faith is the same thing as to be justified *by the blood of Christ*, or made righteous *by his obedience*.† Faith is not the grace wherein we stand, but that by which we *have access* to it.‡ Thus it is, that the healing of various maladies is ascribed, in the new testament, to faith: not that the virtue which caused the cures, proceeded from this as its proper cause; but this was a necessary concomitant, to give the parties *access*

---

* Rom. viii. 1.   1 Cor. i. 30.   Phil. iii. 9.
† Rom. v. 9, 19.   ‡ Rom. v. 2.

to the power and grace of the Saviour, by which only they were healed.

3. The phrase, "counted it for righteousness," does not mean that God thought it to be what it was, which would have been merely an act of justice; but his graciously reckoning it what in itself it was not; viz. a ground for the bestowment of covenant blessings. Even in the case of Phinehas, of whom the same phrase is used in reference to his zeal for God, it has this meaning; for one single act of zeal, whatever may be said of it, could not entitle him, and his posterity after him, to the honour conferred upon them.* And with respect to the present case, "the phrase, as the apostle uses it, (says a great writer) manifestly imports, that God of his sovereign grace, is pleased, in his dealings with the sinner, to take and regard that which indeed is not righteousness, and in one who has no righteousness, so that the consequence shall be the same as if he had righteousness, and which may be from the *respect which it bears* to something which is indeed righteousness."† The faith of Abram, though of a holy nature, yet contained nothing *in itself* fit for a justifying righteousness: all the adaptedness which it possessed to

---

* Psal. cvi. 31. compared with Num. xxv. 12, 13.
† President *Edwards's* Sermons on Justification: Dis. i. p. 9.

that end was the respect which it had to the Messiah, on whom it terminated.*

4. Though faith is not our justifying righteousness, yet it is a necessary concomitant, and mean of justification; and being the grace which above all others honours Christ, it is that which above all others God delights to honour. Hence it is that justification is ascribed to it, rather than to the righteousness of Christ without it. Our Saviour might have said to Bartimeus, 'Go thy way, *I* have made thee whole.' This would have been truth, but not the whole of truth which it was his design to convey. The necessity of faith in order to healing would not have

---

* From the above remarks, we may be able to solve an apparent difficulty in the case of Cornelius. He "feared God," and "his alms and prayers came up for a memorial before God;" he must therefore have been at that time in *a state of salvation:* yet after this he was directed to send for Peter, who should "tell him words by which he and all his house *should be saved.*" (Acts x. 2, 4. xi. 14.) What Abram was in respect of justification before he heard and believed what was promised him concerning the Messiah, Cornelius was in respect of salvation before he heard and believed the words by which he was to be saved. Both were the *subjects* of faith according to their light. Abram believed from the time that he left Ur of the Chaldees; (Heb. xi. 8.) and Cornelius could not have "feared God" without believing in him: but the *object* by which they were justified and saved, was not from the first so clearly revealed to them as it was afterwards.

appeared from this mode of speaking, nor had any honour been done, or encouragement given to it: but by his saying, " Go thy way, *thy faith* hath made thee whole," each of these ideas is conveyed. Christ would omit mentioning his own honour, as knowing that faith having an immediate respect to him, amply provided for it.

DISCOURSE XXIII.

RENEWAL OF PROMISES TO ABRAM.

GENESIS XV. 7——21.

Ver. 7. The Lord having promised Abram a numerous offspring, goes on to renew the promise of the land of Canaan for an inheritance; and this by a reference to what had been said to him when he first left the land of the Chaldees. It is God's usual way, in giving a promise, to refer to former promises of the same thing, which would shew him to be of one mind, and intimate that he had not forgotten him, but was carrying on his designs of mercy towards him.

Ver. 8. Abram, however, ventures to ask for a sign by which he may know that by his posterity he shall inherit the land. This request does not appear to have arisen from unbelief;

but having lately experienced the happy effects of a sign, (ver. 5.) he hopes thereby to be better armed against it.

Ver. 9. The purport of the answer seems to be, 'Bring me an offering, which I will accept at thy hand, and this shall be the sign.' It is in condescension to our weakness that the Lord has given us sensible signs, as in the ordinance of baptism and the supper, in addition to his promises. If it were desirable to Abram to know that he should inherit the earthly Canaan, it must be much more so to us to know that we shall inherit the heavenly Canaan; and God is willing that the heirs of promise should on this subject have strong consolation, and therefore has confirmed his word with an oath.

Ver. 10. Abram, obedient to the divine command, takes of the first and best of his animals for a sacrifice. Their being *divided* in the midst was the usual form of sacrificing when a *covenant* was to be made. Each of the parties passed between the parts of the animals; q. d. thus may I be cut asunder, if I break this covenant! This was called, *making a covenant by sacrifice.**
This process therefore, it appears, was accompa-

---

* Jer. xxxiv. 18, 19. Psal. l. 5.

nied with a solemn covenant between the Lord and his servant Abram.

Ver. 11. Having made ready the sacrifices, he waited, perhaps, for the fire of God to consume them, which was the usual token of acceptance; but meanwhile the birds of prey came down upon them, which he was obliged to drive away. Interruptions, we see, attend the father of the faithful in his most solemn approaches to God; and interruptions of a different kind attend believers in theirs. How often do intruding cares, like unclean birds, seize upon that time, and those affections, which are devoted to God! Happy is it for us, if by prayer and watchfulness, we can drive them away, so as to worship him without distraction.

Ver. 12—16. By the account taken together, it appears as if this was a day which Abram dedicated wholly to God. His first vision was before day-light, while the stars were yet to be seen: in the morning he prepares the sacrifices, and while he is waiting, the sun goes down, and no immediate answer is given him. At this time he falls into a deep sleep, and now we may expect that God will answer him as he had done before, "by vision." But what kind of vision is it? Not like that which he had before; but "lo, an horror of great darkness falls upon him." This might be designed in part to impress his mind with an awful reverence of God; for those who rejoice in him must rejoice with trembling: and partly to give him what he had asked for, a *sign;* not merely that his seed should inherit the land, but of the way in which this promise should be accomplished; namely, by their first going down and enduring great affliction in Egypt. The light must be preceded by darkness. Such appears to be the interpretation given of it in the words which follow: "Know of a surety, that thy seed shall be a stranger in a land that is not theirs, *and shall serve them, and they shall afflict them four hundred years.*"* Egypt is not named, for prophecy requires to be delivered with some degree of obscurity, or it might tend to defeat its own design: but the thing is certain, and God will in the end avenge their cause. It is remarkable how the prophecies gradually open and expand, beginning with what is general, and proceeding to particulars. Abram had never had so much revealed to him before, as to times and circumstances. He is given to un-

---

* These four hundred years are reckoned by Ainsworth to have commenced from the time of Isaac's being weaned, when the son of Hagar, the Egyptian, mocked. So that as soon as Abram's seed, according to the promise, was born, he began to be *afflicted*, and that by one of *Egyptian* extraction.

derstand that these things shall not take place in his day; but that he should first "go to his fathers," and that "in peace, and be buried in a good old age;" but that "in the fourth generation" after their going down, they should return. It is enough to die such a death as this, though we see not all the promises fulfilled. The reason given for their being so long ere they were accomplished, is, that "the iniquity of the Amorites was not yet full." There is a fitness in all God's proceedings, and a wonderful fulness of design, answering many ends by one and the same event. The possession of Canaan was to Israel a promised good, but to the Canaanites a threatened evil. It is deferred towards both till each be prepared for it. As there is a time when God's promises to his people are ripe for accomplishment, so there is a time when his forbearance towards the wicked shall cease, and they often prove to be the same. The fall of Babylon was the deliverance of Judah; and the fall of another Babylon will be the signal for the kingdoms of this world becoming the kingdoms of our Lord, and of his Christ.

Ver. 17. After this, when the sun was set, and it was dark, Abram, perhaps still in vision, has the sign repeated in another form. He sees a "smoaking furnace," and a "burning lamp."

The design of these, as well as the other, seems to be to shew him what should take place hereafter. The former was an emblem of the affliction which his posterity should endure in Egypt, that "iron furnace;"* and the latter might denote the light that should arise to them in their darkness. If, like the pillar of fire in the wilderness, it were an emblem of the divine Majesty, its "passing through" the parts of the divided sacrifices would denote God's entering into covenant with his servant Abram, and that all the mercy which should come upon his posterity would be in virtue of it.

Ver. 18. That which had been hinted under a figure, is now declared in express language. "The same day Jehovah made a *covenant* with Abram," making over to his posterity, as by a solemn deed of gift, the whole land in which he then was, defining with great accuracy its exact boundaries; and this notwithstanding the afflictions which they should undergo in Egypt. Thus the burning lamp would succeed and dispel the darkness of the smoking furnace.

* Deut. iv. 20.

DISCOURSE XXIV.

SARAI's CROOKED POLICY FOR THE ACCOMPLISHMENT OF THE PROMISE.

GENESIS XVI.

VER. 1—3. We have had several renewals of promises to Abram; but as yet no performance of them. Ten years had elapsed in Canaan, and things remained as they were. Now, though Abram's faith had been strengthened, yet that of Sarai fails. At her time of life, she thinks, there is no hope of seed in the ordinary way: if therefore the promise be fulfilled, it must be in the person of another. And having a handmaid whose name was Hagar, she thinks of giving her to Abram to wife. Unbelief is very prolific of schemes; and surely this of Sarai is as carnal, as foolish, and as fruitful of domestic misery as could almost have been devised. Yet such was the influence of evil counsel, especially from such a quarter, that "Abram hearkened to her voice." The father of mankind sinned by hearkening to his wife, and now the father of the faithful follows his example. How necessary for those who stand in the nearest relations, to take heed of being snares instead of helps one to another! It was a double sin: first, of distrust; and secondly, of deviation from the original law of marriage, and which seems to have opened a door to polygamy. We never read of two wives before, except those of Lamech, who was of the descendents of Cain; but here the practice is coming into the church of God. Two out of three of the patriarchs go into it; yet neither of them of their own accord. There is no calculating in how many instances this ill example has been followed, or how great a matter this little fire kindled. The plea used by Sarai in this affair shews how easy it is to err by a misconstruction of providence, and following that as a rule of conduct, instead of God's revealed will. "The Lord (says she) hath restrained me from bearing:" and therefore I must contrive other means for the fulfilment of the promise! But why not enquire of the Lord? As in the crowning of Adonijah, the proper authority was not consulted.

Ver. 4, 5. The consequence was what might have been expected: the young woman is elated with the honour done her, and her mistress is despised in her eyes. And now, when it is too late, Sarai repents, and complains to her husband; breaking out into intemperate language, accusing him as the cause, as though he must needs have secretly encouraged her: "My wrong be upon thee!" Nor did she stop here; but taking it for granted that her husband would not hear her, goes on to appeal to God himself: "The Lord judge between me and thee!" Those who are first in doing wrong, are often first in complaining of the effects, and in throwing the blame upon others. Loud and passionate appeals to God, instead of indicating a good cause, are commonly the marks of a bad one.

Ver. 6. Abram on this vexing occasion is meek and gentle. He had learned that a soft answer turneth away wrath; and therefore he refrained from upbraiding his wife, as he might easily have done, preferring domestic peace to the vindication of himself, and the placing of the blame where it ought to have laid. It is doubtful however, whether he did not yield too much in this case: for though, according to the custom of those times, Hagar was his wife only with respect to cohabitation, and without dividing the power with Sarai; yet she was entitled to protection, and should not have been given up to the will of one who on this occasion manifested nothing but jealousy, passion, and caprice. But he seems to have been brought into a situation wherein he was at a loss what to do; and thus, as Sarai is punished for tempting him, he also is punished with a disordered house for having yielded to the temptation. And now Sarai, incited by revenge, deals hardly with Hagar; much more so, it is likely, than she ought: for though the young woman might have acted vainly and sinfully, yet her mistress is far from being a proper judge of the punishment which she deserved. The consequence is, as might be expected, she leaves the family, and goes into a wilderness. Indeed it were "better to dwell in a wilderness than with a contentious and angry woman." But as Sarai and Abram had each reaped the fruits of their sin, Hagar in her turn reaps the fruit of hers. If creatures act disorderly, God will act orderly and justly in dealing with them.

Ver. 7, 8. Hagar however, though an Egyptian, shall reap advantage from her connexion with Abram's family. Other heathens might have brought themselves into trouble, and been left to grapple with it alone; but to her an angel from heaven is sent, to direct and relieve her. Bending her course towards Egypt, her native country, and finding a spring of water in the wilderness, she sat down by it to refresh herself. While in this situation, she hears a voice, saying, " Hagar, Sarai's maid, whence comest thou; and whither wilt thou go?" She would perceive by this language that she was known, and conclude that it was no common voice that spoke to her. He that spoke to her is called, "the angel of the Lord:" yet he afterwards says, "*I* will multiply thy seed exceedingly." It seems therefore not to have been a created angel, but the same divine personage who frequently appeared to the fathers. In calling Hagar "Sarai's maid," he seems tacitly to disallow of the marriage, and to lead her mind back to that humble character which she had formerly sustained. The questions put to her were close, but tender, and such as were fitly addressed to a person fleeing from trouble. The first might be answered, and was answered: " I flee from the face of my mistress Sarai." But with respect to the last, she is silent. We know our present grievances, and so can tell "whence we came," much better than our future lot, or "whither we are going." In many cases, if the truth were spoken, the answer would be, from bad to worse.—At present, this poor young woman seems to have been actuated by mere natural principles, those of fleeing from misery. In all her trouble, there appears nothing like true religion, or committing her way to the Lord: yet she is sought out of him whom she sought not.

Ver. 9, 10. The counsel of God here was, to return and submit. Whorefore? She had done wrong in despising her mistress, and must now be humbled for it. Hard as this might appear, it was the counsel of wisdom and mercy: a connexion with the people of God, with all their faults, is far preferable to the best of this world, where God is unknown. If we have done wrong, whatever temptations or provocations we may have met with, the only way to peace and happiness is to retrace our footsteps, in repentance and submission.—For her encouragement, she is given to expect a portion of Abram's blessing, of which she must have often heard, namely, a numerous offspring: and by the manner in which this was promised, "*I* will multiply thy seed," she would perceive that the voice which spake to her was no other than that of Abram's God.

Ver. 11. With respect to the child of which she was then pregnant, it is foretold that it should be a son, and that his name should be called *Ishmael, God shall hear*, from the circumstance of God having "heard her affliction." God is not said to have heard her prayer; for it does not appear that she as yet had ever called upon his name: she merely sat bewailing herself, as not knowing what would become of her. Yet lo, the ear of mercy is open to affliction itself! The groans of the prisoner are heard of God; not only theirs who cry unto him, but in many cases, theirs who do not.

Ver. 12. The child is also characterized, as " a wild man;" a bold and daring character, living by his bow in the wilderness, and much engaged in war; "his hand being (as it were) against every man, and every man's hand against him:" yet that he should maintain his ground notwithstanding, " dwelling in the presence of all his brethren," and dying at last in peace.* Nor was this prophecy merely intended to describe Ishmael, but his posterity. Bishop Newton, in his dissertations on the prophecies, has shewn that such has been the character of the Arabians, who descended from him, in all ages: a wild and warlike people, who under all the conquests of other nations by the great powers of the earth, remained unsubdued.

Ver. 13, 14. The effect of this divine appearance on Hagar, was to bring her to the knowledge and love of God: the account, at least, wears such an aspect. She, who, for any thing that appears, had never prayed before, now addresses herself to the angel who spake to her,

* See chap xxv. 17. 18.

and whom she considers as "Jehovah;" calling him by an endearing name, the meaning of which is, *thou God seest me*. She did not mean by this to acknowledge his omniscience, so much as his mercy, in having *beheld* and pitied her affliction. On his withdrawing, she seems to have "looked after him," with faith, and hope, and affectionate desire; and reflecting upon what had passed, is overcome with the goodness of God towards her, exclaiming, "Have I also here looked after him that seeth me!" It was great mercy for God to have *looked* on her, and heard her afflictive moans; but it was greater to draw her heart to "look after him;" and greater still that he should do it *here*, in the wilderness, when she had lived so many years where prayer was wont to be made, in vain. Under the influence of these impressions, she calls the well by which she sat down, "Beer-lahai-roi," a name which would serve as a memorial of the mercy. Let this well, as if she had said, be called Jehovah's well, *the well of him that liveth, and seeth me!* Thus God in mercy sets that right, which, through human folly, had been thrown into disorder. Hagar returns and submits, bears Abram a son when he is fourscore and six years old, and he, on being informed of the prophecy which went before, called his name Ishmael.

DISCOURSE XXV.

GOD's COVENANT WITH ABRAM AND HIS SEED.

GENESIS xvii.

THIRTEEN years elapse, of which nothing is recorded. Hagar is submissive to Sarai, and Ishmael is growing up; but as to Abram, things after all wear a doubtful aspect. It is true God hath given him a son; but no intimations of his being the son of promise. No divine congratulations attend his birth; but on the contrary, Jehovah, who had been used to manifest himself with frequency and freedom, now seems to carry it reservedly to his servant. It is something *like* the thing which he had believed in; but not *the thing* itself. He has seen, as it were, a wind, a fire, and an earthquake; but the Lord is not in them.

Ver. 1. After this, when he was ninety-nine years old, the Lord again appeared to him, and reminded him of a truth which he needed to have re-impressed; namely, his *almighty power*. It was not for want of considering this, that he had had recourse to crooked devices in order to accomplish the promise. This truth is followed by an admonition; "Walk before me, and be thou perfect;" and which admonition implies a serious reproof. It was like saying, 'Have recourse no more to unbelieving expedients: keep thou the path of uprightness, and leave me to fufil my promise in the time and manner that seem good to me!' What a lesson is here afforded us, never to use unlawful means under the pretence of being more useful, or promoting the cause of God. Our concern is to walk before him, and be upright, leaving him to bring to pass his own designs in his own way.

Ver. 2, 3. Abram having been admonished, the promise is renewed to him; and the time drawing near in which the seed should be born, the Lord declares his mind to make a solemn *covenant* with him, and to multiply him exceedingly. Such language denotes great kindness and condescension, with large designs of mercy. Abram was so much affected with it as to "fall on his face, and in that posture "the Lord talked with him."

Ver. 4—6. It is observable that the last time in which mention is made of a covenant with Abram,* God made over to his posterity the land of Canaan for a possession: but the design of this is more extensive, dwelling more particularly on their being "multiplied and blessed." The very idea of a covenant is expressive of peace and good will;† and in this, and some other instances, it is not confined to the party, but extends to others for his sake. Thus, as we have seen, God made a covenant of peace, which included the preservation of the world: but it was with one man, even Noah, and the world was preserved for his sake.‡ And the covenant in question is one that shall involve great blessings to the world in all future ages: yet it is not made with the world, but with Abram. God will give them blessings; but it shall be through him. Surely these things were designed to familiarize the great principle on which our salvation should rest. It was the purpose of God to save perishing sinners; yet his covenant is not originally with them, but with Christ. With him it stands fast; and for his sake they are accepted and blessed. Even the blessedness of Abram himself, and all the rewards conferred on him, were for his sake. He was justified, as we have seen, not by his own righteousness, but by faith in the promised Messiah.

* Gen. xv. 18.   † Ch. xxvi. 28. xxx. 44.   ‡ Ch. vi. 18.

Gen. 17.] COVENANT WITH ABRAM. 205

Moreover: A covenant being a solemn agreement, and indicating a design to walk together in amity, it was proper there should be an understanding, as we should say, between the parties. When Israel came to have a king, "Samuel told them the manner of the kingdom, and wrote it in a book, and laid it before the Lord." Thus as Abram is about to commence the father of a family, who were to be God's chosen people, it was fit at the outset that he should not only be encouraged by promises, but directed how he and his descendents should conduct themselves.

The first promise in this covenant is, that he shall be "the father of many nations;" and as a token of it, his name in future is to be called ABRAHAM. He had the name of a *high* or eminent *father*, from the beginning; but now it shall be more comprehensive, indicating a very large progeny. By the exposition given of this promise in the new testament,* we are directed to understand it not only of those who sprang from Abraham's body, though these were many nations; but also of all that should be "of the faith of Abraham." It went to make him the father of the church of God in all future ages; or, as the apostle calls him, "the heir of the

* Rom. iv. 16, 17.

world." In this view he is the father of many, even of "a multitude of nations." All that the christian world enjoys, or ever will enjoy, it is indebted for it to Abraham and his seed. A high honour this, to be the father of the faithful, the stock from which the Messiah should spring, and on which the church of God should grow. It was this honour that Esau despised, when he sold his birth-right; and here lay the *profaneness* of that act, which involved a contempt of the most sacred of all objects,—the Messiah, and his everlasting kingdom!

Ver. 7—14. The covenant with Abraham was not confined, as has been observed already, to his own person, but extended to his posterity after him in their generations. To ascertain the meaning of this promise, we can proceed on no ground more certain than fact. It is fact, that God in succeeding ages took the seed of Abraham to be a peculiar people unto himself, above all other nations; not only giving them "the land of Canaan for a possession," but himself to be *their God, King*, or *temporal* Governor. Nor was this all: it was amongst them that he set up his *spiritual* kingdom; giving them his lively oracles, sending to them his prophets, and establishing amongst them his holy worship; which great advantages were, for many ages in a manner, confined to them: and what was still more, the great body of those who were eternally saved, previously to the coming of Christ, were saved from amongst them. These things taken together were an immensely greater favour than if they had all been literally made kings and priests. Such then being the *facts*, it is natural to suppose that such was the meaning of the promise.*

* As an Antipædobaptist I see no necessity for denying that spiritual blessings were promised, *in this general way*, to the natural seed of Abraham; nor can it, I think, be fairly denied. The Lord engaged to do that which he actually did; namely, to take out of them, rather than other nations, a people for himself. This, I suppose, is the *seed* promised to Abraham; to which the apostle refers when he says, "They which are the children of the flesh, these are not the children of God; but the children of the promise are counted for the *seed*. (Rom. ix. 8.) By " the children of the promise" he did not mean the elect in general, composed of jews and gentiles, but the elect from amongst the jews. Hence he reckons himself "an Israelite, of the seed of Abraham, and the tribe of Benjamin," as a living proof that " God had not cast away his people whom he foreknew." Rom. xi. 1, 2.

But I perceive not how it follows from hence, that God has promised to take a people from amongst the natural descendents of believers, in distinction from others. What was promised to Abraham, was neither promised nor fulfilled to every good man. Of the posterity of his kinsman Lot, nothing good is recorded. It is true, the labours of those parents who "bring up their children in the nurture and admonition of the Lord," are ordinarily blessed to the conversion of some of them: and

As a sign or token of this solemn covenant with Abraham and his posterity, "every man-child amongst them was required to be circumcised in the flesh of his foreskin;" and not only their own children, but those of their "servants, born in their house, or bought with their money." This ordinance was the mark by which they were distinguished as a people in covenant with Jehovah, and which bound them by a special obligation to obey him. Like almost all other

the same may be said of the labours of faithful ministers, wherever providence stations them. But as it does not follow in the one case, that the graceless inhabitants are more in covenant with God than those of other places, neither does it follow in the other, that the graceless offspring of believers are more in covenant with God than those of unbelievers. " New-testament saints have nothing more to do with the Abrahamic covenant, than the Old-testament believers who lived prior to Abraham."

I am aware that the words of the apostle in Gal. iii. 14, " the blessing of Abraham is come on the gentiles, through Jesus Christ," are alleged in proof of the contrary. But the meaning of that passage, I conceive, is not, that through Jesus Christ every believer becomes an Abraham, a *father* of the faithful; but that he is reckoned among his *children:* not a *stock*, on which the future church should grow; but a *branch*, partaking of the root and fatness of the olive-tree. So, however, the context appears to explain it—" They which are of faith are *the children* of faithful Abraham." ver. 7.

But if it were granted, that the blessing of Abraham is so come on the believing gentiles, as not only to render them bles-

positive institutions, it was also prefigurative of mental purity, or "putting off the body of the sins of the flesh." A neglect of it subjected the party to a being cut off from his people, as having broken God's covenant.

Ver. 15, 16. As Abram's name had been changed to Abraham, a similar honour is conferred on Sarai, who in future is to be called

sed as his spiritual children, but to insure a people for God from amongst their natural posterity, rather than from those of others; yet it is not *as* their natural posterity that they are individually entitled to any one spiritual blessing; for this was more than was true of the natural seed of Abraham. Nor do I see how it follows from hence, that we are warranted to baptize them in their infancy. Abraham, it is true, was commanded to circumcise his male children; and if we had been commanded to baptize our males, or females, or both, or any example of the kind had been left in the new testament, we should be as much obliged to comply in the one case, as he was in the other. But we do not think ourselves warranted to reason from circumcision to baptism; from the circumcision of males to the baptism of males and females; and from the circumcision of the children of a nation, (the greater part of whom were unbelievers) and of "servants born in the house, or bought with money," to the baptism of the children of believers. In short, we do not think ourselves warranted in matters of positive institution, to found our practice on analogies, whether real or supposed; and still less on one so circuitous, dissonant, and uncertain as that in question. Our duty, we conceive, is, in such cases, to follow the precepts and examples of the dispensation under which we live.

Sarah. The difference of these names is much the same as that of her husband, and corresponds with what had been promised to them both on this occasion. The former meant *my princess,* and was expressive of *high* honour in her own family; but the latter *a princess,* and denoted a more *extensive* honour, as it is here expressed, "a mother of nations." This honour conferred on Sarai would correct an important error into which both she and her husband had fallen; imagining that all hope was at an end, of a child being born of her; and therefore, that if the promise were fulfilled, it must be in Ishmael. But not only must Abram become Abraham, "the father of many nations;" but Sarai Sarah, "the mother of nations;" and this not by her handmaid, as she had vainly imagined, but God would "give him a son also *of her,* and kings of people should be *of her.*"

Ver. 17, 18. The effect of this unexpected promise on Abraham was, that he "fell on his face and laughed." The term does not here indicate lightness, as we commonly use it; but joy, mingled with wonder and astonishment. "Shall a child be born, (saith he) unto him that is a hundred years old? And Sarah, that is ninety years old, bear?" In another case,* it implied a

---

* Chap. xviii. 12, 13.

mixture of doubting; but not in this. Abraham believed God, and was overcome with joyful surprise.—But a doubt immediately occurs, which strikes a damp upon his pleasure: 'the promise of another son destroys all my expectations with respect to him who is already given! Perhaps he must die, to make room for the other; or if not, he may be another Cain, who went out from the presence of the Lord.' To what drawbacks are our best enjoyments subject in this world; and in many cases, owing to our going before the Lord in our hopes and schemes of happiness! When his plan comes to be put in execution, it interferes with ours; and there can be no doubt, in such a case, which must give place. If Abraham had waited God's time for the fulfilment of the promise, it would not have been accompanied with such an alloy: but having failed in this, after all his longing desires after it, it becomes in a manner unwelcome to him! What can he do or say in so delicate a situation? Grace would say, Accept the divine promise with thankfulness. But nature struggles: the bowels of the father are troubled for Ishmael. In this state of mind he presumes to offer up a petition to heaven: "Oh that Ishmael might live before thee!" Judging of the import of this petition by the answer, it would seem to mean, either that God would condescend to withdraw his promise of another son, and let Ishmael be the person; or if that cannot be, that his life might be spared, and himself and his posterity be amongst the people of God, sharing the blessing, or being "heir with him"* who should be born of Sarah. To *live*, and to live *before God*, according to the usual acceptation of the phrase, could not, I think, mean less than one or other of these things. It was very lawful for him to desire the temporal and spiritual welfare of his son, and of his posterity after him, in submission to the will of God: but in a case wherein natural affection appeared to clash with God's revealed designs, he must have felt himself in a painful situation; and the recollection that the whole was owing to his own and Sarai's unbelief, would add to his regret.

Ver. 19—27. As Abraham's petition seemed to contain an implied wish that it would please God to withdraw his promise of another son, the answer to it contains an implied, but peremptory denial, with a tacit reflexion on him for having taken Hagar to be his wife—"And God said, Sarah thy wife shall bear thee a son *indeed.*" As if he should say, she is thy wife, and ought to have been thine only wife; and verily it shall be in a son born of her that

* See chap. xxi. 10.

the promise shall be fulfilled. It is also intimated to him, that this should be no grief to him; but that he should call his name Isaac, that is, *laughter*, or *gladness*, on account of the joy which his birth should occasion. And as Abraham's petition seemed to plead that Ishmael and his posterity might at least be "heir with" Isaac, so as to be ranked amongst God's covenant people, this also by implication is denied him. "I will establish my covenant *with him*, for an everlasting covenant, and with his seed after him." Ishmael, while he is in Abraham's family, shall be considered as a branch of it, and as such be circumcised; but the covenant of peculiarity should not be established with him and his descendents, but with Isaac exclusively. As many, however, who were included in this covenant had no share in eternal life, so many who were excluded from it might notwithstanding escape eternal death. The door of mercy was always open to every one that believed. In every nation, and in every age, he that feared God, and wrought righteousness, was accepted of him.

But shall no part of this petition be granted? Yes. "As for Ishmael, I have heard thee: Behold, I have blessed him, and will make him fruitful, and will multiply him exceedingly:

twelve princes shall he beget, and I will make him a great nation . . . . but my covenant will I establish with Isaac, whom Sarah shall bear unto thee."—And having said thus much, the very time of his birth is now particularly named: it shall be "at this set time in the next year." Here ended the communications between the Lord and his servant Abraham; and it appears that from this time he was satisfied. We hear nothing more like an objection to the divine will, nor any wish to have things otherwise than they were. On the contrary, we find him immediately engaged in an implicit obedience to the command of circumcision. His conduct on this occasion furnishes a bright example to all succeeding ages, of the manner in which divine ordinances should be complied with.—There are three things in particular in the obedience of Abraham worthy of notice.—(1.) It was *prompt.* "In the self-same day that God had spoken unto him," the command was put in execution. This was "making haste, and delaying not to keep his commandments." To treat the divine precepts as matters of small importance, or to put off what is manifestly our duty to another time, is to trifle with supreme authority. So did not Abraham. —(2.) It was *punctilious.* The correspondence between the command of God, and the obedience of his servant, is minutely exact. The words of the former are, "*Thou* shalt keep my covenant, *and thy seed* after thee .... and *he that is born in thy house, or bought with money* of any stranger, which is not of thy seed." With this agrees the account of the latter: "In the self-same day was Abraham circumcised, and Ishmael his son; and all the men of his house, born in the house, and bought with money of the stranger, were circumcised with him." A rigid regard to the revealed will of God, enters deeply into true religion: that spirit which dispenses with it, though it may pass under the specious name of liberality, is antichristian.—(3.) Lastly: It was yielded in *old age*, when many would have pleaded off from engaging in any thing new, or different from what they had before received: and when, as some think, it would be a further trial to his faith as to the fulfilment of the promise. "Ninety and nine years old was Abraham when he was circumcised." It is one of the temptations of old age to be tenacious of what we have believed and practised from our youth; to shut our eyes and ears against every thing that may prove it to have been erroneous or defective, and to find excuses for being exempted from hard and dangerous duties. But Abraham to the last was ready to receive farther instruction, and to do as he was commanded, leaving consequences with God. This shews that the admonition to "walk before him, and be perfect," had not been given him in vain.

DISCOURSE XXVI.

ABRAHAM ENTERTAINING ANGELS, AND INTERCEDING FOR SODOM.

GENESIS xviii.

VER. 1—3. The time drawing nigh that the promise should be fulfilled, God's appearances to Abraham are frequently repeated. That which is here recorded seems to have followed the last at a very little distance. Sitting one day in a kind of porch, at his tent door, which screened him from the heat of the sun, " he lift up his eyes, and lo, three men" stood at a little distance from him. To him they appeared to be three strangers on a journey, and as such he treated them. His conduct on this occasion is held up in the epistle to the Hebrews as an example of *hospitality;* and an admirable example it affords. His generosity on this occasion is not more conspicuous than the amiable manner in which it was expressed. The instant he saw them, he rises up, as by a kind of instinctive courtesy, to bid them welcome to his tent, and that in the most respectful manner. Though an old man, and they perfect strangers to him, he no sooner saw them than he "ran to meet them from the tent door, and bowed himself toward the ground;" and observing one of them, as it should seem, presenting himself to him before the other, he said to him, "My Lord, if now I have found favour in thy sight, pass not away, I pray thee, from thy servant."

Ver. 4, 5. And whereas they were supposed to be weary, and overcome with the heat, he persuades them to wash their feet, and sit down under the shade of the spreading oak near his tent, and take a little refreshment, though it were but a morsel of bread to comfort their hearts; after which they might go forward on their journey. Something may be said of the customs of those times and countries, and of there being then but few, if any inns, for the accommodation of strangers: but it certainly affords a charming specimen of patriarchal urbanity, and an example of the manner in which kindness and hospitality should be shewn. To impart relief in an ungracious and churlish manner, destroys the value of it. We see also in this conduct, the genuine fruits of true religion. That which in worldly men is mere complaisance, dictated often by ambition, in Abraham was kindness, goodness, sympathy, and humbleness of mind. It is to the honour of religion that it produces those amiable dispositions which the worst of men are constrained, for their own reputation, to imitate. If such dispositions, and such behaviour were universal, the world would be a paradise.

Ver. 6—8. The supposed strangers having consented to accept the invitation, the good old man, as full of pleasure as if he had found a prize, resolves to entertain them with something better than "a morsel of bread," though he had modestly used that language. Hastening to Sarah, he desires her to get three measures of fine meal, and bake cakes upon the hearth; while he, old as he was, runs to the herd, and fetches a calf, tender and good, and gives it to one of his young men, with orders to kill and dress it immediately. And now, the table being spread beneath the cooling shade of the oak, the veal, with butter and milk to render it more palatable, is placed upon it, and Abraham himself waited on his guests. Such was the style of patriarchal simplicity and hospitality. As yet, Abraham does not appear to have suspected what kind of guests he was entertaining. He might probably be struck from the first with their mien and appearance, which seem to have excited his highest respect; yet he considered them merely as strangers, and as such entertained them. It was thus that he "entertained angels unawares."

Ver. 9, 10. But while they sat at dinner under the tree, enquiry was made after Sarah his wife. Abraham answered, "Behold, she is in the tent." This enquiry must excite some surprise; for how should these strangers know the name of Abraham's wife, and her new name too; and why should they enquire after her? But if the enquiry must strike him with surprise, what followed must have a still greater effect—He who was the first in the train on their arrival, and whom he had addressed in terms of the highest respect, now adds, "I will certainly return unto thee, according to the time of life, and lo, Sarah thy wife shall have a son." This language must remind him of the promise which he had so lately received,* and convince him that the speaker was no other than Jehovah, under the appearance of a man. In the progress of the old-testament history we often read of similar appearances; particularly to Jacob at Peniel, to Moses at the bush, and to Joshua by Jericho. The divine personage who in this manner appeared to men, must surely have been no other than the Son of God, who thus occasionally assumed the form of that nature, which it was his intention, in the fulness of time, actually to take upon him. It was thus, that "being in the form of God, he thought it not robbery

---

* Chap. xvii. 21.

to be equal with God"—that is, he spake and acted all along *as God*, and did not consider himself in so doing as arrogating any thing which did not properly belong to him.

Ver. 11—15. Sarah having over-heard what was said concerning her, and knowing that according to the ordinary course of things she was too old to have a son, laughed within herself at the saying. She supposed however, that as it was to herself, the whole was unknown: but it was not. The same word is used as was before used of Abraham, but it was not the same thing. His laughter was that of joy and surprise: hers had in it a mixture of unbelief, which called forth the reproof of Jehovah. "Jehovah" (the same personage who is elsewhere called an angel, and a man) "said unto Abraham," in the hearing of his wife, "Wherefore did Sarah laugh?" And to detect the sinfulness of this laughter, he points out the principle of it—it was saying, "Shall I of a surety bear a child who am old;" which principle he silences by asking, "Is any thing too hard for Jehovah?" And then solemnly repeats the promise, as that which ought to suffice: "At the time appointed I will return unto thee, according to the time of life, and Sarah shall have a son." This language, while it proved that he who uttered it was a discerner of the thoughts and intents of the heart, covered Sarah's face with confusion. In her fright she denies having laughed; but the denial was in vain. He who knew all things replied, "Nay, but thou didst laugh." We may imagine that what merely passes in our own minds has in a manner no existence, and may almost persuade ourselves to think we are innocent: but in the presence of God all such subterfuges are no better than the fig-leaves of our first parents. When he judgeth, he will overcome.

Ver. 16—19. "The men," as they are called, according to their appearance, now take leave of the tent, and go on their way towards Sodom. Abraham, loth to part with them, went in company, as if to bring them on their way. While they were walking together, Jehovah, in the form of a man, said unto the other two, who appear to be created angels, "Shall I hide from Abraham the thing which I do?" Two reasons are assigned for the contrary.—First: The importance of his character. He was not only the friend of God, but the father of "a great nation," in which God would have a special interest, and through which "all other nations should be blessed." Let him ~~him~~ be in the secret.—Secondly: The good use he would make of it. Being previously disclosed to him, he would be the more deeply impressed by it: and according to his tried and approved conduct as the head of a family, would be concerned to impart it as a warning to his posterity in all future ages. As the wicked extract ill from good, so the righteous will extract good from ill. Sodom's destruction shall turn to Abraham's salvation: the monument of just vengeance against their crimes shall be of perpetual use to him and his posterity, and contribute even to the "bringing of that good upon them, which the Lord had spoken concerning them." The special approbation with which God here speaks of family religion, stamps a divine authority upon it, and an infamy upon that religion, or rather irreligion, which dispenses with it.

Ver. 20, 21. JEHOVAH having resolved to communicate his design to Abraham, proceeds to inform him as follows—"Because the cry of Sodom and Gomorrha is great, and because their sin is very grievous, I will go down now, and see whether they have done altogether according to the cry of it which is come unto me; and if not, I will know." This language, though spoken after the manner of men, contains much serious and important instruction. It teaches us, that the most abandoned people are still the subjects of divine government, and must sooner

Gen. 18.] ABRAM'S INTERCESSION. 223

or later give an account; that impiety, sensuality and injustice are followed with a *cry* for retribution; that this cry is often disregarded by earthly tribunals; that where it is so, the prayers of the faithful, the groans of the oppressed, and the blood of the slain, constitute a cry which ascendeth to heaven, and entereth into the ears of the Lord of Sabaoth; and finally, that in executing judgment, though God will regard these cries, especially where they *wax* greater and greater; as this is said to have done,* yet as they may be partial and erroneous, he will not proceed by them as a rule, but will avail himself of his own omniscience, that the worst of characters may have no cause to complain of injustice.

Ver. 22—33. It is natural to suppose that the mind of Abraham must be forcibly impressed with this intimation. He would feel for his poor ungodly neighbours; but especially for Lot, and other righteous men, whom he might hope, would be found amongst them. At this juncture, "the men," that is, two out of the three,† went towards Sodom: but the third, who is called "Jehovah," continued to converse with Abraham. The patriarch standing before him, and being now aware that he was in the presence of the Most High, addressed him in the lan-

* Gen. xix. 13.   † Chap. xix. 1.

guage of prayer, or intercession. A remarkable intercession it is.—We remark, (1.) Abraham makes a good use of his previous knowledge. Being made acquainted with the evil coming upon them, he stands in the gap, and labours all he can to avert it. They knew nothing: and if they had, no cries, except the shrieks of desperation, would have been heard from them. It is good having such a neighbour as Abraham; and still better to have an Intercessor before the throne who is always heard. The conduct of the patriarch furnishes an example to all who have an interest at the throne of grace, to make use of it in behalf of their poor ungodly countrymen and neighbours.—(2.) He does not plead that the wicked may be spared for their own sake, or because it would be too severe a proceeding to destroy them; but *for the sake of the righteous who might be found amongst them.* Had either of the other pleas been advanced, it had been siding with sinners against God, which Abraham would never do. Wickedness shuts the mouth of intercession; or if any should presume to speak, it would be of no account. Though Noah, Daniel, and Job should plead for the ungodly, they would not be heard. Righteousness only will bear to be made a plea before God. But how then, it may be asked, did Christ make intercession for *transgressors?* Not by arraigning the divine law, nor by alleging ought in extenuation of human guilt; but by pleading his own obedience unto death!—(3.) He charitably hopes the best with respect to the number of righteous characters even in Sodom. At the outset of his intercession, he certainly considered it as a possible case, at least, that there might be found in that wicked place fifty righteous: and though in this instance he was sadly mistaken, yet we may hope from hence that in those times there were many more righteous people in the world than those which are recorded in scripture. The scriptures do not profess to be a book of life, containing the names of all the faithful; but intimate, on the contrary, that God *reserves* to himself a people, who are but little known even by his own servants.—(4.) *God was willing to spare the worst of cities for the sake of a few righteous characters.* This truth is as humiliating to the haughty enemies of religion as it is encouraging to its friends, and furnishes an important lesson to civil governments, to beware of undervaluing, and still more of persecuting, and banishing men whose concern it is to live soberly, righteously, and godly in the world.* Except the Lord of hosts had left *us* a remnant of such characters, we might ere now have been as Sodom, and made

---

* Chap. vii. 11, p. 85, 86.

like unto Gomorrha! If ten righteous had been found in Sodom, it had been spared for their sakes: but alas, there was no such number! God called Abraham to Haran, and when he left that place, mention is made not only of "the substance which he had gathered," but of "the souls which he had gotten."* But Lot, who went to Sodom of his own accord, though he also gathered substance, yet not a soul seems to have been won over by his residence in the place, to the worship of the true God.

DISCOURSE XXVII.

THE DESTRUCTION OF SODOM AND GOMORRHA.

GENESIS xix.

VER. 1, 2. The two angels who left Abraham communing with Jehovah, went on their way till they came to Sodom. Arriving at the city in the evening, the first person whom they saw appears to have been Lot, who was sitting alone, it should seem, at the gate of the city. They had found Abraham also sitting alone; but it was at his own tent door. Lot, whose house was in the city, had probably no place where he could be out of the hearing of those whose con-

---

* Chap. xii. 5.

versation vexed his righteous soul: he therefore took a walk in the evening, and sat down without the city gate, where he might spend an hour in retirement. Seeing two strangers coming up to him, he behaved in much the same courteous and hospitable manner as Abraham had done. Bowing himself with his face towards the ground, he said, "Behold now, my lords; turn in I pray you, into your servant's house, and tarry all night, and wash your feet, and ye shall rise up early, and go on your ways." This was lovely; and the contrast between this and the conduct of his neighbours, shews, what was suggested in the former chapter, the genuine fruits of true religion. What is said to be the customary hospitality of the age and country, was far from being practised by the other inhabitants of Sodom. But though Lot had given them so kind an invitation, they seem determined not to accept of it—"Nay, (said they) but we will abide in the street all night." This might be either for the purpose of being eye-witnesses of the conduct of the citizens, or to express their abhorrence of the general character of the city; as when the prophet of Judah was sent to Bethel, he was forbidden either "to eat bread, or drink water in that place."*

---

* 1 Kings xiii. 8—17.

Ver. 3. After being "greatly pressed" by Lot, however, they yielded to his importunity, and entered into his house; where he made them a feast, as Abraham had done, and they did eat.

Ver. 4, 5. But while things were going on well with respect to Lot, the baseness of his neighbours soon betrayed itself. A little before bed-time, they beset the house; not for the purpose of robbing, or insulting them in any of the ordinary ways of brutal outrage—this had been bad enough, especially to strangers—but to perpetrate a species of crime too shocking and detestable to be named; a species of crime which indeed has no name given it in the scriptures, but what is borrowed from this infamous place.

Ver. 6—9. The conduct of Lot in going out and expostulating with them, was in several respects praise-worthy. His " shutting the door after him," expressed how delicately he felt for his guests, though at present he does not appear to have considered them in any other light than strangers. It was saying in effect, ' Let not their ears be offended with what passes abroad: whatever is scurrilous, obscene, or abusive, let me hear it, but not them.' His gentle and respectful manner of treating this worst of mobs, is also worthy of notice. He could not respect them on the score of character; but he would try and do so as being still his fellow-creatures, and near neighbours. As such he calls them "brethren," no doubt hoping, by such conciliating language, to dissuade them from their "wicked" purpose. But when to turn off their attention to his guests, he proposed the bringing out of his daughters to them, he appears to have gone too far. It is not for us to go into a less evil in hope of preventing a greater; but rather to consent to no evil. It might be owing to the perturbation of his mind; but probably, if he had not lived in Sodom till his mind was almost familiarised to obscenity, he would not have made such a proposal. Nor had it any good effect. He only got himself more abused for it; and even his gentle remonstrance was perversely construed into obtrusive forwardness, and setting himself up for a judge, who was merely "a sojourner" amongst them. Persuasion has no force with men who are under the dominion of their lusts. So now their resentment burns against him, and they will be revenged on him. They will not be contented now with having the men brought out, but will go in unto them, and break the door open to effect their purpose.

Ver. 10, 11. Such an attempt, and such a perseverance in it must have been proof sufficient to the heavenly messengers that the cry of Sodom had not exceeded the truth. Putting forth their hands therefore, they pulled Lot into the house to them, shut to the door, and smote the people without with blindness. The power and indignation displayed in these acts would convince him that they were no common strangers; and one would have thought, might have struck them with awe, and caused them to desist from their horrid purpose: but they are infatuated. Though supernaturally smitten with blindness, they must still "weary themselves to find the door." Such daring presumption, in the face of heaven, must have filled up the measure of their crimes, and rendered them ripe for destruction.

Ver. 12, 13. Things are now hastening to their awful crisis: but mark the mercy of divine proceedings. Ten righteous men would have saved the city; but there seems to have been only one. Well, not only shall that one escape, but all that belong to him shall be delivered for his sake; or if otherwise, it shall be their own fault. "Sons-in-law, sons, daughters, or whatever he had," are directed to be brought out of this place: for, said they, opening their commission, and as it were reading it to Lot, "we will destroy this place, because the cry of them is waxen great before the face of Jehovah, and Jehovah hath sent us to destroy it."

Ver. 14. Giving full credit to the divine threatening, and deeply impressed with it, Lot went forth to warn his sons-in-law, who had married his daughters. We do not read till now that Lot had a family. It looks as if he had taken his wife from Sodom, soon after having parted from Abraham; and as he must have been there about twenty years, he had daughters, some of whom were married, and two remained with him single. No mention is made of his married daughters being alive at this time; but by the manner in which the others are spoken of in verse 15, "thy two daughters which are *here,*" it is probable they were *elsewhere;* viz. along with their husbands, and perished with them in the overthrow. The warning given to his sons-in-law was abrupt and pointed: "Up, get ye out of this place; for Jehovah will destroy this city! But he seemed to them as one that mocked," or who was in jest. He believed, and therefore spake: but they disbelieved, and therefore made light of it. A striking example this of the ordinary effect of truth upon the minds of unbelievers.

Ver. 15, 16. All this had taken place in one night. Early in the morning, Lot is hastened away from the devoted spot. And as his sons-in-law, and it seems their wives with them, would not hear, he is commanded to leave them; and without farther delay, to take his wife, and his two daughters who were with him, lest he should be consumed in the overthrow of the city. The threatening part of this language would probably not have been addressed to him, had he not discovered a reluctance to depart. I hope it was not his worldly substance that clave to him, much less any attachment to that wicked city; but rather that it was his daughters and their husbands who could not be persuaded to accompany him, that occasioned this strong conflict. It was on this account, I suppose, that he is said to have "lingered;" and his deliverers were at last obliged to lay hold upon his hand, and upon the hand of his wife, and upon the hand of his two daughters, and (Jehovah being merciful unto him) by force, in a manner, to set them without the city. Such has been the struggle in many minds, when called to leave all, and flee from the wrath to come; and such the mercy of God towards them.

Ver. 17. Having been so far saved, almost in spite of himself, he is now solemnly charged to "escape for his life, not so much as to look behind him, nor stay in all the plain; but to escape to the mountain, lest he should be consumed." This was continuing to be mercifully severe; and such are our Lord's commands which require us to deny self, take up the cross, and follow him. It was better for Lot to be thus warned off the ground, than to have been consumed upon it: and we had better cut off a right hand, or pluck out a right eye, than be cast into hell.

Ver. 18—22. Lot was certainly a righteous man; but in times of trial his graces do not appear to the best advantage. He is directed to flee to the mountain, and he had better have been there all his days than where he was; but he pleads hard to live in a city, and hopes he may be excused in this desire, seeing it was "a little one." Had he properly confided in God, he would have gone to the mountain without hesitation: but his faith is weak, and his fears prevail, that if he go thither, "some evil will take him, and he shall die." This his imbecility, however, is graciously passed over; his request is granted, and the city spared for his sake. Nor was this all. The angel kindly hastens his escape to this city, (formerly called Bela, but from hence Zoar, that is, *little*) for that "he could do nothing till he should have come thither." All this was merciful, very merciful; and proves not only that the Lord knoweth how to deliver the godly out of temptation, but also that their blood is precious in his sight.

Ver. 23—25. By the time that Lot entered into Zoar, the sun was risen upon the earth. It promised perhaps to be a fine day; and the inhabitants of Sodom, after their night's revel, would be going forth to do as at other times. But lo, on a sudden, floods of fire and brimstone from the Lord out of heaven descend upon this and the neighbouring city of Gomorrha, utterly consuming them, and all their inhabitants! Some have supposed this tremendous judgment to have been effected by a volcanic eruption in the neighbourhood, the lava of which, first ascending high into the atmosphere, and then descending upon the devoted cities, destroyed them.—If so it were, God's hand was in it, directing and timing its operations, no less than if it were accomplished without the interference of any second cause.

Ver. 26. The Lord delivered just Lot; and his whole family, as we have seen, had much mercy shewn them for his sake. But favour may be shewn to the wicked, yet will they not learn righteousness. Some refuse to go with him, and those that did go, proved to him a grief and a snare. His wife is said to have "looked back from behind him," during their journey, and was instantly struck dead, and remained upon the spot a petrified monument of divine vengeance. It may be thought a hard fate for a mere glance of the eye: but that glance, no doubt, was expressive of unbelief, and a lingering desire to return. Probably she was of much the same mind as her sons-in-law, and attributed the whole to the resentment of the strangers, whom her husband was weak enough to believe. It is certain that her example is held up by our Lord as a warning against *turning back*, which intimates that such was the meaning of her look.

Ver. 27—29. Abraham having made intercession, though the issue of it gave him but little hope of success, yet is anxious to see what will be the end of these things. Unable it seems to rest in his bed, he arose early the next morning, and went to the place where he had stood before the Lord. From having a view of the plain, he beheld, and lo, the smoke of the country went up as the smoke of a furnace. He had not mentioned Lot by name in his intercession, though doubtless it had respect to him; and the Lord so far hearkened to his prayer as to deliver that good man in answer to it. Lot could not pray for himself, for he was not aware of his danger till it came in a manner upon him. What a mercy it is to have an Intercessor who knows all the evils which are coming upon us, and prayeth for us that our faith fail not! But to return to Lot—

Ver. 30. On leaving Sodom he was very earnest to have Zoar granted him for a refuge, and to be excused from going to dwell in the mountain: yet now all on a sudden he went up out of Zoar, and dwelt in the mountain, and that for the very reason he had given for a contrary choice. Then he feared some evil would take him, if he went to the mountain; now he " fears to dwell in Zoar." It is well to know that the way of man is not in himself, and that it is not in man that walketh to direct his steps. Our wisdom is to refer all to God, and to follow wherever his word and providence lead the way. But why did not Lot return to Abraham? There was no occasion now for strife about their herds; for he had lost all, and but just escaped with his life. Whatever was the reason, he does not appear to have made a good choice. Had he gone to the mountain when directed, he might have hoped for preserving mercy: but going of his own accord, and from a motive of sinful distrust, evil in reality overtakes him. His daughters, who seem to have contracted such habits in Sodom as would prepare them for any thing, however unnatural, draw him into intemperance and incest, and thus cover his old age with infamy. The offspring of this illicit intercourse were the fathers of two great, but heathen, nations; viz. the Moabites, and the children of Ammon.

The dishonourable end of this good man shews that we are never out of danger while we are upon earth. He whose righteous soul was grieved with the filthy conversation of the wicked, while in a city, is drawn into the same kind of evils himself, when dwelling in a cave! His whole history also, from the time of his leaving Abraham, furnishes an affecting lesson to the heads of families in the choice of habitations for themselves or their children. If worldly accommodations be preferred to religious advantages, we have nothing good, but every thing evil to expect. We may, or we may not lose our substance as he did; but, what is of far greater consequence, our families may be expected to become mere heathens, and our own minds contaminated with the examples which are continually before our eyes. Such was the harvest which Lot reaped from his well-watered plain; and such are the fruits very commonly seen in those who follow his example!

DISCOURSE XXVIII.

ABRAHAM AND ABIMELECH.

GENESIS XX.

VER. 1. After the affecting story of Lot, we return to Abraham. When he and his kinsman parted, he pitched his tent in the plains of Mamre, and appears to have continued there nearly twenty years. At length he removes again, journeying southward, and taking up his residence for a time at Gerar, which was then a royal city of the Philistines.

Ver. 2. And here we find him a second time saying of Sarah his wife, "she is my sister." His sin in so speaking seems to be much greater than it was before.—For, (1.) He had narrowly escaped the first time. If God had not remarkably interposed in his favour, there is no saying what would have been the consequence. The repetition of the same fault looked like presuming upon providence.—(2.) Sarah was now with child, and that of a son of promise: he might therefore surely have trusted God to preserve their lives in the straight-forward path of duty, instead of having recourse to his own crooked policy. But he did not. There are exceptions in every human character, and often in the very thing wherein they in general excel. The consequence was, Abimelech, king of Gerar, sent and took her, probably by force, to be one of his wives. We should have thought that the age of Sarah might have exempted both her and her husband from this temptation: but human life was then much longer than it is now; and she was a beautiful woman, and we may suppose carried her years better than many. Be that as it may, she is involved in a difficulty from which she cannot get clear, nor can Abraham tell how to deliver her. It has been observed, that when wicked men deviate from truth, they will very commonly get through with it: but if a good man think to do so, he will as commonly find himself mistaken. If once he leave the path of rectitude, he is entangled, and presently betrays himself. The crooked devices of the flesh are things in which he is not sufficiently an adept, and conscience will often prevent his going through with them. God also will generally so order things that he shall be detected, and put to shame at an early stage, and that in mercy to his soul; while sinners are left to go on in their evil courses with success.

Ver. 3—7. Man's wisdom leads him into a pit, and God's wisdom must draw him out. God has access to all men's minds, and can impress them by a dream, an affliction, or any way he thinks proper. He did thus by Abimelech. Dreams in general are mere vanity, the excursions of imagination, unaccompanied with reason: yet these are under the controul of God, and have in many instances been the medium of impressing things of great importance on the mind. Abimelech dreamed that he heard the voice of the Almighty, saying unto him, "Behold, thou art a dead man for the woman which thou hast taken; for she is a man's wife!" Whether Abimelech was an idolater, I know not: but this I know, that if in countries called christian, every adulterer were *a dead man*, many would be numbered with the dead who now glory in their shame. And though human laws may wink at this crime, it is no less heinous in the sight of God than when it is punished with death. Abimelech, conscious that he had not come near the woman, answered in his dream, "Lord, wilt thou slay also a righteous nation? Said he not unto me, She is my sister? And she, even she herself said, He is my brother. In the integrity of my heart, and innocency of my hands have I done this."—The first sentence in this answer appears to contain a reference to the recent and awful event of Sodom's overthrow, which must have greatly impressed the surrounding country. It is as if he had said, 'I am aware that thou hast slain a nation notorious for its filthy and unnatural crimes; but we are not such a nation; and in the present case, all that has been done was in perfect ignorance. Surely thou wilt not slay the innocent.'—The answer of God admits his plea of ignorance, and suggests that he was not charged with having yet sinned, but threatened with death in case he persisted now that he was informed of the truth. It is intimated however, that if he had come near her, he should in so doing have sinned *against God*, whether he had sinned against Abraham or not; and this perhaps owing to her being in a state of pregnancy, of which, in that case, he could not have been ignorant. But God had mercifully withheld him from thus sinning against him, for which it became him to be thankful, and without delay to "restore the man his wife." It was also added that the man was "a prophet," or one who had special intercourse with heaven; and who, if he restored his wife, would pray to God for him, and he should live: but if he withheld her, he should surely die, and all that belonged to him.

We see in this account,—(1.) That absolute ignorance excuses from guilt: but this does not prove that all ignorance does so, or that it is in itself excusable. Where the powers and means of knowledge are possessed, and ignorance arises from neglecting to make use of them, or from aversion to the truth, it is so far from excusing, that it is in itself sinful.—(2.) That great as the wickedness of men is upon the face of the earth, it would be much greater, were it not that God by his providence in innumerable instances "withholds" them from it. The conduct of intelligent beings is influenced by motives; and all motives which are presented to the mind are subject to his disposal. Hence we may feel the propriety of that petition: "Lead us not into temptation, but deliver us from evil."

Ver. 8. Abimelech awaking, is deeply impressed with his dream. He rises early, calls together the principal people about him, and imparts particulars to them; at the rehearsal of which they are "sore afraid." Some afflictions had already been laid upon them, of which they seem to have been aware; (ver. 18.) and considering the late tremendous judgments of God upon Sodom, with the terrific dream of the king just rehearsed, it is no wonder they should be seized with fear.

Ver. 9, 10. After speaking to his servants, he next sent for Abraham to converse the matter over. His address to the patriarch is pointed, but temperate: "What hast thou done unto us? And what have I offended thee, that thou hast brought on me, and on my kingdom a great sin? Thou hast done deeds unto me that ought not to be done . . . . What sawest thou, that thou hast done this thing?" We are grieved to find Abraham in such a situation. How honourable did he appear before the king of Sodom, and the king of Salem; but how dishonourable before the king of Gerar! Sin is the reproach of any people; and the greater and better the man, the greater is the reproach.

Ver. 11—13. But let us hear his apology. "And Abraham said, Because I thought surely the fear of God is not in this place, and they will slay me for my wife's sake. And yet indeed, she is my sister: she is the daughter of my father, but not the daughter of my mother; and she became my wife. And it came to pass when God caused me to wander from my father's house, that I said unto her, this is thy kindness which thou shalt shew unto me: at every place whither we shall come, say of me, he is my brother."—According to his account, to be sure, there was nothing against Abimelech in particular, and this might serve to appease him: and with respect to God, or his "doing deeds that ought not to be done," what he had said was not a lie; but it was *equivocation*. Many things of this sort pass among men; but they will not bear a strict scrutiny. If our words, though in some sense true, yet are designed to convey what is not true, as was the case in this instance, we are guilty of doing what ought not to be done.

Ver. 14, 15. Abimelech, satisfied with this answer, so far as respected himself, restored Sarah to her husband, and that with a trespass-offering, like that which was afterwards presented by his countrymen with the ark;* adding with great courteousness, "Behold, my land is before thee: dwell where it pleaseth thee:" for he saw that the Lord was with him.

Ver. 16—18. He did not part with Sarah, however, without giving her a word of reproof. In calling Abraham her "brother," he made use of her own language in a sarcastic way; and tells her that her husband should be to her as a vail, that she should look on none else, and none else should look on her. Some have rendered the words, "It, that is, the silver, shall be to thee a covering for the eyes, unto all that are with

---

* 1 Sam. xi. 3.

thee, and to all other." As if he had given it to buy her a vail, which might prevent all such mistakes in future. Take this, (q. d.) and never go without a vail again, nor any of your married servants. So she was reproved.

The issue was, Abraham prayed, and the Lord answered him, and healed the family of Abimelech. He would feel a motive for prayer in this case which he did not when interceding for Sodom: for of this evil he himself had been the cause.

DISCOURSE XXIX.

THE BIRTH OF ISAAC, &c.

GENESIS xxi.

Ver. 1. Abraham still sojourning in the land of the Philistines, at length sees the promise fulfilled. It is noted with some degree of emphasis, as forming a special epoch in his life, that "the Lord visited Sarah as he had said, and the Lord did unto Sarah as he had spoken." Such a kind of language is used of his posterity being put in possession of the promised land: "The Lord gave them rest round about, according to all that he sware unto their fathers—there failed not aught of any good thing which the Lord had spoken unto the house of Israel: all came to pass."* And such will be our language sooner or later, concerning all the good things promised to the church, or to us as individuals.

Ver. 2. Two things are particularly noticed in the birth of this child:—It was in Abraham's "old age," and "at the set time of which God had spoken to him." Both these circumstances shewed the whole to be of God. That which comes to us in the ordinary course of things may *be* of God; but that which comes otherwise, manifestly *appears to be so.* One great difference between this child and the son of Hagar consisted in this: the one was "born after the flesh," that is, in the ordinary course of generation; but the other, "after the spirit," that is, by extraordinary divine interposition, and in virtue of a special promise.† Analogous to these were those jews, on the one hand, who were merely descended from Abraham *according to the flesh;* and those, on the other, who were "not of the circumcision only, but also walked in the steps of the faith of their father Abraham."‡ The former were the children of the bond-woman, who were cast out: the latter of the free-woman,

* Josh. xxi. 44, 45.   † Gal. iv. 23, 29.
‡ Rom. iv. 12.

who being "his people whom he foreknew, were not cast away," but were counted for the seed.*

Ver. 3, 4. The name by which this extraordinary child should be called was *Isaac*, according to the previous direction of God. It signifies *laughter*, or *joy*, and corresponds with the gladness which accompanied his birth. Children are ordinarily "an heritage of the Lord."— On account of the uncertainty of their future character however, we have reason to rejoice with trembling: but in this case it was joy in a manner unmixed; for he was born under the promise of being "blessed, and made a blessing."—But what a difference between the joy of Abraham at the birth of a child, and that which is commonly seen amongst us! His was not that vain mirth, or noisy laughter, which unfits for obedience to God: on the contrary, he circumcised his son when he was eight days old, not in conformity to custom, but "as God had commanded him."

Ver. 5—7. The sacred writers seldom deal in reflexions themselves; but will often mention those of others. Moses having recorded the fact, that "Abraham was a hundred years old when his son Isaac was born unto him," tells us of the joyful sayings of Sarah:—"God, saith she,

* Gal. iv. 28—31. Rom. ix. 7, 9. xi. 1, 2.

hath made me to laugh, so that all who hear will laugh with me—Who would have said unto Abraham, that Sarah should have given children suck? For I have borne him a son in his old age!" Yes, God had made her to laugh, and that without any of her crooked measures; and not merely with a private, but a public joy: for "all that hear shall laugh with her."

Ver. 8. For awhile nothing remarkable occurred: the child grew, and all went on pleasantly. When the time came for his being weaned, "a great feast was made," in token of joy that he had passed the most delicate, and dangerous stage of life.

Ver. 9. But the joy of that day was embittered. The son of Hagar being stung with envy, cannot bear such an ado about this child of promise. So he turns it into ridicule, probably deriding the parents and the child, and the promise together; and all this in the sight of Sarah! Thus he that was born after the flesh began at an early stage to *persecute* him that was born after the spirit; and thus Sarah's crooked policy in giving Hagar to Abraham, goes on to furnish them with new sources of sorrow. From what is said of Hagar in chapter xvi. we conceived hopes of her; but whatever she was her son appears at present to be a bitter enemy to God, and his people.

Ver. 10—13. The consequence was, Sarah was set on both the mother and the son being banished from the family. Abraham had earnestly desired that Ishmael might *live before God:* but Sarah says, He "shall not be heir with her son, with Isaac." This resolution on the part of Sarah might be the mere effect of temper: but whatever were her motives, the thing itself accorded with the design of God; though therefore it was grievous to Abraham, he is directed to comply with it. The Lord would indeed make a nation of Ishmael, because he was his seed; but "in Isaac should his seed be called." We must not refuse to join in doing what God commands, however contrary it may be to our natural feelings, nor on account of the suspicious motives of some with whom we are called to act.

Ver. 14. Impressed with these principles, the father of the faithful without further delay, rose early the next morning, probably before Sarah was stirring, and sent away both the mother and the son. His manner of doing it, however, was tender, and kind. Giving Hagar a portion of bread, and a bottle of water, he

k

committed them to Him who had in effect promised to watch over them. And now for a little while we take leave of Abraham's family, and observe the unhappy Hagar and her son, wandering in the wilderness of Beersheba.

Ver. 15, 16. It was doubtless the design of Hagar when she set off, to go to Egypt, her native country; but having to travel through a desert land, where there was ordinarily no water, it was necessary she should be furnished with that article. Whether " the wilderness of Beersheba," as it was called at the time when Moses wrote the narrative, was directly in her way, or whether she went thither in consequence of having "wandered," or lost her way; so it was, that she was here reduced to great distress. The bread might not be exhausted, but the water was; and no spring being to be found in this inhospitable place, she and Ishmael appear to have walked about, till he, overcome of thirst, could walk no longer. She had supported him, it seems, as long as she could; but fearing he should die in her arms, she cast him under a shrub, just to screen him from the scorching sun, and " went and sat herself down over against him, a good way off, as it were a bow shot: for she said, Let me not see the death of the child! And she sat over against him, and lifted up her voice and wept."

Ver. 17, 18. A more finished picture of distress we shall seldom see. The bitter cries and flowing tears of the afflicted mother, with the groans of her dying son, are heard, and seen, and felt, in a manner as though we were present. And wherefore do they cry? Had there been any ear to hear them, any eye to pity them, or hand to help them, these cries and tears might have been mingled with hope: but as far as human aid was concerned, there was no place for this. Whether any of them were directed to heaven, we know not. We could have wished, and should almost have expected, that those of the mother, at least, would have been so; for surely she could not have forgotten Him who had seen, and delivered her from a similar condition about sixteen years before, and who had then promised to "multiply her seed," and to cause this very child to "dwell in the presence of all his brethren."* But whether any of these expressions of distress were directed to God, or not, the groans of the distressed reached his ear. "God heard the voice of the lad: and the angel of God called to Hagar out of heaven, and said unto her, What aileth thee, Hagar? Fear not; for God hath heard the voice of the lad, where he is. Arise,

---

* See on Chap. xvi. 13, 14.

lift up the lad, and hold him in thine hand: for I will make him a great nation.

Ver. 19. At this instant, lifting up her eyes, she saw a spring of water, which before she had overlooked; and filling her bottle from it, returned to the lad, and gave him drink. To God the Lord belong the issues from death. He maketh strong the bands of the mocker; and again he looseth his prisoners, and delivereth those that were appointed to die. If Ishmael were at any future time possessed of true religion, he must look back upon these humbling but gracious dispensations of the God of his father Abraham with very tender emotions.

Ver. 20, 21. Whether Hagar and her son continued any longer in the wilderness of Beersheba, we are not informed: it would rather seem that they left it, and prosecuted their journey. They did not however settle in Egypt, though in process of time she took a wife for him from that country, but in the "wilderness of Paran," where the providence of God watched over him, and where he lived, and perhaps maintained his mother by the use of the bow. But to return—

Ver. 22—24. Abraham still continued to sojourn in the land of the Philistines; not indeed at Gerar, but within a few miles of it. Here he was visited by king Abimelech, who, attended by the captain of his host, in the most friendly manner, in behalf of himself, and his posterity, requested to live in perpetual amity with him. " God is with thee, saith he, in all that thou doest. Now therefore swear unto me here by God, that thou wilt not deal falsely with me, nor with my son, nor with my son's son: but according to the kindness that I have done unto thee, thou shalt do unto me, and to the land wherein thou hast sojourned. And Abraham said, I will swear."—Observe, (1.) The *motive* that induces this friendly request; he "saw that God was with him." Probably the news of the extraordinary birth of Isaac had reached the court of Abimelech, and became a topic of conversation. 'This, said he, is a great man, and a great family, and will become a great nation: the blessing of heaven attends him. It is our wisdom, therefore, to take the earliest opportunity to be on good terms with him!' Had Abimelech's successors always acted on this principle towards Israel, it had been better for them: for whether they knew it, or not, God in blessing Abraham had promised to "bless them that blessed him, and to curse them that cursed him."—(2.) The *solemnity* with which he wished the friendship to be confirmed: " swear unto me by God" . . . .

It is a dictate of prudence very common among magistrates to require men to swear by a name which the party holds sacred. In this view Abimelech certainly acted a wise part; for whoever made light of God's name, the party here concerned would not.—(3.) Abraham's cheerful and ready compliance. I hope he did not need to be sworn not to deal falsely; but as posterity was concerned, the more solemn the engagement the better. The friend of God has no desire but to be the friend of man.

Ver. 25, 26. Now that they are entering into closer terms of amity however, it is proper that if there be any cause of complaint on either side, it should be mentioned, and adjusted, that nothing which is past at least may interrupt their future harmony. Abraham accordingly makes mention of "a well of water which Abimelech's servants had violently taken away." In this country, and to a man whose substance consisted much in cattle, a spring of water was of consequence; and to have it taken away by mere violence, though it might be borne with from an enemy, yet is not to be overlooked where there is professed friendship. In this matter Abimelech fairly and fully exonerates himself: " I wot not, saith he, who hath done this thing; neither didst thou tell me, neither yet heard I of it but to-

Gen. 21.] BIRTH OF ISAAC. 255

day." Public characters cannot always be accountable for the misdeeds of those who act under them: they had need take care however, what sort of servants they employ, as while matters are unexplained, that which is wrong is commonly placed to their account.

Ver. 27—32. Abraham, satisfied with the answer, proceeds to enter into a solemn covenant with Abimelech, and as it should seem, a covenant by sacrifice.* The "sheep and oxen" appear to have been presented for this purpose; and the "seven ewe lambs" were probably a consideration to him, as lord of the soil, for a rightful and acknowledged propriety in the well. Having mutually sworn to this covenant of peace, the place where it was transacted was from hence called "Beersheba," *the well of the oath*, or the well of *seven*, alluding to the seven lambs which were given as the price of it. Matters being thus adjusted, Abimelech and Phichol, the chief captain of his host, took leave and departed.

Ver. 33, 34. Abraham being now quietly settled at Beersheba, "planted a grove, and called there on the name of Jehovah, the everlasting God." The grove might be for the

* See on Chap. xv. 9, 10.

shading of his tent, and perhaps for a place of worship. Such places were afterwards abused to idolatry; or if otherwise, yet became unlawful when the temple was erected. The use which Abraham made of it was worthy of him. Such was his common practice: wherever he pitched his tent, there he reared an altar to the Lord. A lovely example this, to all those who would tread in the steps of the faith of Abraham. It does not appear however, that this was a common, but rather a special act of worship; somewhat like that of Samuel, when he set up a stone between Mizpeh and Shen, and called it Ebenezer, saying, "Hitherto the Lord hath helped us." There are periods in life in which we are led to review the dispensations of God towards us, with special gratitude, and renewed devotion. In this situation Abraham continued "many days;" but still he is a "sojourner," and such he must continue in the present world.

DISCOURSE XXX.

ABRAHAM TEMPTED TO OFFER UP HIS SON ISAAC.

GENESIS xxii.

When Isaac was born, Abraham might be apt to hope that his trials were nearly at an end: but if so, he was greatly mistaken. It is not enough, that in consequence of this event, he is called to give up Ishmael: a greater trial than this is yet behind.

"And it came to pass after these things that God did tempt Abraham."—Many temptations had assailed him from other quarters, out of which God had delivered him: and does he after this himself become his tempter? As "God cannot be tempted with evil, so neither (in one sense) tempteth he any man." But he sees fit to *try* the righteous; and very frequently those most who are most distinguished by their faith and spirituality. So great a value doth the Lord set upon the genuine exercises of grace, that all the grandeur of heaven and earth is overlooked, in comparison of "a poor and contrite spirit, which trembleth at his word:"* it is no wonder therefore that he should bring his servants into situations which, though trying to them, are calculated to draw forth these pleasant fruits.

In discoursing upon this temptation of Abraham, I shall deviate from my usual practice of expounding verse by verse. I shall notice the trial itself—the conduct of the patriarch under it—the reward conferred upon him—and the general design of the whole.

First, with respect to *the trial itself.* The *time* of it is worthy of notice. The same things may be more or less trying as they are connected with other things. If the treatment of Job's friends had not been preceeded by the loss of his substance, the untimely death of his children, the cruel counsel of his wife, and the heavy hand of God, it had been much more tolerable: and if Abraham's faith and patience had not been exercised in the manner they were anterior to this temptation, it might have been somewhat different from what it was. It is also a much greater trial to be deprived of an object when our hopes have been raised, and in a manner accomplished respecting it, than to have it

* Isai. lxvi. 1, 2.

altogether withheld from us. The spirits of a man may be depressed by a heavy affliction: but if he be nearly recovered, and experience a relapse; if again he recovers, and again relapses, this is much more depressing than if no such hopes had been afforded him. "Thou hast lifted me up (said the Psalmist) and cast me down!" Now such was the temptation of Abraham. It was *"after these things* that God did tempt Abraham"—that is, after five-and-twenty years waiting; after the promise had been frequently repeated; after hope had been raised to the highest pitch; yea, after it had been actually turned into enjoyment; and when the child had lived long enough to discover an amiable and godly disposition. Verse 7.

The shock which it was adapted to produce upon his natural affections, is also worthy of notice. The command is worded in a manner as if it were designed to harrow up all his feelings as a father: "Take now thy *son,* thine *only son* (of promise) Isaac, *whom thou lovest*"—Or, as some read it, "Take now that son . . . that only one of thine . . . whom thou lovest . . . that ISAAC!" And what! Deliver him to some other hand to sacrifice him? No: be thou thyself the priest: go "offer him up for a burnt-offering!" When Ishmael was thirteen years old, Abraham could have been well contented to have gone without another son: but when he was born, and had for a number of years been entwining round his heart, to part with him in this manner must, we should think, be a rending stroke. Add to this, Isaac's having to carry the wood, and himself the fire and the knife; but above all, the cutting question of the lad, asked in the simplicity of his heart, without knowing that he himself was to be the victim: "Behold the fire, and the wood; but where is the lamb for a burnt-offering?" This would seem to be more than human nature could bear.

But the shock which it would be to natural affection is not represented as the principal part of the trial; but rather what it must have been to his *faith*. It was not so much his being his *son*, as his *only son of promise;* his Isaac, in whom all the great things spoken of his *seed* were to be fulfilled. When called to give up his other son, God condescended to give him a reason for it:* but here no reason is given. In that case, though Ishmael must go, it is because he is not the child of promise; "for in Isaac shall thy seed be called." But if Isaac goes, who shall be a substitute for him?

* Gen. xxi. 12.

Let us next observe *the conduct of Abraham* under this sharp trial. In general we see no opposition, either from the struggles of natural affection, or those of unbelief: all bow in absolute submission to the will of God. *We* may depict to ourselves how the former would revolt, and how the latter would rise up in rebellion, and what a number of plausible objections might have been urged; but there is not a single appearance of either *in Abraham.*—We have here then a surprising instance of the efficacy of divine grace, in rendering every power, passion, and thought of the mind subordinate to the will of God. There is a wide difference between this, and the extinction of the passions. This were to be deprived of feeling; but the other is to have the mind assimilated to the mind of Christ, who though he felt most sensibly, yet said, "If this cup may not pass from me, except I drink it, thy will be done!"

No sooner had the father of the faithful received the heavenly mandate, but without further delay he prepares for the journey. Lot lingered even when his own deliverance was at stake: but Abraham "rose early in the morning," in prompt obedience to God. He had to go three day's journey ere he reached the appointed spot; a distance perhaps of about sixty miles. Sarah seems to have known nothing of it. He takes only two young men with him, to carry what was necessary; and on his arrival within sight of the place, they were left behind. "Abide you here, said he, with the ass, and I and the lad will go yonder and worship, and come again to you." This would intimate that he wished not to be interrupted. In hard duties and severe trials, we should consider that we have enough to struggle with in our minds, without having any interruptions from other quarters. Great trials are best entered upon with but little company. Such was the precaution taken by our Lord himself. It is admirable to see how in this trying hour Abraham possessed his soul. He lays the wood upon his son—takes the fire, and the knife—they go both of them together— he evades the cutting question of Isaac so as to prevent disclosure, and yet in such a manner as to excite resignation to God—built the altar, stretched forth his hand, and took the knife with an intention to slay his son!

But what did he mean by telling his two servants that he and the lad would "come again to them?" These words, compared with those of the apostle in Hebrews xi. 17. explain the whole story. They shew that Abraham from the first believed that the lad would in some way be restored to him, because God had said, "In Isaac shall thy seed be called." He expected no other than that he should have to slay him, and that he would be burnt to ashes: but if so it were, he was persuaded that he should receive him again,—"Accounting that God was able to raise him up even from the dead." Such was the victory of faith!

Take notice, in the next place, of *the reward conferred upon him*. At the very moment when he was about to give the fatal stroke, and to which Isaac seems to have made no resistance, the angel of the Lord who visited him at Mamre, and with whom he had interceded in behalf of Sodom, called unto him to forbear: "For now I know, saith he, that thou fearest God, seeing thou hast not withheld thy son, thine only son from me." The Lord knew the heart of Abraham before he had tried him; but he speaks after the manner of men. It is by a holy and obedient reverence of the divine authority that faith is made manifest. As a sinner, Abraham was justified by faith only: but as a professing believer, he was justified by the works which his faith produced. This accounts, I apprehend, for what is said by Paul on the first of these subjects, and by James on the last. They both allege the example of Abraham: but the one respects him as *ungodly*, the other as *godly*. In the first instance he is justified by faith, exclusive of works, or as having reference merely to the promised seed: in the last by faith, as producing works, and thereby proving him to be the friend of God.*

Abraham being thus agreeably arrested in his design, makes a pause, and "lifting up his eyes, sees a ram caught in a thicket by his horns." Him he takes as provided of God, and "offers him for a burnt-offering instead of his son." This extraordinary deliverance so impressed his mind, that he called the name of the place "Jehovah-Jireh," *the Lord will see, or provide.* And this name seems to have become a kind of proverb in Israel, furnishing not only a memorial of God's goodness to Abraham, but a promise that he would interpose for them that trust in him in times of extremity. To all this the Lord adds a repetition of the promised blesing. The angel of the Lord who called unto him before, "called unto him a second time, saying, By myself have I sworn, saith the Lord; for because thou hast done this thing, and hast not withheld thy son, thine only son, that in blessing I will bless thee, and in multiplying I

---

* Rom. iv. 3—5. James ii. 21—24.

will multiply thy seed as the stars of the heaven, and as the sand upon the sea shore; and thy seed shall possess the gate of his enemies; and in thy seed shall all the nations of the earth be blessed, because thou hast obeyed my voice." (ver. 15—18.) Though the things here promised be much the same as had been promised before; yet they are more than a mere repetition. The terms are stronger than had ever been used on any former occasion, and as such, more expressive of divine complacency. " Blessing, I will bless thee &c." is a mode of speaking which denotes, I will greatly bless thee.* It is also delivered in the form of an oath, that it may be a ground of strong consolation: and the same things which were promised before are now promised as the reward of this singular instance of obedience, to express how greatly God approved of it.

A few remarks on *the general design of the whole*, will conclude this subject. Though it was not the intention of God to permit Abraham actually to offer a human sacrifice; yet he might mean to assert his own right as Lord of all to require it, as well as to manifest the implicit obedience of faith in the conduct of his servant. Such an assertion of his right would manifest his *goodness* in refusing to exercise it.

* Genesis iii. 16.

Hence, when children were sacrificed to Moloch, who had no such right, Jehovah could say in regard of himself, "It is what *I* commanded not, nor spake it, neither came it into my mind."* God never accepted but one human sacrifice; and blood in that case was not shed at his command, but by the wicked hands of men. It is necessary however, that we should resign our lives, and every thing we have to his disposal. We cannot be said to love him supremely, if father or mother, or wife or children, or our own lives be preferred before him. The way to enjoy our temporal comforts is to resign them to God. When we have in this manner given them up, and receive them again at his hand, they become much sweeter, and are accompanied with blessings of greater value.

But in this transaction there seems to be a still higher design; namely, to predict in a figure the great substitute which God in due time should *see and provide*. The very place of it, called "the mount of the Lord," (ver. 14.) seems to have been marked out as the scene of great events; and of that kind too in which a substitutional sacrifice was offered and accepted. Here it was that David offered burnt-offerings, and peace-offerings, and called upon the Lord;

* Jer. xix. 5.

and he answered him from heaven by fire upon the altar of burnt-offering, and commanded the angel of death to put up his sword.* It was upon the same mountain that Solomon was afterwards directed to build the temple.† And if it were not at the very spot, it could not be far distant that the Saviour of the world was crucified. Mount Moriah was large enough to give name to a tract of land about it. (ver. 2.) Mount Calvary therefore was probably a lesser mountain, which ascended from a certain part of it. Hither then was led God's own Son, his only Son, whom he loved, and in whom all nations of the earth were to be blessed; nor was he spared at the awful crisis by means of a substitute, but was himself freely delivered up as the substitute of others. One reason of the high approbation which God expressed of Abraham's conduct might be, its affording some faint likeness of what would shortly be his own.

The chapter concludes with an account of Nahor's family, who settled at Haran. Probably this had not been given, but for the connexion which it had with the church of God. From them, Isaac and Jacob took them wives; and it is as preparatory to those events that the genealogy is recorded.

* 1 Chron xxi. 26, 27.   † 2 Chron. iii. 1.

DISCOURSE XXXI.

THE DEATH AND BURIAL OF SARAH.

GENESIS xxiii.

We have no such account of the death of any woman before, or of the respect paid to her memory, as is here given of Sarah. She was not without her faults, and who is? But she was upon the whole a great female character. As such her name stands recorded in the new testament amongst the worthies, and the memory of her was more than usually blessed.

Ver. 1, 2. Observe, (1.) The *time* of her death. She was younger by ten years than Abraham, and yet died thirty-eight years before him. Human life is a subject of very uncertain calculation: God often takes the youngest before the eldest. She lived, however, thirty-seven years after the birth of Isaac, to a good old age, and went home as a shock of corn ripe in its season.—(2.) The *place*. It was anciently called Kirjath-Arba, afterwards Hebron, situated in the plain of Mamre, where Abraham had lived more than twenty years before he went into the land of the Philistines, and whither he had since returned.* Here Sarah died, and here Abraham "mourned" for her. We may take notice of the *forms* of it. He "*came* to mourn;" i. e. he came into her tent where she died, and looked at her dead body: his eye affected his heart. There was none of that false delicacy of modern times which shuns to see, or attend the burial of near relations. Let him see her, and let him weep: it is the last tribute of affection which he will be able in that manner to pay her. We should also notice the *sincerity* of it: he "wept." Many affect to mourn who do not weep; but Abraham both "mourned and wept." Religion does not stop the course of nature, though it moderates it: and by inspiring the hope of a blessed resurrection, prevents our being swallowed up of overmuch sorrow.

Ver. 3, 4. From mourning, which was commonly accompanied with a sitting on the ground,† Abraham at length "stood up from before his dead," and took measures to bury her. It is proper to indulge in weeping for a time, but there is a time for it to abate; and it is well there is. The necessary cares attending life are often a merciful mean of rousing the

* See on Chap. xiii. 18. † Job. i. 20. ii. 13. Lam. i. 1.

mind from the torpor of melancholy. But see what a change death makes: those faces which once excited strong sensations of pleasure, require now to be buried. " out of our sight." In those times, and long afterwards, they appear to have had no public burying-places; and Abraham being often removed from place to place, and not knowing where his lot might be cast at the time, had not provided one. He had therefore at this time a burying-place to seek. As yet he had none inheritance in the land, though the whole was given him in promise. We see him here pleading for a grave as "a stranger and a sojourner." This language is commented upon by the apostle to the Hebrews: " They confessed (says he) that they were strangers and pilgrims on the earth; and they that say such things declare plainly that they seek a country."* Abraham did not sustain this character alone, nor merely on account of his having no inheritance in Canaan; for Israel when put in possession of the land were taught to consider it as properly *the Lord's*, and themselves as strangers and sojourners *with him* in it. † Even David, who was king of Israel, made the same confession. ‡

* Heb. xi. 13, 14. † Lev. xxv. 23.

‡ Psal. xxxix. 12.

Ver. 5—16. One admires to observe the courteous behaviour between Abraham and the Canaanites, for Heth was a son of Canaan. On his part, having signified his desire, and received a respectful answer, he "bowed himself to them;" and when he had fixed upon a spot in his mind, he does not ask it of the owner, but requests them to entreat him on his behalf; expressing also his desire to give him the full value of it, and refusing to accept it otherwise. Nor is there any thing wanting on their part; but every thing appears generous and lovely. Abraham calls himself a stranger, and a sojourner; but they call him "a mighty prince amongst them;" give him the choice of their sepulchres; offer any one of them gratis; and when he insisted on paying for it, mention its value in the most delicate manner, intimating that such a sum was as nothing between them. Were commerce conducted on such principles, how pleasant would it be! How different from that selfish spirit described by Solomon, and still prevalent amongst men. "Naught, naught, saith the buyer: but when he is gone his way, then he boasteth." Civility, courtesy, and generosity adorn religion. The plainness of christianity is not a rude and insolent one: it stands aloof from flattery, but not from obliging behaviour. Some who are very courteous to strangers, are very much the reverse to those about them: but Abraham's behaviour to his neighbours is no less respectful than it was to the three strangers who called at his tent. It is painful to add however, that civility and courtesy may be where there is no religion. However it may tend to smooth the rugged paths of life, and however much we are indebted to the providence of God for it; yet this alone will not avail in the sight of God.

Ver. 17—20. Respecting the purchase of this sepulchre, I conceive it was *an exercise of faith.* Jacob and Joseph after him had certainly an eye to the promise, in requesting their bones to be carried up from Egypt. A sepulchre was like an earnest, and indicated a persuasion of future possession.* It would tend also to endear the land to his posterity. This was so much a dictate of nature, that Nehemiah could urge it to a heathen king, whom no religious considerations would probably have influenced:† and when to this was added, the *character* of those who should be there deposited, it would render the country still more endearing. Heathens venerate the dust of their forefathers; but contemplate it without hope. It is not so with believers: those who should lie in this sepulchre, walked with God in their generations;

* Isai. xxii. 16. † Neh. ii. 3.

and though dead, yet *lived* under the promise of a glorious resurrection.

Upon the whole, it is natural to wish to mingle dust with those whom we love—" Where thou diest, there will I be buried." And sometimes with those whom we only respect—" When I am dead, (said the old prophet of Bethel to his sons) bury me in the sepulchre wherein the man of God is buried, and lay my bones beside his bones." But after all, the chief concern is with whom we shall rise!

DISCOURSE XXXII.

ABRAHAM SENDING HIS SERVANT TO OBTAIN A WIFE FOR ISAAC.

GENESIS XXIV.

The last chapter contained a funeral; this gives an account of a marriage. Such are the changes of human life! Let not this minute narrative seem little in our eyes: it was thought by the Spirit of God to be of more importance than all that was at that time going on among the great nations of antiquity. It is highly interesting to trace great things to their small beginnings; and to them that love Zion it must be pleasant to observe the minute turns of providence in respect of its first fathers.

Ver. 1—9. Abraham being now an old man, and having lost the partner of his life, feels anxious to adjust his affairs, that he may be ready to follow her. "The Lord had blessed him in all things," and he had doubtless much to dispose of: but the greatest blessing of all related to his seed, and this occupies his chief attention. Aware that character as well as happiness greatly depended on a suitable connexion, he was desirous that before he died he might discharge this part of the duty of a father. Calling to him therefore his eldest servant, who was already steward of his affairs, and in case of death must have been his trustee in behalf of Isaac, he bound him in a solemn oath respecting the wife that he should take to him. We are not here told the servant's name; but by the account which is given of him, compared with chapter xv. 2, it is not unlikely that it was Eliezer of Damascus.

The characters of men are not so easily ascertained from a few splendid actions, as from the ordinary course of life, in which their real dispositions are manifested. In this domestic concern of Abraham we see several of the most prominent features of his character.—(1.) His decided aversion to idolatry: "I will make thee swear by Jehovah, the God of heaven, and the God of the earth, that thou shalt not take a wife unto my son of the daughters of the Canaanites amongst whom I dwell." Had Abraham then contracted a prejudice against his neighbours? This does not appear by what occurred between them in the last chapter. He does not complain of their treatment of him, but of his God. He has no objection to an exchange of civilities with them; but to take their daughters in marriage, was the sure way to corrupt his own family. The great design of God in giving the land to Abraham's posterity was the eventual overthrow of idolatry, and the establishment of his true worship on earth. To what purpose then was he called from amongst Chaldean idolaters, if his son join affinity with those of Canaan? Such, or nearly such, were the sentiments which dictated the address to his servant. "The Lord God of heaven, *who took me from my father's house* . . . *and sware unto me, saying, Unto thy seed will I give this land,* he shall send his angel before thee."—(2.) His godliness. There does not appear in all this concern the least taint of worldly policy, or any of those motives which usually govern men in the settlement of their children. No mention is made of riches, or honours, or natural accomplishments; but merely of what related to God. Let not the woman be a daughter of Canaan, but of the family of Nahor, who had forsaken Chaldean idolatry, and with Milcah his wife had settled in Haran, and who was a worshipper of the true God.*—(3.) His faith, and obedience. The servant being about to bind himself by oath, is tenderly concerned lest he should engage in more than he should be able to accomplish. "Peradventure, saith he, the woman will not follow me into this land: must I needs bring thy son again to the land whence thou camest?" No: as Isaac must not marry a daughter of Canaan, neither must he leave Canaan to humour a daughter of Haran: for though Canaan's daughters are to be shunned, yet Canaan itself is to be chosen as the Lord's inheritance bestowed on the promised seed. Nor do these supposed difficulties at all deter Abraham: "The Lord God of heaven, saith he, who took me from my father's house, and from the land of my kindred, and who spake unto me, and sware unto me, saying, Unto thy seed will I give this land, HE shall send his angel before thee, and thou shalt take a wife unto my son from thence." On the ground of this promise, he would send him away, fully acquitting him of his oath, if the party should prove

* Chap. xxxi. 53.

A WIFE FOR ISAAC.

unwilling; only charging him not to bring Isaac to Haran, as he had before charged him not to marry him to a daughter of Canaan.

Ver. 10—14. Abraham's servant having on the above terms consented to take the oath, now betakes himself to his journey. No time seems to have been lost; for his heart was in the business. He did not trouble his aged master in things of inferior moment; but having all his affairs entrusted to him, adjusts those matters himself. Taking with him ten camels, and of course a number of attendants, partly for accommodation, and partly, we may suppose, to give a just idea of his master's substance, he set off for Mesopotamia, to the city of Nahor. Nothing remarkable occurs by the way: but arriving on a summer's evening at the outside of the city, he espies a well. Here he causes his camels to kneel down for rest, and with a design as soon as opportunity offered, to furnish them with drink. Now it was customary in those countries for the women at the time of the evening to go out to draw water. Of this Abraham's servant is aware. And having placed himself and his camels by the well in a waiting posture, he betakes himself to prayer for divine direction. Light as men make of such concerns in common, there are few things of greater importance, and in which there is greater need for imploring the guidance and blessing of heaven. Upon a few minute turns at this period of life, more depends than can possibly be conceived at the time. Young people! Pause a moment, and consider .... Think of the counsel of God .... "In all thy ways acknowledge him, and he shall direct thy paths." That which is done for life, and which may involve things of another life, requires to be done well; and nothing can be done well in which the will of God is not consulted, and his blessing implored. Let us each pause a few minutes too, and notice the admirable prayer of Abraham's servant. Truly he had not lived with Abraham in vain!—Observe, (1.) The *character* under which he addresses the great Supreme: "Oh Jehovah, God of my master Abraham." He well knew that Jehovah had entered into covenant with Abraham, and had given him exceeding great and precious promises. By approaching him as a God in covenant, he would find matter for faith to lay hold upon: every promise to Abraham would thus furnish a plea, and turn to a good account. Surely this may direct us in our approaches to a throne of grace, to make mention of a greater than Abraham, with whom also God is in covenant, and for whose sake the greatest of all blessings may be expected. The God and Father

Gen. 24.] A WIFE FOR ISAAC. 279

of our Lord Jesus Christ is to us what the God of Abraham was to Eliezer; and in the name of our Redeemer we may pray and hope for every thing that is great and good.—(2.) The *limitation* of the prayer to the present time: " Send me good speed *this day.*" We may in a general way ask for grace for our whole lives; but our duty is more especially to seek direction at the time we want it. Our Lord teaches us to pray for daily bread as the day occurs.—(3.) The *sign* which he presumed to ask for; that the damsel to whom he should say so and so, and who should make such and such answers, should be the person whom the Lord had appointed for his servant Isaac. In this he might be under extraordinary influence, and his conduct therefore afford no example to us. The sign he asked however, was such as would manifest the qualifications which he desired and expected to find in a companion who should be worthy of his master's son; namely, industry, courtesy, and kindness to strangers.—(4.) The *faith* in which the prayer was offered. He speaks all along under a full persuasion that the providence of God extended to the minutest events, to the free actions of creatures, and even to their behaviour, of which at the time they are scarcely conscious. His words are also full of humble confidence that God would direct him in a matter of so much consequence to his church in all future ages. I believe, if we were to search the scriptures through, and select all the prayers that God has answered, we should find them to have been the prayers of faith.

Ver. 15—28. While he was speaking, a damsel, with a pitcher upon her shoulder, came towards the well. By her appearance he is possessed of the idea that she is the person, and that the Lord hath heard his prayer. He said nothing to her till she had gone down to the well, and was come up again. Then he ran towards her, and addressed her in the words which he had resolved to do, intreating permission to drink a little water of her pitcher. To this she chearfully consented, and offered her assistance to give drink also to his camels; all exactly in the manner which he had prayed for. The gentleness, chearfulness, assiduity, and courtesy manifested towards a stranger, of whom she at present could have no knowledge, is truly admirable. The words in which it is described are picturesque and lively in the highest degree. We need only read them in order to feel ourselves in the midst of the pleasing scene— " And she said, Drink my lord: and she hasted, and let down her pitcher upon her hand, and gave him drink. And when she had given him drink, she said, I will draw for thy camels also, until they have done drinking. And she hasted, and emptied her pitcher into the trough, and ran again unto the well to draw, and drew for all his camels." This conduct, in itself so amiable, and so exactly in unison with the previous wishes of the man, struck him with a kind of amazement, accompanied with a momentary hesitation, whether all could be true. "Wondering at her, he held his peace, to wit, whether the Lord had made his journey prosperous or not."—We pray for blessings, and when our prayers are answered, we can scarcely believe them to be so. There are cases in which the mind, like the eye by a great and sudden influx of light, is overpowered. Thus Zion, though importunate in prayer for great conversions, yet when they come, is described as being in a manner confounded with them: "Thine heart shall fear, and be enlarged .... thou shalt say in thine heart, who hath begotten me these?"* Recovering from his astonishment, and being satisfied that the Lord had indeed heard his prayer, he opens his treasures, and presents the damsel with certain eastern ornaments, which he had provided for the purpose; enquiring at the same time after her kindred, and whether they had room to lodge him. Being told in answer, that she was "the daughter of

* Isai. lx. 5. xlix. 21.

Bethuel, the son of Nahor and Milcah," and that they had plenty of accommodation for him and his company, his heart is so full that he cannot contain himself, but even in the presence of Rebecca, and perhaps, of the men who were with him, " bowed down his head and worshipped, saying, Blessed be Jehovah, God of my master Abraham, who hath not left destitute my master of his mercy and his truth: I being in the way, Jehovah led me to the house of my master's brother!"—We see here not only a grateful mind, equally disposed to give thanks for mercy, as to pray for it; but a delicate and impressive manner of communicating to Rebecca a few particulars which he wished her to know. His words were addressed to the Lord; but being spoken in her hearing, she would perceive by them who he was, whence he came, and that the hand of the God of Abraham was in the visit, whatever was the object of it. Full of joyful surprize, she runs home, with the bracelets upon her hands, and tells the family of what had passed. But here I must break off for the present, and leave the conclusion of this interesting story to another discourse.

DISCOURSE XXXIII.

ABRAHAM SENDING HIS SERVANT TO OBTAIN A WIFE FOR ISAAC. (CONTINUED.)

GENESIS xxiv. 29——67.

VER. 29—31. As yet no one suspects the object of the visit: but all hearts are full, and there is much running hither and thither. No mention is made at present of Bethuel, or of Milcah: they were aged people, and the affairs of the family seem principally to have devolved on its younger branches. Laban appears to have taken a very active part in this business. Hearing his sister's tale, and seeing the ornaments upon her hands, he is all alive, and runs towards the well to welcome the man into his house. By the account which is afterwards given of Laban, it is perhaps more than probable that these golden ornaments had great influence on what would otherwise appear a very generous behaviour. His whole history shews him to have been a mercenary man; and we frequently see in such characters the truth of Solomon's remarks: "A man's gift maketh room for him—It is as a precious stone in the eyes of him that hath it:

whithersoever it turneth, it prospereth."* If a man be in straits, he is coldly treated; but if once he begin to rise in the world, he becomes another man, and his company and acquaintance are courted. Such is the spirit of this world. But whatever were Laban's motives, he carried it very kindly to Abraham's servant. Finding him at the well, modestly waiting for a further invitation from some of the heads of the family, he accosted him in language that would have befitted the lips of a much better man: "Come in thou blessed of the Lord: wherefore standest thou without? For I have prepared the house, and room for the camels." It becomes us to bless, and bid welcome to those whom the Lord hath blessed; nor must we confine it to those whom he hath blessed with outward prosperity: a christian spirit is in the sight of God of great price, and ought to be so in ours.

Ver. 32, 33. On this becoming invitation, the man goes into the house; and we see Laban very attentive. First, he ungirds the poor beasts which had borne the burdens, and furnished them with provender: then provides water for the man, and those who were with him, to wash their feet; and after this, sets meat before him. All this is proper. But the good man's heart is

* Prov. xviii 16. xvii. 8.

full; and he cannot eat till he has told his errand. Such are the feelings of a servant of God whose heart is in his work. Where this is the case, personal indulgence will give place to things of greater importance. "I will not give sleep to mine eyes, (said David) nor slumber to mine eye-lids, till I find out a place for Jehovah, a habitation for the mighty God of Jacob." While the woman of Samaria was gone to tell her neighbours of the man who had told her all things that ever she did, his disciples, knowing how weary and faint he must have been, "prayed him to eat:" but seeing the Samaritans flocking down the hill to hear the word of God, he answered, "I have meat to eat that ye know not of . . . my meat is to do the will of him that sent me, and to finish his work . . . Say ye not there are yet four months, and then cometh harvest? Behold . . . lift up your eyes, and look" on yonder companies . . . "the fields are white already to harvest!"

Ver. 34, 35. Being requested to tell his tale, the servant begins by informing them who he is. His prayer to *the God of his master Abraham,* in the hearing of Rebecca, might possibly have superseded the necessity of this part of his statement; but lest it should not, he tells them expressly. "I am Abraham's servant." He was an upright man, and upright men do not conceal who they are. He was also a humble man, and humble men are not ashamed to own their situation in life, though it be that of a servant. A vain man might have talked about himself, and that he was the first servant of the house, the steward that ruled over all that Abraham had, and that all his master's goods were in his hand.* But not a word of this is heard; for his heart was set on his errand. He has no objection, however, to tell of the glory of his master; for this would tend to promote the object; nor does he fail to acknowledge the hand of God in it. "The Lord hath blessed my master greatly." And if they were worthy to be connected with Abraham, this would tend farther to promote the object; yea, more than all the riches and glory of Abraham without it.

Ver. 36. And now for the first time he makes mention of *Isaac*. A messenger less ingenuous might have given a hint of this kind to the damsel when he presented her with the "ear-ring, and bracelets:" but so did not Abraham's servant. Not an intimation of the kind is given till he is before her parents. In their presence, and that of the whole family, he frankly makes mention of his master's son; and as his object

* See Esther v. 10—12.

was to recommend him to their esteem, and to prepossess Rebecca in his favour, it is admirable to see how he accomplishes his end. All is in the form of a simple narrative; yet every moving consideration is worked into it that the subject will admit of. In only this single verse we observe four circumstances touched upon, each of which would have a powerful effect—He was the son of the highly honoured Abraham—by the much-loved Sarah—in their old age—(of course he himself must be young)—and was made heir of all his father's substance.

Ver. 37, 38. From hence he proceeds to a still more explicit mention of the object of his journey, mixing with it such grounds or reasons as must ingratiate both his master, and his master's son in their esteem, and so tend to accomplish his design. He informs them that Abraham was utterly averse to his son's being united with a daughter of Canaan; so much so, that he even made him solemnly swear upon the subject. The family at Haran might possibly have thought ere now that Abraham had forgotten his old friends, and formed new connexions: but they would perceive by this that he had not. There is a charming delicacy in his introducing the subject of marriage. He speaks of "a wife being taken" for his master's son; but first mentions it in reference to the daughters of Canaan, whom he must *not* take, before he suggests any thing of the person he wished to take; thus giving them to infer what was coming ere he expressed it. And now having intimated the family whom his master preferred, he represents him as speaking of them in the most affectionate language—" My father's house, my kindred."

Ver. 39—41. Next he repeats what passed between his master and himself, as to the supposed willingness or unwillingness of the party; and here also we see much that will turn to account. In expressing Abraham's persuasion in the affair, he appeals to their piety. It was saying in effect, the hand of God is in it; and this with godly minds would be sure to weigh. Indeed it did weigh; for when required to give an answer, it was this: "The thing proceedeth from the Lord." Religion, thus mingled with natural affection, sanctifies it, and renders sweetness itself more sweet. In repeating also the words of Abraham, " thou shalt take a wife for my son *of my kindred, and of my father's house,*" he touches and re-touches the strings of fraternal love. And in that he intimates that his master had laid nothing more upon him than to tell his tale, and leave the issue to the Lord, he gives them to understand that whether they were willing or unwilling, he should be clear of his oath. In this and several other parts of this pleasant story, our thoughts must needs run to the work of Christ's servants in espousing souls to him. They may be clear of the blood of all men, though sinners may be unwilling; and it is their duty to tell them so, that while on the one hand they allure them by exhibiting the glory of their Master, they may on the other convince them that their message is not to be trifled with. Both are means appointed of God to bring them to Christ; and if the Lord be with them in their work, such will be the effect.

Ver. 42—49. The *repeating* of the interview with Rebecca at the well, was all admirably in point, and of a tendency to bring the matter to a crisis. 'I came to the well—I called on the God of my master Abraham—I asked for a sign —a sign was given me—every thing answered to my prayer—judge ye—let Rebecca judge —whether the hand of the Lord be not in it? And now, if ye will deal kindly and truly with my master, tell me: and if not, tell me, that I may turn to the right hand, or to the left.'

Ver. 50—52. With this simple, but interesting account, the whole family is overcome:

one sentiment bows every mind. Rebecca says nothing: but her heart is full. It is an affair in which little or nothing seems left for creatures to decide. "The thing (say they) proceedeth from the Lord: we cannot speak unto thee good or bad. Behold, Rebecca is before thee; take her, and go, and let her be thy master's son's wife, as the Lord hath spoken!" Such was the happy result of this truly religious courtship; and the good man, who saw God in all things, still keeps up his character. Hearing their words, he bowed himself to the earth, and worshipped God! How sweet would all our temporal concerns be rendered, if they were thus intermixed with godliness!

Ver. 53. The main things being settled, he, according to the customs of those times, presents the bride elect with "jewels of silver, jewels of gold, and raiment," suited to the occasion; and farther to conciliate the esteem of the family, "he gave also to her brother, and to her mother precious things." Presents when given from sincere affection are very proper, and productive of good effects. It is by a mutual interchange of kind offices that love is often kindled, and always kept alive. Our Saviour accepted the presents which were offered him, not only of food, but raiment, and even the anointing of his feet.

Where love exists, it is natural and grateful to express it in acts of kindness.

Ver. 54—58. The good man would not eat till he had told his errand: but now that his work is done, he and the men who were with him both eat and drink: and doubtless it would add to the enjoyment of their meal, to know that the Lord had made their way prosperous. The next morning, having accomplished his object, the diligent and faithful servant wants to be going. To this proposal however, though honourable to him as a servant, the mother and the brother object; pleading for a few days, ten at least, ere they parted; nor does their objection seem to be unreasonable. Though willing upon the whole that she should go; yet parting is trying work, especially when they considered that they might never see her more in this world, as in truth they never did. The man, however, knows not how to consent to it; but entreats that he might not be "hindered, seeing the Lord had prospered his way." Whether we consider him as too pressing, in this case, or not, we may lay it down as a general rule, never to hinder those who are engaged in a right way, and who have received manifest tokens that God hath blessed them in it. The case being somewhat difficult, and neither of the parties disposed to disoblige the other, they consent to leave it to the decision of the damsel herself. A few days to take leave of her friends could not, we may suppose, have been disagreeable to her; but seeing as she did, so much of God in the affair, and the man's heart so deeply set upon it; feeling also her own heart entirely in it, she would not so much as seem to make light of it, or hinder it even for an hour; but, far from all affectation, answered, "I will go."

Ver. 59, 60. And now, preparation is made for her departure. Before she goes she must be provided with a "nurse." Rebecca's having been employed in drawing water, we see, was no proof of the poverty of her parents, but rather of the simplicity of the times. Daughters were not yet taught to be so delicate as scarcely to *adventure to set the sole of their foot upon the ground.* But now that she is going to leave her family, it is desirable that she should have one of its domestics who had probably been brought up with her from her childhood, who in times of affliction would kindly wait on her, and at all times be a friend and companion. The name of this nurse was Deborah. We hear no more of her till we are told of her death. She appears to have survived her mistress, and to have died in the family of Jacob, much lamented.* To an

* Chap. xxxv. 8.

Gen. 24.] A WIFE FOR ISAAC. 293

affectionate nurse, they added a parting blessing. The language used in it shews that Abraham's servant had told them of the promises which God had made to his master, and which were to be fulfilled in Isaac and his posterity. They speak as believing the truth of them, and as having their hearts full of hope and joy, amidst the natural sorrow which must have attended the parting scene. "They blessed Rebecca, and said unto her, Thou art our sister; be thou the mother of thousands of millions, and let thy seed possess the gate of those that hate them!"

Ver. 61—63. Taking leave of Haran, they go on their way towards Canaan. A little before their arrival at Hebron, they are unexpectedly met by a person who was taking an evening walk. This was no other than Isaac. It may be thought that he was looking out in hopes of meeting them; but we are expressly told that his walk was for another purpose, namely, to "meditate." It is a word which is sometimes used for prayer, and hence it is so rendered in the margin of our bibles. He was a man of reflexion and prayer, and in the cool of the evening it might be common for him to retire an hour to converse, as we should say, with himself, and with his God. Admitting that the thought might occur, 'I may possibly see my father's servant on his return,' still his object would be on such an important turn in his life, to commit the matter to God. Those blessings are likely to prove substantial and durable, which are given us in answer to prayer.

Ver. 64, 65. Rebecca having espied a stranger approaching towards them, enquires of her guide whether he knew him; and being told that it was no other than his young "master," she modestly alighted from the camel, and took a vail and covered herself. This eastern head-dress might in the present instance answer a double purpose: First, it would express her subjection to her husband, as being already his espoused wife. Secondly, it would prevent that confusion which the exposure of her person, especially in so sudden and unexpected a manner, must have occasioned.

Ver. 66, 67. Isaac observing her to have put on her vail, very properly avoids addressing himself to her; but walking awhile with the servant by himself, heard the whole narrative of his journey, and which appears to have wrought on his mind as the former had wrought on that of Rebecca. And now the marriage is consummated. " Isaac brought her into his mother Sarah's tent, and took Rebecca, and she became his wife, and he loved her: and Isaac was comforted after his mother's death." In this tender manner is the admirable story closed. Who can forbear wishing them all happiness? The union of filial and conjugal affection is not the least honourable trait in the character of this amiable man. He "brought her into his mother Sarah's tent;" and was then, and not till then, comforted for his loss of her. Dutiful sons promise fair to be affectionate husbands: he that fills up the first station in life with honour, is thereby prepared for those that follow. God in mercy sets a day of prosperity over against a day of adversity. Now he woundeth our spirits by dissolving one tender union, and now bindeth up our wounds by cementing another.

DISCOURSE XXXIV.

ABRAHAM's MARRIAGE WITH KETURAH, AND DEATH; ISHMAEL's POSTERITY AND DEATH; WITH THE BIRTH AND CHARACTERS OF ESAU AND JACOB.

GENESIS XXV.

This chapter gives an account of several changes in the families of Abraham, Ishmael, and Isaac. In each the sacred writer keeps his eye on the fulfilment of the great promise to the father of the faithful,

Ver. 1—6. The marriage of Abraham to Keturah is an event which we should not have expected. From the last account we had of him, charging his servant respecting the marriage of his son Isaac, we were prepared to look for his being buried, rather than married. I do not know that it was a sin: but it is easy to see in it more of man than of God. No reason is given for it; no marks of divine approbation attend it; five-and-thirty years pass over with little more than recording the names of his children, and that not from any respect to the connexion, but to shew the fulfilment of the divine promise of multiplying his seed. During this last period of his life, we see nothing of that extraordinary strength of faith by which he was formerly distinguished; but, like Sampson when he had lost his hair, he is become weak like another man. While the promise of Isaac was pending, and while Abraham was employed in promoting that great object, the cloud of glory accompanies all his movements: but this being accomplished, and his mind diverted to something else, the cloud now rests upon Isaac; and he must walk the remainder of his journey in a manner without it.

Who Keturah was we are not told: probably she was one of his family. She and Hagar are called "concubines." This does not mean however, that they were not his lawful wives, but that they occupied a less honourable station than Sarah, who was a fellow-heir with him in the promise. Keturah bare Abraham six sons, amongst whose descendents were preserved in some measure the knowledge and fear of the true God. From one of them, namely, Midiam, descended Jethro, the father-in-law of Moses; and it is not improbable that Job and his friends had the same general origin.

We have seen how the last thirty-five years of Abraham's life fall short of what it was in former periods: it is pleasant however to observe, that his sun does not set in a cloud. There are several circumstances which shed a lustre upon his last end. Amongst others, his regard for Isaac, constituting him his heir, and settling his other sons at a sufficient distance from him, shews that his heart was still with God's heart; or that he whom the Lord had chosen was the object to whom his thoughts were chiefly directed. He was not wanting in paternal goodness to any of his children. Though Ishmael was sent away, and as it would seem by the other parts of the history, with nothing: yet it is here plainly intimated that his father "gave gifts" to him, as well as the sons of Keturah.

Probably he visited and provided for him in the wilderness of Paran, and gave him a portion when he married. But God's covenant being established with Isaac, *his* settlement in Canaan is that to which all the others are rendered subservient. All this shews that his faith did not fail; that he never lost sight of the promise in which he had believed for justification; but that as he had lived, so he died.

Ver. 7—10. Let us notice the death and burial of this great and good man. His death is expressed by a common, but impressive scripture phrase; "he gave up the ghost:" and his burial by another; "he was gathered to his people." The one is the parting of body and soul; the other the mingling of our dust with that of our kindred who have gone before us. Even in the grave it is natural to wish to associate with those whom we have known and loved on earth; and still more in the world to come. When all the sons of Adam shall be assigned their portion, each in a sense will be gathered to his people!—The inscription on his tomb, if I may so call it, was, "He died in a good old age." On this I have two remarks to offer.—(1.) It was *according to promise.* Upwards of four-score years before this, the Lord told Abraham in vision, saying, "Thou shalt go to thy fathers in peace:

thou shalt be buried in a good old age.* In every thing, even in death, the promises are fulfilled to Abraham.—(2.) It is language that is *never used of wicked men*, and *not very commonly of good men*. It is used of Gideon, and of David;† and I know not whether of any other. The idea answers to what is spoken by the psalmist, "They shall bring forth fruit in old age;" or that in Job, "Thou shalt come to thy grave in a full age, like as a shock of corn cometh in in his season."—Isaac and Ishmael are both present at his funeral. We have no account of their having seen each other before from the day that Ishmael was cast out as a mocker; but whether they had or not, they met at their father's interment. Death brings those together who know not how to associate on any other occasion, and will bring us all together sooner or later.—Finally, the place where they buried him was the same as that in which he had buried his beloved Sarah.

Ver. 11. The death and burial of so great and good a man as Abraham must have made an impression upon survivors: howbeit, the cause of God died not. "It came to pass after the death of Abraham, that God blessed his son

---

* Gen. xv. 15.   † Judges viii. 32.   1 Chron. xxix. 28.

Isaac." Isaac was heir to the promise; and though all flesh withereth and fadeth like the grass, yet the word of the Lord shall stand for ever. We shall hear more of Isaac soon: at present we are only told in general that he "dwelt by the well Lahai-roi." It was necessary in those countries to fix their residence by a well; and it is no less necessary, if we wish to live, that we fix ours near to the ordinances of God. The well where Isaac pitched his tent was distinguished by two interesting events:—(1.) The merciful appearance of God to Hagar, from whence it received its name; *the well of him that liveth and seeth me.** Hagar or Ishmael, methinks, should have pitched a tent there, that it might have been to them a memorial of past mercies: but if they neglect it, Isaac will occupy it. The gracious appearance of God in a place, endears it to him, let it have been to whom it may.—(2.) It was the place from the way of which he first met his beloved Rebecca:† there therefore they continue to dwell together.

Ver. 12—18. A short account is here given of Ishmael's posterity, and of his death. His sons were numerous and great; they had their "towns and their castles;" nay more, they are denominated "twelve princes, according to their

---

* Gen. xvi. 14. † Chap. xxiv. 62.

nations." Thus amply was fulfilled the promise of God concerning him: "Behold, I have blessed him, and will make him fruitful, and will multiply him exceedingly: twelve princes shall he beget, and I will make him a great nation."* But this is all. When a man leaves God and his people, the sacred historian leaves him. After living in prosperity a hundred and thirty-seven years, "he gave up the ghost, and died;" and was gathered unto his people." As this language is applicable to men whether good or bad, no conclusion can be drawn from it in favour of his having feared God. It is added, that "he died in the presence of all his brethren;" that is, in peace, or with his friends about him, which, considering how his " hand had been against every man, and" of course "every man's hand against him," was rather surprising: but so it had been promised of the Lord to his mother at *the well* Lahai-roi—" He shall dwell in the presence of all his brethren."† So he lived, and so he died, an object of providential care for his father's sake; but as to any thing more, the oracles of God are silent.

Ver. 19—23. The history now returns to the son of promise. Forty years old was he when he took Rebecca to wife; and for twenty

* Gen. xvii, 20. † Chap. xvi. 12.

years afterwards he had no issue. We should have supposed that as the promise partly consisted in a multiplication of his seed, the great number of his children would have made a prominent part of his history. When Bethuel, and Milcah, and Laban took leave of Rebecca, saying, "Be thou the mother of thousands of millions," they doubtless expected to hear of a very numerous family. And she herself, and her husband would, as believing the divine promise, expect the same. But God's thoughts are not as our thoughts, nor his ways as our ways. Abraham's other sons abound in children, while he in whom his seed is to be as the stars of heaven for multitude, lives childless. In this manner God had tried his father Abraham; and if he be heir to his blessings, he must expect to inherit a portion of his trials. God bestows his mercies upon wicked men without waiting for their prayers: but his conduct is somewhat different with them that fear him. Isaac had received Rebecca in answer to prayer; and let him not expect to receive seed by her in any other way. Well, the good man is led to pray: "Isaac entreated the Lord for his wife, because she was barren; and the Lord was entreated of him, and Rebecca conceived." During the time of her pregnancy she was the subject of some extraordinary sensations, which filling her mind with perplexity, she "enquired of the Lord." Both the entreaty of Isaac, and the enquiry of Rebecca might be improper in ordinary cases; but as it was not the natural desire of children that prompted him, so neither was it an idle curiosity that excited her; they each kept in view the promise of all nations being blessed in their posterity, and therefore were not only solicitous for children, but anxious concerning every thing which seemed indicative of their future character. And as Isaac had received an answer to prayer, so it is revealed to Rebecca that the sensations which she felt were signs of other things—that she was pregnant of twins—that they should become "two nations" —and not only so, but "two *manner* of nations" —lastly, that "the elder should serve the younger." The struggle between these children, which was expressive of the struggles that should in after ages take place between their posterity, furnished another instance of the opposition between the seed of the woman and the seed of the serpent, both which are commonly found in most religious families. Paul introduces this case as an instance of the sovereignty of God in the dispensation of his grace. The rejection of a great part of the jewish nation was to some a stumbling-block. It seemed to them as if the word of promise to the fathers had taken none effect. The apostle in answer maintains that it was not the original design of God in the promise to save all Abraham's posterity; but on the contrary, that from the beginning he drew a line of distinction between Isaac and Ishmael, Jacob and Esau, though each were alike descended from him according to the flesh. To a farther supposed objection, that such a distinction between children, while they were yet unborn, reflected on the *righteousness* of God, he contents himself with denying the consequence, and asserting the absolute right of God to have mercy on whom he will have mercy.*

Ver. 24—28. As there were extraordinary sensations during the pregnancy of the mother, so in the birth of the children there was a certain circumstance which betokened that the one should prevail over the other; and that not only in his person, but in his posterity. Hence the prophet Hosea, reproaching the degenerate sons of Jacob, says of him, "*He* took his brother by the heel in the womb . . . and by his strength had power with God"—But, as if he should say, are you worthy of being called his children?†

From the circumstances attending the birth of a child, it was common in those ages to derive their names; and thus it was in the present

---

* Rom. ix. 6—16.   † Hos. xii. 3.

instance. The first-born, from his colour, was called *Esau*, i. e. *red:* the younger, from the circumstance of his taking hold of his brother's heel, was called *Jacob*, a *supplanter*. Both these names were prophetic. Esau was of a *sanguine* disposition, and his posterity the Edomites always cherished a most *cruel* and *bloody* antipathy against Israel. In allusion to this, when the enemies of the church are punished, they are not only represented as Edomites, but God is described as giving them as it were blood for blood .... "Who is this that cometh from Edom, with dyed garments from Bozrah? ... Wherefore art thou *red* in thine apparel, and thy garments like him that treadeth in the wine-fat? I have trodden the wine-press alone; and of the people there was none with me: for I will tread them in mine anger, and trample them in my fury, and their *blood* shall be sprinkled upon my garments, and I will stain all my raiment."* Jacob on the other hand, supplanted his brother in the affair of the birth-right, as we shall see presently. As his having hold of his brother's heel seemed as if he would have drawn him back from the birth, and have been before him, so his mind in after life appeared to aspire after the blessing of the first-born, and never to have rested till he had obtained it.

* Isai. lxiii, 1—6.

As they grew up they discovered a different turn of mind. Esau was the expert huntsman, quite "a man of the field;" but Jacob was simple-hearted, preferring the more gentle employment of rearing and tending cattle. The partiality of Isaac towards Esau on account of his venison, seems to have been a weakness rather unworthy of him: that of Rebecca towards Jacob appears to have been better founded: her preference was more directed by the prophecies which had gone before of him, choosing him whom the Lord had chosen.

Ver. 29—34. In process of time a circumstance arose in the family which in its consequences was very serious. Jacob was one day boiling some pottage, perhaps for his dinner; for he lived mostly upon herbs. Just then came in Esau from hunting, very faint and hungry, and had a great mind to Jacob's pottage. Its very colour corresponding with his sanguine disposition seemed to take his fancy; on which account he was called Edom, a name commonly applied to his posterity, and of similar import with that which was first given to him. There seems, at first sight, to be something ungenerous in Jacob's availing himself of his brother's hunger in the manner he did; and if there were, however it may reflect dishonour upon him, it reflects none upon the event. God often brings his purposes to pass by means which on man's part are far from justifiable. The Reformation was a great and good work, and we may wish to vindicate every measure which contributed to it; but that is more than we can do. God's thoughts are not as our thoughts, nor his ways as our ways. It will be found that "he is holy in all *his* ways, and righteous in all *his* works:" but this is more than can be said of his best servants, in any age of the world. A close inspection of this affair however, will convince us that whether Jacob was right as to the *means* he used, or not, his *motives* were good, and those of Esau were evil.—Observe, particularly, (1.) The birthright attached to seniority.—(2.) It ordinarily consisted in the excellency of dignity, the excellency of power, and a double portion.*—(3.) These privileges of the first-born were in several instances forfeited by the misconduct of the parties; as in the case of Cain, Reuben, &c.—(4.) There was in the family of Abraham a peculiar blessing which was supposed to be attached to the birthright, though God in several instances put it into another direction. This blessing was principally spiritual and distant, having respect to the setting up of God's kingdom, to the birth of the Messiah, or in other words, to all those

* Gen. xlix. 3. Deut. xxi. 17.

great things included in the covenant with Abraham. This was well understood by the family: both Esau and Jacob must have often heard their parents converse about it. If the birthright which was bought at this time had consisted in any temporal advantages of dignity, authority, or property to be enjoyed in the life-time of the parties, Esau would not have made so light of it as he did, calling it "*this* birth-right," and intimating that he should soon die, and then it would be of no use to him.* It is a fact too, that Jacob had none of the ordinary advantages of the birthright during his life-time. Instead of a double portion, he was sent out of the family with only "a staff" in his hand, leaving Esau to possess the whole of his father's substance. And when more than twenty years afterwards he returned to Canaan, he made no scruple to ascribe to his brother the excellency of dignity, and the excellency of power, calling him "my lord Esau," and acknowledging himself as his "servant." The truth is, the question between them was, which should be heir to the blessings promised in the covenant with

---

* He could not mean surely, that he should then die of hunger, unless he eat of the pottage; for that is scarcely conceivable, while he had full access to all the provision in Isaac's house: but that in a little time he should be dead; and then of what account would these fine promises be to him?

Abraham. This Jacob desired, and Esau despised; and in despising blessings of so sacred a nature, and that for a morsel of meat, he was guilty of profaneness.* The spirit of his language was, 'I cannot live upon promises: give me something to eat and drink; for to-morrow I die.' Such is the spirit of unbelief in every age; and thus it is that poor deluded souls continue to despise things distant and heavenly, and prefer to them the momentary gratifications of flesh and sense.

From the whole we may perceive in this case a doctrine which runs through the scriptures, namely, that while the salvation of those that are saved is altogether of grace, the destruction of those that are lost will be found to be of themselves. From what is recorded of Jacob he certainly had nothing to boast of; neither had Esau any thing to complain of. He lost the blessing; but not without having first despised it. Thus when the apostle had asserted the doctrine of election, and grounded it upon God's absolute right to have mercy on whom he would have mercy, he nevertheless proceeds to ascribe the cause of the overthrow of them that perish merely to themselves. "But Israel which followed after the law of righteousness, hath not

* Heb. xii. 15—17.

attained to the law of righteousness. Wherefore? Because they sought it not by faith; but as it were by the works of the law: for they stumbled at that stumbling stone."* I am aware that when we preach in this manner, many are ready to accuse us of inconsistency. 'You preach the doctrine of election, say they; but before you have done, you destroy your own work, by telling the unconverted that if they perish, the fault will lie at their own door.' We answer, it is enough for us to teach what the scriptures teach. If we cannot conceive how the purposes of God are to be reconciled with the agency and accountableness of man, let us be content to be ignorant of it. The scriptures teach both; and true wisdom will not aspire to be wise above what is written.

DISCOURSE XXXV.

ISAAC AND ABIMELECH.

GENESIS xxvi.

WE saw Abraham in a great variety of situations, by means of which sometimes his excellencies and sometimes his failings became the more conspicuous. Isaac has hitherto been but

* Rom. ix. 12—16, 31, 32,

little tried, and therefore his character is at present but little known. In this chapter, however, we shall see him roused from his retirement, and brought into situations in which, if there be some things to lament, there will be many to admire.

Ver. 1—6. We now see him *in affliction*, by reason of " a famine in the land, beside the first famine that was in the days of Abraham." There seem to have been more famines in the times of the patriarchs than usual; and which must not only be afflictive to them in common with their neighbours, but tend more than a little to try their faith. Every such season must prove a temptation to think lightly of the land of promise. Unbelief would say, *It is a land that eateth up the inhabitants:* it is not worth waiting for. But faith will conclude that he who hath promised to give it, is able to bless it. Thus Abraham believed, and therefore took every thing patiently; and thus it is with Isaac. He first went to Abimelech, king of the Philistines, at Gerar. His father Abraham had found kind treatment there about a hundred years before, and there was a covenant of peace between them.* It seems however, as if he had thought of going as far as Egypt; but the Lord appeared to him at Gerar,

* Genesis xxi.

and admonished him to put himself under his direction, and go no where without it—" Dwell, saith he, in the land that I shall tell thee of: sojourn in this land, and I will be with thee, and I will bless thee." In times of trouble we are apt to cast, and forecast, what we shall do: but God mercifully checks our anxiety, and teaches us by such dispensations in all our ways to acknowledge him. To satisfy Isaac that he should never want a guide, or a provider, the Lord renews to him the promises which had been made to his father Abraham. Had he met with nothing to drive him from his retreat by the well of Lahai-roi, he might have enjoyed more quiet; but he might not have been indulged with such great and precious promises. Times of affliction, however disagreeable to the flesh, have often proved our best times.

Two things are observable in this solemn renewal of the covenant with Isaac.—(1.) *The good things promised.* " I will be with thee, and will bless thee: for unto thee and unto thy seed I will give all these countries, and I will perform the oath which I sware unto Abraham thy father. And I will make thy seed to multiply as the stars of heaven, and will give unto thy seed all these countries: and in thy seed shall all the nations of the earth be blessed." The sum of these blessings is, the land of Canaan, a numerous progeny, and what is the greatest of all, the Messiah, in whom the nations should be blessed. On these precious promises Isaac is to live. God provided him with bread in the day of famine; but he " lived not on bread only, but on the words which proceeded from the mouth of God." It was in reference to such words as these that Moses said unto Hobab, " We are journeying to the place of which the Lord said, I will give it you: come thou with us, and we will do thee good; for the Lord hath spoken good concerning Israel."—(2.) *Their being given for Abraham's sake:* " Because that Abraham obeyed my voice, and kept my charge, my commandments, my statutes, and my laws." We are expressly informed in what manner this patriarch was accepted of God, namely, as " believing on him who justifieth the ungodly;" and this accounts for the acceptance of his works. The most " spiritual sacrifices" being offered by a sinful creature, can no otherwise be acceptable to God than *by Jesus Christ:* for, as President EDWARDS justly remarks, " It does not consist with the honour of the majesty of the king of heaven and earth, to accept of any thing from a condemned malefactor, condemned by the justice of his own holy law, till that condemnation be removed."

But a sinner being accepted as believing in Jesus, his works also are accepted for his sake, and become rewardable. It was in this way, and not of works, that Abraham's obedience was honoured with so great a reward. The blessings here promised are called "the *mercy* to Abraham."* Hence we perceive the fallacy of an objection to the new-testament doctrine of our being forgiven and blessed in Christ's *name*, and for *his sake;* that this is no more than was true of Israel, who were blessed and often forgiven for the sake of Abraham. "Instead of this fact making against the doctrine in question," says a late judicious writer, "it makes for it: for it is clear from hence that it is not accounted an improper, or unsuitable thing in the divine administration, to confer favours on individuals, and even nations, *out of respect to the piety of another to whom they stood related.* But if this principle be admitted, the salvation of sinners out of respect to the obedience and sufferings of Christ, cannot be objected to as unreasonable. To this may be added, that every degree of divine respect to the obedience of the patriarchs was in fact no other than respect to the obedience of Christ, in whom they believed, and through whom their obedience, like ours, became acceptable. The

---

* Mic. vii. 20.

light of the moon which is derived from its looking, as it were, on the face of the sun, is no other than the light of the sun itself reflected. But if it be becoming the wisdom of God to reward the righteousness of his servants, and that many ages after their decease, so highly, (which was only borrowed lustre) much more may he reward the righteousness of his Son from whence it originated, in the salvation of those that believe in him."*

The renewal of these great and precious promises to Isaac in a time of famine, would preserve him from the fear of perishing, and be more than a balance to present inconveniences. It is not unusual for our heavenly Father to make up the loss of sensible enjoyments by encreasing those of faith. We need not mind where we "sojourn," nor what we endure, if the Lord "will be with us and bless us." When Joseph was sold into a strange land, and unjustly cast into prison, it was reckoned a sufficient antidote to add, "but the Lord was with Joseph."†

Ver. 6—11. After so extraordinary a manifestation of the Lord's goodness to Isaac, we might

* *Williams's Letters to Belsham,* pp. 156—158.

† Genesis xxxix.

have supposed he would have dwelt securely and happily in Gerar: but great mercies are often followed with great *temptations*. The abundance of revelations given to Paul were succeeded by a thorn in the flesh, a messenger of Satan sent to buffet him. It is said of our Lord himself, after the heavens were opened, and the most singular testimony had been borne to him at Jordan, "*Then* was Jesus led up of the Spirit into the wilderness to be tempted of the devil."* Heavenly enjoyments are given us in this world, not merely to comfort us under present troubles, but to arm us against future dangers; and happy is it for us if they be so improved.

Isaac had generally lived in solitude; but now he is called into company, and company becomes a snare. "The men of the place asked him of his wife." These questions excited his apprehensions, and put him upon measures for self-preservation that involved him in sin.—Observe, (1.) He did not sin by thrusting himself into the way of temptation; for he was necessitated, and directed of God to go to Gerar. Even the calls of necessity and duty, may, if we be not on our watch, prove ensnaring; and if so, what must those situations be in which we have no call to be found?—(2.) The temptation

* Matt. iv. 1.

of Isaac is the same as that which had overcome his father, and that in two instances. This rendered his conduct the greater sin. The falls of them that have gone before us are so many rocks on which others have split; and the recording of them is like placing buoys over them, for the security of future mariners.—(3.) It was a temptation that arose from the beauty of Rebecca. There is a vanity which attaches to all earthly good. Beauty has often been a snare both to those who possess it, and to others. In this case, as in that of Abraham, it put Isaac upon unjustifiable measures for the preservation of his own life; measures that might have exposed his companion to that which would have been worse than death. Man soon falls into mischief when he sets up to be his own guide.

And now we see, what we are grieved to see, a great and good man let down before heathens, and reproved by them for his dissimulation. He had continued at Gerar " a long time" uninterrupted, which sufficiently shewed that his fears were groundless: yet he continued to keep up the deception, till the king observing from his window some freedoms he took with Rebecca, from which he inferred that she was his wife. The conduct of Abimelech on this occasion was as worthy of a king, as that of Isaac had been unworthy of a servant of God.

Ver. 12—17. Things being thus far rectified, we see Isaac engaged in the primitive employment of husbandry; and the Lord blessed him, and encreased him, so that he became the envy of the Philistines. Here again we see how vanity attaches to every earthly good: prosperity begets *envy*, and from envy proceeds *injury*. The wells which Abraham's servants had digged, Isaac considered as his own, and made use of them for his flocks: but the Philistines, out of envy to him, "stopped them up, and filled them with earth." Had they drank of them, it might have been excused; but to stop them up was downright wickedness, and a gross violation of the treaty of peace which had been made between a former Abimelech and Abraham. The issue was, the king perceiving the temper of his people, entreated Isaac quietly to depart. The reason he gave for it, that "he was much mightier than they," might be partly to apologize for his people's jealousy, and partly to soften his spirit by a compliment. If Isaac was so great as was suggested, he might, instead of removing at their request, have disputed it with them: he might have alleged the covenant made with his father, the improvement of his lands, &c. But he was a peaceable man, and therefore without making words, removed to the "valley of Gerar," either beyond the borders of Abimelech's territory, or at least farther off from the metropolis. A little with peace and quietness is better than much with envy and contention.

Ver. 18—22. Isaac, though removed to another part of the country, yet finds " wells of water which had been digged in the days of Abraham his father, and which the Philistines had stopped up after his death." It seems wherever Abraham went, he improved the country; and wherever the Philistines followed him, their study was to mar his improvements, and that for no other end than the pleasure of doing mischief. Isaac however is resolved to open these wells again. Their waters would be doubly sweet to him for their having been first tasted by his beloved father; and to shew his filial affection still more, he "called their names after the names by which his father had called them." Many of our enjoyments, both civil and religious, are the sweeter for being the fruits of the labour of our fathers; and if they have been corrupted by adversaries since their days, we must restore them to their former purity. Isaac's servants also digged *new wells,* and which occasioned new strife. While we avail ourselves of the labours of our forefathers, we ought not to rest in them, without making farther progress, even though it expose us to many unpleasant disputes. *Envy* and *strife* may be expected to follow those whose researches are really beneficial, provided they go a step beyond their forefathers. But let them not be discouraged: the wells of salvation are worth striving for; and after a few conflicts, they may enjoy the fruits of their labours in peace. Isaac's servants dug two wells, which, from the bitter strife they occasioned, were called Esek and Sitnah, *contention* and *hatred:* but peaceably removing from these scenes of wrangle, he at length digged a well for which "they strove not." This he called Rehoboth, saying, "Now the Lord hath made *room* for us, and we shall be fruitful in the land."

Ver. 23—25. The famine being now over, Isaac returned to Beersheba, the place where he and his father had lived many years before.* It may seem strange, after God had made room for him at Rehoboth, that the next news we hear is, that he takes leave of it. This however might be at some distance of time, and Beersheba was to him a kind of home. Here, the very first night he arrived, the Lord appeared to him, probably in vision, saying, "I am the God of Abraham thy father: fear not, for I am with thee, and will bless thee, and multiply thy seed for my servant Abraham's sake." Isaac was attached

* Chap. xxi. 31—33.

to the wells which his father had digged, and to the place where he had sojourned; and doubtless it would add endearment to the very name of Jehovah himself that he was the God of Abraham, especially as it would remind him of the covenant which he had made with him. A self-righteous spirit would have been offended at the idea of being blessed *for another's sake;* but he who walked in the steps of his father's faith would enjoy it: and by how much he loved him for whose sake the blessing was bestowed, by so much the greater would his enjoyment be. The promises are the same for substance as were made to him on his going to Gerar. The same truths are new to us under new circumstances, and in new situations. To express the grateful sense he had of the divine goodness, he arose and "built an altar, and called upon the name of the Lord:" and now the very place being rendered doubly dear to him, "*there* he pitched his tent, and *there* his servants digged a well." Temporal mercies are sweetened by their contiguity to God's altars, and by their being given us after we have first sought the kingdom of God and his righteousness.

Ver. 26—31. One would not have expected after driving him, in a manner, out of their country, that the Philistines would have had any thing more to say to him. Abimelech, however, and some of his courtiers pay him a visit. They were not easy when he was with them, and now they seem hardly satisfied when he has left them. I believe they were afraid of his growing power, and conscious that they had treated him unkindly, wished for their own sakes to adjust these differences before they proceeded any farther. Isaac, while they acted as enemies, bore it patiently as a part of his lot in an evil world: but now they want to be thought friends, and to renew covenant with him, he feels keenly, and speaks his mind. "Wherefore come ye to me, seeing ye hate me, and have sent me away from you?" We can bear that from an avowed adversary, which we cannot bear from one in habits of friendship. *It was not an enemy that reproached me; then I could have borne it.* To this they answer, "We saw certainly that the Lord was with thee." Had they any regard then for Isaac's God, or for him on that account? I fear they had not: they felt however a regard to themselves, and a kind of respect for him which is very commonly seen in men of no religion towards them that fear the Lord. We do not blame them for wishing to be on good terms with such a man as Isaac: but they should not have pretended to have "done unto him nothing but good," when they must know, and he must have felt the contrary. But this is the very character of a self-righteous heart, when seeking reconciliation with God, as well as man. It palliates its sin, and desires peace in return for its good deeds, when in fact its deeds are evil. Isaac being of a peaceable spirit admits their plea, though a sorry one, and treated them generously. Next morning they arose; and having solemnly renewed covenant with each other, parted in peace.

Ver. 32, 33. The same day in which Abimelech and his courtiers took leave, the news came out of the field that Isaac's servants had discovered a well. It is the same well as they are said to have digged in verse 25, only there the thing is mentioned without respect to the time. Here we are told that the news of the discovery of the well arrived immediately after the mutual oath which had been taken between Isaac and Abimelech, and he for a memorial of the event called it "Shebah," *an oath;* and a city being afterwards built on the spot was from hence, it seems, called "Beer-shebah," *the well of the oath.* Indeed this name had been given it by Abraham above a hundred years before, and that on a similar occasion: but what was now done would serve to confirm it.

Ver. 34, 35. The Lord had promised to "multiply Isaac's seed;" and they are multiplied in the person of Esau; howbeit not to the encrease of comfort, either in him or in Rebecca. Esau went into the practice of polygamy, and took both his wives from among the Canaanites. Whether he went into their idolatrous customs, we are not told, nor whether they lived in the father's family. However this might be, their ungodly, and some think undutiful behaviour, was a grief of mind to their aged parents. Isaac entreated the Lord for his wife when she bare no children: and now that they have children grown up, one of them occasions much *bitterness of spirit:* this indeed is not uncommon. Such an issue of things in this instance would tend to turn away the hopes of Isaac from seeing the accomplishment of Abraham's covenant in the person of his first-born son, to whom he appears to have been inordinately attached. By other instances of the kind, God teaches us to beware of excessive anxiety after earthly comforts, and in receiving them to rejoice with trembling.

End of Vol. I.

EXPOSITORY DISCOURSES

ON

THE BOOK OF

GENESIS,

INTERSPERSED WITH

PRACTICAL REFLECTIONS.

BY ANDREW FULLER.

VOL. II.

Printed by J. W. Morris, Dunstable,
FOR J. BURDITT, 60, PATERNOSTER-ROW,
London:
SOLD ALSO BY W. BUTTON, 24, PATERNOSTER-ROW; WILLIAMS AND SMITH, STATIONERS' COURT; AND T. GARDINER, PRINCES STREET.

1806.

CONTENTS.

VOL. II.

DISCOURSE XXXVI.
Chap. xxvii.

Page.
Jacob's obtaining the blessing - - - - - - 1

DISCOURSE XXXVII.
Chap. xxviii.

Jacob's departure from Beersheba - - - - - 16

DISCOURSE XXXVIII.
Chap. xxix.

Jacob's arrival at Haran - - - - - - 27

DISCOURSE XXXIX.
Chap. xxx. xxxi. 1—16.

Jacob in Haran - - - - - - - - - 36

DISCOURSE XL.
Chap. xxxi. 17—55.

Jacob's departure from Haran - - - - - - 48

CONTENTS.

DISCOURSE XLI.
Chap. xxxii.

Jacob's fear of Esau—His wrestling with the Angel — Page 62

DISCOURSE XLII.
Chap. xxxiii.

Jacob's interview with Esau, and arrival in Canaan — 73

DISCOURSE XLIII.
Chap. xxxiv.

Dinah defiled, and the Shechemites murdered - - 83

DISCOURSE XLIV.
Chap. xxxv. xxxvi.

Jacob's removal to Bethel—God's renewal of covenant with him—the death of Deborah, Rachel, and Isaac—Esau's generations - - - - - 93

DISCOURSE XLV.
Chap. xxxvii.

Joseph sold for a slave - - - - - - - - 109

DISCOURSE XLVI.
Chap. xxxviii. xxxix.

The conduct of Judah—Joseph's promotion and temptation - - - - - - - - - - - - - 123

DISCOURSE XLVII.
Chap. xl.

Joseph in prison - - - - - - - - - - 137

DISCOURSE XLVIII.
Chap. xli.

Joseph's advancement - - - - - - - - - 145

DISCOURSE XLIX.
Chap. xlii.

The first interview between Joseph and his brethren 157

DISCOURSE L.
Chap. xliii.

The second interview between Joseph and his brethren 172

DISCOURSE LI.
Chap. xliv. 1—17.

The cup in Benjamin's sack - - - - - - - 184

DISCOURSE LII.
Chap. xliv. 18—34.

Judah's intercession - - - - - - - - - 193

DISCOURSE LIII.
Chap. xlv.

Joseph making himself known to his brethren - - 202

DISCOURSE LIV.
Chap. xlvi.

Jacob's going down into Egypt - - - - - - 211

DISCOURSE LV.
Chap. xlvii.

Joseph's conduct in the settlement of his brethren, and in the affairs of Egypt - - - - - - 220

CONTENTS.

DISCOURSE LVI.
Chap. xlviii.

Page.

Joseph's interview with his dying father, with the blessing of his sons - - - - - - - - - 230

DISCOURSE LVII.
Chap. xlix.

Jacob's blessings on the tribes - - - - - - - 239

DISCOURSE LVIII.
Chap. l.

The burial of Jacob, and the death of Joseph - - 258

CONCLUSION - - - - - - - - - - - 269

EXPOSITORY DISCOURSES,

&c.

VOL. II.

DISCOURSE XXXVI.

JACOB's OBTAINING THE BLESSING.

GENESIS xxvii.

BEFORE we entered on the history of Isaac, we met with some painful events respecting the departure of Ishmael: but in the introduction to the history of Jacob, we find things much more painful. In the former instance we found him that was rejected a mocker; but in this we see in the heir of promise a supplanter. This deviation from rectitude, though it changes not the divine purpose, but on the contrary, is overruled for its accomplishment, yet sows the seed of much evil in the life of the offender. Isaac retained his place in the family; but Jacob was obliged to depart from it. When the former was of age to be married, an honourable embassy was sent to bring it about: but the latter is necessitated to go by himself, as one that had just escaped with his life. There is a deep mystery in the system of providence, and much eventual good brought out of great evils.

Ver. 1—4. Isaac was now about a hundred and thirty-seven years of age, and " his eyes were dim, so that he could not see." He therefore called Esau his eldest son, and said, " Behold now, I am old, I know not the day of my death . . . take I pray thee thy weapons . . . and go out to the field, and take me some venison; and make me savoury meat, such as I love, and bring it to me that I may eat, that my soul may bless thee before I die." Isaac lived forty-three years after this: but as it was unknown to him, he did very properly in settling his affairs. The day of our death is concealed from us for the very purpose that we may be always ready: and when life is upon the wane, especially, it becomes us to do what we do quickly. The above account however does not appear greatly to his honour. His partiality towards Esau would seem to imply a disregard to what had been revealed to Rebecca; and his fondness for the venison has the appearance of weakness.

But passing this, there are two questions which require an answer—Wherein consisted the blessing which was now about to be bestowed; and why was savoury meat required in order to the bestowment of it? Respecting the first, I might refer to what has been said already on the birthright.* There was, no doubt, a common blessing to be expected from such a father as Isaac on all his children, and a special one on his firstborn: but in this family there was a blessing superior to both. It included all those great things contained in the covenant with Abraham, by which his posterity were to be distinguished as God's peculiar people. Hence that which Isaac did is said to have been done " in faith," and was prophetic " of things to come."† The faith of this good man was however at first much interrupted by natural attachment. Desirous of conferring the blessing on Esau, he gives him directions as to the manner of receiving it. And here occurs the second question, Why was " savoury meat" required in order to the bestowment of the blessing? The design of it seems to to have been not merely to strengthen animal nature, but to enkindle affection. Isaac is said to have *loved* Esau on account of his venison:‡ this therefore would tend, as he supposed, to

---

* Chapter xxv. 29—34. † Heb. xi. 20. ‡ Chapter xxv. 23.

revive that affection, and so enable him to bless him with all his heart. It seems however to have been but a carnal kind of introduction to so divine an act; partaking more of the flesh than of the Spirit, and savouring rather of that natural affection under the influence of which he at present acted, than of the faith of a son of Abraham.

Ver. 5—10. Rebecca overhearing this charge of Isaac to his son Esau, takes measures to direct the blessing into another channel. This is a mysterious affair. It was just that Esau should lose the blessing, for by selling his birth-right he had despised it. It was God's design too that Jacob should have it. Rebecca also knowing of this design, from its having been revealed to her that "the elder should serve the younger," appears to have acted from a good motive. But the scheme which she formed to correct the error of her husband was far from being justifiable. It was one of those crooked measures which have too often been adopted to accomplish the divine promises; as if the end would justify, or at least excuse the means. Thus Sarah acted in giving Hagar to Abraham; and thus many others have acted under the idea of being *useful* in promoting the cause of Christ. The answer to all such things is that which God addressed to Abrah-

I am God Almighty; walk before me, and be thou perfect. The deception practised on Isaac was cruel. If he be in the wrong, endeavour to convince him; or commit it to God, who could turn his mind, as he afterwards did that of Jacob, when blessing Ephraim and Manasseh: but do not avail yourself of his loss of sight to deceive him. Such would have been the counsel of wisdom and rectitude: but Rebecca follows her own.

Ver. 11—13. We ought not to load Jacob with more of the guilt of this transaction than belongs to him. He was not first in the transgression. His feelings revolted at it when it was proposed to him. He remonstrated against it. Considering too that it was against the advice, or rather the command of a parent, such remonstrance would seem to go far towards excusing him. But no earthly authority can justify us in disregarding the authority of God. Moreover, the remonstrance itself is founded merely on the *consequences* of the evil, and not on *the evil itself.* What a difference between this reasoning, and that of his son Joseph. " I shall bring a *curse* upon me," said he, " and not a blessing." " How can I do this great wickedness," said the other, " and sin against God !"— The *resoluteness* of Rebecca is affecting : " Upon

me be thy curse, my son : only obey my voice."
Surely she must have presumed upon the divine
promise, which is a dangerous thing: our Lord
considered it as tempting God.* Those who do
evil under an idea of serving God, commonly go
to the greatest lengths. It was in this track that
the Lord met Saul in his way to Damascus.

Ver. 14—17. If Jacob's remonstrance had
arisen from an aversion to the evil, he would not
so readily have yielded to his mother as he did:
but to resist temptation with merely the calculation of consequences, is doing nothing. Rebecca
takes the consequence upon herself, and then he
has no more to object, but does as she instructs
him. She also performs her part; and thus between them the scheme is executed. What labour
and contrivance are required to dissemble the
truth, and carry on a bad cause. Uprightness
needs no such circuitous measures.

Ver. 18—24. Jacob now enters upon the
business. And first, with all the artifice of his
mother, she cannot guard him at all points. He
is obliged to *speak*, and he could not counterfeit
his brother's voice. " My father," said he—The
patriarch starts . . . " Who art thou my son ?"

* Matt. iv. 7.

It was the voice of one of his sons, but not of him whom he expected. And now what can Jacob answer? He must either confess the deception, or persist in it at all events. He chooses the latter. One sin makes way for another, and in a manner impels us to commit it. " Jacob said, I am Esau thy first-born ... I have done according as thou badest me ... Arise, I pray thee, sit, and eat of my venison, that thy soul may bless me." Isaac, still suspicious, enquires how he came so soon. The answer intimates, that by a special interposition of his father's God he had met with early success! It is not easy to conceive of any thing more wicked than this. It was bad enough to deal in so many known falsehoods: but to bring in the Lord God of his father in order to give them the appearance of truth, was much worse, and what we should not have expected but from one of the worst of men. There is something about falsehood which though it may silence, yet will not ordinarily satisfy. Isaac is yet suspicious, and therefore desires to feel his hands; and here the deception answered. The hands, he thinks, are Esau's; but still it is mysterious, for " the voice is Jacob's." Were it not for some such things as these, we might overlook the wisdom and goodness of God in affording us so many marks by which to detect imposture, and distinguish man from man. Of all the multitudes of faces, voices, and figures in the world; no two are perfectly alike: and if one sense fail us, the others are frequently improved. Such was the strength of Isaac's doubts, that he would not be satisfied without directly asking him again, "Art thou my very son Esau," and receiving for answer, "I am." After this he seems to have thought it must be Esau, and therefore proceeded to bless him.

The adversaries of revelation may make the most they can of these narrations: evil as was the conduct of Jacob, and of Rebecca, the history of it contains the strongest internal evidence that it is written by inspiration of God. Had it been a cunningly devised fable, it would have been the business of the writer to have thrown the faults of this his great ancestor into the shade: but the scriptures do not profess to describe perfect characters: they represent men and things as they were. We feel for the imposition practised on Isaac; and yet it was no doubt a chastisement to him for his ill-placed partiality for Esau on grounds so unworthy of him, and to the disregarding of what God had revealed concerning them.

Ver. 25—29. It was of the Lord that Jacob should have the blessing, notwithstanding the

Gen. 27.] THE BLESSING. 9

unwarrantable means he had used to obtain it. In pronouncing it, Isaac was supernaturally directed; otherwise it would not have corresponded with what afterwards actually befel his posterity, which it manifestly does; nor would he have felt himself unable to revoke it. It is observable however, that the blessing is expressed in very general terms. No mention is made of those distinguishing mercies included in the covenant with Abraham; and this might be owing to his having Esau in his mind, though it was Jacob who was before him. He could not be ignorant how that young man had despised these things, and this might be a check to his mind while he thought he was blessing him. Moreover, his attachment to Esau, to the disregard of the mind of God, must have greatly weakened and injured his own faith in these things: it might therefore be expected that the Lord would cause a comparative leanness to attend his blessing, corresponding with the state of his mind.

Ver. 30—33. Jacob had scarcely left the room when Esau, returning from the chase, enters it, and presents his father with his venison. This at once discovers the imposition. Isaac is greatly affected by it. At first, when he heard his voice, he was confounded ... " Who art thou?" And when he perceived that it was indeed his " first-born son Esau," he " trembled very exceedingly," and said, " Who, where is he that hath taken venison and brought to me, and I have eaten of all before thou camest, and have blessed him?" Such a shock must have been more than he knew how to sustain. To ascertain the sensations of which it was composed, we must place ourselves in his situation. As an aged and afflicted man, the imposition which had been practised on him would excite his *indignation.* Yet a moment's reflexion would convince him that the transfer of the blessing must have been *of the Lord;* and consequently, that he had all along been acting against his will in seeking to have it otherwise. Two such considerations rushing upon his mind in the same instant, sufficiently account for all his feelings: it was to him like a place where two seas met, or as the running of subterraneous fires and waters, the commotion of which causeth the earth to tremble. It must have appeared to him as a strong measure permitted of God for his correction; and that he had thus caused him to do that against his choice which should have been done without it. Viewing it in this light, and knowing the blessing to be irrevocable, he, like a good man, acquiesced in the will of God, saying, " Yea, and he shall be blessed."

THE BLESSING.

Ver. 34—40. The " very exceeding trembling" of Isaac is now followed by "a great and exceeding bitter cry" on the part of Esau. Nothing he had ever met with seems to have affected him like it. But how is it, that he who made so light of the birthright, as to part with it for a morsel of meat, should now make so much of the blessing connected with it? It was not that he desired to be a servant of the Lord, or that his posterity should be his people, according to the tenor of Abraham's covenant: but as he that should be possessed of these distinctions would in *other respects* be superior to his brother, it became an object of emulation. Thus we have often seen religion set at nought, while yet the advantages which accompany it have been earnestly desired; and where grace has in a manner crossed hands by favouring a younger or inferior branch of a family, envy and its train of malignant passions have frequently blazed on the other side.—It was not as the father of the holy nation, but as being "lord over his brethren," that Jacob was the object of Esau's envy. And this may farther account for the blessing of Isaac on the former dwelling principally upon *temporal advantages*, as designed of God to cut off the vain hopes of the latter, of enjoying the *power* attached to the blessing, while he despised the blessing itself.

When Esau perceived that Jacob must be blessed, he entreated to be blessed *also:* " Bless me, even me also, oh my father!" One sees in this language just that partial conviction of there being something in religion, mixed with a large portion of ignorance, which it is common to see in persons who have been brought up in a religious family, and yet are strangers to the God of their fathers. If this earnest request had extended only to what was consistent with Jacob's having the pre-eminence, there *was* another blessing for him, and he had it: but though he had no desire after the best part of Jacob's portion, yet he was very earnest to have had that clause of it reversed, " be lord over thy brethren, and let thy mother's sons bow down to thee." If this could have been granted him, he had been satisfied; for " the fatness of the earth" was all he cared for. But this was an object concerning which, as the apostle observes, " he found no place of repentance," (that is, in the mind of his father,) " though he sought it carefully with tears."* Such will be the case with fornicators and all profane persons, who, like Esau, for a few momentary gratifications in the present life, make light of Christ, and the blessings of the gospel. They will cry with a great and exceeding bitter

---

* Heb. xii. 15—17.

cry, saying, Lord, Lord, open unto us! But they will find no place of repentance in the mind of the Judge, who will answer them, I know you not whence ye are: depart from me ye workers of iniquity!

Esau's reflections on his brother for having twice supplanted him, were not altogether without ground: yet his statement is exaggerated. It was not accurate to say, " he took away my birthright," as though he had robbed him of it, seeing he himself had so despised it as to part with it for a morsel of meat: and having done so, whatever might be said of Jacob's conduct in the sight of God, *he* had no reason to complain.

Ver. 41. Esau obtained, as we have seen, a blessing, and some relief on the score of subjection; yet because he could not gain his point, but the posterity of Jacob must needs have the ascendency, there is nothing left for him but to " *hate* him for the blessing wherewith his father blessed him." He was not ignorant of Isaac's partiality: he must therefore have known that it was not owing to him, nor even to Jacob's subtilty, that the first dominion was given him. He must have perceived from what his father had said that the thing *was of the Lord,* and therefore could not be reversed. Hence it appears that the hatred of Esau was of the same nature with that of Cain to Abel, and of Saul to David; and operated in the same way: it was directed against him principally on account of his having been an object whom the Lord had favoured. Such also was the motive of the hatred which in after ages subsisted in the Edomites against Israel. As nothing could comfort Esau but the hope of murder, so nothing could satisfy his posterity but to see Jerusalem rased to its foundations.— Isaac had talked of dying, and Esau thought to be sure the time was not far distant; and then during the days of mourning for his father, he hoped for an opportunity of murdering his brother. He might think also that it was best to suppress his resentment till the poor old man was dead, and then it would not be a grief to him. The most cruel designs of wicked men may be mixed with a partiality for those who have been partial to them.

Ver. 42—45. Esau, it seems, had not only " said in his heart," I will slay my brother, but had put his thoughts into words, probably before some of the servants. The hint, however, was carried to Rebecca, and she clearly foresaw what was to be expected. She therefore sent for Jacob and told him of his brother's design, counselling him at the same time to go to her relations at Haran, and tarry there awhile, till Esau's anger should have subsided. The reason which she urges to enforce her counsel is very strong: " Why should I be deprived of you both in one day?" Had Esau's purpose succeeded, the murderer, as well as the murdered, had been lost to her. We see here the bitter fruits which Rebecca begins to reap from her crooked policy: she must part with her favourite son to preserve his life, and will never see him again in this world, though she thinks of sending in a little time to fetch him home.

Ver. 46. By the manner in which things are here related, it appears that Isaac was so infirm as to have lost all the power of management, and that the whole in a manner devolved on Rebecca. She advises Jacob what to do: it is expedient if not necessary, however, before he takes his departure, to obtain his father's concurrence. She does not choose to tell her husband the true reason of her wishes, as that was a tender point, and might lead to a subject which she might think it better to pass over in silence: but knowing that he, as well as herself, had been grieved with Esau's wives,* she judges that the most

---
* Chapter xxvi. 35.

likely means of success would be a proposal for Jacob to go to Haran for the purpose of taking a wife from amongst their relations in that country. She does not propose it, however, directly; but merely expresses her strong disapprobation of his following the example of his brother, leaving it to Isaac to mention positively what should be done. And this, her apparent modesty, answered the end, as we shall see in the following chapter.

DISCOURSE XXXVII.

JACOB's DEPARTURE FROM BEERSHEBA.

GENESIS xxviii.

VER. 1—4. The hint which Rebecca had dropped against Jacob's taking a wife from among the daughters of Heth, quite fell in with Isaac's mind; and knowing that there was but one place for him to go to on such an errand, he determines without delay to send him thither. The account here given of his "calling, blessing, and charging" him, is very much to his honour. —The first of these terms implies his reconciliation to him; the second, his satisfaction in what had been done before without design; and the last, his concern that he should act in a manner worthy of the blessing which he had received.

How differently do things issue in different minds. Esau, as well as Isaac, was "exceedingly" affected by what had lately occurred: but the "bitter cry" of the one issued in a settled hatred, while the "trembling" of the other brought him to a right mind. He had been thinking matters over ever since, and the more he thought of them, the more satisfied he was that it was the will of God; and that all his private partialities should give place to it.

One sees in what he now does that his heart is in it. He not only blesses him, but invokes the blessing of Almighty God to attend him— "God Almighty bless thee, and make thee fruitful, and multiply thee, that thou mayest be a multitude of people; and give thee the blessing of Abraham, to thee, and to thy seed with thee, that thou mayest inherit the land wherein thou art a stranger, which God gave unto Abraham." Who does not perceive the difference between this blessing and the former? In that he was thinking of one person, and blessing another: in this he understands what he is about. Then his mind was straitened by carnal attachment: now it is enlarged by faith. The rich promises of Abraham's covenant seem there to have been almost forgotten: but here they are expressly named, and dwelt upon with delight. Of what importance it is for our minds to be kept one with God's mind; and what a difference it makes in the discharge of duty! We may pray, or preach, after a manner, while it is otherwise; and God may preserve us from uttering gross error: but what we deliver will be miserably flat and defective, in comparison of what it is when a right spirit is renewed within us.

Ver. 5—9. The departure of Jacob was attended by many painful and humiliating circumstances, as well it might; for these are the necessary consequences of sin. The parting scene to Isaac was tender; but Jacob and his mother must have felt something more than tenderness. As to Esau, it is not likely that he was present. He was near enough however to eye his motions, and by some means to make himself acquainted with every thing that passed. Probably he expected more supplanting schemes were forming, and longed for the time when a fair opportunity should offer for his being revenged on the supplanter. But when he found that his father had blessed him, and charged him not to take a wife of the daughters of Canaan, and that he had obeyed his voice, and was gone to Padan-aram, it seems to have wrought in a way that we should scarcely have expected. Finding himself left in the possession of all the substance of the family, and Jacob out of his way, he thinks he has now only to please his father, and notwithstanding the loss of this birthright, and blessing, all will be his. And now, to accomplish his end, he carefully notices the means by which Jacob succeeded in pleasing his parents. One great advantage which he had gained over him, as he perceived by his father's "charge," was in reference to marriage. He had obeyed the voice of his father and his mother, and was gone to take a wife from the family of Bethuel. 'I will take another wife then,' said Esau to himself, 'if that will please them; and as they seem attached to their *relations*, it shall be from amongst them. Moreover, as Jacob, who is his mother's favourite, intends to marry into her family, I who am my father's, will marry into his.' See what awkward work is made when men go about to please others, and promote their worldly interests by imitating that in which they have no delight. Ignorance and error mark every step they take. Esau was in no need of a wife, for he had two already; nor did his parents desire him to add to the number; nor would they be gratified by his connexion with the apostate family of Ishmael; nor was it principally on account of Bethuel's being a *relation* that Abraham's family took wives from his.—In short, he is out in all his calculations; nor can he discover the prin-

ciples which influence those who fear the Lord. Thus have we often seen men try to imitate religious people for the sake of gaining esteem, or some way promoting their selfish ends: but instead of succeeding, they have commonly made bad worse. That which to a right mind is as plain as the most public highway, to a mind perverted shall appear full of difficulties. "The labour of the foolish wearieth every one of them, because he knoweth not how to go to the city."*
—But to return—

Ver. 10, 11. The line of promise being now fully ascertained, Jacob becomes the hero of the tale. He was now about seventy-seven years old; and though his brother Esau had two wives, yet he was single. The posterity of Ishmael and Esau encreased much faster than those of Isaac and Jacob. It seemed to be the design of God that the promise should be slow in its operations, that it might try the faith of his servants. Setting out from his father's house at Beersheba, we find Jacob journeying towards Haran, a distance of about five hundred miles. Without a servant to attend him, or a beast to carry him, or any other accommodation, except, as he afterwards informs us, a "staff" to walk with, he pursues his solitary way. Having travelled one

* Eccles. x. 15.

whole day, the sun being set, he alighted on a certain place where he took up his abode for the night. The place was called Luz, and is said to have been "a city." (ver. 19.) Jacob, however, does not seem to have entered it; but for some reason chose to sleep in the open air in its suburbs. Sleeping abroad is a custom very common in the east, and less dangerous than in colder climates. The stones which he used for a pillow might preserve him from the damp of the ground; but, we should think, must have contributed but little to rest his weary body.

Ver. 12—15. During the night he had a very extraordinary dream, almost every particular of which is introduced by the sacred writer with the interjection "behold!" "He dreamed, and behold a ladder set upon the earth, and the top of it reached to heaven: and behold, the angels of God ascending and descending on it. And behold, Jehovah stood above it, and said, I am Jehovah, God of Abraham thy father, and the God of Isaac: the land whereon thou liest, to thee will I give it, and to thy seed; and thy seed shall be as the dust of the earth, and thou shalt spread abroad to the west and to the east, and to the north and to the south: and in thee and in thy seed shall all the families of the earth be blessed. And behold, I am with thee, and will keep thee in all places whither thou goest, and will bring thee again into this land; for I will not leave thee until I have done that which I have spoken to thee of."

We might have been at a loss in ascertaining the meaning of the latter, if the great medium of communion between heaven and earth had not almost expressly applied it to himself. "Hereafter," said he to Nathaniel, "ye shall see heaven open, and the angels of God ascending (that is to heaven,) and descending (that is to the earth,) upon the Son of Man."* Our Lord's design appears to have been to foretel the glory of gospel times, in which, through his mediation, heaven should as it were be opened, and a free intercourse established between God, angels, and men. But it may be asked, what analogy there could be between this, and that which was revealed to Jacob? I answer, we have seen that the Messiah was not only included in the promises to Abraham, but that he made a principal part of them; and as these promises were now renewed to Jacob, though we had read nothing of his vision of the ladder, yet we should have known that they looked as far forward as to him, and to that dispensation in which "all the families of the earth should be blessed" in him. As it is, we

* John i. 51.

may conclude that what was *seen* in vision was of the same general import as what was *heard* in the promises which followed. It was giving the patriarch a glimpse of that glory which should be accomplished in his seed.

There was something very *seasonable* in this vision, and in the promises which accompanied it. Jacob had lately *acted* an unworthy part, and if properly sensible of it, must have been very unhappy. His father, it is true, had blessed him, and of course forgiven him; but till God has done so too, he can enjoy no solid peace. Now such was the present vision: it was the Lord his God saying Amen to his father's blessing.* He was taking leave of Canaan, and if he had calculated on human probabilities, he was never likely to return to it, at least during the life-time of Esau: but by the gift of the land on which he lay, to him and to his seed, he was taught to expect it, and to consider himself only as a sojourner at Haran.—Considering his age too, there seemed but little probability of his having a numerous offspring. If the blessing consisted in this, it seemed much more likely to be fulfilled in his brother than in him: but he was hereby assured that "his seed should be as the dust of the earth," spreading abroad in every direction.

* Comp. ver. 3, 4, with ver. 13, 14.

—The thought also of leaving his father's house, and of going among strangers, must needs have affected him. During his solitary walk from Beersheba, he had doubtless been thinking of his lonely condition, and of the difficulties and dangers which he had to encounter. How seasonable then was the promise, "Behold, I am with thee, and will keep thee in all places whither thou goest, and will bring thee again into this land."—Finally, the present was a new epoch in his life, and as an heir of promise, a kind of commencement of it. In this character he must, like his predecessors, live by faith. Esau's blessing was soon fulfilled; but Jacob's related to things at a great distance, and which none but "God Almighty" could bring to pass. How seasonable then were those precious promises which furnished at his outset a ground for faith to rest upon! "I will not leave thee till I have done that which I have spoken to thee of."

Ver. 16—22. Awaking from sleep in the night-time, and reflecting on his dream, he was greatly affected, as well he might. "Surely," exclaimed he, "Jehovah is in this place, and I knew it not! And he was afraid, and said, How dreadful is this place! This is none other than the house of God, and this is the gate of heaven!" q. d. 'Surely this is no common dream! God is in it! God is near! I went to sleep as at other times, expecting nothing; and lo, ere I was aware, God hath visited me!' Feeling himself as in the presence of the Divine Majesty, he trembles—the place seems to be holy ground—the temple of Jehovah, the suburbs of heaven! Whether he slept after this, we are not told: be that as it may, he "rose early in the morning;" and deeply impressed with what had passed, resolved to perpetuate the remembrance of it. Taking the stone which he had lain upon, he set it up for a pillar, or monument; and that he might consecrate it to the future service of the Lord, "poured oil upon the top of it." This done, he gave the place a new name. Instead of "Luz," which signifies an almond, or nut tree, probably on account of a number of those trees growing near it, he called it "Bethel," *the house of God.*

Finally: He closed this extraordinary vision by a solemn vow, or dedication of himself to God. "And Jacob vowed a vow, saying, If God will be with me, and will keep me in this way that I go, and will give me bread to eat, and raiment to put on, so that I come again to my father's house in peace; then shall Jehovah be my God, and this stone which I have set for a pillar shall be God's house; and of all that thou shalt give me, I will surely give the tenth unto thee."—The *terms* of this solemn vow were not of Jacob's dictating to the Almighty, but arose out of his own gracious promises; and so furnish a lovely example of the prayer of faith. God had promised to be with him, to keep him, to bring him again into the land, and not to leave him. Jacob takes up the precious words, saying, If God will thus be with me, and keep me, and provide for me, and bring me home in peace, then in return will I be his for ever. We may pray for things which God hath not promised, *in submission to his will*, as Abraham interceded for Sodom, and Moses for the idolaters at Horeb: but when we ask for that which he hath engaged to bestow, we approach him with much greater encouragement.—The *order* of what he desired is also deserving of notice. It corresponds with our Saviour's rule, to seek things of the greatest importance first. By how much God's favour is better than life, by so much his being *with us*, and *keeping us*, is better than food and raiment. A sense of this will moderate our desires for inferior things, as it did Jacob's. A little with the fear of the Lord is better than great treasures with trouble. If God be with us, and keep us, the mere necessaries of life will make us happy.—The *vow itself* contains an entire renunciation of idolatry, and a taking Jehovah to be his God. And inasmuch as it looks forward to his return to Canaan, it includes a solemn promise to maintain the worship of God in his family. Then he would rear an altar to him in Bethel, and consecrate the tenth of all his substance to his cause.

In the course of the history we shall perceive the use that Jacob made of this vision, and that which the Lord made of the vow which here he vowed to him. But I conclude with only remarking, that in the former chapter we saw much of man; but in this we have seen much of God. In the works of the one, sin abounded: in those of the other, grace hath much more abounded.

DISCOURSE XXXVIII.

JACOB's ARRIVAL AT HARAN.

GENESIS XXIX.

Ver. 1. Jacob's second day's journey was very different from the first: then he had a heavy burden, but now he has lost it. His outset from Bethel is expressed by a phrase which signifies he *lifted up his feet;* that is, he went lightly and cheerfully on. Nothing more is recorded of his journey, but that "he came into the land of the people of the east."

Ver. 2—10. The first object that struck him was a well, with three flocks of sheep lying by it, ready to be watered. The shepherds coming up, rolled away the stone from the well's mouth, watered the flocks, and then put the stone again in his place. Jacob, who had hitherto looked on, now began the following conversation with them, " My brethren, whence be ye? Of Haran. Know ye Laban, the son of Nahor? We know him. Is he well? He is well; and behold, Rachel his daughter cometh with the sheep." On this, Jacob suggests that it was too soon to gather all the flocks together, as they did at night; and that there was much time yet for their being again led forth to pasture. " Water ye the sheep, said he, and go and feed them." It might appear somewhat out of character for a stranger to be so officious as to direct them how to proceed with their flocks : but the design was, I apprehend, to induce them to depart, and to leave him to converse with Rachel by herself. They tell him however, that they must stop till all the flocks are watered; Rachel's, it seems, as well as the rest. Such probably was the custom, that the well might be left secure. While they were talking, Rachel came up. The sight of the daughter of his mother's brother affected him. He could have wished that so tender an interview had been by themselves;

but as this could not be, he in the presence of the shepherds, went and "rolled away the stone from the well's mouth, and watered her flock;" which being done, he "kissed Rachel, and lift up his voice and wept." The tears shed on this occasion must have arisen from a full heart. We cannot say that the love which he afterwards bore to Rachel did not commence from his first seeing her. But however that might be, the cause of this weeping was of another kind: it was her being "the daughter of his *mother's* brother," that now affected him. Every thing that revived *her* memory, even the very flocks of sheep that belonged to *her* brother, went to his heart. Nor did he wish to be alone with Rachel, but that he might give vent without reserve to these sensations.

Ver. 12—14. It must have excited surprise in Rachel's mind, to see a stranger so attentive in watering her flock, and still more so to receive from him so affectionate a salutation: but now, having relieved his heart by a burst of weeping, he tells her who he is;—he is her father's near kinsman, Rebecca's son! And now we may expect another very tender interview. Rachel ran and told her father; and the father "ran to meet him, and embraced him, and kissed him, and brought him to his house." After an interchange of salutations, Jacob tells him his whole story; and Laban seems much affected with it, and speaks to him in affectionate language, "Surely thou art my bone, and my flesh."

Ver. 15—20. During the first month of his stay, Jacob employed himself about his uncle's business; but nothing was said with respect to terms. On such a subject it was not for Jacob to speak: so Laban very properly intimated that he did not desire to take advantage of his near relationship, that he should serve him any more than another man for nothing. Tell me, said he, what shall be thy wages. This gives Jacob an opportunity of expressing his love to Rachel. Aware that he had no dowry, like his father Isaac, he could not well have asked her, but for such an opportunity as this being afforded him. It was humiliating however, to be thus in a manner obliged to earn his wife before he could have her. This is twice afterwards referred to in the scriptures as an instance of his low condition. It was a part of the confession required to be made by every Israelite when he presented his basket of first fruits before the Lord, "A Syrian, *ready to perish*, was my father!"* And when in the days of Hosea they were grown haughty, the prophet reminds them that "Jacob

* Deut. xxvi. 5.

fled into the country of Syria, and Israel *served* for a wife, and for a wife he *kept sheep.*"* Half the generosity which Laban's words seemed to express would have given Jacob the object of his choice, without making him wait seven years for her. It was very proper for the one to offer it; but it was mean and selfish for the other to accept it. If he had really esteemed his daughters, and on this account set a high value on them, he would not afterwards have imposed two where one only was desired. But his own private interest was all he studied. In his sister Rebecca's marriage there were presents of gold and silver, and costly raiment, besides an assurance of the Lord having greatly blessed the family, and that Isaac was to be the "heir." These were things which wrought much on Laban's mind. He could then say, "Behold, Rebecca is before thee, take her, and go, and let her be thy master's son's wife." But here are none of these moving inducements. Here is a man, it is true, and he *talks* of promised blessings: but he is poor, and Laban cannot live upon promises. He perceives that Abraham's descendants are partial to his family, and he is resolved to make his market of it. The sight of the very flocks of Laban, as being his *mother's* brother, interested Jacob's heart; but he would soon find that Laban will

* Hosea xii. 12.

make him pay for his attachments. Such however was the love he bore to Rachel, that he took all in good part, and consented to *serve* seven years for her. Nay, such was the strength of his affection, that " they seemed unto him but a few days." Some would suppose that love must operate in a contrary way, causing the time to appear long rather than short; and therefore conclude, that what is here spoken is expressive of what it appeared *when it was past:* but the phraseology seems rather to denote what it appeared *at the time.* The truth seems to be this: when there is nothing to obstruct a union, love is impatient of delay; but when great difficulties interpose, it stimulates to a patient and resolute course of action in order to surmount them. Where the object is highly valued, we think little of the labour and expense of obtaining it. *Love endureth all things.*

Ver. 21—24. At the expiration of the time, Jacob demanded his wife, and preparation is made accordingly for the marriage. Laban, like some in their gifts to God, is not wanting in ceremony. He "made a feast," gave his daughter a handmaid, and went through all the forms: but the gift itself was a deception: it was not Rachel, but Leah that was presented. It seems somewhat extraordinary that Jacob should be capable of being thus imposed upon. Perhaps the veil which was then worn by a woman on her marriage might contribute to his not perceiving her. It was a cruel business on the part of Laban; yet Jacob might see in it the punishment of his having imposed upon his father. In such a way God often deals with men, causing them to reap the bitter fruits of sin even when they have lamented and forsaken it. *When thou shalt make an end to deal treacherously, they shall deal treacherously with thee.* Isai. xxxiii. 1.

Ver. 25—30. Jacob perceiving by the light of the morning how he had been deceived, remonstrated; but it was to no purpose. The answer of Laban was frivolous. If the custom of the country was as he alleged, he ought to have said so from the first: but it is manifest that he wanted to dispose of both his daughters in a way that might turn to his own advantage. Hence he adds, " Fulfil her week, and I will give thee this also." These words would seem to intimate that he had seven years longer to stay for Rachel; but this does not agree with other facts. Jacob was twenty years in Haran.* At the end of fourteen years Joseph was born.† At that time Rachel had been a wife without bearing any children for several years.‡ The

* Gen. xxxi. 41. † chap. xxx. 25. ‡ ch. xxxi. 22, 24.

two marriages therefore must have been within a week of each other; and the meaning of Laban's words must be, 'Fulfil the seven days' feasting for Leah, and then thou shalt have Rachel, and shalt serve me seven years after the marriage on her account.' With this perfectly agrees what is said in verse 30, in which he is said to have "gone in *also* unto Rachel," denoting that it was soon after his having gone in unto Leah; and in which the seven years' service is spoken of as following his marriage to her.—This proposal on the part of Laban was as void of principle as any thing could well be. His first agreement was ungenerous, his breach of it unjust; and now to extort seven years' more labour, or withhold the object agreed for, was sordid in the extreme. Jacob had no desire for more wives than one: yet as polygamy was at that time tolerated, and as the marriage had been consummated, though ignorantly, with Leah, he could not well put her away: yet neither could he think of foregoing Rachel. So he acceded to the terms, notwithstanding their injustice, and was married also to Rachel; and Bilhah was given to her for a handmaid. But it was to him a sore trial, and that which laid the foundation of innumerable discords in his family, of which the succeeding history of it abounds. The following prohibition to Israel seems to have been occasioned by this unhappy example in their great ancestor: *Thou shalt not take a wife to her sister, to vex her, to uncover her nakedness, besides the other, in her life time.* Lev. xviii. 18.

Ver. 31—35. That Leah, who was never the object of Jacob's choice, and who must have had a share in the late imposition, should be "hated" in comparison of Rachel, is no more than might be expected: yet it is worthy of notice how God balances the good and ill of the present life. Leah is slighted in comparison of Rachel: but God gives children to her while he withholds them from the other; and children in a family whose chief blessing consisted in a promised *seed,* were greatly accounted of. The names given to the children were expressive of their mother's state of mind; partly as to her affliction for want of an interest in her husband's heart, and partly, we hope, as to her piety, in viewing the hand of God in all that befel her. Four children were born of her successively; namely, Reuben, Simeon, Levi, and Judah: and thus God was pleased to put more abundant honour on the part that lacked. The name of the last of these children, though given him by his mother merely under an emotion of thankfulness, yet was not a little suited to the royal tribe, from whence also the Messiah should descend. Of this his father was made acquainted by revelation when he blessed his sons. "Judah, (said he) thou art he whom thy brethren shall *praise*—the sceptre shall not depart from Judah, nor a lawgiver from between his feet, until Shiloh come; and unto him shall the gathering of the people be!"

One sees in the conduct of both Jacob and Leah under their afflictions, a portion of that patience which arose from a consciousness of their having brought them upon themselves. They were each buffeted in this matter for their faults; and being so, there was less of praiseworthiness in their taking it patiently. Yet when compared with some others, who in all their troubles are as bullocks unaccustomed to the yoke, we see what is worthy of imitation.

DISCOURSE XXXIX.

JACOB IN HARAN.

GENESIS XXX. xxxi. 1—16.

Though every part of Scripture is given by inspiration of God, and is profitable for various purposes; yet I conceive it is no disparagement from its real value to say, that every particular passage in it is not suited for a public exposition.

On this ground I shall pass over the thirtieth chapter, with only two or three general remarks.

First: The domestic discords, envies, and jealousies, between Jacob's wives, serve to teach us the wisdom and goodness of the christian law, that "every man have his own wife," as well as every woman her own husband. No reflecting person can read this chapter without being disgusted with polygamy, and thankful for that dispensation which has restored the original law of nature, and with it, true conjugal felicity.

Secondly: Though the strifes and jealousies of Jacob's wives were disgusting, yet we are not to attribute their desire of children, or the measures which it put them upon for obtaining them, to mere carnal motives. Had it been so, there is no reason to believe that the inspired writer would have condescended to narrate them. "It would," as an able writer observes, "have been below the dignity of such a sacred history as this is, to relate such things, if there had not been something of great consideration in them." The truth appears to be, they were influenced by the promises of God to Abraham; on whose posterity were entailed the richest blessings, and from whom the Messiah was in the fulness of time to descend. It was the belief of these promises that rendered every pious female in those times emulous of being a mother. Hence also both Leah and Rachel are represented as praying to God for this honour, and when children were given them, as acknowledging the favour to have proceeded from him. Ver. 17, 18, 22.

Thirdly: The measure which Jacob took to obtain the best of the cattle would at first sight appear to be selfish, and disingenuous; and if viewed as a mere human device, operating according to the established laws of nature, it would be so: but such it was not. As when unbelievers object to the curse of Noah upon his son, that it was the mere effect of revenge, we answer, let them curse those who displease them, and see whether any such effects will follow; so if they object to the conduct of Jacob as a crafty device, we might answer, let them make use of the same, if they be able. I believe it will not be pretended that any other person has since made the like experiment with success. It must therefore have been by a special direction of God, that he acted as he did.* And this will acquit him of selfishness, in the same manner as the divine command to the Israelites to borrow of the Egyptians acquits them of fraud. Both were extraordinary interpositions in behalf of the

* Chap. xxxi. 10—12.

injured; a kind of divine reprisal, in which justice was executed on a broad scale. And as the Egyptians could not complain of the Israelites, for that they had freely lent, or rather given them their jewels, without any expectation of receiving them again; so neither could Laban complain of Jacob, for that he had nothing more than it was freely agreed he should have; nor was he on the whole injured, but greatly benefited by Jacob's services.

Chap. xxxi. 1, 2. It is time for Jacob to depart; for though Laban has acknowledged, in the hope of detaining him, that the Lord had "blessed him for his sake;"* yet there is at this time much envy and evil-mindedness at work in the family against him, overlooking all their gains, and dwelling only upon his. Mercenary characters are not contented to prosper with others, but think much of every thing that goes beside themselves. If a poor tenant, or a servant thrive under them, they will soon be heard murmuring, "He hath taken away all that was ours, and of that which was ours hath he gotten all this glory." If Laban's sons only had murmured thus, Jacob might have borne it; but their father was of the same mind, and carried it unkindly towards him. He had been very willing to part

* Chap. xxx. 27.

with his daughters, more so indeed than he ought to have been; but Jacob's increase of cattle under him touches him in a tender part.

Ver. 3. The Lord had promised to "be with Jacob, and to keep him in all places whither he went;" and he makes good his promise. Like a watchful friend at his right hand, he observes his treatment, and warns him to depart. If Jacob had removed from mere personal resentment, or as stimulated only by a sense of injury, he might have sinned against God, though not against Laban. But when it was said to him, "Return unto the land of thy fathers, and to thy kindred, *and I will be with thee,*" his way was plain before him. In all our removals, it becomes us so to act as that we may hope for the divine presence and blessing to attend us; else, though we may flee from one trouble, we shall fall into many, and be less able to endure them.

Ver. 4—13. And now, being warned of God to depart, he sends for his wives into the field, where he might converse with them freely on the subject, without danger of being overheard. Had they been servants, it had been sufficient to have imparted to them his will; but being wives, they require a different treatment. There is an authority which scripture and nature give to the man over the woman; but every one who deserves the name of a man will exercise it with a gentleness and kindness that shall render it pleasant, rather than burdensome. He will consult with her as a friend, and satisfy her by giving the reasons of his conduct. Thus did Jacob to both his wives and who by such kind conduct forgot the differences between themselves, and cheerfully cast in their lot with him.

The reasons assigned for leaving were, partly the treatment of Laban, and partly the intimations from God. "I see your father's countenance, (says he) that it is not towards me as before." It is wisely ordered that the countenance shall in most cases be an index to the heart; else there would be much more deception in the world than there is. We gather more of men's disposition towards us from looks, than from words; and domestic happiness is more influenced by the one, than by the other. Sullen silence is often less tolerable than contention itself, because the latter, painful as it is, affords opportunity for mutual explanation.—But while Jacob had to complain of Laban's cloudy countenance, he could add, "The God of my father hath been with me." God's smiles are the best support under man's frowns: if we walk in the light of his countenance, we need not fear what man can do unto us. He then appeals to his wives, as to the faithfulness and diligence with which he had served their father, and the deceitful treatment he had met with in return. "Ye know, that with all my power I have served your father; and your father hath deceived me, and changed my wages ten times." Next he alleges the good hand of his God upon him, that he had not suffered him to hurt him; but in whatever form his wages were to be, had caused things in the end to turn to his account; and that the purport of this was revealed to him by a dream before it came to pass, in which he saw the cattle in those colours which were to distinguish them as his hire.—Moreover, that he had very lately had another dream,* in which the angel of God directed him to observe the fact as accomplished, of which he had before received only a pre-intimation; and accounted for it, saying, "I have seen all that Laban doeth unto thee." In alleging these things in his defence, Jacob said in effect, 'If your father's cattle have of late been given to me, it is not my doing, but God's, who hath seen my wrongs, and redressed them.'—

* I am aware that the dreams in verses 10, 11, are generally considered as one and the same. But those who thus consider them are not only obliged to interpret those as one which the text represents as two, but what is said by the angel in the 12th and 13th verses as two speeches, which manifestly appear to be one.

Finally: He alleges as the grand reason of his departure, the command of God. The same angel who had directed him to observe the accomplishment of his former dream, at the same time added, " I am the God of Bethel, where thou anointedst the pillar, and vowedst a vow unto me: now arise, get thee out from this land, and return unto the land of thy kindred."

Let us pause, and observe with attention this important passage. *I am the God of Bethel!* Such words could never have been uttered by a created angel; nor does the appearing in the form of an angel, or messenger, accord with the scripture account of God the Father: it must therefore have been the Son of God, whose frequent appearances to the patriarchs afforded a prelude to his incarnation. Paul, speaking of Christ in his preincarnate character, says, that *being in the form of God*, he thought it not robbery to be equal with God.* But to what does the apostle refer? When or where had he appeared equal with God? In such instances as these, no doubt, wherein he constantly spake of himself, and was spoken to by his servants, *as God;* and in a manner which evinces that he accounted it *no usurpation* of that which did not belong to him.

* Phil. ii. 6.

I am the God of Bethel! When at Bethel, the Lord said, *I am Jehovah, God of Abraham thy father, and the God of Isaac.** He might have said the same now; but it was his pleasure to direct the attention of his servant to the *last*, and to him the most interesting of his manifestations. By giving him hold of the last link in the chain, he would be in possession of the whole. The God of Bethel was the God of his fathers, Abraham and Isaac; the God who had entered into covenant with the former, had renewed it with the latter, and again renewed it with him. What satisfaction must it afford, to be directed by such a God!

It is also observable, that in directing Jacob's thoughts to the vision at Bethel, the Lord reminds him of those solemn acts of his own, by which he had at that time devoted himself to him —"I am the God of Bethel, *where thou anointedst the pillar, and vowedst a vow unto me.*" It is not only necessary that we be reminded of God's promises for our support in troubles, but of our own solemn engagements, that the same affections which distinguished the best seasons of our life may be renewed, and that in all our movements we may keep in view the end for which we live.—The object of the vow was, that *Jehovah*

* Chap. xxviii. 13.

should be his God; and whenever he should return, that *that stone should be God's house.* And now that the Lord commands him to return, he reminds him of his vow. He must not go to Canaan with a view to promote his own temporal interest, but to introduce the knowledge and worship of the true God. This was the great end which Jehovah had in view in all that he did for Abraham's posterity, and they must never lose sight of it.

Ver. 14—16. Jacob, having given the reasons for his proposed departure, paused. The women, without any hesitation, acquiesce, intimating that there was nothing in their father's house that should induce them to wish to stay in it. It is grievous to see the ties of nature dissolved in a manner by a series of selfish actions. I am not sure that Rachel or Leah were clear of this spirit towards their father: their words imply that they were sufficiently on their own side. Yet the complaints which they make of him were but too well founded. The sordid bargain which he had made with Jacob, exacting fourteen years labour from him as the price of his daughters, appears to have stung them at the time; and now that an opportunity offers, they speak their minds without reserve. They felt that they had been treated more like slaves than daughters, and that he had not consulted their happiness, any more than their husband's, but merely his own interest. Moreover, they accuse him of having "devoured all their money." Instead of providing for them as daughters, which the law of nature required,* he seems to have contrived to get all that private money which it is common to allow a son or a daughter while residing with their parents, into his hands, and had kept them in a manner pennyless. Hence they allege that all the riches which had been taken from him and given to their husband, were theirs, and their children's in right; and that God, knowing their injuries, had done this to redress them. Upon the whole, their mind is that Jacob should go, and they will go with him.

We have seen some things in the history of these women which have induced us to hope well of them, notwithstanding their many failings: but though in this case it was their duty to comply with the desire of their husband, and to own the hand of God in what had taken place between their father and him; yet there is something in their manner of expressing themselves that looks more like the spirit of the world, than the spirit which is of God. A right spirit would

* 2 Cor. xii. 14.

have taught them to remember that Laban, whatever was his conduct, was still their father. They might have felt it impossible to vindicate him; but they should not have expatiated on his faults in such a manner as to take pleasure in exposing them. Such conduct was but too much like that of Ham towards his father. And as to their acknowledging the hand of God in giving their father's riches to their husband, this is no more than is often seen in the most selfish characters, who can easily admire the divine providence when it goes in their favour. The ease however with which all men can discern what is just and equitable towards themselves, renders the love of ourselves a proper standard for the love of others, and will sooner or later stop the mouth of every sinner. Even those who have no written revelation have this divine law engraven on their consciences: they can judge with the nicest accuracy what is justice to them, and therefore cannot plead ignorance of what is justice from them to others.

DISCOURSE XL.

JACOB'S DEPARTURE FROM HARAN.

GENESIS xxxi. 17----55.

VER. 17—21. Jacob having consulted with his wives, and obtained their consent, the next step was to prepare for their departure. Had Laban known it, there is reason to fear he would either have detained him by force, or at least have deprived him of a part of his property. He must therefore, if possible, depart without his knowledge. At that time Laban was three day's journey from home, at a sheep-shearing. Jacob taking advantage of this, effected his escape. The women returning from the field, collected their matters together in a little time; and being all ready, Jacob rose up, set his family upon the camels, and with all his substance, set off for his father's house in the land of Canaan. Being apprehensive that Laban would pursue him, he passed over the Euphrates, and hastened on his way towards mount Gilead.

Gen. 31.] JACOB'S DEPARTURE. 49

I do not know that we can justly blame Jacob for this his sudden and secret departure: but when we read of Rachel's availing herself of her father's absence to "steal his images," a scene of iniquity opens to our view! What then, is the family of Nahor, who left the idolatrous Chaldees; the family to which Abraham and Isaac repaired, in marrying their children, to the rejection of the idolatrous Canaanites; is this family itself become idolaters? It is even so. But is Rachel, the beloved wife of Jacob, not only capable of stealing, but of stealing images? Some, reluctant to entertain such an opinion of her, have supposed she might take them away to prevent their ill effects on her father's family: but subsequent events are far from justifying such a supposition. It is a fact that these teraphim afterwards proved a snare to Jacob's family, and that he could not go up to Bethel till he had cleansed his house of them.* But had the family of Laban cast off the acknowledgement of Jehovah, the one true God? This does not appear, for they make frequent mention of him. Both Rachel and Leah on the birth of their children were full of apparently devout acknowledgements of him; and we were willing from thence to entertain a hope in favour of their piety. Laban also, notwithstanding his

* Chap. xxxv. 1—3.

keeping these images in his house, could afterwards invoke Jehovah to watch between him and Jacob. (ver. 49.) The truth seems to be, they were like some in after times, who *sware by the Lord, and by Malcham;** and others in our times, who are neither cold nor hot, but seem to wish to serve both God and mammon. The teraphim that Rachel stole were not public idols, set up in temples for worship; but, as some think, little images of them, a kind of household gods. Laban's family would probably have been ashamed of publicly accompanying the heathen to the worship of their gods; but they could keep images of them in their house, which implies a superstitious respect, if not a private homage paid to them.

This dividing of matters between the true God and idols has in all ages been a great source of corruption. A little before the death of Joshua, when Israel began to degenerate, it was in this way. They did not openly renounce the acknowledgement of Jehovah, but kept images of the idols in the countries round about them in their houses. Of this the venerable man was aware; and therefore, when they declared, saying, *We will serve Jehovah, for he is our God,* he answered, *Ye cannot serve Jehovah, for he is*

* Zeph. i. 5.

a holy God, he is a jealous God: he will not forgive your transgressions, nor your sins. And when they replied, *Nay, but we will serve Jehovah,* he answered, *Put away the strange gods that are among you:* as if he should say, You cannot serve God and your idols—If Jehovah be God, follow him; but if Baal, follow him. What is popery? It does not profess to renounce the true God; but abounds in images of Christ, and departed saints. What is the religion of great numbers among protestants, and even protestant dissenters? They will acknowledge the true God in words; but their hearts and houses are the abodes of spiritual idolatry. When a man, like Laban, gives himself up to covetousness, he has no room for God or true religion. The world is his god; and he has only to reside amongst gross idolaters, in order to be one, or at least a favourer of their abominations.

Ver. 22—30. The news of Jacob's abrupt departure was soon carried to Laban, who collecting all his force, immediately pursued him. It was seven days however, ere he came up with him. Without doubt, he meditated mischief. He would talk of his regard to his children and grand-children, and how much he was hurt in being prevented from taking leave of them: but that which lay nearest his heart was the substance which Jacob had taken with him. This, I conceive, he meant by some means to recover. And if he had by persuasion or force, induced the family to return, it had been only for the sake of this. But the night before he overtook Jacob, God appeared to him in a dream, and warned him not only against doing him harm, but even against "speaking to him," that is, on the subject of returning to Haran, "either good or bad." From this time his spirit was manifestly overawed, and his heart smitten as with a palsy. Overtaking Jacob at mount Gilead, he begins with him in rather a lofty tone, but faulters as he proceeds, dwelling upon the same charges over and over again. "What hast thou done, (said he) that thou hast stolen away unawares to me, and carried away my daughters as captives taken by the sword? Wherefore didst thou flee away secretly, and steal away from me, aud didst not tell me, that I might have sent thee away with mirth and with songs, with tabret and with harp? And hast not suffered me to kiss my sons and my daughters? Thou hast now done foolishly in so doing." In all this he means to insinuate that Jacob had no cause to leave him on account of any thing *he* had done; that where there was so much secresy there must be something dishonourable, and that in pursuing him, he was only moved by affection to his children. He adds, "It is in the power of my hand to do you hurt; but the God of your father spake unto me yesternight, saying, "Take thou heed that thou speak not to Jacob, either good or bad." Without doubt, Laban's company was much more powerful than that of Jacob, and he meant to impress this idea upon him, that his forbearance might appear to be the effect of generosity; nay, it is possible he might think he acted very religiously, in paying so much deference to the warning-voice of his God. He concludes by adding, "And now, though thou wouldest needs be gone, because thou sore longedst after thy father's house; yet wherefore hast thou stolen my gods?" The manner in which he accounts for his desire to be gone, has an appearance of candour and sympathy; but the design was to insinuate that it was not on account of any ill treatment he had received from *him*, and perhaps to give an edge to the heavy charge with which his speech is concluded. It was cutting to be accused of theft; more so of having stolen what he abhorred; and for the charge to be preferred by a man who wished to make every possible allowance, would render it more cutting still. Jacob felt it, and all his other accusations, as his answers sufficiently indicate.

Ver. 31, 32. With respect to the reiterated complaints of the *secresy* of his departure, Jacob answers all in a few words—It was " because I was afraid: for I said, peradventure thou wouldst take by force thy daughters from me." This was admitting his power, but impeaching his justice: and as *he* had dwelt only upon the taking away of his daughters, so *Jacob* in answer confines himself to them. Laban might feel for the loss of something else besides his daughters; and Jacob when he left Haran might be afraid for something else: but as the charge respected only them, it was sufficient that the answer corresponded to it. If by withholding the women he could have detained him and his substance, his former conduct proved that he would not have been to be trusted.—With respect to the gods, his answer is expressive of the strongest indignation. He will not deign to disown the charge; but desires that all his company might be searched, saying, "With whomsoever they are found, let him not live!" It was worthy of an upright man to feel indignant at the charge of stealing, and of a servant of God at that of stealing idols. But unless he had been as well assured of the innocence of all about him, as he was of his own, he ought not to have spoken as he did. His words might have proved a sorer trial to him than he was aware of.

Though Laban had not expressly charged him with fraud in any thing, except the gods; yet having dwelt so much upon the *privacy* of his departure, as to intimate a general suspicion, Jacob answers also in a general way : " Before our brethren, discern thou what is thine with me, and take it to thee." It was unpleasant to be thus pursued, accused, and searched; but it was all well. But for this, his uprightness would have appeared in a more suspicious light.

Ver. 33—42. Laban accepts the offer, and now begins to search. Going from tent to tent he hopes to find at least his gods. Rachel's policy, however, eludes his vigilance: " He searched, but found not the images." No mention is made of his going amongst the cattle, which proves he had no suspicion of being wronged in respect of them. During the search, Jacob looked on, and said nothing : but when nothing was found that could justify the heavy charges which had been preferred against him, his spirit was provoked. " He was wroth, and chode with Laban." Hard words, and cutting interrogations follow. " What is my trespass, and what is my sin, that thou hast so hotly pursued after me? Whereas thou hast searched all my stuff, what hast thou found of all thy houshold stuff? Set it here before my brethren, and thy brethren, that they may judge betwixt us both!" He goes on, and takes a review of his whole conduct towards him for twenty years past, and proves that he had been very hardly dealt with, summing up his answer in these very emphatic terms —"Except the God of my father, the God of Abraham, and the fear of Isaac had been with me," notwithstanding all thy talk of sending me away with mirth and with songs, with tabret and with harp, " surely thou hadst sent me away now empty. God hath seen mine affliction, and the labour of mine hands, and rebuked thee yesternight!" Laban made a merit of obeying the dream; but Jacob improves it into an evidence of his evil design, for which God had " rebuked" him, and pleaded the cause of the injured.

Ver. 43—53. Laban, whose spirit was checked before he began, was now confounded. He quite gives up the cause, and wishes to make up matters as well as he can. He cannot help prefacing his wish, however, with a portion of vain boasting, and affected generosity. "These daughters are my daughters, and these children my children, and these cattle my cattle, and all that thou hast is mine: and what can I do this day unto these my daughters, or unto their children which they have borne?" As if he had said, ' Yes, yes, God hath given you many things; but remember they were all mine, and you have obtained them under me. Let us have no more disputes however; for though I am come so far, and possess so great a force, yet how can I find in my heart to hurt my own children? Come therefore, and let us make a covenant, and be good friends.'

Jacob makes no reply to Laban's boasting, but lets it pass: and though he had felt so keenly, and spoken so warmly, yet he consents to a covenant of peace. Anger may rise in the breast of a wise man; but it *resteth* only *in the bosom of fools.* He said nothing; but expressed his mind by actions. He first "took a stone, and set it up for a pillar;" then said to his brethren, "Gather stones: and they took stones, and made a heap, and did eat together," in token of reconciliation, upon it. This done, Laban called it "Jegar-sahadutha," and Jacob "Galeed;" the one was the Syriac, and the other the Hebrew word for the same thing; that is, *the heap of witness.* It was also called "Mizpah," *a beacon,* or *watch-tower.* The meaning of these names in reference to the present case is explained by Laban, as being the elder man, and the leading party in the covenant. "This heap, said he, is a *witness* between me and thee this day—Jehovah *watch* between me and thee, when we are absent one from another. If thou shalt afflict my daughters, or if thou shalt take other wives besides my daughters, no man is with us: see, God is witness betwixt me and thee." To this he added, " Behold this heap, and behold this pillar—this heap be witness, and this pillar be witness, that I will not pass over this heap to thee, and that thou shalt not pass over this heap and this pillar unto me, for harm. The God of Abraham, and the God of Nahor, the God of their father judge betwixt us." To this covenant Jacob fully assented, and sware by the fear of his father Isaac; that is, by the God whom Isaac feared.

We are surprised to hear a man who had been seven days in pursuit of certain stolen gods, speak so much, and in so solemn a manner about Jehovah: but wicked men will on some occasions utter excellent words. After all, he could not help manifesting his attachment to idolatry. When speaking to Jacob of Jehovah, he calls him "the God of *your* father," in a manner as if he was not *his* God; and in swearing to the solemn covenant which had been made between them, he does not appear to have invoked Jehovah as the *only* true God. It is very observable, that though he makes mention of "the God of Abraham," yet it is in connexion with "Nahor," and their father, i. e. Terah: but when Abraham was with Nahor and Terah, they were idolaters. To this purpose we read in Joshua: *Thus saith the Lord God of Israel; Your fathers dwelt on the other side of the flood in old time, even Terah the father of Abraham, and the father of Nahor; and they served other gods.** "The God of Abraham, and Nahor, and Terah," therefore, were words capable of a very ill construction. Nor does Jacob appear to be ignorant of Laban's design in thus referring to their early ancestors; and therefore, that he might bear an unequivocal testimony against all idolatry, even that of Abraham in his younger years, he would swear only by "the fear of his father Isaac," who had never worshipped any other than the true God. It were worth while for those who plead for *antiquity* as a mark of the true church, to consider that herein they follow the example of Laban, and not of Jacob.

Ver. 54, 55. Laban had professed his regret that he had not an opportunity to enjoy a day of feasting and of mirth at parting with his children. Such a parting would hardly have been seemly, even in a family which had no fear of God before their eyes. Jacob however makes a *religious* feast previous to the departure of

* Joshua xxiv. 2.

his father-in-law. " He offered sacrifices upon the mount Galeed, and called his brethren," that is the whole company, " to eat bread: and they did eat bread, and tarried all night in the mount. And early in the morning Laban rose up, and kissed his sons and his daughters, and blessed them: and Laban departed, and returned unto his place." This parting proved final. We hear no more of Laban, nor of the family of Nahor. They might for several ages retain some knowledge of Jehovah; but mixing with it the superstitions of the country, they would in the end sink into gross idolatry, and be lost among the heathens.

On observing the *place* from which Balaam the son of Beor is said to have been sent for to curse Israel, namely, *Pethor* of Mesopotamia,* or *Aram*,† or as it is frequently called *Padan-aram*, and that it is the same with that in which Laban dwelt, I have been inclined to think he might be one of his descendants. He is supposed to have lived about two hundred and eighty years after Jacob's departure from that country, which in those ages would not include above two or three generations. The opinion of ancient jewish writers, though often fabulous, yet when agreeing with what is otherwise pro-

* Deut. xxiii. 4. † Num. xxiii. 7.

bable, may serve to strengthen it. "The Targum of Jonathan on Num. xxii. 5, and the Targum on 1 Chron. i. 44, make Balaam to be Laban himself; and others say he was the son of Beor, the son of Laban."* The first of these opinions, though in itself utterly incredible, yet may so far be true as to hit upon the family from which he descended; and the last, allowing perhaps for a defect of one generation, appears to me to be highly probable.—Add to this, the teraphim, or images which Laban kept in his house, and which he would doubtless replace on his return, are supposed to be a sort of "talismans, were consulted as oracles, and in high esteem with the Chaldeans, and Syrians, a people given to astrology, and by which they made their divinations. Hos. iii. 4. Zech. x. 2."† According to this, Balaam the soothsayer would only tread in the steps of his ancestors; not utterly disowning Jehovah, but devoted to the abominations of the heathen.

If the above remarks be just, they shew in a strong point of light *the progress of apostasy and corruption.* Laban imitated the corruptions of his ancestors, some of whom were good men; and his decendants improved upon him. Thus you will often see a man who has descended

* See *Gill* on Num. xxii. 5.   † Ibid. Gen. xxxi. 19.

from religious parents, but whose heart is entirely taken up with the world: He keeps up the forms of godliness, though he denies the power; but mixes with them all the evil that he can rake up from the examples of his forefathers, with considerable additions of his own. The next generation improves upon him, having less of the form of religion, and more conformity to the world. The third throws off both the form and the power, retaining no vestige of the religion of their ancestors, excepting a few speculative notions, learnt from a few old books and sayings, and which have no other influence upon them than to enable them to be more wicked than their neighbours, by sinning against somewhat of superior light. How important is it for good men to act in character in their families, inasmuch as every evil which they practise will be re-acted and encreased by their carnal posterity!

DISCOURSE XLI.

JACOB's FEAR OF ESAU—HIS WRESTLING WITH THE ANGEL.

GENESIS xxxii.

Ver 1, 2. The sacred writer, pursuing the history of Jacob, informs us that he went on his way, and the angels of God met him.

And when he saw them, he said, "This is God's house: and he called the name of that place Mahanaim." That the angels of God are *ministering spirits, sent forth to minister for them who shall be heirs of salvation,* is truth clearly revealed in the scriptures: but this their ministry has seldom been rendered visible to mortals. *The angel of Jehovah,* it is said, *encampeth round about them that fear him, and delivereth them.* But I do not recollect that any of these celestial guardians have *appeared* in this character to the servants of God, except in times of *imminent danger.* When a host of Syrians encompassed Dothan, in order to take Elisha, his servant was alarmed, and exclaimed, *Alas, master, how shall we do?* The prophet answered, *Fear not: for they that be with us are more than they that be with them.* Yet there was no earthly force to protect them. But when in answer to the prophet's prayer, *the young man's eyes were opened, he saw the mountain full of horses, and chariots of fire round about Elisha.** In this case God's hosts became visible, to allay the fear of man's hosts. Thus it was also in the present instance. Jacob had just escaped one host of enemies, and another is coming forth to meet him. At this juncture God's host makes its appearance, teaching him to whom he owed his late escape, and

* 2 Kings vi. 17.

that he who had delivered, did deliver, and he might safely trust would deliver him. The angels which appeared on this occasion are called God's host, in the singular: but by the name which Jacob gave to the place, it appears that they were divided into two, encompassing him as it were before and behind; and this would correspond with the two hosts of adversaries, which at the same time, and with almost the same violent designs, were coming against him; the one had already been sent back without striking a blow, and the other should be the same. This however was not expressly revealed to Jacob, but merely a general account afforded him: for it was not the design of God to supersede other means, but to save him in the use of them.

Ver. 3—5. Jacob has as yet heard nothing of his brother Esau, except that he had settled "in the land of Seir, the country of Edom;" but knowing what had formerly taken place, and the temper of the man, he is apprehensive of consequences. He therefore resolves on sending messengers before him, in order to sound him, and if possible to appease his anger. These messengers are instructed what they shall say, and how they shall conduct themselves on their arrival, all in a way to conciliate. "Thus shall ye speak unto my lord Esau. Thy servant Jacob saith thus: I have sojourned with Laban, and staid there until now. And I have oxen, and asses, flocks, and men-servants, and women-servants: and I have sent to tell my lord, that I may find grace in thy sight."—Observe, (1.) He declines the honour of precedency given him in the blessing, calling Esau "his *lord*." Isaac had said to him, "Be lord over thy brethren, and let thy mother's sons bow down to thee:" but Jacob either understood it of spiritual ascendency, or if of temporal, as referring to his posterity rather than him. He therefore declines all disputes on that head.—(2.) He would have him know that he was not come to claim the *double portion*, nor even to divide with him his father's inheritance; for that God had given him plenty of this world's goods without it. Now as these were the things which had so greatly provoked Esau, a relinquishment of them would tend more than any thing to conciliate him.

Ver. 6—12. The messengers had not proceeded far, ere they met Esau coming forth to meet his brother Jacob, and four hundred men with him! It would seem by the account, that they went and delivered their message to him. But however that was, they appear to have been struck with the idea that he was coming with a hostile design, and therefore quickly returned, and informed their master of particulars. We are surprised that Jacob's journey, which had taken him but about a fortnight, and had been conducted with so much secresy, should yet have been known to Esau. His thirst for revenge must have prompted him to great vigilance. One would think he had formed connexions with persons who lived in the way, and engaged them to give him information of the first movements of his brother. However this was, "Jacob was greatly afraid," and even "distressed." This term with us is sometimes lightly applied to the state of mind produced by ordinary troubles; but in the scriptures it denotes a sore strait, from which there seems to be no way of escape. This distress would probably be heightened by the recollection of his sin, which first excited the resentment of Esau. There is no time however to be lost. But what can he do? Well, let us take notice what a good man will do in a time of distress, that we may, as occasion requires, follow his example.—First: He uses all possible precaution, "dividing the people that were with him, and the flocks, and herds, and camels, into two bands; saying, If Esau come to the one company and smite it, then the other company which is left shall escape." Secondly: He bebetakes himself to prayer; and as this is one of the scripture examples of successful prayer, we shall do well to take particular notice of it.—Observe, (1.) He approaches God *as the God of his father;* and *as such, a God in covenant.* " Oh God of my father Abraham, and God of my father Isaac!" This was laying hold of the divine faithfulness: it was the prayer of faith. We may not have exactly the same plea in our approaches to God; but we have one that is more endearing, and more prevalent. The God and Father of our Lord Jesus Christ, is a character which excites more hope, and in which more great and precious promises have been made than in the other.—(2.) As *his own God,* pleading what he had promised to *him*—" Jehovah who saidst unto me, return unto thy country, and to thy kindred, and I will deal well with thee." Jehovah has never made promises to us in the same extraordinary way as he did to Jacob: but whatever he hath promised to believers in general, may be pleaded by every one of them in particular, especially when encountering opposition in the way which he hath directed them to go.—(3.) While he celebrates the great mercy and truth of God towards him, he acknowledges himself *unworthy* of the least instance of either. The worthiness of *merit* is what every good man, in every circumstance, must disclaim: but that which he has in view, I conceive, is that of *meetness.* Looking back to his own unworthy conduct, especially that which preceded and occasioned his passing over Jordan with a " staff " only in his hand, he is affected with the returns of mercy and truth which he had met with from a gracious God. By sin he had reduced himself in a manner to nothing; but God's goodness had made him great. As we desire to succeed in our approaches to God, we must be sure to take low ground; humbling ourselves in the dust before him, and sueing for relief as a matter of mere grace.— Finally: Having thus prefaced his petition, he now presents it. " Deliver me, I pray thee, from the hand of my brother, from the hand of Esau; for I fear him, lest he will come and smite me, and the mother with the children." This was doubtless the petition of a kind husband, and a tender father: it was not as such only, nor principally however, but as a believer in the promises, that he presented it: the great stress of the prayer turns on this hinge. It was as though he had said, ' If my life, and that of the mother, with the children, be cut off, how are thy promises to be fulfilled?' Hence he adds, " And thou saidst, I will surely do thee good, and make thy *seed* as the sand of the sea, which cannot be numbered for multitude." It is natural for us as husbands and as parents to be importunate with God for the well-being of those who are so nearly related to us: but the way to obtain mercy for them is to seek it in subordination to the divine glory.

Gen. 32.] JACOB'S FEAR OF ESAU. 69

Ver. 13—30. Jacob and his company seem now to have been north of the river Jabbok, near to the place where it falls into the Jordan. Here he is said to have "lodged that night." Afterwards we read of his "rising up," and sending his company "over the ford."* Probably it was during one single night that the whole of what follows in this chapter occurred. The messengers having returned towards evening, he divided his company into two bands, and then committed his cause to God. After this he halted for the night: but whatever sleep might fall to the lot of the children, or rest to the beasts of burden, there was but little of either for him. First, he resolves neither to flee, nor fight; but to try the effect of *a present.* Upwards of five hundred head of cattle were sent off in the night, under the care of his servants; and to produce the greater effect, they were divided into droves, with a space between drove and drove. Having sent off the present, he seems to have tried to get a little rest: but not being able to sleep, he "rose up," and took his whole family, and all that he had, and sent them over the ford of Jabbok. Every servant presenting his drove in the same words, would strike Esau with amasement. It would seem as if all the riches of the east were coming to him: and every one

* Verse 22.

concluding by announcing his master as coming behind them, would work upon his generosity. He expected, it is likely, a host of armed men, and felt resolved to fight it out: but instead of an army, here is a present worthy of a prince, and the owner coming after it with all the confidence of a friend, and kindness of a brother.

Whether he thought it would express more friendship, and be better taken, to be at the trouble of crossing the ford in order to meet Esau, than to oblige Esau to cross it in order to meet him; or whatever was his reason, so he acted: and the family being all over the river, "he himself staid behind." Here it was that he met with that extraordinary appearance on which he wrestled with the angel, and prevailed. The account is as follows—"And Jacob was left alone; and there wrestled a man with him until the breaking of the day. And when he saw that he prevailed not against him, he touched the hollow of his thigh; and the hollow of Jacob's thigh was out of joint, as he wrestled with him. And he said, Let me go, for the day breaketh. And he said, I will not let thee go, except thou bless me. And he said unto him, What is thy name? And he said, Jacob. And he said, Thy name shall be called no more Jacob, but Israel; (that is, a *prince of God)* for as a prince hast thou power with God and with men, and hast prevailed. And Jacob asked him, and said, Tell me, I pray thee, thy name: and he said, Wherefore is it that thou dost ask after my name? And he blessed him there. And Jacob called the name of the place Peniel: for I have seen God face to face, and my life is preserved."

On this singular manifestation of God to his servant, we offer the following remarks:—(1.) It does not appear to be a vision, but a literal transaction. A personage, in the form of a man, really wrestled with him, and permitted him to prevail so far as to gain his object.—(2.) Though the form of the struggle was corporeal, yet the essence and object of it were spiritual. An inspired commentator on this wrestling says, "He wept and made supplication to the angel."* That for which he strove was a blessing, and he obtained it.—(3.) The personage with whom he strove is here called "a man," and yet in seeing him, Jacob said, "I have seen God face to face, and my life is preserved." Hosea, in reference to his being a messenger of God to Jacob, calls him "the angel:" yet he also describes the patriarch as having "power with God." Upon the whole, there can be no doubt but that it was the same divine personage who appeared to him

* Hosea xii. 4.

at Bethel, and at Padan-aram; who *being in the form of God,* again thought it no usurpation to appear *as God.*—(4.) What is here recorded had relation to Jacob's distress, and may be considered as an answer to his evening supplications. By his "power with God," he had "power with men:" Esau, and his hostile company, were conquered at Peniel.—(5.) The change of his name from "Jacob" to "Israel," and the "blessing" which followed, signified that he was no longer to be regarded as having obtained it by *supplanting* his brother, but as a *prince of God,* who had wrestled with him for it, and prevailed. It was thus that the Lord pardoned his sin, and wiped away his reproach. It is observable too, that this is the name by which his posterity are afterwards called.—Finally: The whole transaction furnishes an instance of believing, importunate, and successful prayer. As Jacob would not let the angel go, except he blessed him, and as the latter, though to convince him of his power he touched the hollow of his thigh, and put it out of joint, yet suffered himself to be overcome by him; so every true Israelite pleads the promises of God, with an importunity that will take no denial, and God is pleased to suffer himself in this manner to be as it were overcome.

Ver. 30—32. What a night was this to Jacob! What a difference between what he felt the past evening, on the return of the messengers, and what he now felt! Well might he wonder and exclaim, "I have seen God face to face, and my life is preserved!" Passing over Peniel, however, to rejoin his family, just as the sun rose upon him, "he halted upon his thigh." This would be a memorial to him of his own weakness, as well as of the power and goodness of God, who instead of touching a single part, might, as he intimated, have taken away his "life." The law which afterwards prevailed in Israel, of not eating of the sinew which shrank, might be of divine origin, as it corresponds with the genius of the ceremonial economy.

DISCOURSE XLII.

JACOB's INTERVIEW WITH ESAU, AND ARRIVAL IN CANAAN.

GENESIS xxxiii.

Ver. 1—4. No sooner had Jacob passed over the ford of Jabbok, and rejoined his family, but lifting up his eyes, he saw his brother approaching him, and four hundred men with him. He hast just time before he comes up, to arrange his family, placing the children with their respective mothers, and those last for whom he has the tenderest affection. This circumstance shews that though he treated Esau with the fullest confidence, yet he was still secretly afraid of him. He must however put the best face he can upon it, and go on to meet him. This he does; and as he had by his messengers acknowledged him as his "lord," so he will do the same by "bowing down to him." His object was to satisfy him that he made no claim of that kind of pre-eminence which the other's heart was set upon, but freely gave it up. And this seems to have had the desired effect on Esau's mind; for though he did not bow in return to his brother, since that had been relinquishing his superiority; yet "he ran to meet him, and embraced him, and fell on his neck, and kissed him:" nor could such an unexpected meeting fail to dissolve both of them in tears! It is pleasant and affecting to see the bitter heart of Esau thus melted by a kind and yielding conduct. We must not forget that God's hand was in it, who turneth the hearts of men as rivers of water: but neither must we overlook the means by which it was effected. *A soft tongue,* saith Solomon, *breaketh the bone.** On which our commentator *Henry* remarks, with his usual pith, "Hard words, we say, break no bones, and therefore we should

* Prov. xxv. 15.

bear them patiently; but it seems soft words do, and therefore we should, on all occasions, give them prudently." Treat men as friends, and you make them so. Pray but as Jacob did, and be as obliging and condescending as he was, and you will go through the world by it.

Ver. 5—7. The two brothers having wept over each other, Esau, lifting up his eyes, saw the women and children, and enquired who they were? Jacob's answer is worthy of him. It savours of the fear of God which ruled in his heart, and taught him to acknowledge him even in the ordinary concerns of life. They are, saith he, " the children which God hath graciously given thy servant." " Then the handmaidens came near, they and their children, and they bowed themselves. And Leah also, with her children, came near, and bowed themselves: and after came Joseph near, and Rachel, and they bowed themselves." Had this been done to Jacob, methinks he would have answered, *God be gracious unto you my children!* But we must take Esau as he is, and rejoice that things are as they are. We have often occasion to be thankful for civilities, where we can find nothing like religion. One cannot help admiring the uniformly good behaviour of all Jacob's family. If one of them had failed, it might have undone all the good which his ingratiating conduct had done: but to their honour it is recorded, they all acted in unison with him. When the head of a family does right, and the rest follow his example, every thing goes on well.

Ver. 8. But Esau desires to know the meaning of these droves of cattle being sent to him. The answer is, "These are to find grace in the sight of my lord." This would express how high a value he set upon his favour, and how much he desired to be reconciled to him; and so tended to conciliate. We might, in most cases, purchase peace and good-will from men at a much cheaper rate than this; a few shillings, nay often, only a few kind words would do it: and yet we see for the want of these, strifes, contentions, law-suits, and I know not what evil treatment, even between those who ought to love as brethren. But if the favour of man be thus estimable, how much more that of God? Yet no worldly substance, nor good deeds of ours, are required as the price of this; but merely the receiving of it as a free gift, through Him who hath given himself a sacrifice to obtain the consistent exercise of it towards the unworthy.

Ver. 9—11. The reply of Esau to this obliging answer was, "I have enough, my brother, keep that thou hast unto thyself." There might be in this language pretty much of a high spirit of independence. Whatever effect Jacob's present had had upon him, he would not be thought to be influenced by any thing of that kind; especially as he had great plenty of his own. Jacob, however, continued to urge it upon him, not as if he thought he needed it, but as a token of good-will, and of his desire to be reconciled. He did not indeed make use of this term, nor of any other that might lead to the recollection of their former variance. He did not say that he should consider the acceptance of his present as a proof that he was cordially reconciled to him: but what he did say, though more delicately expressed, was to the same effect. Such I conceive to be the import of the terms, "If now I have found grace in thy sight, then receive my present at my hand." The receiving of a present at another's hand is perhaps one of the greatest proofs of reconciliation. Every one is conscious that he could not receive a present at the hand of an enemy. And upon this principle no offerings of sinful creatures can be accepted of God, till they are reconciled to him by faith in the atonement of his Son. To find grace in the sight of Esau, and to have his present accepted as a token of it, was the desire of Jacob. To these ends he further assures him how highly his favour was accounted of, and that to have seen his face in the manner he had, was to him next to seeing "the face of God." This was strong language, and doubtless it was expressive of strong feelings. Reconciliation with those whom we have long been at variance with, especially when it was through our own misconduct, is, as to its effect upon the mind, next to reconciliation with God.—Finally: He entreats him to accept what he had presented, as his "blessing;" (so a present was called when accompanied with love, or good will*) and the rather because God had graciously blessed him, and given him "enough;" nay more, had given him *all things*. Esau on this accepted it; and as far as we know, the reconciliation was sincere and lasting.

Ver. 12—15. Esau proposes to be going, and to guard his brother and his family through the country. The proposal was doubtless very friendly, and very honourable; and appears to have contained an invitation of Jacob and his family to his house in Seir: but Jacob respectfully declines it, on account of the feebleness of the cattle, and of the children. There is no reason that I know of for supposing Jacob had any other motive than that which he alleged; and this is

* See Joshua xv. 19. 1 Sam. xxv. 27. 2 Kings v. 15.

expressive of his gentleness as a shepherd, and his tenderness as a father. There are many persons with whom we may wish to be on good terms, who nevertheless, on account of a difference of character, taste or manners, would be very unsuitable companions for us. Jacob proposes going to Seir after his arrival; and this he probably did, though we read not of it. We have no account of his visiting his father Isaac till he had been several years in Canaan; yet to suppose him capable of such a neglect, were not only injurious to his character, but contrary to what is implied by Deborah, one of Isaac's family, being found in his house at the time of her death.* Esau's first proposal being declined, he next offers to leave a part of his men, as a guard to Jacob's company: but this also he respectfully declines, on the ground of its being unnecessary; adding, "Let me find grace in the sight of my lord"—which I conceive was equal to saying, Let me have thy favour, and it is all I desire.

Ver. 16—20. The two brothers having parted friendly, Esau returns to Seir, and Jacob journeyed to a place east of Jordan, where he stopped awhile, and built a house for his family, and booths for his cattle. Upon this spot a city

* Chap. xxxv. 8.

was afterwards built, and called "Succoth;" that is, *booths*, from the circumstance above related.* He did not stop here however with a design to abide; for he was commanded to return " to the land of his kindred," that is to Canaan, and he was as yet not in Canaan: but finding it a country abounding with rich pasture, he might wish to refresh his herds, and take time for enquiry into a more suitable place for a continued residence. Hence when after this he passed over Jordan, and "came to Shalem, a city of Shechem, in the land of Canaan," it is said to be " when he came from Padan-aram;" intimating that till then he had not arrived at the end of his journey. " Shalem" is considered by *Ainsworth*, and some others, not as the name of a city, but as a term denoting the *peace and safety* with which Jacob arrived. Hence they render it, " He came *in safety*, or *in peace*, to the city of Shechem." It is an argument in favour of this translation, that we have no account of a city called Shalem near to Shechem. All agree that it could not be the place where Melchizedek reigned, as it was forty miles distant from it; and as to that near Enon, where John was baptising,† it was not in the neighbourhood of Shechem, but of Jordan. This rendering also gives additional propriety and force to the phrase, "When he

* Josh. xiii. 27. Judges viii. 5. † John iii. 23.

came from Padan-aram." It is a declaration to the honour of him who had said, "Behold, I am with thee, and will keep thee in all places whither thou goest, and will bring thee again into this land." He arrived *in peace* at his journey's end, notwithstanding the dangers and difficulties he met with by the way.

Shechem, before which Jacob pitched his tent, was a city called after the name of the son of Hamor, its king, of whom we shall presently hear more. It is the same place as that which in the new testament is called *Sychar*.* Here he bought "a parcel of a field," that neither he nor his cattle might trespass on the property of others. This field was afterwards taken from him, it should seem, by the Amorites; and he was under the necessity of recovering it *by his sword and his bow;* which having accomplished, he bequeathed it to his son Joseph. I have sometimes thought that this parcel of ground might be designed to exhibit a specimen of the whole land of Canaan. When the Most High divided to the nations their inheritance, he marked out an allotment for the children of Israel:† but the Canaanites taking possession of it, were obliged to be dispossessed by the rightful owners, with the sword and with the bow.

* John iv. 5. † Deut. xxxii. 8.

But that which requires the most particular notice, is, that "he erected there an altar, and called it El-elohe-Israel;" i. e. *God, the God of Israel.* It was worthy of this great and good man publicly to acknowledge God, after so many signal deliverances, and soon after his arrival. His first purchasing a piece of ground, and "there" erecting his altar, was like saying, Whenever this whole country shall be in possession of my posterity, let it in this manner be devoted to God. Nay, it was as if he had then taken possession of it in the name of the God of Israel, by setting up his standard in it. It is the first time also in which he is represented as availing himself of his *new name,* and of the *covenant blessing* conferred upon him under it. The name given to the altar was designed, no doubt, to be a memorial of both; and whenever he should present his offerings upon it, to revive all those sentiments which he had felt when wrestling with God at Peniel. It were no less happy for us, than consistent with our holy profession, if every distinguishing turn of our lives were distinguished by renewed resignations of ourselves to God. Such times and places would serve as memorials of mercy, and enable us to recover those thoughts and feelings which we possessed in our happiest days.

DISCOURSE XLIII.

DINAH DEFILED, AND THE SHECHEMITES MURDERED.

GENESIS xxxiv.

The arrival of Jacob in Canaan promised fair for a holy and happy residence in it. Laban no more oppresses him, and the breach between him and his brother Esau is healed. But alas, foreign troubles being removed, domestic ones take place of them. He had but one daughter, and she is defiled. He had many sons, and the greater part of them are deceitful and cruel. What with the conduct of the one, and the other, his heart must be sorely grieved. It was not however till he had lived six or seven years in the neighbourhood of Shechem that these troubles came upon him; for in less time than this the two brethren could not have arrived at man's estate: and there is reason to believe that from his first settlement at this place, his mind began to sink into a state of spiritual declension. One would think, if he had had a proper sense of things, he could not have continued so long to expose a family of young people to the contageous influence of a heathen city. It was next to the conduct of Lot, when he took up his residence in Sodom.

Ver. 1, 2. It is natural to suppose that the younger branches of the family, hearing every thing that was going on among the youth of the place, would think it hard if they must not go amongst them. Whether the sons formed acquaintances among the Shechemites, we know not; but Dinah on a certain occasion, must needs " go out to see the daughters of the land." She wished no doubt to be acquainted with them, to see and be seen of them, and to do as they did. It might not be to a ball, nor a card party; but I presume it was to some merry-making of this kind: and though the daughters of the land were her professed companions, yet the sons of the land must have assembled with them, else how came Shechem there? Young people, if you have any regard for your parents, or for yourselves, beware of such parties! The consequence was what might have been expected. Shechem was the son of the " prince of the country," and men of rank and opulence are apt to think themselves entitled to do any thing which their inclinations prompt them to. The young woman was inexperienced, and unused to company of this kind; she therefore fell an easy prey to the seducer. But could Dinah have gone without the consent, or connivance of her parents, at least of one of them? We should think she could not. I fear Leah was not clear in this matter.

Ver. 3, 4. The story is such as must needs excite indignation: some circumstances, however, bad as it is, tend in a certain degree to alleviate it. The young man is not like Amnon by Tamar: he is attached to her, and applies to his father Hamor to obtain her for him to wife. Had this been done at first, all had been honourable: but a bad beginning seldom admits of a good ending. And though a respectful application was immediately made to the parents of the damsel, yet she herself was at the same time detained in Shechem's house. But let us observe the effect of this disgraceful transaction.

Ver. 5—24. The news soon reached Jacob's ear. His sons were in the field: he felt much no doubt, but said nothing till they returned. He did not however foresee what would follow, or he would not have reserved the utterance of his grief to them. But probably he knew not what to do. If Leah had connived at her daughter's visit, he would not know how to speak to her; and as to Rachel, the jealousies between the sisters might prevent his speaking freely to the one on the concerns of the other. So he held his peace till his sons should return. Meanwhile, Hamor, and it seems his son with him, came out of the city to Jacob, to commune with him on the subject, and to ask the young woman in marriage. It had been well if he and Jacob had settled it; and this to all appearance they might have done; but scandal, with its swift wings, reaching the young men in the field, brought them home before the usual time; so that Hamor and his son had scarcely entered Jacob's door, ere they followed them. Had Jacob and Hamor conversed the matter over by themselves, or Jacob and his sons by themselves, their anger might have been somewhat abated: but all meeting together, there was no vent for the first strong feelings of the mind; and such feelings when suppressed, like subterraneous fires, must find their way, and very commonly issue in some dreadful explosion. The young men said little, but thought the more. The real state of their minds is thus described—" And the men were grieved, and they were very wroth, because he had wrought folly in Israel in lying with Jacob's daughter, which thing ought not to be done." There certainly was cause for great displeasure; and provided it had been directed against the sin, frankly avowed, and kept within the limits of equity, great displeasure ought to have been manifested. Light as heathens, and other wicked men, may make of fornication, it is an evil and a bitter thing. To the honour of Jacob and his posterity, he that was guilty of it amongst them, was said to have " wrought folly in Israel," and to have done that which "ought not to be done." It might be from the present early example that this phraseology became proverbially descriptive of a fornicator;* and a great advantage it must be to any people where the state of society is so far influenced by principles of honour and chastity, as by common consent to brand such characters with infamy. It was proper that the brothers of the young woman should be " grieved:" it was not unnatural that they should be " wroth:" but wherefore did they feel thus strongly? Was it for the sin committed against God, or only for the shame of it in respect of the family? Here alas, they failed; and this it was that prompted them to all their other wickedness. Jacob was grieved, and displeased, as well as they; but his grief and displeasure wrought not in the manner theirs did. The reserve which they assumed while Hamor and his son were speaking, concealed behind it the most deadly resentment. They heard all that was said; (and many fine things were said, both by the father as a politician, in favour of intermarriages between the

* 2 Sam. xiii. 12.

families in general, and by the son as a lover, in order to gain the damsel) they heard it, I say, with much apparent coolness, and stated their objections in a manner as if there was nothing between them but the compliance with a certain ceremony, and as though they felt nothing for their sister that should hinder their entering into a covenant of peace with him who had seduced her. But all was "deceit;" a mere cover to a bloody design which they appear to have formed for the purpose of revenge; "because he had defiled Dinah their sister."

The deceitful proposal however succeeded: "their words pleased Hamor, and Shechem, Hamor's son." So they go about forthwith to persuade the citizens into a compliance with them; not as a matter of principle, but of policy, as a measure which would contribute to the country's good. They also succeed; the Shechemites are circumcised; and all seems to bid fair for an amicable issue.

But let us pause, and reflect on the right and wrong in these transactions. What was the line of conduct that Hamor and Shechem should have pursued? They ought no doubt, in the first place, to have restored the young woman to her parents; and at the same time to have acknowledged the great injury done to her, and to the family, and expressed their sorrow on account of it. Till they had done this, they had no reason to expect any thing like reconciliation on the part of Jacob, or his sons. But it is likely the young man being of so honourable a family, and the sin of fornication being so common in the country, made them think these punctilios might be dispensed with in the present instance. And being wholly under the influence of sensual and worldly motives, they are prepared to profess any religion, or profane any institution, however sacred, so that they may accomplish their selfish ends.—But what was the line of conduct which ought to have been pursued by Jacob and his sons? If the one had taken a greater share in the conversation, and the other a less, it had been more to the honour of both; and might not have issued in the manner it did. It is very proper for brothers to consider themselves as guardians of a sister's honour; but not in such a way as to supersede the authority, or silence the counsel of a father. The answer to the question, whether Dinah should be given in marriage to Shechem, belonged to the parents, and not to the brothers. With respect to the displeasure which required to be expressed, it ought to have been confined to words; and if the proposed marriage could not be acceeded to, they should, as they said, have "taken their sister, and been gone." As to their objection on the score of circumcision, there appears to have been no such law established as yet in Jacob's family. It is true, they were discouraged from marrying with the devotees of idolatry; but the circumcision of the Shechemites was merely a form; and had they been suffered to live, would have produced no change in respect of this. Could they indeed have been induced to renounce their idolatrous practices, and to cast in their lot with Israel, the good had overbalanced the evil: but religion was no part of the young men's concern: the whole was a mere pretence, to cover their malignant designs.

Ver. 25—29. The result was shocking. Simeon and Levi, two of Dinah's brethren by the same mother, as well as father, availing themselves of the present incapacity of the Shechemites to resist them, took each man his sword, and slew all the males of the city, with Hamor, and Shechem his son, and took their sister out of his house, and went their way! Nor was this cruel business to be attributed to the two brothers only; for the rest were so far accessory as to join in plundering the city, and taking captive all the females.

Alas, how one sin leads on to another, and like flames of fire, spreads desolation in every direction! Dissipation leads to seduction; seduction produces wrath; wrath thirsts for revenge; the thirst of revenge has recourse to treachery; treachery issues in murder; and murder is followed by lawless depredation! Were we to trace the history of illicit commerce between the sexes, we should find it, more perhaps than any other sin, terminating in blood. We may read this warning truth not only in the life of David and his family, but in what is constantly occurring in our own times. The murder of the innocent offspring by the hand of the mother, or of the mother by the hand of the seducer; or of the seducer by the hand of a brother, or a supplanted rival—are events which too frequently fall under our notice. Nor is this all, even in the present world. Murder seldom escapes detection: a public execution therefore may be expected to close the tragical process!

Ver. 30, 31. It is some relief to find the good old man expressing his disapprobation of these proceedings: "Ye have troubled me," says he to Simeon and Levi, " to make me stink among the inhabitants of the land—and I being few in number, they shall gather themselves together against me; and I shall be destroyed, I and my house." Both Abraham and Isaac had carried it peaceably in all places where they pitched their tents, and by their good conduct had recommended true religion, and gained great respect amongst the heathen. It was Jacob's desire to have trod in their steps; but his sons were children of Belial, who knew not the Lord; yet being so nearly akin to him, his character is implicated by their conduct. Their answer is insolent in the extreme: " Should he deal with our sister (say they) as with a harlot?" As if their father had no proper concern for the honour of his children, and cared not what treatment they met with, so that he might be at peace, and maintain his credit.

But how is it that Jacob should dwell only upon the *consequences* of the sin, and say nothing on the sin itself? Probably because he knew them to be so hardened in wickedness that nothing but consequences, and such as affected their own safety too, would make them feel. It is certain that he did abhor the deed, and that with all his soul. Of this he gave a most affecting proof upon his dying bed, when instead of blessing the two brethren with the rest of his children, he in a manner cursed them; or at least, branded their conduct with perpetual infamy,

Simeon and Levi, said he, *are brethren; instruments of cruelty are in their habitations. Oh my soul, come not thou into their secret; unto their assembly, mine honour, be not thou united: for in their anger they slew a man, and in their self-will they digged down a wall. Cursed be their anger, for it was fierce, and their wrath, for it was cruel: I will divide them in Jacob, and scatter them in Israel!* *

We read no more of Dinah, except her bare name: probably she died single. Her example affords a loud warning to young people to beware of visiting in mixed companies, or indulging in amusements by which they put themselves in the way of temptation.

DISCOURSE XLIV.

JACOB's REMOVAL TO BETHEL—GOD's RENEWAL OF COVENANT WITH HIM—THE DEATH OF DEBORAH, RACHEL, AND ISAAC—ESAU's GENERATIONS.

GENESIS XXXV. XXXVI.

There is a greater diversity in the life of this patriarch than in that of Abraham, and much greater than in that of Isaac. If he did

* Chapter xlix. 5.

not attain to *the days of the years of the life of his fathers*, the records of his pilgrimage are not less useful than either of them.

Ver. 1. It might have been expected that Jacob would leave Shechem, on account of what had taken place; yet he would not know whither to flee: but "God said unto him, Arise, go up to Bethel, and dwell there: and make there an altar unto God that appeared unto thee when thou fleddest from the face of Esau thy brother." This admonition appears to resemble that which was addressed to Abram, *Walk before me, and be thou perfect;** that is, it implies a reproof, and was intended to lead Jacob to reflect upon his conduct. There were two things in particular which required his serious consideration.—(1.) Whether he had not neglected to perform his vow. He had solemnly declared in the presence of God, that if he would be with him, and keep him in the way he went, and give him bread to eat, and raiment to put on, then Jehovah should be his God: and that the stone which he then set up for a pillar should be God's house.† Now God had performed all these things on his part; but Jacob had not been at Bethel, even though he had now resided in Canaan about seven years. And what was worse, though Jehovah had been

* Chap. xvii. 1.   † Chap. xxviii. 20—22.

his God, so far as respected himself; yet his house was not clear of idols! Rachel's stolen teraphim had proved a snare to the family. At the time Laban overtook him, Jacob knew nothing of them; but he appears to have discovered them afterwards; and yet, till roused by this divine admonition, he never interposed his authority to have them "put away."—(2.) Whether the late lamentable evils in his family had not arisen from this cause. Had he gone sooner to Bethel, his house had been sooner purged of the "strange gods" that were in it; and his children had escaped the taint which they must of necessity impart. At first the gods of Laban were hid by Rachel, and none of the family except herself seemed to know of them: but now Jacob had to speak to his "household, and to all that were with him," to cleanse themselves. Moreover, had he gone sooner to Bethel, his children might have been out of the way of temptation, and all the impure and bloody conduct in which they were concerned, have been prevented. From the whole, we see the effects of spiritual negligence, and of trifling with temptation. Do not neglect God's house, nor delay to keep his commandments. He that puts them off to a more convenient season, has commonly some idols about him which it does not suit him just yet to put away.

Ver. 2, 3. No sooner is Jacob admonished to go to Bethel, than he feels the necessity of a reformation, and gives command for it. This proves that he knew of the corrupt practices of his family, and had too long connived at them. We are glad however to find him resolved at last to *put them away.* A constant attendance on God's ordinances is *dwelling* as it were in Bethel; and it is by this that we detect ourselves of evils which we should otherwise go on in without thought or concern. It is *coming to the light,* which will *manifest our deeds, whether they be wrought in God,* or not. Wicked men may reconcile the most sacred religious duties with the indulgence of secret sins; but good men cannot do so. They must wash their hands in innocency, and so compass God's altar.* Jacob not only commands his household to put away their idols, but endeavours to impress upon them his own sentiments. "Let us arise (saith he) and go up to Bethel; and I will make there an altar unto God, who answered me in the day of my distress, and was with me in the way which I went." He is decided for himself, and uses all means to persuade his family to unite with him. His intimating that God had heretofore "answered him in the day of his distress," might be designed not only to shew them the propriety

* Psalm xxvi. 6.

of what he was about to do, but to excite a hope that God might disperse the cloud which *now* hung over them on account of the late impure and bloody transaction.

Ver. 4. Considering the evils which prevailed in this family, and the bewitching nature of idolatry, it is rather surprising to observe the readiness with which they consent to give it up. But no doubt the hand of the Lord was in it. When Jacob spake as he ought to speak, their hearts were bowed before him. Difficulties which in a languid state of mind seem insurmountable, are easily got over when once we come to act decidedly for God: and those whom we expected to oppose the good work, shall frequently be found willing to engage with us in it. They not only gave their gods, but even their "ear-rings," which in those times were convertible, and often, if not always, converted to purposes of idolatry.* But why did Jacob bury them? We may think they might have been melted down, and converted to a better use: but that was expressly forbidden by the Mosaic law,† and it seems the patriarchs acted on the same principle. But why did he not utterly destroy them? Perhaps it would have been better if he had. I hope however, he hid them

* Exod. xxxii. 2. Hos. ii. 13. † Deut. vii. 25.

where they were found no more.—Upon the whole, we see at this time a great change for the better in Jacob's family. He should not have been reluctant, or indifferent, to going up to Bethel; for it appears to have been the design of God to make it one of his best removals. It was a season of grace, in which God not only blessed him, but caused even those that *dwelt under his shadow to return.* I have more hope of Rachel and Leah's having relinquished all for the God of Israel from this time, than from any thing in the former part of their history.

Ver. 5. We now see Jacob and his family on their journey. It would appear to the cities round about that the slaughter of the Shechemites was the cause of this removal; their " not pursuing them" being ascribed to " the terror of God being upon them," implies, that the public indignation was so excited against them, that if they dare, they would have cut them off. The kind care which God exercised on this occasion was no less contrary to the parent's fears, than to the deserts of his ungodly children; and its being extended to them *for his sake*, must, if they had any sense of things, appal their proud spirits, and repress the insolence with which they had lately treated him.

Ver. 6, 7. Arriving at Bethel in safety, Jacob, according to his vow, "built there an altar" unto Jehovah, and gave it a name which God had graciously given himself; namely, "Elbethel," *the God of Bethel.* This altar, and this name would serve as a perpetual memorial of God's having "appeared to him when he fled from the face of his brother." And as at that time many great and precious promises were made to him, it would be natural for him to associate with the idea of "the God of Bethel," that of a God *in covenant;* the God of Abraham, the God of Isaac, and the God of Jacob.

Ver. 8. While Jacob and his family were at Bethel, their enjoyments seem to have been interrupted by the death of "Deborah, Rebecca's nurse." Some particulars are here implied, which are not recorded in the history. Deborah did not belong to the family of Jacob, but to that of Isaac. Jacob must therefore have been and visited his father; and finding his mother dead, and her nurse far advanced in years, more fit to be nursed herself than to be of any use to her aged master, he took her home, where she would meet with kind attentions from her younger country-women, and probably furnished his father with another more suitable in her place. Nothing is said of her from the time she left

Padan-aram with her young mistress; but by the honourable mention that is here made of her, she seems to have been a worthy character. The death of an aged servant, when her work was done, would not ordinarily excite much regret. To have afforded her a decent burial was all that in most cases would be thought of: but Jacob's family were so much affected by the event, as not only to weep over her grave, but to call the very tree under the shadow of which she was interred, "Allon-bachuth," *the oak of weeping.* It is the more singular too, that the family who wept over her was not that in which she had lived, in what we should call her best days; but one that had merely taken her under their care in her old age. It is probable however, that the sorrow expressed at her interment was on account not only of her character, but her office, or her having been "Rebecca's nurse." The text seems to lay an emphasis upon these words. The sight of the daughter of Laban, *his mother's brother*, and even of his sheep, had interested Jacob's heart;* much more would the burial of her nurse. In weeping over her grave, he would seem to be weeping over that of his beloved parent, and paying that tribute of affection to her memory, which providence had denied him at the time of her decease.

* Chap. xxix. 10.

Ver. 9—15. During the seven years in which Jacob resided at Shechem we do not find a single instance of God's manifesting himself to him, except that of admonishing him to depart. But now that he is come to Bethel, and performed his vow, "God appeared unto him again,—and blessed him." But how is it that this is said to be "when he came out of Padan-aram?" The design of the phrase, I apprehend, is not to convey the idea of its being at the time of his return from that country, or immediately after it; but to distinguish it from that appearance of God to him in the same place where he now was, in his way thither. He appeared to him at Bethel when he was going to Padan-aram; and now he "appeared to him again" at the same place, *when he was come out of it.** The whole account given in these verses of the appearance of God to Jacob, and of his conduct in return, describes a solemn and mutual *renewal of covenant.* There is nothing material in what is here said to him, but what had been said before; and nothing material which he did, but what had been done before; but the whole was now as it were consolidated and confirmed.—(1.) God had before told him that his name should no more be called Jacob, but Israel:† this

---

* So the passage is rendered by *Ainsworth.*
† Chap. xxxii. 28.

honour is here *renewed*, and the renewal of it contained an assurance that he should still go on to prevail.—(2.) God had before declared that the promises made to Abraham should be fulfilled in him and his posterity :* this declaration is here *renewed*, and prefaced with an assertion of his own all-sufficiency to fulfil them.—(3.) When God had before appeared to him, he set up a pillar of stone, and poured oil upon it, and called the name of the place Bethel:† this process he now *renewed*, with the addition of a drink-offering, for which on his first journey he probably had not the materials.—These renewals of promises, and acknowledgments, may teach us not to be so anxious after new discoveries, as to overlook those which we have already obtained. God may "appear to us" by the revival of known truths, as well as by the discovery of what was unknown; and we may glorify him as much by *doing our first works*, as by engaging in something which has not been done before. Old truths, ordinances, and even places, become new to us when we renew communion with God in them.

Ver. 16—20. We are not told the reason of Jacob's leaving Bethel. Probably he was directed to do so. However this might be, his remov-

---

* Chap. xxviii. 13, 14. † Chap. xxviii. 18, 19.

al in the present instance was accompanied with a very painful event, namely, the loss of his beloved Rachel, and that in the prime of life. Journeying from Bethel, and within a little of Ephrath, or Bethlehem, she " travailed, and had hard labour." The issue was, the infant was spared, but the mother removed. Thus she that had said, " Give me children, or I die," died in child-birth!

Several circumstances which attended this afflictive event are deserving of notice.—(1.) The words of the midwife: " Fear not: thou shalt have this son also." When Rachel bare her first son, she called him Joseph, that is, *adding;* " for," said she, by a prophetic impulse, " the Lord shall add to me another son."* It is probably in reference to this that the midwife spake as she did. Her words, if reported to Jacob, with the recollection of the above prophetic hint, would raise his hopes, and render his loss more affecting, by adding to it the pain of disappointment. They appear to have no influence however on Rachel. She has the sentence of death in herself, and makes no answer: but turning her eyes towards the child, and calling him Ben-oni, *the son of my sorrow,* she expires! —(2.) The terms by which her death is described

* Chap. xxx. 24.

—" It came to pass, *as her soul was in departing*" .... An ordinary historian would have said, as she was dying, or as she was ready to expire: but the scriptures delight in an impressive kind of phraseology, which at the same time shall both instruct the mind and affect the heart. It was by means of such language, on various occasions, that the doctrine of a future state was known and felt from generation to generation among the Israelites, while the heathen around them, with all their learning, were in the dark upon the subject.—(3.) The change of the child's name—" She called his name Ben-oni; but his father called him Benjamin." The former, though very appropriate at the time, yet if continued, must tend perpetually to revive the recollection of the death of his mother; and of such a monitor Jacob did not stand in need. The name given him, signified, *the son of my right hand;* that is, a son of the most tender affection and delight, inheriting the place which his mother had formerly possessed in his father's heart. If the love of God be wanting, that of a creature will often be supreme; and where this is the case, the loss of the object is frequently known to leave the party utterly inconsolable: but though the affection of a good man may be very strong, and his sorrow proportionably deep; yet he is taught to consider that every created good is only lent him; and that his generation work being as yet unfulfilled, it is not for him to feed melancholy, nor to pore over his loss with a sullenness that shall unfit him for duty, but rather to divert his affections from the object that is taken, and direct them to those that are left.—(4.) The stone erected to her memory, and which appears to have continued for many generations. Burying her in the place where she died, " Jacob set a pillar upon her grave ; " and that was the pillar of Rachel's grave when her history was written. It was near this place, if not upon the very spot, that the tribe of Benjamin afterwards had its inheritance: and therefore it is that the people who lived in the times of Jeremiah are called *Rachel's children.** The babes which Herod murdered are also so called; and she herself, though long since dead, is supposed to rise, as it were, out of her grave, and witness the bloody deed: yea more, to stand upon it, and weep, refusing to be comforted, because they were not!

Ver. 21. It is proper that Jacob, or, as he is now called, Israel, after having interred his beloved Rachel, should remove to some little distance, at least, from her grave. " The tower of Edar," near to which he next spread his tent,

* Jer. xxxi. 15.

was in the neighbourhood of Bethlehem. In removing however from the scene of one sorrow, he is soon overtaken by another. While dwelling in that land, a criminal intercourse took place between Reuben and Bilhah, his father's wife. It was done in secret; but "Israel heard of it." For this his unnatural wickedness, Reuben was afterwards cursed as a tribe, and the heavier on account of his being the first-born of the family.* By his conduct however, in reference to his brother Joseph,† he seems to have obtained at least a mitigation of his punishment: for Moses in blessing the tribes, said of him, *Let Reuben live, and not die, and let not his men be few.*‡ Yet even here he does but *live:* no idea is suggested that he should ever *excel;* and with this the history of his tribe in after ages perfectly accords.

Ver. 22—26. The history will henceforward principally respect *the sons of Jacob*, as being the fathers of the twelve tribes of Israel. We have here therefore at the outset a particular account of them, as descended from the different wives of their father Jacob.

---

* Chap. xlix. 4.   † Chap. xxxvii. 20, 22.
‡ Deut. xxxiii. 6.

Gen. 35.] DEATH OF ISAAC. 107

Ver. 27—29. Before the sacred writer however proceeds to narrate their history, he finishes two other subjects, that the thread of the story may not be broken. One of them is the conclusion of the life of Isaac; and the other, which is contained in the thirty-sixth chapter, a brief sketch of the family and temporal prosperity of Esau. If the first of these events had been introduced in the order of time, it would have fallen in the midst of the history of Joseph; for it occurred about twelve or thirteen years after his being sold into Egypt. There are not many particulars concerning it. Jacob seems to have been sent for just in time to witness his father's decease. By the years of his life, namely, " a hundred and fourscore," it appears that he must have lived fifty-seven years in a state of blindness and inactivity. This is one of the mysteries of providence which often strikes us: an aged and afflicted person, whose usefulness appears to us at an end, shall have his life prolonged, while a hundred active young people around him shall be cut off. We know not the reason of these things in the present state; but we may know it hereafter.

Chap. xxxvi. With respect to Esau, he and his brother had been together at their father's funeral, and for aught appears were on brotherly terms. In the course of this chapter we find them separated; not however from any difference arising between them, but on account of their great prosperity. Their riches are said to have been "more than that they might dwell together; and the land wherein they were strangers could not bear them, because of their cattle."

The account which is here given of him and his posterity is however a kind of leave taken of them: we shall hear no more of Esau, nor of his descendants, but as enemies to the people of God. It is remarkable that three times in this chapter when Esau is spoken of, we meet with the phrase "This is Edom," and once, "He is Esau, the father of the Edomites."* We have seen that the name of Edom was given him on account of his *sanguinary* disposition;† and as this was notoriously the character of the Edomites especially towards Israel, it would seem as if the holy Spirit would have it well remembered that the bitterest enemies of the church of God descended from this man. He seems to be marked as the father of persecutors, in some such manner as Ahaz is marked for his wickedness of another kind, *This is that king Ahaz.*‡

* Verse. 1, 9, 19, 43. † Chap. xxv. 24—34.
‡ Chron. xxviii. 22.

Finally: It is remarkable that Esau, though he had despised and lost his birthright, yet was prospered in his life-time, and for several generations, more than his brother. While the latter was a servant at Padan-aram, he established his dominion in mount Seir; and while the descendants of the one were groaning under Egyptian bondage, those of the other were formed into an independant kingdom, and had eight kings in succession, "before there reigned any king over the children of Israel." In this manner did God order things, to shew, it may be, that the most valuable blessings require the greatest exercise of faith and patience.

DISCOURSE XLV.

JOSEPH SOLD FOR A SLAVE.

GENESIS xxxvii.

We now enter on the very interesting history of Joseph, a history in which I feel not pleasure only, but a portion of dismay; and this because I have but little hope of doing justice to it. It is a history, perhaps unequalled, for displaying the various workings of the human mind, both good and bad, and the singular providence of God in making use of them for the accomplishment of his purposes.

Ver. 1. Jacob is represented as *dwelling in the land wherein his father was a stranger.* The character of sojourners was common to the patriarchs: it is that which Jacob afterwards confessed before Pharaoh; on which the apostle remarks, that "they who say such things declare plainly that they seek a country."

Ver. 2. The "generations of Jacob" seem here to mean his family history: so the word is used of Adam, chapter v. 1. And Joseph being, as we should say, the chief hero of the tale, it begins with him. It was the design of the sacred writer, in the course of his narration, to tell of all the great events of that family; as of their going down into Egypt, remaining there for a number of years, and at last being brought out by the mighty hand of God: at present his object is to lead us to the origin of these events, as to the spring-head of a great river, or to describe the minute circumstances by which they were brought about.

Joseph was distinguished by his early piety. His brethren were most, if not all of them, very wicked; and he being frequently with them in the field, saw and heard such things as greatly affected him. We are not told what they were: the oracles of God have thrown a veil over them till the judgment day. Suffice it for us to know, that the mind of this godly youth was hurt by their conversation and behaviour, and that he could not be easy without disclosing particulars to his father. In this he was to be commended: for though a child should not indulge, nor be indulged by his parents, in reporting every trivial tale to the disadvantage of his brothers or sisters; yet where wickedness is acted, it ought not to be concealed. The parents should know it, that they may correct it; or if that cannot be, that they may be enabled to counteract its effects. But that which was commendable in him produced hatred in them. They would perceive that he did not join them when in company, and perhaps the carriage of their father would lead them to suspect that this his favourite son had been their accuser. In this, the outset of Joseph's story, we perceive a striking resemblance between him and our Lord Jesus Christ, whom *the world hated, because he testified of it that the works thereof were evil.**

Here therefore, before I proceed any further, I would offer a few words on the question, Whether Joseph is to be considered as *a type of Christ?*—I am far from thinking that every point of analogy which may be traced by a live-

* John. vii. 7.

ly imagination, was designed as such by the holy Spirit; yet neither do I think that we are warranted to reject the idea. We have already seen that God prepared the way for the coming of his Son, by a variety of *things,* in which the great principles of his undertaking were prefigured, and so rendered familiar to the minds of men;* and he pursued the same object by a variety of *persons,* in whom the life and character of Christ were in some degree previously manifest. Thus Melchisedec prefigured him as a priest, Moses as a prophet, and David as a king; and I cannot but think that in the history of Joseph there is a portion of designed analogy between them. But to return—

Ver. 3, 4. The hatred of Joseph's brethren on account of his reports was not diminished, but heightened by his father's partiality towards him. It is much less difficult to account for this partiality, than to justify it, or at least the method of expressing it. He was the son of the beloved Rachel ; and though Benjamin was in this respect equal to him, yet he was but a child, and had as yet discovered nothing as to character: he therefore would be out of the question. Joseph seems to have been the only one in the family who had hitherto discovered

* See the Notes on Chap. vi. 18. xvii. 4.

either the fear of God, or the duty of a child. From these considerations his father might be allowed to love him with a peculiar affection; but his clothing him with "a coat of many colours," was a weakness calculated only to excite envy and ill will in his brethren. If he had studied to provoke these dispositions, he could scarcely have done it more effectually. The event was, that the hatred of the brothers could no longer be concealed, nor could they speak in the usual strain of civility to Joseph.

Ver. 5—11. Another circumstance occurred, which tended still more to heighten the enmity; namely, certain *dreams* which Joseph had at this time, and which he in the simplicity of his heart related to his brethren. These were divine intimations of his future advancement, and were remarkably fulfilled in Egypt, about twenty-three years afterwards. But at present they inflamed a resentment already too strong; and even his father thought it necessary to chide what seemed a little presumptuous in his son. Yet as Jacob felt a check on this occasion, and "observed the saying," suspecting, it should seem, that there might be more in it than he was at present aware of; so, I apprehend, his sons had a secret persuasion that these dreams were prophetic: but that which softened the father, only hardened and inflamed the sons. Their hatred had originated in religion; and the thought of God having determined to honour him, provoked them the more. Such were the operations of malice in Cain towards Abel, in Esau towards Jacob, in Saul towards David, and in the scribes and pharisees towards the Lord of glory.

Ver. 12—17. Things now approach fast to a crisis. It seems as if the vale of Hebron, where Jacob now was, did not contain sufficient pasturage for his flocks: the young men therefore take them to Shechem, a distance, it is said, of about sixty miles, and the place where they lived for the first seven years after their return from Padan-aram. Jacob feeling anxious about them, and the cattle, (as well he might, considering the part they had acted there) proposes to Joseph that he should go and enquire, and bring him word of their welfare; to which the latter with cheerful obedience consents. Arriving at Shechem, he finds they had left it, with the flocks; and being informed by a stranger that they were gone to Dothan, a distance of about eight miles, he proceeds thither.

Ver. 18—22. The sight of Joseph, while he was yet afar off, rekindles all the foul passions of his brethren, and excites a conspiracy against him. "Behold," say they, with malignant scorn, "this dreamer cometh! Come now, let us slay him!"—In some cases sin begins upon a small scale, and encreases as it advances: but the very first proposal in this case is murder! This shews the height to which their hatred had been previously wrought up, and which, now that opportunity offered, raged like fire with uncontroulable fury. But have they no apprehensions as to consequences? What tale are they to carry home to their father? Oh, they are at no loss for this. Malice has two intimate friends always at hand to conceal its dark deeds; viz. artifice and falsehood. "We will cast him into some pit, (say they) and we will say some evil beast hath devoured him: and we shall see what will become of his dreams!" Who will say that the workers of iniquity have no knowledge? They have all the cunning as well as the cruelty of the old serpent. See how they wrap it up. But what do they mean by that sarcastic saying, *we shall see what will become of his dreams!* If they had considered them as feigned through ambition, they would not have felt half the resentment. No, they would have winked at it as a clever piece of deceit, and have had a fellow feeling for him. I doubt not but they considered these dreams as the intimations of heaven, and their language included nothing less than a challenge of the Almighty! But is it possible, you may say, that they could think of thwarting the divine counsels? It is possible, and certain that men have been so infatuated by sin, as to attempt to do so. Witness Pharaoh's pursuit of Israel, after all that he had seen and felt of the divine judgments; Saul's attempts on David's life; Herod's murder of the children of Bethlehem; and the conspiracy of the Jews against Christ, who, as many of them knew, had raised Lazarus from the dead, and done many miracles. Yes, we will kill him, say they, and then let God advance him to honour if he can! But they shall see what will become of his dreams. Yes, they shall see them accomplished, and that by the very means they are concerting to overthrow them. Thus, though the kings of the earth take counsel together against the Lord, and against his Anointed, saying, Let us break their bands asunder, and cast away their cords from us; yet He that sitteth in the heavens shall laugh at them, the Lord shall have them in derision. Joseph's brethren, like the sheaves in the dream, should make obeisance to him; and at the name of Jesus every knee shall bow, and every tongue confess that he is Lord, unto the glory of God the Father.

In this bloody council there was one dissentient. God put it into the heart of *Reuben*, though in other respects none of the best of characters, to oppose their measures: and being the elder brother, his opinion must have somewhat the greater weight. He appears to have utterly disapproved of their intention, and wished earnestly to get the lad safe out of their hands, that he might deliver him to his father, though perhaps through fear of his own life he made only a partial opposition. His counsel, however, saved his life, and he was doubtless raised up on this occasion for the very purpose, for Joseph's time was not yet come.

Ver. 22—24. All that had hitherto taken place was during the time that Joseph was absent. Glad to have caught the sight of them, he was walking towards them in the simplicity of his heart, while they were taking counsel to destroy him! He arrives. Like beasts of prey, they immediately seize him, and tear off the envied *coat of many colours*. It was not enough to injure him: they must also insult him. Thus Jesus was stripped and degraded before he suffered. Now it was, as they afterwards confessed one to another in the Egyptian prison, that they " saw the anguish of his soul, when he besought them, and would not hear:" now it was that Reuben interceded on his behalf, saying, "Do not sin against the child;

but they would not hear."* No, they would not hear: "they took and cast him into a pit"— probably, a hole in the earth, both dark and deep; for he does not appear to have been able to get out again. It was however empty, or without water. Whether they knew of this circumstance or not, God knew it; and it seems to have been known to Reuben when he made the proposal of his being cast into it, seeing he hoped by this means to save his life.

Ver. 25—28. Having thus far gratified their revenge, they retire, and with hardened unconcern *sit down to eat bread.* It is probable that they both ate and drank, and made merry; and it may be partly in allusion to this that certain characters, in the times of the prophet Amos, are described as drinking wine in bowls, and anointing themselves with the chief ointments, but were *not grieved for the affliction of Joseph.* †

At this juncture a company of merchants appeared, who were going down to Egypt. They are called Ishmaelites, and also Midianites: they were it seems a mixed people, composed of both. On the sight of them a thought occurs to the mind of Judah, that they had better sell their brother for a slave than murder him; and

* Chap. xlii. 21, 22. † Amos vi. 6.

which he proposes to the rest. His proposal contains words of mercy, but it was mercy mixed with covetousness. I am not sure that Judah felt any tenderness towards Joseph, as being his "brother, and of his flesh," any more than his name-sake did in selling Christ: it is not unusual for covetous men to urge their objects under a shew of generosity and kindness. But if he did, it was the "profit" that wrought upon the company. The love of money induced them to sell their brother for a slave; and the same principle carries on the same cruel traffic to this day. So they sold Joseph for "twenty pieces of silver," the value of which was about twenty shillings of our money, and which was ten shillings less than the price of a slave.* A goodly price at which they valued him! But let not Joseph complain, seeing a greater than he was sold by Judas Iscariot for but a little more.

Ver. 29, 30. In this iniquitous transaction Reuben was absent. I suppose, while they were eating and drinking, he stole away from their company with the intention of going by himself to the pit, and delivering Joseph; and to the pit he went: but taking a circuitous course, it may be, to prevent suspicion, he was too late!

* Exod. xxi. 32.

At this he is greatly affected, rends his garments, returns to the company, and exclaims, "The child is not : and I, whither shall I go!" But though he spake like a brother, and an elder brother, who was obliged to give account to his father, yet it appears to have made no impression on them. Like the scribes and pharisees, they were ready to answer, *See thou to that!*

Ver. 31—36. They feel not for Joseph, nor for Reuben; but have some concern about themselves, and immediately fall upon a stratagem wherewith to deceive their father. A kid is slain, and the coat of Joseph is dipt in its blood. This is to be carried home, and shewn to Jacob, with the addition of a lie, saying, they had " found" it; and thus the poor old man was to be persuaded that some evil beast had devoured him. Who will say that the workers of iniquity have no knowledge? Yet one cannot but remark the difficulty of supporting a feigned character. To have done it completely, they should first have seen their father without the coat, broke it to him by degrees, affected to grieve with him for the loss, and at last have presented the coat with apparent reluctance, as that which must harrow up his feelings. Instead of this, the whole is done in the most unfeeling and undutiful manner that it could be—"This have we found, (say they) know now whether it be *thy* son's coat, or no!" They could not deny themselves the brutal pleasure of thus insulting their father, even in the hour of his distress, for his former partiality. Wicked dispositions often make men act like fools: hence it is that murderers commonly betray themselves. The disguise of hypocrisy is generally very thin: truth only is throughout consistent. This disguise however, thin as it was, seemed at present to answer the end. Jacob knew the bloody garment, and said, "It is my son's coat; an evil beast hath devoured him: Joseph is without doubt rent in pieces." No, it is no evil beast, but men more cruel than tygers that have done towards him what is done: but thus Jacob thought, and thus he mourned. We are ready to wonder how Reuben could keep his counsel; yet with all his grief he did so: perhaps he might be afraid for his own life. Whatever was the cause however, of Jacob's being thus imposed upon, it was wisely ordered that he should be so. The present concealment of many things contributes not a little to the accomplishment of the divine counsels, and to the augmentation of future joy.

Jacob's mourning is deep and durable: when after a time, his sons and his sons' wives rose up to comfort him, he refused to be comforted; resolving to die a mourner, and to welcome the grave, which, though a land of darkness, should be dear to him, because his beloved Joseph was there! "Thus his father wept for him."

From the whole, one sees already with admiration, the astonishing machinery of providence. The malignant brothers seem to have obtained their ends: the mercenary merchants, who care not what they deal in so that they get gain, have also obtained theirs; and Potiphar, having got a fine young slave, has obtained his. But what is of greater importance, God's designs are by these means all in train for execution. This event shall issue in Israel's going down to Egypt; that in their deliverance by Moses; that in the setting up of the true religion in the world; and that in the spread of it among all nations by the gospel. *The wrath of man shall praise the Lord, and the remainder thereof will he restrain.*

DISCOURSE XLVI.

THE CONDUCT OF JUDAH—JOSEPH's PROMOTION AND TEMPTATION.

GENESIS xxxviii. xxxix.

If we turn aside with the sacred writer, for a few minutes, and notice the conduct of Judah about this time, we shall perceive new sources of sorrow for the poor old patriarch. This young man, whatever was the cause, must needs leave his father's family; and wandering towards the south, entered into the house of one Hirah, an inhabitant of Adullam, with whom he formed an intimate acquaintance. If all the brethren had dispersed, and mingled amongst the heathen, if we consider only their state of mind, there had been nothing surprising in it. While tarrying here, he saw a young female, whose father's name was Shuah; and though he had joined in objecting to his sister's marriage with Shechem, yet he makes no scruple of taking this Canaanitish woman to be his wife; and that without at all consulting his father. The children which he had by this marriage were such as might be expected; and the loose life which he himself led, aided in it as he was, by his *friend* the Adullamite, was that of a man, who, weary of the restraints of religion, had given himself up to his propensities.

Yet it is observable how he keeps up the customs of his father's family, by directing his younger son to take the widow of the eldest, that he might raise up seed unto his brother; and though he himself indulged in licentiousness, yet he can feel indignation, and even talk of "burning" his daughter-in-law for the same thing. Thus we have often seen men tenacious of ceremonies, while living in the grossest immorality; and quick to censure the faults of others, while blinded to their own.

The odious wickedness committed in this family might not have been recorded but for the purpose of chronology, and to shew what human nature is till it is renewed by the grace of God. How this connexion between Judah and his *friend* the Adullamite came to be broken, we know not; but finding him afterwards in his father's house, we hope it was so. Even while he continued on that side of the country, he had some remorse of conscience, particularly when discovering the supposed harlot to be his daughter Tamar. "She hath been (said he) more righteous than I."

But we return to the history of Joseph—

Chap. xxxix. We left him in Egypt, sold to Potiphar, a captain of the guard; and here we find him. He was sent beforehand as a saviour; and like the Saviour of the world, was not sent in state, but in the form of a servant.

Nothing is said of the grief of mind which he felt on the occasion, but this must needs have been great. A youth of seventeen, torn from his father, enslaved to all appearance for life, and that amongst idolaters, where the true God was utterly unknown! If the day of Jacob's departure from his father's house was "the day of his distress,"* what must Joseph's have been? The archers may well be said to have *sorely grieved him!*

Ver. 2, 3. But here is a remedy equal to this or any other disease: *the Lord was with Joseph!* God can make up any loss, sustain under any load, and render us blessed in any place. To this Moses alludes, in his dying blessing upon the tribe of Joseph—" Blessed of the Lord

* Chap. xxxv. 3.

be his land, for the precious things of heaven .... for the precious things of the earth .... and for the *good will of him that dwelt in the bush: let the blessing come upon the head of Joseph, and upon the top of the head of him that was separated from his brethren!*" If we be but in the path of duty, we have nothing to fear. Whatever wrongs we suffer, if we be but kept from doing wrong, we shall enjoy the peace of God in our hearts, and all will come to a good issue. What a difference is there between the case of Joseph and that of Jonah! They were both in trouble, both absent from God's people, and among the heathen: but the sufferings of the one were for righteousness sake, while those of the other were of his own procuring.

God makes Joseph *prosperous*—He must then have submitted with cheerfulness to his lot, studied to make himself agreeable and useful to his master, and applied attentively to business. Herein he was an example of resignation to the will of God in afflictive circumstances. Fretfulness greatly aggravates the ills of life, while a cheerful submission to the will of God alleviates them. The *prosperity* attending Joseph was *manifest:* his master sees it, and sees that "Jehovah is with him," and that it is his hand which blesses all he does. This is a circumstance not a little to Joseph's honour; for it implies that he made no secret of his religion. He must have refused to join in Egyptian idolatry, and have avowed himself a worshipper of Jehovah, the only true God. In many cases, for a poor unprotected slave to have done this, would have cost him his life: but the Lord was with Joseph, and had all hearts in his hand. Potiphar observing that the religion of the young man turned to his account, like many irreligious masters in the present day, makes no objection to it. This holds up a most encouraging example to religious servants, to recommend the gospel by their fidelity and diligence; and to all christians to be faithful to God, even when there are no religious friends about them, to watch over them. This is walking with God.

Ver. 4. The effect of this is, Joseph comes into favour, and is promoted over all the other servants. From a slave he is made a steward, a steward not only of the household, but over all his master's affairs, and this though but a youth.

Ver. 5. And now, as Potiphar favours the Lord's servant, the Lord will not be behind-hand with him, but will favour him. From this time forward every thing is blessed and prospered *for*

Joseph's sake. We see here that it is good to be connected with them that fear God, but much better to cast in our lot with them. In that case we shall not only gain by them for this life, but, as Moses told Hobab, whatever good thing the Lord doth to them, shall be done to us. Here also we see the promise to Abraham fulfilled in his posterity: he not only blesses them, but *makes them a blessing*. Such was Jacob to Laban; such is Joseph to Potiphar, and afterwards to all Egypt; such has Israel been to the world, who from them derive a Saviour, and all that they possess of true religion. Even the casting away of them has proved the reconciling of the world, and how much more shall the receiving of them at a future day be as life from the dead!—It might also be the design of God, by this as well as other of his proceedings, to set forth under a figure the method in which he would bless the world; namely, *for the sake of another that was dear unto him.* Potiphar was not blessed for his own sake, or on account of any of his good deeds; but for the sake of Joseph. Even his receiving Joseph into favour was not *that on account of which* he was blessed, though that was necessary to it: it was *Joseph* to whom the eye of the Lord was directed; he looked on him, and blessed Potiphar. So, *that for the sake of which* we are accepted and saved, is not any works of righteousness which we have done, nor even our believing in Christ, though this is necessary to it; but the name and righteousness of Jesus. Thus in both cases, grace is displayed, and boasting excluded.—Finally: It was a proverb in Israel, that "when it goeth well with the righteous, the city rejoiceth." This was singularly exemplified in the prosperity of Joseph, and still more in the exaltation of Christ. From the day that he was made head over all principalities and powers, from that time forward the Lord hath blessed the world *for his sake.*

Ver. 6. So great was the confidence which Joseph's fidelity inspired in his master, that all his concerns were left in his hands, and for his own part he did nothing but enjoy the prosperity which was thus bestowed upon him. This circumstance might be wisely ordered to prepare this lovely youth for his future station. He was now brought into business, and inured to management: had he been raised to his last post first, he might have been less qualified to fill it. Sudden advancements are seldom safe.

Under all this prosperity, what may we suppose to be the state of Joseph's mind? No doubt his thoughts would sometimes glance to the vale of Hebron, and he would ask himself, 'How does my father bear the rending stroke; and what is become of my poor wicked brethren?' But as to himself, so far as it was possible to be happy in a strange land, happy he must have been. God was with him, every thing he did prospered, and every thing he met with was extremely flattering. Indeed there are few characters who, at his period of life expecially, could bear such a tide of success. We see in him nothing assuming or overbearing towards his fellow servants, nor forgetful of his God. If, however, any thing of this kind should have been at work in his heart, he will soon meet with that which shall recal him to a right mind. A sharp temptation approaches, in which his virtue and patience shall be put to the proof. After a day of prosperity, let us expect a day of adversity; for God hath set the one over against the other, even in the lot of his most favoured servants.

Ver. 7—9. Joseph's goodly and well-favoured countenance excites the lawless desires of a faithless woman, who in violation of her marriage vows, and of all the modesty and decency which should distinguish her sex, tries to seduce him. In such a situation, how many young men would have been carried away! Nay, how many are so, where the temptation is far less powerful. His conduct on this occasion is a proof of great grace, and exhibits to all posterity an example of what may be done by closely walking with God.

The first attack upon him is repelled with a modest but severe remonstrance, exactly suited to his situation. Let us examine it minutely. There are four things in it worthy of admiration. —(1.) He is silent with respect to the wickedness of the tempter. He might have reproached her for the indelicacy, the infidelity, and the baseness of her proposal: but he confines himself to what respected *his own* obligation, and what would be his own sin. In the hour of temptation it is enough for us to look to ourselves. It is remarkable that all our Lord's answers to the tempter, as recorded in the fourth chapter of Matthew, are in this way. He could have accused him of insolence, and outrage; but he barely refuses to follow his counsels, because thus and thus *it was written.*—(2.) He considers his obligation as rising in proportion to his high station: "There is none greater in this house than I." Some young men would have drawn a contrary conclusion from the same premises, and on this ground have thought themselves entitled to take the greater liberties; but this is the true use to be made of power, and riches, and every kind of trust.—(3.) He considers it as heightened by the generosity and kindness of his master, who withheld nothing else from him. Eve reasoned at first on this principle; (chap. iii. 2.) and had she kept to it, she had been safe. When we are tempted to covet what God has forbidden, it were well to think of the many things which he has not forbidden, but freely given us.—(4.) He rises from created to uncreated authority: It would not only be treachery to my master, but "wickedness, great wickedness, and sin against God." In the hour of temptation it is of infinite importance what view we take of the evil to which we are tempted. If we suffer our thoughts to dwell on its agreeableness, as Eve did concerning the forbidden fruit, its sinfulness will insensibly diminish in our sight, a number of excuses will present themselves, and we shall inevitably be carried away by it: but if we keep our eye stedfastly on the holy will of God, and the strong obligations we are under to him, that which would otherwise appear a little thing, will be accounted what it is, a *great wickedness*, and we shall revolt at the idea of sinning against him. This is the armour of God wherewith we shall stand in the evil day.

Ver. 10. This remonstrance however, strong as it was, has no lasting effect upon the woman: for sin, and this sin in particular, is outrageous in its operations. Joseph therefore finds it necessary to shun her company, carefully avoiding, as much as possible, to be with her any where alone.—This shewed, First, *great sincerity:* for if we throw ourselves in the way of temptation, or be not careful to shun it when occasions offer, in vain do we talk against sin.—Secondly, *great wisdom:* for though he had been kept hitherto, he was not sure that he should be so in future. —Thirdly, *great resolution and perseverance:* for it is not every one who withstands a temptation in the first instance, that holds out to the end. Eve repelled the tempter on his first onset, but was carried away by the second. Job endured a series of trials, and sinned not; yet afterwards spake things which he ought not.—Finally, *great grace.* "Can a man go upon hot coals, and his feet not be burned?" No, if we voluntarily *go* into temptation, we shall assuredly be hurt, if not ruined by it: but when God by his providence *leads* us into it for the trial of our graces, we may hope to be kept in it, and brought victorious out of it.

Ver. 11—20. If we were told of a young man in Joseph's situation, we should probably advise his leaving the family; but circumstanced as he was, that might be impossible. He was a bought servant, however exalted; and therefore was not at liberty to leave. Nor could he speak on the subject to his master without ruining his peace for ever. He therefore kept it to himself, and went on as well as he could, watching and praying, no doubt, lest he should enter into temptation. One day, being under the necessity of going into the house about business, his mistress renewed her solicitations; on which he fled from her presence as before: but as he was escaping, she caught a piece of his garment, and kept it by her. Wantonness being disappointed, and pride wounded, the whole is now turned into hatred and revenge. She will work his overthrow, that she will! Mark how the cunning of the old serpent operates. The servants are called in to witness how she had been mocked, or as we should say, insulted by this Hebrew. If they knew nothing from other quarters, it was very natural they should think it was so; and thus they were every thing but eye-witnesses of Joseph's guilt. Presumptive evidence is certainly very strong against him. Yet with all this cunning, like other hypocrites, she does not do it completely. She should have pretended how much she felt for the insult offered to her husband, as well as to herself: but the truth will come out after all the pains taken to conceal it. How disrespectfully she speaks of him to the servants, half attributing the pretended insult to him. "See (saith she) HE hath brought a Hebrew unto us, to mock us!" Such language not only betrayed the alienation of her heart from her husband, but tended to set the servants against him. Nothing but truth is consistent throughout. If these servants possessed only a moderate share of good sense, they must have seen through this thin disguise, whether they chose to speak their minds or not.

The scheme however took. Potiphar thought the story so plausible, that there could be no doubt of its being true. His wrath therefore was kindled, and without farther ceremony, he took him and committed him to prison. He had, being fired with anger, no ear to hear what could be said on the other side; and perhaps Joseph might think that nothing he could say would be regarded; or if it were, it must ruin his master's peace of mind: he would therefore go in silence to prison, trusting in God to vindicate his injured character.

But what an affecting reverse of condition. Poor young man! A stranger in a strange land, without a friend to speak for him, or care about him. Behold him confined in the dungeon, and think what must have been his reflexions. 'Oh, if my father knew of this, what would he feel on my account! How mysterious are the ways of providence, that by an inflexible adherence to righteousness, I should be brought into this horrible place!' He was not only confined in a *dungeon*,* but as we are told in the 105th psalm, *his feet were hurt with fetters, being laid in iron.* This last phrase is very emphatic. Calvin renders it, *The iron entered into his soul.* Not only were his feet galled, but his heart was grieved; and probably he expected nothing but death.

Ver. 21—23. But, as under his former affliction, so under this, "The Lord was with Joseph." What was once said to Abraham, might now be said to him: *I am God all-sufficient: walk before me, and be thou perfect.* All will be right at last. Where providence leads us into difficulties and hardships, grace can sustain us under them; and if we suffer for righteousness sake, as Joseph did, we may be assured it will be so. Nothing shall eventually harm us, if we be followers of that which is good. In a little time Joseph obtains favour in the eyes of the keeper of the prison, as he had done before in those of Poti-

* Chapter xl. 15.

phar. And now he has an opportunity of showing the power of true religion in the prison, by his fidelity, his tenderness, and his worship of the only true God. It might be wisely ordered too, that he should go into his high station by way of a prison: he might not otherwise have been so well qualified to feel for his brethren, and for other prisoners. Nor would he have been in the way of his future advancement, if he had not been there. Before honour is humility: the Lord of glory himself obtained not the crown, but by first enduring the cross.

DISCOURSE XLVII.

JOSEPH IN PRISON.

GENESIS xl.

WE left Joseph in prison; but by the good hand of God upon him, its hardships are greatly mitigated. At first he is thrown into a dungeon, and laid in irons; but now he is made a kind of steward or overseer of the other prisoners. Yet it is a prison still, and he desires to be free; but he must wait awhile. God will deliver him in his own time and way. This chapter contains the story of the means by which his deliverance was effected.

Ver. 1, 2. Two of Pharaoh's officers offend their lord, for which they are committed to prison — the chief butler, and the chief baker. Whether they suffered justly, for having attempted to poison the king, which was often done in heathen countries; or merely on account of unfounded suspicion; whether, if there were any thing actually attempted, it was *their* doing, or some of the under butlers and bakers, for whose conduct they might be responsible, we know not; but imprisoned they were.

Ver. 3, 4. The prison into which they were sent is called the house of *the captain of the guard.* This title is more than once before given to Potiphar.* It is not improbable that it was him, and that the keeper was a person employed under him. If so, it is very probable that Potiphar was reconciled to Joseph. There is little reason to think that his wife would long conceal her character; and that being known, would operate in Joseph's favour: and though he might not wish to release him out of prison, for his own credit, yet he might be induced to connive at the keeper's kindness to him.—It is remarkable, that the prison to which these persons were sent should be the same as that wherein Joseph was confined. In this we see the hand of God,

* Chap. xxxvii. 36.   xxxix. 1.

ordering all events. They might have been sent to another place of confinement; but then the chain had been broken. On how many little incidents, of which the parties at the time think nothing, do some of the greatest events depend. If they had gone to another prison, Joseph might have died where he was, and no provision been made for the seven years of famine; and Jacob and his family, with millions of others, have perished for want; and so all the promises of their becoming a great nation, and of the Messiah springing from amongst them, and all nations being blessed in him, would have been frustrated. But he that appoints the end, appoints all the means that shall lead to it; and not one of them, however small or incidental, shall be dispensed with.—In this prison Joseph is said to have *served* the chief butler, and the chief baker; that is, he carried them their daily provisions, and so was in the habit of seeing them every day, and conversing with them.

Ver. 5—8. One morning, when he went to carry them their usual food, he finds them more than ordinarily dejected, and kindly enquires into the reason of it. It appears from hence that Joseph was not a hard-hearted overseer: unlike many petty officers, whose overbearing conduct towards their inferiors is the most intolerable, he sympathizes with the sorrowful, and makes free with them. The fear of God produces tenderness of heart, and compassion towards men, especially to the poor and the afflicted. On enquiry he found that they had each had a *dream;* and which, by the circumstances attending them, they considered as extraordinary. Both of them dreamed, and both in one night; both their dreams related to their past employments, and seemed therefore to be ominous of their future destiny: yet they knew not what to make of them, and had no interpreter at hand who could instruct them. Such was the cause of their dejection. Though the greater part of dreams be vanity, yet in all ages and places God has sometimes impressed the mind of man by these means; and especially, it would seem, in countries which have been destitute of divine revelation. We have many instances of this in the book of Daniel, and by which, as in this case, the servants of God came in request, and the glory of God eclipsed the powers of idolatry.

But what kind of interpreters did these men wish for? Such, no doubt, as Pharaoh on his having dreamed, called for; namely, the magicians, and the wise men of Egypt: and because they had no hopes of obtaining them in their present situation, therefore were they sad. Here lies the force of Joseph's question: "Do not interpretations belong to GOD?" Which was a reproof to them for looking to their magicians instead of him: hence also he offered himself as the servant of God to be their interpreter.

It is worthy of notice that what Joseph's interpretation was to the dreams of the butler and the baker, that the oracles of God are to the notices and impressions on the human mind by the light of nature and conscience. Man in every age and country has felt in himself a consciousness of his being what he ought not to be, a fearfulness of having in another state to give an account, with many other things of the kind: but all is uncertainty. He only knows enough, if he regard it not, to render him inexcusable; and if he regard it, to make him miserable. It is only in the scriptures that the mind of God is revealed.

Ver. 9—15. The butler first tells his dream, which Joseph interprets of his deliverance and restoration to office: and having told him this good news, he very naturally throws in a request on behalf of himself. There is no proof or symptom of impatience in this; but patience itself may consist with the use of all lawful means to obtain deliverance. The terms in which this request is made are modest, and exceedingly impressive: *Think on me when it shall be well with thee, and shew kindness, I pray thee, unto me, and make mention of me unto Pharaoh, and bring me out of this house.* He might have asked for a place under the chief butler, or some other post of honour or profit: but he requests only to be delivered from *this house.* He might have reminded him how much he owed to his sympathetic and kind treatment; but he left these things to speak for themselves, using no other language than that of humble entreaty: *I pray thee, shew kindness unto me!* In pleading the exalted situation in which the chief butler was about to be reinstated, he gently intimates the obligations which people in prosperous circumstances are under, to think of the poor and the afflicted; and christians may still farther improve the principle, not to be unmindful of such cases in their approaches to the King of kings. This plea may also direct us to make use of His name and interest, who is exalted at the right hand of the Majesty on high. It was on this principle that the dying thief presented his petition. *Lord remember me when thou comest into thy kingdom!* A petition which the Lord of glory did neither refuse nor forget: and still he liveth to make intercession for us.

Joseph, in order to make a deeper impression upon the butler's mind, tells him a few of the outlines of his history—" I was *stolen* (says he) from the land of the Hebrews." But was this a *just* account? Did not the Ishmaelites *buy* him? They did; but it was of them who had no right to sell him, and therefore it was in reality stealing him. Such, you know, would be the purchase of a child by a kidnapper of an unprincipled nurse; and such is the purchase of slaves to this day on the coast of Africa. The account was not only just, but *generous*. In making use of the term *stolen*, without any mention of particulars, he seems to have intended to throw a veil over the cruelty of his brethren, whom he did not wish to reproach to a stranger. And the same generous spirit is discovered in what he says of his treatment in Egypt. We have seen in a former discourse how this great and good man refused to reproach his tempter, confining himself to what was his own duty; and now when he had suffered so much through her base and false treatment, and when it might have been thought necessary to expose her in order to justify himself, he contents himself with asserting his own innocence—*And here also I have done nothing that they should put me into the dungeon.* What an example is here afforded us of temperateness and forbearance, under the foulest and most injurious treatment! Such was Joseph's request, and such his pleas to enforce it. If there had been any gratitude, any bowels of mercy, or any justice in the butler's heart, surely he must have thought of these things.

Ver. 16—19. But before telling us the issue of the above, the sacred writer informs us of the request of the baker. Observing the success of his companion, he is encouraged to tell *his* dream also; but here is a sad reverse. In three days his life will be taken from him! Whether he would suffer justly or unjustly, we know not; but as his death was so near, it was an advantage for him to know it: and if he had been properly affected, he had now an opportunity of enquiring at the hand of a servant of God, concerning his eternal salvation.

Ver. 20—23. The third day after these things, being Pharaoh's birth-day, both these prisoners were brought forth. Whether they were put to a formal trial, or whether their fate was determined by the mere will of the king, we are not informed; but the chief butler was reinstated in his office, and the chief baker hanged, according to the word of the Lord by his servant Joseph.

We should now have expected to read of the chief butler's intercession to the king in behalf of an amiable and injured young Hebrew, whom he had met with in prison. But instead of this we are told, *Yet did not the chief butler remember Joseph, but forgot him!* Alas, what a selfish creature is man! How strangely does prosperity intoxicate and drown the mind. How common is it for people in high life to forget the poor, even those to whom they have been under the greatest obligations. Well, be it so; Joseph's God did not forget him: and we, amidst all the neglects of creatures, may take comfort in this, Jesus does not neglect us. Though exalted far above all principalities and powers, he is not elated with his glory, so as to forget his poor suffering people upon earth. Only let us be concerned not to forget him. He who needs not our esteem, as we do his, hath yet in love condescended to ask us to do thus and thus *in remembrance of him!*

DISCOURSE XLVIII.

JOSEPH's ADVANCEMENT.

GENESIS xli.

VER. 1—14. Hope deferred maketh the heart sick. It is not the intenseness of our trials, but the duration of them, that is the greatest test of patience. *Two full years* longer Joseph must remain in prison. How long he was at the house of Potiphar before he was sent to this dismal place, I do not recollect that we are informed; but we learn that it was thirteen years in the whole: for when he came out of Egypt he was but seventeen, and was thirty when he stood before Pharaoh. God seldom makes haste to accomplish his designs. His movements, like those of a comet, fetch a large compass, but all comes right at last. The time is now come for Joseph's advancement, and God makes way for it by causing Pharaoh himself to dream. Abraham made a point of not laying himself under obligation to the king of Sodom; and though Joseph in the grief of his soul would gladly have been obliged to both Pharaoh and the Butler for his deliverance, yet will God will so order it that he shall be obliged to neither of them. Pharaoh shall send for him; but it shall be *for his own sake.* Though a poor friendless young man himself, yet he is a servant of the great King, and must maintain the honour of his Lord. It might be for this that God suffered the butler to forget him, that he might not take, from a thread to a shoe-latchet, what was theirs; and that the king of Egypt might not have to say, I have made Israel rich. Abraham and his posterity were made to impart blessedness to mankind, rather than to receive it from them. If it be more blessed to give than to receive, theirs it is to be thus blessed, and thus honoured. Oh, the depth of the wisdom and goodness of God; not only in giving, but in withholding his gifts till the time when they shall best subserve the ends for which they are conferred!

And now that the set time to favour Joseph is come, events rise in quick succession. Pharaoh's mind is impressed with an extraordinary dream—the same is repeated in another form—each appears to portend something of importance—his spirit is troubled—he sends for his magicians, and wise men; but their wisdom fails them—all are nonplused——What is to be done? Just now it occurs to the butler that this had once been his own case—'Oh, and I have forgotten my kind and worthy friend! Stupid creature! That is the man for the king.'—Obtaining an audience, he confesses the whole truth, and ingenuously acknowledges his faults. Joseph is now sent for in haste. He shaves himself, changes his raiment, and obeys the summons. Thus in a few hours he is delivered from the dungeon, and introduced to the court of what was then perhaps the first nation upon earth. Were we unacquainted with the event, with what anxious solicitude should we follow him; and even as it is, we cannot wholly divest ourselves of these feelings.

Ver. 15—24. Being introduced to the king, he is told for what cause he is sent for. "I have (said Pharaoh) dreamed a dream, and there is none that can interpret it: and I have heard say of thee that thou canst understand a dream to interpret it." The meaning of this was, that he had a case in hand which baffled all the wise men of Egypt, but that from what he had heard of Joseph, he supposed he might be a wiser man, or more deeply skilled in occult science, than any of them. Such a compliment from a king would have been too much for a vain mind: if he had affected to disclaim superior wisdom, it would have been done in a manner which betrayed what lurked within. But Joseph feared God; and is the same man in a palace as in a prison. *It is not in me,* said he; God *shall give Pharaoh an answer of peace.*—In this brief answer we see a spirit of genuine *humility,* disclaiming all that kind of wisdom for which Pharaoh seemed very willing to give him credit, or indeed any other, but what God gave him. We see also a *disinterested concern to glorify the true God,* in the face of the mightiest votaries of idolatry, and who had power to do what they pleased with him. It is observable, he does not say the God of Abraham, Isaac, or Jacob, or the God of the Hebrews. Such language might have been understood by Pharaoh and his courtiers as setting up one titular deity in opposition to others, the God of his country against the gods of Egypt: but he simply says God; a term which would lead their thoughts to the One great Supreme, before whom all idols would fall to the ground. Thus with great wisdom, modesty and firmness, he states truth, and leaves error to fall of its own accord. In assuring Pharaoh that God would give him an answer of *peace*, he would remove all fear from his mind of an unfavourable interpretation, which he might have some reason to apprehend from the butler's report, inasmuch as though he had foretold his restoration to office, yet he had prophetically hanged the chief baker.

Pharaoh's mind being thus relieved and encouraged, he without farther hesitation proceeds to tell his dreams of the fat and lean-fleshed kine, and of the rank and withered ears of corn.

Ver. 25—31. The answer of Joseph is worthy of the man of God. You perceive no shuffling to gain time, no juggling, no peeping and muttering, no words of dark or doubtful meaning:

all is clear as light, and explicit as the day. 'The dreams are one; and they were sent of God to forewarn the king of what he would shortly bring to pass. The seven good kine, and the seven good ears, are seven years of plenty; and the seven evil kine, and thin ears, are seven years of famine. And the reason of the dream being doubled is to express its certainty, and the near approach of the events signified by it.'

Ver. 32—36. Having made the matter plain, and so relieved the king's mind, he does not conclude without offering a word of counsel; the substance of which was to provide from the surplus of the seven good years, for the supply of the seven succeeding ones. If he had only interpreted Pharaoh's dreams, he might have gratified his curiosity, but that had been all. Knowledge is of but little use any farther than as it is converted into practice.

With respect to the advice itself, it carried with it its own recommendation. It was no more than what common prudence would have dictated to any people. If they had doubted Joseph's interpretation of the dreams, and whether any such years of plenty and of scarcity would follow, yet they could not even upon this supposition object to his counsel: for nothing was to be expended, nor done, but upon the actual occurrence of the plenteous years; and which, as they were to come first, afforded an opportunity of which wisdom would have availed itself, if there had been no dreams in the case, to provide for a time of want. Nor is there any reason, from what we know of Joseph's character, to suspect him of interested designs, like those of Haman, who wished to recommend himself. He appears to have had no end in view but the good of the country where God had caused him to sojourn.

Ver. 37, 38. Happily for Egypt, Pharaoh and his ministry saw the propriety of what was offered, and readily came into it. It is a sign that God has mercy in store for that people whose rulers are open to receive good counsel, and know how to appreciate the worth of good men. As Joseph had recommended a wise man to be employed in the business, Pharaoh without farther hesitation appeals to his courtiers, whether any man in Egypt was so fit for the work as himself. A man who had not only proved himself wise in counsel, but had also intercourse with GOD, and was inspired of him to reveal the secrets of futurity. Such language proves that Joseph's mentioning the true God to Pharaoh had not been without effect. To this, however, the courtiers make no answer. If they felt a little jealous of this young foreigner, it were not to be wondered at. Such were the feelings of the Babylonish nobles towards Daniel. It were easier to see the goodness of the counsel which left a hope to each man of a new office, than to see that Joseph was the only man in the land that could execute it. They knew very well, that they had not, like him, *the Spirit of God;* but might think themselves capable, nevertheless, of managing this business. However, they silently acquiesce; and Pharaoh proceeds without delay to carry his purposes into effect.

Ver. 39—45. And now all power, except that which is supreme, is put into his hands, over the house, and over the nation; and as the courtiers had probably discovered a secret reluctance, Pharaoh repeats his determination the more earnestly, that as the dream had been repeated to him, the thing might be established, and immediately put in execution. To words were added *signs,* which tended to fix his authority in the minds of the people. The king took his ring from his hand, and put it upon the hand of Joseph, clothed him in fine linen, and put a gold chain about his neck. Nor was this all: he caused him to ride in the second chariot through the streets of the city, and that it should be proclaimed before him, *Bow the knee,* or *tender father.* The Chaldee translates it, as Ainsworth observes, "The father of the king, master in wisdom, and tender in years"—as who should say, Though a youth in age, yet a father in character. In addition to this, Pharaoh uses a very solemn form of speech, such as that which is prefixed, or affixed to many of the divine commands—*I am Pharaoh:* and without thee shall no man lift up his hand or foot in all the land of Egypt!*—Finally: To crown him with respect, he gave him a new name, the meaning of which was, *a revealer of secrets,* and the daughter of a priest, or prince, to be his wife. Pause a moment, my brethren, and reflect . . . . . Who, in reading the preceeding sufferings and present advancement of Joseph, can forbear thinking of HIM, who *for the suffering of death was crowned with glory and honour?—Whom God hath highly exalted, giving him a name which is above every name; that at the name of* JESUS *every knee should bow, of things in heaven, and things in earth, and things under the earth; and that every tongue should confess that Jesus Christ is Lord, to the glory of God the Father?* Surely it was the design of God, by these sweet anologies, to lead the minds of believers imperceptibly on, that when the Messiah should come, they might see in him their Josephs, and Joshuas, and Davids, as well

---

* See Lev. xix.

as their sacrifices, their cities of refuge, and their jubilees, in perfection.

Ver. 46—49. Joseph being thirty years old when he stood before Pharaoh, was just suited for active life. At such a period however, and raised from such a situation, many would have been lifted up to their hurt: but He who enabled him to repel temptation, and endure affliction, enabled him also to bear the glory that was conferred upon him with humility. It is observable, that on going out from the presence of Pharaoh, he did not go hither and thither to shew his greatness; but immediately betook himself to business. New honours, in his account, conferred new obligations. The first thing necessary for the execution of his trust was a general survey of the country; which having taken, he proceeded to execute his plan, laying up grain during the seven plentiful years beyond all calculation.

Ver. 50—52. During these years of plenty, Joseph had two sons by his wife Asenath, both which are significantly named, and express the state of his mind in his present situation. The first he called *Manasseh,* that is, *forgetting; for God,* said he, *hath made me to forget all my toil, and all my father's house.* A change from the extremes of either joy to sorrow, or sorrow to joy, is expressed by the term *forgetfulness;* and a very expressive term it is. *Thou hast removed my soul far off from peace; I* FORGOT *prosperity*—*A woman when she is in travail hath sorrow, because her hour is come: but as soon as she is delivered, she* REMEMBERETH NO MORE *the anguish, for joy that a man is born into the world.** But what, had Joseph forgotten his father's house? Yes, so far as it had been an affliction to him; that is, he had forgotten the cruel treatment of his brethren, so as no longer to lay it to heart.— His second son he called *Ephraim,* that is, *made fruitful; for God,* said he, *hath caused me to be fruitful in the land of my affliction.* In both he eyes the hand of God in doing every thing for him, and gives the glory to him only.

Ver. 53—57. But now the day of prosperity to Egypt is at an end, and the day of adversity cometh: God hath set the one over against the other, to sweep away its fulness, that man should find nothing after him. And now the people being famished for want of bread, resorted to Pharaoh. Had not Pharaoh been warned of this evil beforehand, he might have replied, as Jehoram did to her that cried, "Help my lord, oh king!" *If the Lord do not help thee, whence*

* Lam. iii. 17. John xvi. 21.

shall I help thee? Out of the barn-floor, or out of the wine-press? But provision was made for this time of need; and the people are all directed to *go to Joseph.*—And here, I may say again, Who can forbear thinking of HIM, in whom it hath pleased the Father that all fulness should dwell, and to whom those who are ready to perish are directed for relief?

This sore famine was not confined to Egypt, but extended to the surrounding countries; and it was wisely ordered that it should be so, since the great end for which God is represented as *calling for it** was to bring Jacob's sons, and eventually his whole family, into Egypt; which end would not otherwise have been answered.

Joseph is now filling up his generation work in useful and important labours; and like a true son of Abraham, he is *blessed and made a blessing.* Yet it was in the midst of this career of activity that his father Jacob said with a deep sigh, *Joseph is not!* What a large portion of our troubles would bside, if we knew but the whole truth!

---

* Ps. cv. 16.

DISCOURSE XLIX.

THE FIRST INTERVIEW BETWEEN JOSEPH AND HIS BRETHREN.

GENESIS xlii.

THINGS now approach fast to a crisis. We hear but little more of the famine, but as it relates to Jacob's family, on whose account it was sent. It is remarkable that all the three patriarchs, Abraham, Isaac, and Jacob, experienced a famine while sojourning in the land of promise; a circumstance sufficient to try their faith. Had they been of the disposition of the spies in the times of Moses, they would have concluded it to be a land which ate up the inhabitants, and therefore not worth accepting: but they believed God, and thought well of whatever he did.

Ver. 1, 2. Jacob and his family have well nigh exhausted their provision, and have no prospect of recruiting it. They had money, but corn was not to be had for money in their own country. They could do nothing therefore, but *look one at another* in sad despair. But Jacob, hearing that there was corn in Egypt, rouses them from their torpor. His words resemble those of the four lepers: "Why sit we here until we die?" It is a dictate of nature not to despair while there is a door of hope; and the principle will hold good in things of everlasting moment. Why sit we here, poring over our guilt and misery, when we have heard that with the Lord there is mercy, and with him there is plenteous redemption? How long shall we take counsel in our soul, having sorrow in our hearts daily? Let us trust in his mercy, and our hearts shall rejoice in his salvation.

Ver. 3, 4. The ten brethren immediately betake themselves to their journey. They are called *Joseph's brethren*, and not Jacob's sons, because Joseph is at present the principal character in the story. But when Benjamin is called *his brother*, there is more meant than in the other case. It would seem to be assigned as the reason why Jacob was unwilling to part with him, that he was the only surviving child of Rachel, and brother of him that was not! As mischief had befallen him, he was afraid the same should befal his brother, and therefore wished the young men to go without him. Jacob does not say, 'Lest you should do him mischief, as I fear you did his brother'.... but I suspect there was something of this at the bottom; and which, when afterwards urged by a kind of necessity to part

with Benjamin, came out. *Me ye have bereaved
. . . . Joseph is not!* (ver. 36.) At first he appears to have thought that some evil beast had devoured him: but upon more mature observation and reflexion, might see reason to suspect at least, whether it was not by some foul dealing on on their part that he had come to his end. As nothing however could be proved, he at present kept his suspicions to himself, and the matter passed, as it had done from the first, that mischief in some unknown way had befallen him.

Ver. 5. Nothing is said of their journey, except that a number of their countrymen went with them on the same errand; for the famine was in the land of Canaan. Such a number of applicants might possibly excite fears in their minds, lest there should not be enough for them all. Such fears however, if they existed in this case, were unnecessary; and must always be unnecessary, where there is enough and to spare.

Ver. 6. Now Joseph being governor of the land, they find him on their arrival fully employed in serving the Egyptians. He had assistants; but his eye pervaded every thing. As soon as they could get access to the governor, they according to the eastern custom, bow themselves before him, with their faces to the earth.

Ver. 7. We may wonder that Joseph could live all this time in Egypt, without going to see his father or his brethren. We might indeed allege, that while with Potiphar, he had probably neither opportunity nor inclination; when in prison, he was not allowed to go beyond its walls; and when advanced under Pharaoh, his hands were so fully employed that he could not be spared. We know that when his father was to come down to him, he could only send for him; and when he went to bury him, there was great formality required to attend his movements, a number of the Egyptians going with him. But it was doubtless ordered of God that he should not go, but that his brethren should come to him; for on this depended the issue of the whole affair. And now comes on the delicate part of the story: *Joseph saw his brethren, and knew them.* What must have been his feelings! The remembrance of the manner in which he parted from them, two-and-twenty years ago, the events which had since befallen him, their prostration before him, and the absence of Benjamin, from which he might be apprehensive that they also had made away with him,—altogether, must have been a great shock to his sensibility. Let him beware, or his countenance will betray him. He feels the danger of this, and therefore immediately puts on a stern look, speaks roughly to them, and affects to take them for spies. By this innocent piece of artifice, he could interrogate them, and get out of them all the particulars that he wished, without betraying himself, which he could not have done by any other means. The manner in which he asked them, *Whence come ye?* Would convey to them an idea of suspicion as to their designs. It was like saying, 'Who and what are you? I do not like your looks.' Their answer is humble and proper, stating the simple truth . . . . . . they came from Canaan, and had no other design in view than to buy food.

Ver. 8. *Joseph knew his brethren,* and felt for them, notwithstanding his apparent severity: *but they knew not him!* It was wisely ordered that it should be so, and is easily accounted for. When they last saw each other, they were grown to man's estate, but he was a lad; they were probably in much the same dress, but he was clothed in vestures of fine linen, with a golden chain about his neck; and they had only one face to judge by, whereas he had ten, the knowledge of any one of which would lead to the knowledge of all. Now Joseph sees, without being seen; and now he remembers his dreams of the sheaves, and of the stars.

Ver. 9—14. Determined to continue at present unknown, and yet wishing to know more of them, and of matters in Canaan, Joseph still speaks under an assumed character, and affects to be dissatisfied with their answer. *Ye are spies*, saith he; *to see the nakedness of the land are ye come.* They modestly and respectfully disown the charge, and repeat the true, and only object of their coming; adding, what is very much in point, *We are all one man's sons.* This was saying, 'Ours is not a political, but a domestic errand: we are not sent hither by a king, but by a father, and merely to supply the wants of the family.' Still he affects to disbelieve them; for he does not know enough yet. He therefore repeats his suspicions, in order to provoke them to be more particular: as if he should say, 'I will know all about you before I sell you corn, or send you away.' This had the desired effect. *Thy servants*, say they, *are, or were, twelve brethren, the sons of one man in the land of Canaan; and behold, the youngest is this day with our father, and one is not.* This is deeply interesting, and exquisitely affecting to Joseph. By this he learns that his father was yet alive, and his brother too: oh, these are joyful tidings! This was the drift of his questions, as they afterwards tell their father Jacob—"The man asked us straitly of our state, and of our kindred, saying, Is your father yet alive? Have ye another brother? And we told him according to the tenor of these words."* But what must have been his sensations at the mention of the last words, *One is not!* .... Well, he conceals his feelings, and affects to turn their account of matters against them. They had not told all the truth at first. It seemed at first there were only ten of them, and now there were eleven: *That is what I said unto you, saying, ye are spies.*

Ver. 15, 16. He now proposes to prove them. *By the life of Pharaoh,* saith he, *ye shall not go hence, except your youngest brother come hither. Send one of you and fetch him, that your words may be proved, whether there be any truth in you; or else, by the life of Pharaoh, surely ye are spies.* Some supposed that Joseph had learned the manners of the Egyptians by living amongst them, or that he would not thus have sworn by the life of Pharaoh: but I see no ground for any such thing. We might as well say, that he had learned to speak untruth, because he really had no such suspicions as he feigned; or that he had learned magic, seeing he afterwards talked of *divining;* or that our Saviour had learned the proud and haughty spirit of the jews, who treated the gentiles as dogs, because for the sake of try-

* Chap. xliii. 7.

ing the woman of Canaan he made use of that kind of language. The truth is, Joseph acted under an assumed character. He wished to be taken for an Egyptian nobleman, with whom it was as common to swear by the life of Pharaoh, as it was afterwards for a Roman to swear by the fortune of Cæsar.

But wherefore does Joseph thus keep up the deception; and why propose such methods of proving them? I suppose at present his wish is to *detain* them. Yes, they must not leave Egypt thus: had they done this, he might have seen them no more; yet he had no other cause to assign but this, without betraying the truth, which it was not a fit time to do at present.

Ver. 17, 18. 'Take these men up,' said Joseph to his officers, 'and put them into a place of safe custody; it is not proper they should be at large.' Here they lie three days; a period which afforded him time to think what to do, and them to reflect on what they had done. On the third day he paid them a visit, and that in a temper of more apparent mildness. He assures them that he has no designs upon their life, nor any wish to hurt their family; and ventures to give a reason for it which must to them appear no less surprising than satisfying: *I fear God.*

What, an Egyptian nobleman know and fear the true God! If so, they have no injustice to fear at his hands; nor can he withhold food from a starving family. The fear of God will ever be connected with justice, and humanity to man. But how mysterious an affair! If he be a good man, how is it that he should treat us so roughly? How is it that God should suffer him so to mistake our designs? Severity from the hand of goodness is doubly severe. Their hearts must surely by this time have been full. Such were the methods which this wise man made use of to agitate their minds, and to touch every spring of sensibility within them; and such were the means which God by him made use of to bring them to repentance. This indeed is his ordinary method of dealing with sinners: now their fears are awakened by threatenings, or adverse providences, in which death sometimes stares them in the face; and now a little gleam of hope arises, just sufficient to keep the mind from sinking; yet all is covered with doubt and mystery. It is thus, as by alternate frost, and rain, and sun-shine, upon the earth, that he humbleth the mind, and maketh soft the heart of man.

Ver. 19—24. Joseph, still under a disguise, though he consents that nine out of the ten should go home with provision for the relief of the family, yet that he may have some pledge for their return, insists on one being detained as a hostage till they should prove themselves true men, by bringing their younger brother; and his will at present must be their law. Having thus determined their cause, he withdraws from their immediate company to a little distance, where perhaps he might stand conversing with some other persons, but still within hearing of what passed among them. As he had all along spoken to them by an interpreter, they had no suspicion that he understood Hebrew, and therefore began talking to one another in that language, with the greatest freedom, and as they thought without any danger of being understood. Their full hearts now began to utter themselves. Perhaps their being obliged to speak of Joseph as *not*, might serve to bring him to their remembrance. Whatever it was, the same thoughts had been in all their minds, which probably they could read in each others looks. As soon therefore as one of them broke silence, the rest immediately joined in ascribing all this evil which had befallen them to this cause. They "said one to another, We are verily guilty concerning our brother, in that we saw the anguish of his soul, when he besought us, and we would not hear; therefore is this distress come upon us!" God, in dealing with sinners, usually adapts the punishment to the sin, so as to cause them to read the one in the other. Hence, adverse providences call our sin to remembrance; our own wickedness corrects us, and our backslidings reprove us. They would not hear Joseph in his distress, and now they could not be heard: they had thrown him into a pit, and are themselves now thrown into prison!—These convictions are heightened by the reproaches of Reuben, who gives them to expect blood for blood. Reuben was that, methinks, to his brethren, which conscience is to a sinner; remonstrating at the outset, and when judgment overtakes him, reproaching him, and foreboding the worst of consequences. His words are sharp as a two-edged sword: "Spake I not unto you, saying, Do not sin against the child; and ye would not hear? Therefore, behold also, his blood is required!"—But that which is still more affecting, Joseph hears all, and understands it, and this without their suspecting it. Such words however were too much for the heart of man, at least such a man as he was, to bear: it is no wonder therefore, that he " turned himself about from them and wept!"..... But having recovered himself, he returned to them, and with an austere countenance, took Simeon and bound him before their eyes. This must be cutting work on both sides. On the part of Joseph, it must be a great force put upon his feelings; and on theirs, it would seem a prelude to greater evils. There might be a fitness in taking Simeon rather than any other. He had proved himself a ferocious character by his conduct towards the Shechemites; and therefore it is not unlikely he was one of the foremost in the cruelty practised towards Joseph. Perhaps he was the man who tore off his coat of many colours, and threw him into the pit. If so, it would tend to humble him, and heighten all their fears, as beholding in it the righteous judgment of God.

Ver. 25—28. This done, their sacks are ordered to be filled, and their money restored; not by giving it into their hands however, but by putting it into the mouths of their sacks. But why all this mysterious conduct? Was it love? It was, at the bottom; but love operating at present in a way tending to perplex, confound, and dismay them. It could not appear to them in any other light than as either an oversight, or a design to ensnare, and find occasion against them. It was certain to fill their minds with consternation and fear; and such appears to have been the intention of Joseph from the first. It accords with the wisdom of God, when he means to bring a sinner to a right mind, to lead him into dark and intricate situations, of which he shall be utterly unable to perceive the design; to awaken by turns his fears and his hopes; bring his sin to remembrance; and cause him to feel his littleness, his danger, and his utter insufficiency to deliver his soul: and such, in measure, appears to have been the design of Joseph, according to the wisdom that was imparted to him on this singular occasion. If his brethren had known all, they would not have felt as they did: but neither would they have been brought to so right a state of mind, nor have been prepared, as they were, for that which followed. And if we knew all, with respect to the mysterious dispensations of God, we should have less pain: but then we should be less humbled, and less fitted to receive the mercy which is prepared for us.

It is remarkable how this circumstance operates on their minds. They construe it to mean something against them; but in what way they know not. They do not reproach the man, the lord of the land, though it is likely from his treatment of them that they would suspect some ill design against them: but overlooking second causes, they ask, "What is this that God hath done to us!" To his righteous judgment they attributed what they had already met with;

(ver. 21, 22.) and now it seems to them that he is still pursuing them in a mysterious way, and with a design to require their brother's blood at their hand. Such a construction, though painful for the present, was the most useful to them of any that could have been put upon it.

Ver. 29—35. Arriving at their father's house, they tell him of all that had befallen them in Egypt, that they may account for their coming home without Simeon, and being required when they went again to take Benjamin with them. But the mysterious circumstance of the money being found by the way in their sacks, they appear to have concealed. Mention is made of only one of the sacks being opened; yet by what they afterwards said to the steward,* it appears that they opened them all, and found every man's money in his sack's mouth. But they might think their father would have blamed them for not returning with it when they were only a day's journey from Egypt, and therefore agreed to say nothing to him about it, but leave him to find it out. Hence it is that they are represented, on opening their sacks, as discovering the money in a manner as if they knew nothing of it before; not only participating with their

* Chap. xliii. 21.

father in his apprehensions, but seeming also to join with him in his surprise.

Ver. 36—38. If the discovery of the money affected Jacob, much more the requirement of his darling son. This touches him to the quick. He cannot help thinking of the end that Joseph had come to. The reasons he had had to suspect some foul dealing in that affair, had probably made him resolve long ago that Benjamin should never be trusted in their hands! Yet things are now so circumstanced that he must go with them. It was a distressing case. Jacob speaks, as well he might, in great anguish; having in a manner lost all his earthly hopes, save one; and of that he is now in danger of being deprived. His words have too much peevish sorrow about them: they certainly reflect upon his sons; and the last sentence would almost seem to contain a reflection upon providence. The words, *all these things are against me,* must have some reference to the promise, "I will surely do thee good;" and if so, they were like saying, 'Is this the way? Surely not!'... Yet so it was. The conduct of God towards Jacob is covered with as great a mystery as that of Joseph towards his brethren; but all will be right at last. Much present trouble arises from our not knowing the whole truth.

In mentioning the name of Joseph, Jacob had touched a tender place; an old wound, which providence too had been lately probing. On this occasion, all that were guilty, you will perceive, are silent. Reuben is the only one that speaks, and he dares not touch that subject; but with strong and passionate language, seems to aim to divert his father's mind from it, and to fix it upon Benjamin only: "Slay my two sons, if I bring him not to thee!" This language so far answers the end, as that no more is said of their having *bereaved* him of Joseph: but he still dwells upon his *being dead,* nor can he at present be persuaded to part with his brother. "If mischief (saith he) befall him in the way in which ye go, then shall ye bring down my grey hairs with sorrow to the grave."

DISCOURSE L.

THE SECOND INTERVIEW BETWEEN JOSEPH AND HIS BRETHREN.

GENESIS xliii.

Ver. 1, 2. The relief obtained by the first journey to Egypt is soon exhausted: for "the famine was sore in the land," and therefore nothing of its native productions could be added to the other to make it last the longer. "Go," said Jacob to his sons, "and buy us a little food." Avarice and distrust would have wished for much, and have been for hoarding it at such a time as this: but Jacob is contented with a little, desirous that others should have a part as well as himself; and with respect to futurity, he puts his trust in God.

Ver. 3—5. But here the former difficulty recurs: they cannot, must not, will not go without their younger brother. This is trying. Nature struggles with nature; the affection of the father with the calls of hunger: but the former must yield. Jacob does not appear however, at present, to be entirely willing; wherefore Judah considering it as a fit opportunity, urges the matter, alleging the peremptory language of the man, the lord of the land, on the subject.

Ver. 6, 7. This brings forth one more feeble objection, or rather complaint, and which must be his last: "Wherefore dealt ye so ill with me as to tell the man whether ye had yet a brother?" To which they very properly answer that they could not do otherwise, being so straitly examined; nor was it possible for them to know the use that would be made of it.

Ver. 8—10. While matters were thus hanging in suspense, Judah very seasonably and kindly attempts to smooth the difficulty to his father, by offering in the most solemn manner to be surety for the lad, and to bear the blame for ever, if he did not bring him back and set him before him. In addition to this, he alleges that the life of the whole family depended upon his father's acquiescence, and that they had been too long detained already.

Ver. 11—14. And now Jacob must yield, must yield up his beloved Benjamin, though not without a mixture of painful reluctance: but imperious necessity demands it. He who a few weeks before had said, "My son shall not go down with you," is now upon the whole constrained to part with him. Thus have we often seen the tender relative, who in the first stages of an affliction thought it impossible to sustain the loss of a beloved object, gradually reconciled;. and at length, witnessing the pangs of wasting disease, almost desirous of the removal. Thus it is that the wisdom and goodness of God are seen in our bereavements: the burden which at first threatens to crush us into the grave, being let down gradually upon our shoulders, becomes not only tolerable, but almost desirable.

But mark the manner in which the patriarch acquiesces: his is not the sullen consent of one who yields to fate, but in his heart rebels against it. No, he yields in a manner worthy of a man of God; proposing first that every possible mean should be used to conciliate the man, the lord of the land, and then commits the issue of the whole to God. Just thus he had acted when his brother Esau was coming against him with four hundred men.* "Take of the best fruits of the land in your vessels, and carry down the man a present.... take double money in your hands, and the money that was brought again in the mouth of your sacks.... take also your brother .... and God almighty give you mercy before the man, that he may send away your other brother, and Benjamin. If I be bereaved, I am bereaved!" The fruits of Canaan, especially in a time of famine, would be a great token of respect; the double money might be necessary, as the continuance of the famine might enhance the price of corn; and the restoration of that which was returned would prove their integrity.

But we must not pass over the concluding part without noticing two or three things in particular.—(1.) The *character* under which the Lord is addressed: *God almighty,* or *God all-*

* Chap. xxxii. 6—12.

sufficient. This was the name under which Abraham was blessed: "I am God almighty;" and which was used by Isaac in his blessing Jacob: "God almighty bless thee, and give thee the blessing of Abraham."* It is natural to suppose that Jacob, in putting up this prayer, thought of these covenant promises and blessings, and that it was the prayer of *faith.*—(2.) The *mistake* on which the prayer is founded, which yet was acceptable to God. He prayed for the turning of the man's heart in a way of mercy; but the man's heart did not need turning. Yet Jacob thought it did, and had no means of knowing otherwise. The truth of things may in some cases be concealed from us, to render us more importunate; and this importunity, though it may appear at last to have been unnecessary, yet being right according as circumstances appeared at the time, God will approve of it, and we shall find our account in it.—(3.) The *resignation* with which he concludes: "If I am bereaved, I am bereaved!" It is God's usual way, in trying those whom he loves, to touch them in the tenderest part. Herein the trial consists. If there be one object round which the heart has entwined more than all others, that is it which is likely to be God's rival, and of that we must be deprived. Yet if when it goes, we humbly

---

* Chap. xvii. 1. xxviii. 3, 4.

resign it up into God's hands, it is not unusual for him to restore it to us, and that with more than double interest. Thus Abraham, on giving up Isaac, received him again; and David, on giving up himself to God to do with him as seemed good in his sight, was preserved in the midst of peril.

Ver. 15, 16. Jacob's sons now betake themselves to their second journey, and do as their father directed them. On arriving in Egypt, they are introduced to Joseph. Joseph looking upon them, beholds his brother Benjamin. It is likely his eyes would here be in some danger of betraying his heart; and that being conscious of this, he instantly gives orders to his steward to take these men home to his house, and prepare a dinner, for that they must dine with him at noon. By this means he would be able to compose himself, and to form a plan how to conduct and in what manner to discover himself to them, which it appears by the sequel it was his design at this time to have accomplished. See how fruitful love is of kind contrivance; seeking, and finding opportunities to gratify itself, by closer and closer interviews. Thus when two of John's disciples were kindly asked, "What seek ye;" they answered, "Master, where *dwellest* thou?" As who should say, 'We want to be better acquainted with thee, and to say more than could be said in this public place.' And thus when Jesus himself would commune with his disciples, he saith unto them, "Children, come and dine!"*

Ver. 17, 18. But to Joseph's brethren, things still wear a mysterious and confounding aspect: that which he meant in love, they construed as a design to ensnare and enslave them. The mind, while in a state of dark suspense, is apt to view every thing through a discouraging medium. It will misconstrue even goodness itself, and find fear where no fear is. Thus it is that souls depressed under God's hand, often misinterpret his providences, and draw dismal conclusions from the same things which in another state of mind would afford them relief. When the soul is in such a frame as to *refuse to be comforted*, it will *remember* God, *and be troubled.*†

Ver. 19—23. Being introduced into the house of Joseph however, though it excited their fears, yet it afforded an opportunity, during his absence, of speaking to the steward concerning the money found in their sacks, which was the circumstance that at present most alarmed them. It was wise in them to be first in mentioning this

* John i. 38. xxi. 12.   † Psal. lxxvii. 2, 3.

matter, that if any thing was afterwards said by Joseph about it, they might appeal to the steward, and he could declare on their behalf that they without any accusation had, of their own accord, mentioned the whole business to him, and returned the money.—But the answer of the steward is surprising. He could scarcely have spoken more suitably, if he had been in the secret. I do not suppose he knew that these were Joseph's brethren: but he would know that they were his countrymen, and perceiving the interest which he took in them, and the air of mystery which attended his conduct towards them, he would be at no loss to conclude that there was no ill design against them. It is likely he knew of the money being returned by Joseph's order; and he knew his master too well to suppose that, whatever might be his design in it, he would hurt the poor men for what had been done by his own order. Moreover, this steward, whoever he was, appears to have learnt something by being with Joseph, concerning the true God, the God of the Hebrews. His answer is kind, and wise, and religious. "Peace be unto you, fear not: your God, and the God of your father hath given you treasure in your sacks: I had your money." q. d. 'Let your hearts be at rest: I will be answerable that you paid what was due; enquire no farther about it; providence brought it, and let that satisfy you.' To render them still more at ease, Simeon is brought out of his confinement, and introduced to them; which being done by the order of Joseph, was a proof of his being satisfied. The deliverance of the hostage was an evidence that all was well. Thus the *bringing again from the dead our Lord Jesus, that great Shepherd of the sheep,* was to us a token for good, and therefore is ascribed to God, as *the God of peace.**

Ver. 24, 25. While Joseph is busy about his concerns, and thinking how he shall conduct towards his brethren, they are busy in washing and dressing themselves to appear before him, and in preparing the present which they had brought for him. What was done required to be done in a handsome manner, and they are disposed to do their best.

Ver. 26, 27. And now, the business of the morning being over, Joseph enters. They immediately request his acceptance of the spices and sweet-meats of Palestine, sent as a present by their father, bowing down their faces to the earth, as they had done before. Thus Joseph's dream, which was repeated to him, is repeated in its fulfilment. There is nothing said of his

* Heb. xiii. 20.

manner of receiving it; but doubtless, it was kind and affable. And as they would present it in the name of their father, this would furnish a fair opportunity to enquire particularly respecting him; a subject on which his feelings would be all alive. It is charming to see how he supports the character which he had assumed, that of an Egyptian nobleman, who remembered what they had said about a venerable old man, of whose welfare he very politely enquires. "Is your father well, the old man of whom ye spake? Is he yet alive?"

Ver. 28. They answer very properly, and call their father *his servant*, and again make obeisance. Thus, in them, Jacob himself bowed down to Joseph; and thereby that part of his dream was also fulfilled.

Ver. 29. When Joseph first saw his brethren, his eyes, perhaps without his being aware of it, were fixed on Benjamin. (ver. 16.) But having detected himself in that instance, he appears to be more upon his guard in this. He receives the present, and converses with them about their father's welfare, without once turning his eyes towards his brother. But having done this, he thinks he may venture a look at him. He "lifted up his eyes, and saw his brother Benjamin, his mother's son, and said," to the others, but still under the same disguise, "Is this your younger brother, of whom ye spake unto me?" If he could have waited for an answer, they would doubtless have told him, it was . . . . but his heart is too full. No sooner is the question out of his lips, than, it may be with his hand upon his head, he adds, "God be gracious unto thee, my son!" Oh Joseph, on what tender ground dost thou presume to walk! This benediction, though under the disguise of a good wish from a stranger, was in reality an effusion of a full heart, which in this manner sought for ease. Genuine love longs to express itself.

Ver. 30. This little indulgence of affection however, had well nigh betrayed him. Ardent desires will always plead hard to go a little way, and presume not to go too far: but to indulge them a little, is like letting air into a room on fire. Joseph is so affected by what has passed, that he is obliged to quit the company, and retire into his chamber to weep there.

Ver. 31. Having recovered himself, and washed his face, that they might not discover his tears, he re-enters, and behaves with much hospitality and attention.

Ver. 32—34. And now, I apprehend, it was Joseph's wish to discover himself to his brethren, or rather to enable them to discover him. There are three things in particular while they were at dinner, each tending to this end, and as I conceive, designed for it.—(1.) The order of the tables. One for himself, one for the strangers, and one for the Egyptians. The design of this was to set them a thinking of him, and who he was, or could be? That the Egyptians and Hebrews should eat apart, they could easily account for: but who, or what is this man? Is he not an Egyptian? Yet if he be, why eat by himself? Surely he must be a foreigner . . . . . . (2.) The order in which they themselves were seated: it was "before him," so that they had full opportunity of looking at him; and what was astonishing to them, every man was placed "according to his age." But who can this be that is acquainted with their ages, so as to be able to adjust things in this order? Surely it must be some one who knows us, though we know not him. Or is he a diviner? Who or what can he be? They are said to have "marvelled one at another," and well they might. It is marvellous that they did not from hence suspect who he was.—(3.) The peculiar favour which he expressed to Benjamin, in sending him a mess five times more than the rest. There is no reason to suppose that Benjamin ate more than the rest; but this was the manner of shewing special favour in those times.* It was therefore saying in effect, 'I not only know all your ages, but towards that young man I have more than a common regard...... Look at all this, and look at me ..... Look at me, my brother Benjamin. Dost thou not know me?' But all was hid from them. Their eyes, like those of the disciples towards their Lord, seem to have been holden, that they should not know him. Their minds however are eased from all apprehensions, and they drank, and were cheerful in his company.

DISCOURSE LI.

THE CUP IN BENJAMIN's SACK.

GENESIS xliv. 1—17.

VER. 1, 2. As every measure which Joseph had yet taken to lead his brethren to discover who he was, had failed, he must now have recourse to another expedient to detain them. Their sacks are ordered to be filled, and their beasts laden with as much corn as they can carry, their money restored as before, and a silver cup put into the sack's mouth of the youngest. All this is

---

* See Chap. xlv. 22, 23.

love: but it is love still working in a mysterious way. The object seems to be to *detain* Benjamin, and to *try* the rest.

Ver. 3—6. Having stopped over the night, next morning at break of day, they are dismissed, and set off for home. After the treatment which they had received, we may suppose they were now all very happy. Simeon is restored, Benjamin is safe, and they are well laden with provision for the family. They would now be ready to anticipate the pleasure of seeing their father, and easing his anxious heart. But lo, another dark cloud presently overspreads their sky. They had scarcely got out of the city before the steward overtakes them, and charges them with the heinous crime of having stolen his lord's cup; a crime which would be highly offensive at any time, but much more so after the generous treatment which they had received. And to perplex them the more, he intimates as if his lord was a diviner, and therefore must needs be able to find out stolen property! Such we see was heathenism in those early ages; and such heathenism is found even in christian countries to this day.

Ver. 7—9. At this they are all thunderstruck with surprise: yet conscious of their innocence, they disown the charge, and express the utmost abhorrence at such a conduct. They appeal also to a fact with which the steward was well acquainted, namely, their having brought again the money which they had found in their sacks. Did this conduct comport with the character of thieves? 'Can it be supposed after this, say they, that we should steal out of my lord's house, either silver or gold? Search us throughout. On whomsoever it be found, let him die, and we will all consent to become slaves!' Such was their confidence that the charge was unfounded; and their invoking so severe a penalty, would be a presumptive evidence that it was so.

Ver. 10, 11. The steward, who is well aware of some profound design on the part of his master, though he knew not the whole of it, humours the thing with much address. He accedes to the mode of trial, but softens the penalty, proposing that none but the guilty should suffer, and he nothing more than the loss of his liberty. With this they readily acquiesce; and being stung with reproach, they with indignant sensations hastily unlade every man his beast, in order to disprove the charge. How willing is conscious innocence that things should be searched to the bottom; and how confident of an honourable acquittal!

Ver. 12. And now, search is made from the eldest to the youngest. Ten out of eleven are clear, and enjoy the triumph of a good conscience: but lo, in the sack of the youngest the cup is found! Every thing seems contrived to give an edge to their sorrow. It was when they were leaving Egypt, in high spirits, that they were stopped; and now when they have disproved the charge, except in one instance, lo, that instance fails them! To have their hopes raised within one step of an acquittal, and then to be at once disappointed, was very affecting. "Thou hast lifted me up, and cast me down."*

But what a confounding event! Could they really think for a moment that Benjamin had been guilty of the mean and wicked action which seems to be proved upon him? I do not suppose they could. They must remember having found the money in their sacks' mouths, when, nevertheless, they knew themselves to be innocent. Nay, and in searching for the cup, though nothing is now said of the money, yet they must have found it there a second time. All this would acquit Benjamin in their account. Yet what can they allege in his favour, without reflecting upon his accusers? The article is found upon him; which is a species of proof that seems

* Psal. cii, 10.

to admit of no answer. A deep and dismal silence therefore pervades the company. In very agony they rend their cloaths, reload their beasts, and return into the city. As they walk along, their thoughts turn upon another event; an event which had more than once occurred to their remembrance already. 'It is the Lord! We are murderers: and though we have escaped human detection, yet divine vengeance will not suffer us to live! There, though guilty, we were acquitted: here, though innocent, we shall be condemned!'

Ver. 13—17. Arriving at Joseph's house, where he still was, no doubt, expecting their return, Judah and his brethren fall prostrate before him. Judah is particularly mentioned as having a special interest at stake, on account of his suretyship: but neither he nor his brethren can utter a word, but wait in this humble posture to hear what is said to them.

Joseph having carried matters to this height, once more assumes the tone of a great man highly offended; suggesting withal, that they ought to have known that such a man as he could certainly divine, and that therefore it would be in vain to think of escaping with his property undetected.

As Judah appeared foremost on their entrance, Joseph's words would probably be directed to him, for an answer. But what answer can be given? The surety and the advocate is here dumb: for he had been a party in guilt; not indeed in the present instance, but in another. He can therefore only exclaim, "What shall we say unto my lord! What shall we speak; or how shall we clear ourselves? GOD HATH FOUND OUT THE INIQUITY OF HIS SERVANTS! Behold, we are my lord's servants; both we, and he also with whom the cup is found!" He did not mean by this to plead guilty to the charge; but neither dare he plead innocent, for that would have been accusing the offended party of having ensnared them, and so have made the case still worse; neither was he able to confront the evidence which appeared against his younger brother. What can he say, or do? He can only suggest that it is a mysterious providence, in which it appears to be the design of God to punish them for their FORMER CRIMES. This answer, which was manifestly dictated by what lay uppermost in all their minds, was at the same time the most delicate and modest manner in which he could possibly have insinuated a denial of the charge. While it implied their innocence in the present instance, it contained no reflexion upon others; but an acknowledgement of the divine justice, and a willingness to bear the punishment that might be inflicted upon them, as coming from above. If Joseph had really been the character which he appeared to be, such an answer must have gone far towards disarming him of resentment. How forcible are right words! The simple and genuine utterance of the heart is the most irresistible of all eloquence.

Joseph in answer, disclaims every thing that might wear the appearance of cruelty. No, he will not make bondmen of them, but merely of him on whom the cup was found. Such is the sentence. They may go about their business; but Benjamin must be detained in slavery. Alas, and is this sentence irrevocable? Better all be detained than him; for it will be the death of his father! What can be said, or done? The surety now becomes the advocate, and that to purpose. Such an intercession as that which follows we shall no where find, unless it be in His whom the Father *heareth always*. But I shall here close the present discourse, with only a reflexion or two on the subject.

1. We see a striking analogy between the conduct of Joseph towards his brother Benjamin, and that of Jesus towards his people. "Whom I love, I rebuke and chasten." Benjamin must

have thought himself peculiarly unhappy to be one day marked out as a favourite, and the next convicted as a criminal; and yet in neither instance able to account for it. It might teach him however, when the mystery came to be unravelled, not to draw hasty conclusions from uncertain premises; but to wait and see the issue of things, before he decided upon them. Such a lesson it will be well for us to learn from it. The Lord often brings us into difficulties that he may detain us, as I may say, from leaving him. Were it not for these, he would have fewer importunate applications at a throne of grace than he has. He does not *afflict willingly*, or *from his heart:* * but from necessity, and that he may bring us nearer to him.

2. We see also a striking analogy between Joseph's conduct towards his brethren, and that of the Lord towards us. In all he did, I suppose, it was his design to try them. His putting the cup into Benjamin's sack, and convicting him of the supposed guilt, would try their love to him, and to their aged father. Had they been of the same disposition as when they sold Joseph, they would not have cared for him. Their language would have been somewhat to this effect —'Let this young favourite go, and be a slave

* Lam. iii. 33.

in Egypt. If he have stolen the cup, let him suffer for it. We have a good riddance of him; and without being under the necessity of dealing with him as we did with his brother. And as to the old man, if he will indulge in such partial fondness, let him take the consequence.' But, happily, they are now of another mind. God appears to have made use of this mysterious providence, and of Joseph's behaviour, amongst other things, to bring them to repentance. And the cup being found in Benjamin's sack, would give them occasion to manifest it. It must have afforded the most heart-felt satisfaction to Joseph, amidst all the pain which it cost him, to witness their tender concern for Benjamin, and for the life of their aged father. This of itself was sufficient to excite, on his part, the fullest forgiveness. Thus God is represented as *looking upon a contrite spirit*, and even overlooking heaven and earth for it.* Next to the gift of his Son, he accounts it the greatest blessing he can bestow upon a sinful creature. Now that on which he sets so high a value, he may be expected to produce, even though it may be at the expense of our present peace. Nor have we any cause of complaint, but the contrary. What were the suspense, the anxiety, and the distress of Joseph's brethren, in comparison of that which followed?

* Isai. lxvi. 1, 2.

And what is the suspense, the anxiety, and the distress of an awakened sinner, or a tried believer, in comparison of the joy of faith, or the grace that shall be revealed at the appearing of Jesus Christ? It will then be found that our light affliction, which was but for a moment, has been working for us a far more exceeding and eternal weight of glory.

DISCOURSE LII.

JUDAH's INTERCESSION.

GENESIS xliv. 18—34.

Joseph, in the character of a judge, has sternly decided the cause, that Benjamin, the supposed offender, should be detained a bondman, and the rest may go in peace. But Judah, the surety, wounded to the heart with this decision, presumes as an advocate to plead, not that the sentence may be annulled, but changed with respect to its object. It was a difficult and delicate undertaking: for when a judge has once decided a cause, his honour is pledged to abide by it. He must therefore have felt the danger of incurring his displeasure by attempting to induce him in that stage of the business to alter his purpose. But love to his father, and to his brother, with a recollection of his own engagement, impose upon him the most imperious necessity.

Ver. 18. Prompted by these sentiments, he approaches his judge. His first attempt is to conciliate him: "Oh my lord, let thy servant, I pray thee, speak a word in my lord's ears, and let not thine anger burn against thy servant: for thou art even as Pharaoh." This brief introduction was admirably calculated to soften resentment, and obtain a patient hearing. The respectful title given him, "my lord;" the entreaty for permission to "speak;" the intimation that it should be but as it were "a word;" the deprecation of his anger, as being in a manner equal to that of "Pharaoh;" and all this prefaced with an interjection of sorrow, as though nothing but the deepest distress should have induced him to presume to speak on such a subject, shewed him to be well qualified for his undertaking.

Ver. 19. And now, perceiving in his judge a willingness to hear, he proceeds, not by passionate declamations, and appeals to his generosity, but by narrating a simple tale, and then grounding a plea upon it. Truth is the best weapon wherewith to assail the heart, only let truth be represented in an affecting light. His object, remember, is to persuade the judge so far to reverse the doom, as to accept of him, the surety, for a bondman, instead of the supposed offender. Mark how every thing he says leads to this issue. "My lord asked his servants, saying, Have ye a father, or a brother?" Here the judge is gently reminded that the occasion of this unhappy young man coming at all into Egypt was what *he himself had said.* He does not mean to reflect upon him for it; but he might hope that merely this circumstance would have some weight in softening his resentment against him. It is observable however, that in repeating the questions of Joseph, or their own former answers to him, he does not confine himself to terms. Joseph did not say in so many words, Have ye a father, &c. . . . nor did they make answer in the exact form as is here repeated: but he pretends only to repeat the tenor of what passed, of the justness of which the judge himself would be well acquainted. Nor is this verbal deviation to be attributed merely to the failure of memory: for he avails himself of it to introduce every affecting circumstance that could possibly touch the heart, which if he had adhered to a mere verbal rehearsal, would have been lost. Of this the following words are a remarkable instance.

Ver. 20. "And we said unto my lord, we have a father, an old man, and a child of his old age, a little one; and his brother is dead, and he alone is left of his mother, and his father loveth him." All these things were said, I believe, either expressly or by implication, but *not in this order*. As they were said before, they were merely rays of light diffused in the air; but here they are reduced to a focus, which burns every thing before it! I need not repeat, how every word in this inimitable passage tells, how it touches every principle of compassion in the human mind; in short, how it rises, like a swelling wave, till it overcomes resistance, and in a manner compels the judge to say, in his own mind, 'Well, whatever this young man has done, he must not be detained!'

Ver. 21—29. Having already intimated that the coming of the lad was *occasioned* by the enquiries concerning the family, and made the proper use of that, the advocate proceeds another step, and reminds his judge that it was in *obedience to his command:* "Thou saidst, bring him down to me, that I may set mine eyes upon him." This circumstance, though it conveyed no reflection, any more than the former, yet would work upon a generous mind, not to distress an aged father by taking advantage of an affair which had occurred merely from a willingness to oblige him. To this he adds, that they discovered at the time a *reluctance*, on their father's account, to comply with this part of his request: but he would have no denial, protesting that "except their younger brother came with them, they should see his face no more." Nor was this all: not only did they feel reluctant on their father's account, but he when told of it on their return, felt a still *greater reluctance*. The manner in which he introduces his father's objection, repeating it in his own words, or rather in his own words at different times, reduced as to a focus, is amasing. 'We repeated, q. d. the words of my lord to our father; and when feeling the imperious calls of nature, he requested us to go again, and buy a little food, we answered him that we could not go without our younger brother; for we could gain no admittance except he were with us. On this painful occasion, thy servant our father addressed us as follows'—"Ye know that my wife bare me two sons. The one went out from me, and I said, surely he is torn in pieces, and I saw him not since. And if ye take this also from me, and mischief befal him, ye shall bring down my grey hairs with sorrow to the grave!"

To point out the force of this overwhelming argument requires a view of the human mind, when, like a complicate machine in motion, the various powers and passions of it are at work. The whole calamity of the family arising from obedience to the judge's own command; an obedience yielded to on their part with great reluctance, because of the situation of their aged father; and on his part with still greater, because his brother was as he supposed torn in pieces, and he the only surviving child of a beloved wife; and the declaration of a venerable grey-headed man, that if he lose him it will be his death .... was enough to melt the heart of any one possessed of human feelings. If Joseph had really been what he appeared, an Egyptian nobleman, he must have yielded the point. To have withstood it, would have proved him not a man, much less a man who "feared God," as he had professed to be. But if such would have been his feelings even on that supposition, what must they have been, to know what he knew? What work must it have made upon his mind to be told of Jacob's words: "My wife bare me two sons; and the one went out from me, and I said, surely he is torn in pieces!"

It is also observable with what singular adroitness Judah avoids making mention of this elder brother of the lad, in any other than his father's words. *He* did not say he was torn in pieces. No, he knew it was not so! But his father had once used that language, and though he had lately spoken in a manner which bore hard on him and his brethren, yet this is passed over, and nothing hinted but what will turn to account.

Ver. 30, 31. The inference of what effect the detention of Benjamin would have on the aged parent, might have been left for the judge to make; but it is a part of the subject which will bear a little enlargement, and that to a very good purpose: thus therefore he proceeds. "When I come to thy servant, my father, and the lad be not with us; (seeing that his life is bound up with the lad's life) it will come to pass, when he seeth that the lad is not with us, he will die: and thy servants shall bring down the grey hairs of thy servant, our father, with sorrow to the grave!"—The whole of this intercession taken together, is not one twentieth part the length of what our best advocates would have made of it in a court of justice; yet the speaker finds room to *expatiate* upon those parts which are the most tender, and on which a minute description will heighten the general effect. We are surprised, delighted, and melted with his charming parenthesis: "Seeing his life is bound up with the lad's life." It is true, it does not seem to inform us of any thing which we might not have known without it; but it represents what was before stated, in a more affecting light. It is also remarkable how he *repeats* things which are the most tender; as, " when I come, *and the lad be not with us* . . . . . it shall come to pass, when he seeth that *the lad is not with us*". . . . . . So also in describing the effect which this would produce: " When he seeth that the lad is not with us, *he will die;* and we shall bring down the grey hairs of thy servant, my father, *with sorrow to the grave.*" This last sentence also, not only repeats the death of the aged parent in a more affecting manner than the first, but contains a plea for Benjamin's release founded on the cruel situation of their being otherwise forced, in a manner, to become parricides!

Ver. 32—34. One plea more remains, and which will at once contain an apology for his importunity, and make way for what, with humble submission, he means to propose: this is, "Thy servant became surety for the lad unto my father;" and that it may make the deeper impression, he repeats the terms of it. "If I bring him not unto thee, let me bear the blame for ever." And now, having stated his peculiar situation, he presumes to express his *petition*. But why did he not mention that at first, and allege what he has alleged in support of it? Such might have been the process of a less skilful advocate: but Judah's feelings taught him better. His withholding that till the last, was holding the mind of his judge in a state of affecting suspense, and preventing the objections which an abrupt introduction of it at the beginning might have created. He might,in that case have cut him short, as he had done before, saying, "God forbid that I should do so: the man in whose hand the cup is found, he shall be my servant." But he could not refuse to hear his tale; and by that he was prepared to hear his petition. Thus Esther, when presenting her petition to Ahasuerus, kept it back till she had, by holding him in suspense, raised his desire to the utmost height to know what it was, and induced in him a predisposition to grant it.

But what is Judah's petition? That the crime may be passed over, and that they may all return home to their father? No: "Let thy servant, I pray thee, abide instead of the lad, a bondman to my lord, and let the lad go home with his brethren!" If we except the grace of another, and greater Substitute, never surely was there a more generous proposal! And when to this is added, the filial regard from which it proceeds, "for how shall I go up to my father, and the lad be not with me; lest peradventure, I see the evil that shall come on my father!" This in itself, distinct from all which had gone before it, was enough to overcome every objection.

DISCOURSE LIII.

JOSEPH MAKING HIMSELF KNOWN TO HIS BRETHREN.

GENESIS xlv

Ver. 1-3. The close of Judah's speech must have been succeeded by a solemn pause. Every heart is full; but every tongue is silent. The audience, if they understood the language, would be all in tears. The ten brethren, viewing the whole as the righteous judgement of God upon them, would be full of fearful amasement as to the issue. Benjamin would feel both for his dear father and his beloved brother, who had offered to give himself for him! But what saith the judge? How does he stand affected? I have no doubt but that he must have covered his face during the greater part of the time in which Judah had been pleading: and now this will not suffice. The fire burns within him, and it must have vent. "Cause every man (said he) to depart from me!" And then breaks out in a loud weeping, so that the Egyptians from without heard him. Their minds no doubt must be filled with amasement, and desire to know the cause of this strange affair; while the parties within would be still more confounded, to witness such a burst of sorrow from him, who but awhile before was all sternness and severity. But now the mystery is at once revealed, and that in a few words— I AM JOSEPH!!! DOTH MY FATHER YET LIVE? If they had been struck by an electrical shock, or the most tremendous peal of thunder had instantly been heard over their heads, its effect had been nothing in comparison of that which these words must have produced. They are all struck dumb, and as it were petrified with terror. If he had been actually dead, and had risen, and appeared to them, they could not have felt greatly different. The flood of thoughts which would at once rush in upon their minds is past description. No words could better express the general effect than those which are used: "They could not answer him; for they were troubled at his presence!"

Ver. 4—8. A little mind, amidst all its sympathy, might have enjoyed the triumph which Joseph now had over them who once hated him, and have been willing to make them feel it;

but he has made them feel sufficiently already; and having forgiven them in his heart, he remembers their sin no more, but is full of tender solicitude to heal their wounded spirits. "Come near unto me, saith he, I pray you. And they came near: and he said, I am Joseph your brother, whom ye sold into Egypt." This painful event he does not seem to have mentioned, but for the sake of convincing them that it was he himself, even their *brother* Joseph, and not another; and lest the mention of it should be taken as a reflection, and so add to their distress, he immediately follows it up with a dissuasive from overmuch sorrow. "Now therefore be not grieved, nor angry with yourselves, that ye sold me hither; for God did send me before you to preserve life. For these two years hath the famine been in the land: and yet there are five years in the which there shall be neither earing nor harvest. And God sent me before you to preserve a posterity in the earth, and to save your lives by a great deliverance. So now, it was not you that sent me hither, but God: and he hath made me a father to Pharaoh, &c."

In this soothing and tender strain did this excellent man pour balm into their wounded hearts. A less delicate mind would have talked of forgiving them; but he entreats them to forgive themselves, as though the other was out of the question. Nor did he mean that they should abuse the doctrine of providence to the making light of sin; but merely that they should eye the hand of God in all, so as to be reconciled to the event, though they might weep in secret for the part which they had acted. And it is his desire that they should for the present, at least, view the subject much in that point of light; which would arm them against despondency, and a being swallowed up of overmuch sorrow. Their viewing things in this light would not abate their godly sorrow, but rather increase it: it would tend only to expel the sorrow of the world which worketh death. The analogy between all this, and the case of a sinner on Christ's first manifesting himself to his soul, is very striking. I cannot enlarge on particulars: suffice it to say, the more he views the doctrine of the cross, in which God hath glorified himself, and saved a lost world, by those very means which were intended for evil by his murderers, the better it will be with him. He shall not be able to think sin on this account a less, but a greater evil; and yet he shall be so armed against despondency, as even to *rejoice* in what God hath wrought, while he *trembles* in thinking of the evils from which he has escaped.

Ver. 9—11. It is not in the power of Joseph's brethren to talk at present: he therefore talks to them. And to divert their minds from terror, and gradually remove the effects of the shock, he goes on to tell them they must make haste home to his father, and say thus and thus to him in his name; and invite him and all his family to come down forthwith into Egypt, where he and they shall be well provided for, during the five years' famine yet to come, and where he shall be near unto him.

Ver. 12—15. While he is thus talking with his brethren, they would be apt to suspect whether all could be true, and whether they were not in a dream, or imposed upon in some supernatural way. To obviate these misgivings of mind, he adds, "And behold, your eyes see, and the eyes of my brother Benjamin, that it is my mouth which speaketh unto you. And you shall tell my father of all my glory in Egypt".... The former part of this speech must needs have produced in him a fresh flood of tears. As to them, I know not whether they could weep at present. Nothing is said of the kind; and it is natural to suppose that they had too much fear as yet mingled with their sorrow, to admit of its being vented in this manner. He however, having made mention of *Benjamin,* cannot forbear falling upon his neck, and weeping over him: and Benjamin not feeling that petrifying guilty shock, which must have confounded them, fell upon his neck, and wept with him.

Joseph had said nothing to his brethren of forgiving them; but he would now express as much, and more, by his actions; giving an affectionate *kiss* to every one of them, accompanied with tears of tenderness. This appears more than any thing to have removed their terror, so that now they are sufficiently composed to "talk with him," if not to mingle their tears with his.

Ver. 16—24. The secret being once disclosed within-doors, soon got out; and the news of *Joseph's brethren being come*, flies through the city, and reaches the palace. Pharaoh and his court too, are well pleased with it; or if there were any who might envy Joseph's high honour, they would not dare to express it.

In other cases, Pharaoh had left every thing to Joseph; and Joseph knowing what he had done, and the confidence which he possessed, had given orders in this case; yet to save his feelings in having to invite his own relations, as it were to another man's house, as well as to express the gratitude of the nation to so great a benefactor, the king in this instance comes forward, and gives orders himself. His orders too were more liberal than those of Joseph: he had desired them to bring with them all the property they had; but Pharaoh bids them to disregard their stuff, for that the good of all the land of Egypt was theirs. Joseph had said nothing about the mode of conveyance; but Pharaoh gives orders for waggons, or chariots, as the word is sometimes rendered, to be sent to fetch them.

Joseph however, in executing these orders, gives fresh testimonies of affection, not only in furnishing them with "provisions by the way," but to each man changes of raiment, and to Benjamin his brother three hundred pieces of silver, and five changes of raiment. And to his honoured father, though he could not on account of business go and fetch him, yet he sends him the richest present, viz. ten asses laden with the good things of Egypt, and ten she asses laden with corn, and bread, and meat for him by the way. These things might not be all necessary: Jacob would need no more for himself than any other individual of the family; but as we saw in the mess which was sent to Benjamin, this was the mode at that time of expressing peculiar affection. To all this kindness he added a word of counsel. "See that ye fall not out by the way." Joseph had already heard from Reuben some severe reflections on his brethren,* and might suppose that such things would be repeated when they were alone. One might be accused of this, and another of that, till all their minds would be grieved and wounded. But he that could find in his heart to love them, after all their unworthy conduct, gives them, as I may say, *a new commandment that they should love one another!*

Ver. 25—28. And now the young people betake themselves to their journey, and in a little time arrive at their father's house. Jacob had doubtless been looking and longing for their return, and that with many fears and misgivings of mind. If the matter was announced as suddenly as it is here related, it is not surprising that "Jacob's heart fainted, and that he believed them not!" It must appear too much to be true. The suddenness of the transition would produce an effect like that of fire and water coming in contact: and though he had suspected that Joseph had not been fairly treated by his brethren, yet he never seems to have doubted but that he was dead. It would appear therefore at first as if they meant to tantalize him. Per-

* Chap. xlii. 22.

haps too, we may partly account for this incredulity from the aptness there is in a dejected mind to believe what is against him, rather than what is for him. When they brought him the bloody garment, he readily believed, saying, Joseph no doubt is torn in pieces! But when good news is told him, it seems too good to be true!

They went on however, and told him of all the words of Joseph, that is, of the invitations which he sent by them; and as a proof, pointed to the waggons which were come to take him down. The sight of these overcomes the incredulity of the patriarch, and revives his spirit. "It is enough, said he: Joseph my son is yet alive. I will go and see him before I die!" . . . Yes, this was enough, not only to remove his doubts, but to heal his wounded heart, to set all right, to solve all mysteries, and to satisfy his soul. He had no more wishes on this side the grave. No mention is made of how he received the gifts, or what he said of his son's glory: it was enough for him that he was alive. The less must give way to the greater . . . . He seems to have considered death as near at hand, and as though he had nothing to do but to go and see him, and, like old Simeon by the Saviour, depart in peace.* But he must live a few years longer, and reflect upon the wisdom and goodness of God in all these mysterious events.

DISCOURSE LIV.

JACOB's GOING DOWN INTO EGYPT.

GENESIS xlvi.

The patriarch having resolved to go and see his beloved Joseph, soon gets ready for his journey, and takes with him "all that he had." It was generous in Pharaoh to propose his leaving the stuff behind him, but Jacob was not elated with the riches of Egypt, and might wish to put his friends to as little expence as possible. Those things which Pharaoh would call "stuff," might also have a peculiar value in his esteem, as having been given him in answer to prayer.† What is given us by our best friend, should not be set at nought.

But does not Jacob acknowledge God in this undertaking? It is a very important one, to him, and to his posterity. Surely he does not "use lightness" in such an affair; and "the

* Chap. xlvi. 30.   † Chap. xxviii. 20.

thing which he purposeth, is not according to the flesh."* No, he will solemnly invoke the divine blessing; but not till he had gone one day's journey. He had doubtless privately committed his way to God, and we hope was satisfied as to the path of duty; but he might have a special reason for deferring his *public* devotions till he should arrive at Beersheba. This was a distinguished spot: what had there taken place would tend to assist him in his approaches to God. It was there that Abraham, after many changes and trials, " called on the name of the everlasting God ;" and there that Isaac had the promise renewed to him, " built an altar, and called also upon the name of Jehovah."† This therefore shall be the place where Jacob will offer a solemn sacrifice, and invoke the divine blessing on himself and his children.

Arriving at the appointed place towards evening, he and all his company stop; and having reared an altar, or repaired that which had been built aforetime, " offered sacrifices to the God of his father Isaac." Jacob in his approaches to God, did not forget to avail himself of the covenant made with his forefathers, and of the promises already on record. His coming to this place seems to have been with the very design,

* 2 Cor. i. 17. † Gen. xxi. 33. xxvi. 23—52.

that his eyes, in beholding the surrounding objects, might assist his mind, and affect his heart in the recollection. Nor must we in ours forget to avail ourselves of the covenant of God in Christ, in which is all our salvation. The remembrance of the godliness of our predecessors, also, in like circumstances with ourselves, may have a happy influence on our devotions. It is sweet to a holy mind to be able to say, "He is my God, and I will exalt him: my father's God, and I will build him a habitation!"

Ver. 2—4. Jacob having closed the day by a solemn act of worship, retires to rest; and, as in a former instance, God appeared, and spake to him in visions of the night; calling him twice by name, "Jacob, Jacob!" To which the patriarch answers, "Here am I," ready to hear what God the Lord will speak unto his servant. And he said, "I am God." To one so well acquainted with the divine character as Jacob was, this would be cheering; especially as it would indicate his acceptance of the sacrifice, and his being with him in the way he went. It would seem enough for a godly mind to know that God is with him. But in compassion to Jacob it is added, " the God of thy father. " As such he had sought him; and as such he found him. This language amounted to a renewal of the covenant of Abraham, that *God would bless, and make him a blessing; and that in him, and his seed, all the nations of the earth should be blessed.* And lest this should be thought too general, it is further added, " Fear not to go down into Egypt; for I will there make thee a great nation. I will go down into Egypt; and I will also surely bring thee up again: and Joseph shall put his hand upon thine eyes." Though Jacob's affection to Joseph made him resolve at first to go and see him, yet it is likely he had afterwards some misgivings of mind upon the subject. Abraham went once into Egypt; but he left it under a cloud, and never went again. Isaac, in a time of famine, was forbidden to go.* And though Jacob had sent his sons to buy corn, yet it did not seem to be the place for him. But God removes his fears, and intimates that Egypt is designed to be the cradle of that great nation which should descend from his loins. They were idolaters, and should prove in the end oppressors; but the promise of God to " go with him " was enough. Neither temptation nor persecution need dismay us when we are led into it by the Lord: if he lead us into it, we may hope that he will keep us in it. The Lord in promising Jacob that he would "surely bring him up again," did not mean that he himself should come back

* Chap. xxvi. 2.

again alive; but that his posterity should, after becoming a great nation. With respect to himself, he was given to expect that his beloved Joseph should survive him, and be present at his death to *close his eyes*. But his descendants should be brought back with a high hand: and as what was spoken of bringing him up again, respected them, so that of going down with him, extended to them also.

Ver. 5—7. After so signal an instance of mercy, Jacob can leave Beersheba with a cheerful heart. He is now so far advanced in life however, as to be glad of a carriage to convey him, and of all the kind and dutiful assistance of his sons to accommodate him. Time was when he wanted no accommodation of this sort; but set off on a much longer journey with only a "staff:" but sixty years, toil and trouble, added to the seventy which had gone before, have reduced him to a state of feebleness and debility. Nature is ordained to decay: but if grace do but thrive, it need not be regretted. It is wisely and mercifully ordered, that the strong should bear the infirmities of the weak; and that those who in infancy and childhood have been borne by their parents, should return the kindness due to them under the imbecility of age.

In taking all his substance, as well as all his kindred, he would cut off occasion from those who might be disposed, at least in after times, to reproach the family with having come into Egypt empty handed, and to throw themselves upon the bounty of the country.

Ver. 8—27. The names of Jacob's descendants, who came with him into Egypt, are here particularly recorded. Compared with the families of Abraham and Isaac, they appear to be numerous, and afford a prospect of a great nation: yet compared with those of Ishmael and Esau, they are but few. Three and twenty years ago there was " a company of Ishmaelites," who bought Joseph: and as to Esau, he seems to have become a nation in a little time. We see from hence that the most valuable blessings are often the longest ere they reach us. The just shall live by faith.

There seems to be some difference between the account of Moses and that of Stephen, in Acts vii. 14. Moses says, "All the souls that came with Jacob into Egypt, which came out of his loins, besides his sons' wives, were threescore and six." (ver. 26.) And "all the souls of the sons of Jacob which came into Egypt," i. e. first and last, including Jacob himself, his son

Joseph, and his two sons Ephraim and Manasseh, who came in his loins, "were threescore and ten." (ver. 27.) But Stephen says, "Joseph called his father Jacob to him, and *all his kindred*, threescore and fifteen souls." Moses speaks of him and those who *descended from his loins*, to the exclusion of *his sons' wives;* but Stephen of his "kindred" in general, which would include them.

Ver. 28. Drawing nigh to Egypt, Judah is sent before to apprise Joseph of his father's arrival. Judah had acquitted himself well in a former case of great delicacy, and this might recommend him in the present instance. He who could plead so well for his father, shall have the honour of introducing him. It is fitting too that the father of the royal tribe, and of the Messiah himself, should not be the last in works of honour and usefulness, but rather that he should have the pre-eminence. When enquiry was made in the times of the Judges, "Who shall go up first against the Canaanites?" The Lord answered, "Judah shall go up."*

Ver. 29. Joseph, on receiving the intelligence, makes ready his chariot to go and meet his father: for being in high office he must act

---

* Judges i. 1, 2.

accordingly, else another kind of carriage, or perhaps a staff only, would have satisfied him, as well as his father; but situations in life often impose that upon humble minds which they would not covet of their own accord. The interview is as might be expected, tender and affecting. The account is short, but appropriate. He presents himself to his venerable father; but, unable to speak, "fell upon his neck and wept a good while!" And who that reflects on the occasion can forbear to weep with him?

Ver. 30. As to the good old man, he feels so happy that he thinks of nothing but dying. Perhaps he thought he should die soon: having enjoyed as much as he could desire in this world, it was natural now to wish to go to another. Having seen all things brought to so blessed an issue, both in his circumstances and in the character of his children, it is not surprising that he should now desire to quit the stage. *Lord, now let thy servant depart in peace; for mine eyes have seen thy salvation!* Yet Jacob did not die for seventeen years; a proof this, that our feelings are no certain rule of what shall befal us.

Ver. 31—34. As soon as the tenderness of the interview would permit, Joseph kindly intimates to his father and his brethren what was proper to be done, as to their being introduced to the king; and that they might be prepared for that piece of necessary formality, he gives them some general instructions what to answer. And here it is observable, how careful he is to keep them clear of the snares of Egypt. A high-minded young man would have been for introducing his relations into posts of honour and profit, lest they should disgrace him. But Joseph is more concerned for their purity, than their outward dignity. 'I will go before you, (says he) and will tell the king that you are *shepherds*, and have been so all your lives, and your fathers before you. This will prevent his making any proposals for raising you to posts of honour in the state; and he will at once feel the propriety of assigning you a part of the country which is suited to the sustenance of your flocks and herds, and where you may live by yourselves uncontaminated by Egyptian customs. And, when you come before the king, and he shall ask you of your occupation, then do you confirm what I have said of you: and as the employment of a shepherd is meanly accounted of in Egypt, and those that follow it are despised, and reckoned unfit for the higher offices of the state, this will determine the king to say nothing to you on that subject, but to grant you a place in Goshen.'

Thus while men in general are pressing after the highest stations in life, and sacrificing every thing to obtain them, we see a man who had for nine years occupied one of these posts, and felt both its advantages and disadvantages, carefully directing his dearest friends and relations into another track; acting up to Agur's prayer, "Give me neither poverty nor riches; but give me food convenient." The cool and sequestered path of life is the safest, happiest, and most friendly to true religion. If we wish to destroy our souls, or the souls of our children, let us seek for ourselves and them great things: but if not, it becomes us, having food and raiment, therewith to be content. A rage for amassing wealth, or rising to eminence, is a whirlpool in which millions have perished.

DISCOURSE LV.

JOSEPH's CONDUCT IN THE SETTLEMENT OF HIS BRETHREN, AND IN THE AFFAIRS OF EGYPT.

GENESIS xlvii.

Ver. 1, 2. Joseph having adjusted matters with his father and his brethren, with respect to their appearance before the king, takes with him five of the latter, and introduces them. His object is not merely a compliance with the rules of respect which were proper on such an occasion, but to obtain for them a residence in Goshen, where they might pursue their usual avocations, and be near unto him. To this end he mentions that they were then in that part of the country, with their flocks and their herds; hoping that this might induce the king to consent to their continuance there.

Ver. 3, 4. The young men appearing before Pharaoh, he asked them, as Joseph supposed he would, what was their occupation? A very proper question to be put by a magistrate to young men at any time; but the object in this case seems to have been to ascertain what posts in the state they were qualified to fill. He took it for granted that they were of some lawful calling; and every government has a right to require that those who enjoy its protection should not be mere vagrants, but by their industry contribute in some way to the public good. Their answer accords with their previous instructions: they were " shepherds, both they and their fathers." To this they added what was their wish, if it might please the king, which was, not to be naturalised, but merely to *sojourn* for a season in the country, with their flocks and their herds, which were starved out by the severity of the famine in their own land. This language implies their faith in the divine promises; for they that say such things declare plainly that they seek another country. It would also tend to second the endeavours of Joseph, in removing from the king's mind all thoughts of promoting them to places of honour, and obtaining for them a residence in Goshen. Their answer concludes with an express petition for this object.

Ver. 5, 6. Pharaoh turning himself to Joseph, with much politeness and frankness, thus addressed him. ' Thy father and thy brethren are come unto thee: the land of Egypt is before thee. In the best of the land, in the land of Goshen, seeing they prefer it, let them dwell. And as to promoting them, it does not seem to suit their calling, or their inclinations, to be raised in the manner which I might have proposed on their behalf: I will therefore leave it to you to make them happy in their own way. If there be one or more of them better qualified for business than the rest, let them be appointed chief of my herdsmen.'

Ver. 7—10. The grand object being accomplished, all hearts are at rest, and now Joseph introduces to the king his aged father; not upon business, but merely in a way of respect. When the young men were presented, they *stood* before him; but Jacob, in honour of his years, and in compassion to his infirmities, is placed upon a *seat*. The first object that meets his eyes is Pharaoh, sitting in his royal robes before him. The sight of a prince who had shewn such kindness to him and his, in a time of distress, calls forth the most lively sensations of gratitude, and which he is prompted to express by a solemn blessing! How befitting, and how affecting is this! It was reckoned by the apostle as a truth "beyond all contradiction, that the less is blessed of the better," or greater. In one respect Pharaoh was greater than Jacob, but in another Jacob was greater than him; and Jacob knew it, and thought it no presumption to act upon such a principle. He was a son of Abraham, whose peculiar honour it was, that he and his posterity should be blessings to mankind. "I will bless thee, and thou shalt be a blessing." He was also himself a man who "as a prince, had power with God and men, and prevailed." The blessing of such a man was of no small account: for God suffered not the words of his servants to fall to the ground.

It would seem at first sight, as if Pharaoh was not struck with the blessing, but merely with the venerable aspect of the man, and therefore proceeded to enquire his age: but I incline to think he was chiefly struck with the former. He must have perceived a wide difference between this, and any thing he had ever met with from the Egyptian sages; something heavenly and divine; and as the steward appeared to be well acquainted with the religion of the family, telling the brethren that "their God and the God of their father had given them the treasure in their sack's;"* so we may suppose was Pharaoh himself. He would see also in this solemn blessing, in which Jacob no doubt made use of the name of the Lord, something perfectly correspondent with what might have been expected from the father of "a man in whom was the Spirit of God." If he felt the force of these things, it would overcome him, and render him scarcely able to speak; and hence it would be natural, in order to recover himself, to turn the conversation upon a less affecting topic, enquiring, "How old art thou?" The answer to this question is very pathetic and impressive: "The days of the years of my pilgrimage are a hundred and thirty: few and evil have the days of the years of my life been, and have not attained unto the days of the years of the life of my fathers, in the days of their pilgrimage." We have a

* Chap. xliii. 23.

comment upon this answer, in Heb. xi. 13, 14, where it is called a "confession," and its implication is insisted on: "They that say such things declare plainly that they seek a country." We may see in it a charming example of spirituality, and how such a state of mind will find a way of introducing religion, even in answer to the most simple and common questions. We go into the company of a great man, and come away without once thinking of introducing religion: nay, it would seem to us almost rude to attempt it. But wherefore? Because of our want of spiritual-mindedness. If our spirits were imbued with a sense of divine things, we should think of the most common concerns of life in a religious way; and so thinking of them, it would be natural to speak of them. Jacob, in answer to this simple question, introduces several important truths, and that without any force or awkwardness. He insinuates to Pharaoh, that he and his fathers before him were strangers and pilgrims upon the earth—that their portion was not in this world, but in another—that the life of man, though it extended to a hundred and thirty years, was but a few days—that those few days were mixed with evil: all which, if the king properly reflected on it, would lead him to set light by the earthly glory with which he was loaded, and to seek a crown which fadeth not away. It is admirable to see how all these sentiments could be suggested in so prudent, so modest, so natural, and so inoffensive a manner. If Pharaoh was affected with Jacob's blessing him, and wished by his question to turn the conversation to something less tender, he would be in a manner disappointed. He is now in company with a man, who, talk on what he will, will make him feel; and yet it shall be in a way that cannot hurt him: for he says nothing about him, but speaks merely of himself.

Having thus made a suitable *confession*, the patriarch, whose heart was full, could not take leave of the king without repeating his solemn blessing. Whether Pharaoh ever saw him again, we are not told: but if what was then said had a proper effect, he would remember this interview as one of the most interesting events of his life.

Ver. 11, 12. Joseph having obtained the consent of the king, places his father and his brethren in the situation he intended, and there continued to nourish and cherish them, "as a little child is nourished." And thus he is made, more than at the birth of Manasseh, to forget all his toil, and all the distresses which he had met with in his father's house.

Ver. 13—26. The sacred writer informs us, as a matter by the bye, of the state of things in Egypt during the remaining five years of famine, under Joseph's administration. The famine was so sore in the land, that to purchase the necessaries of life, the inhabitants first parted with all their money; and not only they, but the countries adjacent; so that the king's treasury became greatly enriched. And when money failed, their cattle were required; and last of all their lands, and their persons, save only that the lands of their priests, or princes, were not sold: for being according to the laws of the country considered as a part of the royal household, they were not under the necessity of selling their estates, but were participants of all the advantages which Pharaoh derived by Joseph.

This part of Joseph's conduct has been thought by some very exceptionable, as tending to reduce a nation to poverty and slavery. I am not sure that it was entirely right, though the parties concerned appear to have cast no reflexion upon him. If it were not, it only proves that Joseph, though a good and great man, yet was not perfect. But difference of time and circumstances may render us incompetent to judge of his conduct with accuracy. The following remarks, if they do not wholly exculpate him from blame, may at least serve greatly to extenuate the evil of his conduct.—(1.) He does not appear to have been employed by the country, but by the king only, and that for himself. He did not buy up corn during the plentiful years, at the public expense, but at that of the king, paying the people the full price for their commodities, and as it would seem, out of the king's private purse.—(2.) If the Egyptians had believed the word of God, as the king did, they had the same opportunity, and might have laid by grain enough, each family for itself, during the seven plentiful years, fully to have supplied their own wants during the years of famine. But it seems they paid no regard to the dreams, nor to the interpretation, any more than the antediluvians did to the preparations of Noah. All the plenty which had been poured upon them, according as Joseph had foretold, did not convince them: the only use they made of it was to waste it in luxury as it came. It was just therefore, that they should now feel some of the consequences.—(3.) In supplying their wants, it was absolutely necessary to distribute the provisions not by *gift*, but by *sale;* and that according to what we should call the market price: otherwise the whole would have been consumed in half the time, and the country have perished.—(4.) The slavery to which they were reduced was merely that of being tenants to the king, and who accepted of one-fifth of the produce for his rent. Indeed it was scarcely possible for a whole nation to be greatly oppressed, without being driven to redress themselves; and probably what they paid in after-times as a rent, was much the same thing as we pay in taxes, enabling the king to maintain his state, and support his government, without any other burdens. There is no mention, I believe, in history, of this event producing any ill effects upon the country.—Finally: Whatever he did, it was not for himself, or his kindred, but for the king, by whom he was employed. The utmost therefore that can be made of it to his disadvantage, does not affect the disinterestedness of his character.

Ver. 27, 28. The sacred historian now returning to Israel, informs us that they " dwelt in Goshen, and had possessions, and grew and multiplied exceedingly;" and this during the lifetime of Jacob, who lived seventeen years in Egypt. The vision which he had at Beersheba contained an intimation that he should die in that country, else we may suppose he would have been for returning as soon as the famine had subsided: but Jacob is directed as by the cloud in the wilderness.

Ver. 29—31. And now the time drawing nigh that Israel should die, he sends for his son Joseph, and engages him by a solemn oath to bury him not in Egypt, but in the sepulchre of his fathers. This request was not merely the effect of natural affection, but of faith. As it was by faith that Joseph gave commandment concerning his bones, doubtless this arose from the same principle. The patriarch relying on the covenant made with his fathers, and believing that his posterity would hereafter possess the land, wished to lie amongst them, and to have his body carried up to take a kind of previous possession on their behalf. To this request of his father, Joseph readily consents. The venerable man, however, is not yet at the point of death, but is desirous of setting things in order, that when he comes to die he may have nothing else to think about.

DISCOURSE LVI.

JOSEPH's INTERVIEW WITH HIS DYING FATHER, WITH THE BLESSING OF HIS SONS.

GENESIS xlviii.

Ver. 1. Jacob did not die immediately after having sent for his son Joseph; but he seems at that time to have been confined to his "bed," and probably it was by the same affliction which issued in his death. Joseph, as soon as he was told of his father's being sick, without waiting to be sent for another time, proceeded to the place, and took his two sons to obtain his dying benediction.

Ver. 2. On entering the house, his name is announced; the mention of which gives the venerable patriarch a portion of new life. He " strengthened himself, and sat upon the bed." And now we may expect to hear something worthy of attention. The words of dying men to their children are, or should be, interesting, especially of good men, and still more of men inspired of God.

Ver. 3. The man of God has neither time nor strength to lose in ceremony: he comes therefore immediately to the point. "God almighty, said he, appeared unto me at Luz in the land of Canaan, and blessed me, and said unto me, Behold I will make thee fruitful, and multiply thee; and I will make of thee a multitude of people, and will give this land to thy seed after thee, for an everlasting possession."—Observe, (1.) The appearance at Luz, or Bethel,* if it were not the first time in which God had made himself

---
* Chap. xxviii.

known to Jacob, it was certainly the most remarkable epoch in his life: and almost all that had gone before it, was nothing, or worse than nothing.—(2.) Though the mention of Luz, or Bethel, must ever be sweet to Jacob, and though he could have told what a support the promise there made had been to him through the pilgrimage of life; yet he confines himself at present to the aspect which it bore to his posterity, whom he was now about to bless. The promise made to Abraham's seed involved all the goodness intended for the world in after ages; and this occupies the chief attention of Jacob. The dying words of David dwell upon the same thing: the everlasting covenant, which contained *all his salvation and all his desire*, was that in which God had promised of his seed to raise up the Messiah, whose kingdom should endure to all generations. To see the good of his chosen, to rejoice in the gladness of his nation, and to glory with his inheritance, is enough for a servant of God: and for an aged parent, after seeing much evil in his family, to be able to take leave of them in the full expectation of the divine blessing attending them, is a death which better characters than Balaam might wish to die.—(3.) The mention of Canaan to Joseph was designed to draw off his attention from a permanent settlement in Egypt, and to fix his faith upon the promise; that, like his fathers before him, he might pass his life as a pilgrim till it should be accomplished.

Ver. 4—7. And now, having given this general intimation to Joseph, he solemnly adopts his two sons, Ephraim and Manasseh, as his own, constituting them two tribes in Israel. Thus Joseph had a double portion, the first birthright being taken from Reuben, and given unto him.[*] And thus his sons, as well as himself, were taught to fix their faith and hope not in Egypt, whatever might be their expectations as the descendants of Joseph by an Egyptian princess, but in Canaan, or rather in the promise of the God of Israel. The mention of the death and burial of Rachel might be partly to add another motive of attachment to Canaan, to Joseph; and partly to account for this double portion conferred upon him; she being in the most proper sense his wife, and he in a sense his first-born son.

Ver. 8—11. Jacob had made mention of Ephraim and Manasseh before, but he had not seen them. Lifting up his eyes, he perceives two young men standing by the side of his beloved Joseph, and enquires who they are. "They

---

[*] 1 Chron. v. i. 2.

are my sons, said Joseph, whom God hath given me in this place." On this he requests them to be brought unto him, that he might bless them. He could scarcely see them, for his eyes were dim of age; but his heart was full of tenderness towards them for their father's sake, and for the sake of the hope of which they were heirs: therefore he kissed and embraced them. And being full of holy affection, he looks back upon his past sorrows, and admires the grace of God towards him and his. "I had not thought," said he to Joseph, " to see thy face; and lo, God hath shewed me also thy seed." How much better is God to us than our fears! Only let us wait with faith and patience, and our desponding thoughts will be turned into songs of praise.

Ver. 12—14. After this affectionate embrace, Joseph brought forth the two young men from between his father's knees, and bowed himself with his face to the earth, in token of thankfulness for the kindness conferred upon himself and his sons, and in expectation of a further blessing. And having probably observed the order in which his father had spoken of them, putting Ephraim before Manasseh, (ver 5.) he wished to correct it as a mistake, snd therefore placed the young men according to their age, Ephraim towards Israel's left hand, and Manasseh towards his right hand, and in this manner presented them before him. But the conduct of the patriarch was not thus to be corrected. God, from whom the blessing proceeded, directed him in this case to cross hands. Nor is this the only instance in which the order of nature is made to give way to that of grace; for of this, Jacob himself had been an example.

Ver. 15, 16. In this attitude Jacob proceeds to bless the lads. "And he blessed Joseph, and said, God, before whom my fathers Abraham and Isaac did walk, the God which fed me all my life long unto this day; the Angel which redeemed me from all evil, bless the lads! And let my name be named on them, and the name of my fathers, Abraham and Isaac; and let them grow into a multitude in the midst of the earth." —Observe, (1.) Though Ephraim and Manasseh were each constituted heads of tribes, yet they were blessed *in the person of their father Joseph:* "He blessed Joseph, &c." In this, as in many other instances, God would exemplify the great principle on which he designed to act in blessing mankind in the name and for the sake of another. —(2.) Jacob, though now amongst the Egyptians, and kindly treated by them, yet makes no mention of their gods, but holds up to his posterity *the living and true God.* In proportion as Egypt was kind to the young people, such would be their danger of being seduced: but let them remember the dying words of their venerable ancestor, and know from whence their blessedness cometh.—(3.) The God whose blessing was bestowed upon them was not only the true God, but *the God of their fathers;* a God in covenant with the family, who loved them, and was loved and served by them. " God, before whom my fathers, Abraham and Isaac, did walk." How sweet and endearing the character; and what a recommendation of these holy patterns to the young people! Nor was he merely the God of Abraham and Isaac, but Jacob himself also could speak well of his name; adding, " The God who fed me all my life long unto this day!" Sweet and solemn are the recommendations of aged piety. " Speak reproachfully of Christ," said the persecutors to Polycarp, when leading him to the stake. " Eighty six years I have served him," answered the venerable man, " during all which time he never did me any injury: How then can I blaspheme him who is my King, and my Saviour?" Hearken, oh young people, to this affecting language! It is a principle dictated by common prudence, " Thine own friend, and thy father's friend, forsake not:" and how much more forcibly does it apply to the God of your fathers!—(4.) This

God is called "the Angel who redeemed him from all evil." Who this was it is not difficult to decide. It was the Angel, no doubt, with whom Jacob wrestled and prevailed, and concerning whom he said, "I have seen God face to face, and my life is preserved.*—(5.) The blessing of God under all these endearing characters is invoked upon the lads, their forefathers' names put upon them, and abundant encrease promised to them. Surely it is good to be connected with them that fear God: yet those only who are of faith will ultimately be blessed with their faithful predecessors.

Ver. 17—20. Joseph's enjoyment of this sweet and solemn blessing was sadly interrupted by the unpleasant circumstance of his father's crossing his hands, and he could not refrain from respectfully remonstrating. Thus our frail minds are liable to be ruffled by some trivial event, even on the most solemn occasions, and so to lose the advantage of some of the happiest opportunities. Jacob however is not to be dissuaded. He had been guided by an unseen hand; and like Isaac, after having blessed him, he could not repent. "I know it my son, said he, I know it.... He shall be great; but his younger brother shall be greater than he." God is as

* Chap. xxii. 24—30.   Hos. xii. 2.

immutable as he is sovereign. It does not become us to contend with him; and it is to the honour of Joseph that as soon as he perceived his father knew what he did, believing him to be directed from above, he acquiesced. Hence the patriarch went on without further interruption, saying, "In thee shall Israel bless, saying, God make thee as Ephraim, and as Manasseh!"

Ver. 21. A word or two more to Joseph, and the present interview is closed. "I die," said Israel; "but God shall be with you, and bring you again into the land of your fathers." All that he had said before tended to break off their attachment to Egypt, and to fix their faith in the divine promise: such also was the design of these words. How satisfactory it is to a dying saint to consider that God lives, and will carry on his cause without him, as well as with him. The great JOHN OWEN, two days before he died, which was in 1683, a time when popery and arbitrary power threatened to overspread the land, thus wrote in a letter to a friend—"I am leaving the ship of the church in a storm; but whilst the great Pilot is in it, the loss of a poor underrower will be inconsiderable."

Ver. 22. One more special token of love is added to Joseph's portion, namely, a parcel of ground which had been originally bought of the sons of Hamor; but as it would seem, being seized by some of their descendants, Jacob was necessitated to recover it by force of arms.* This portion he gave to Joseph, and the tribe of Ephraim afterwards possessed it.† The hazard at which this portion was obtained would no doubt endear it to Joseph; for we prize those things which they who were dear to us acquired at a great expense. On this principle we have often been admonished to hold fast our civil liberties. On this principle especially, it becomes us to value our religious advantages, for which so much blood has been shed. And on this principle we are called to prize, more than any thing, the hope of the gospel, to obtain which our Saviour laid down his life!

DISCOURSE LVII.

JACOB's BLESSINGS ON THE TRIBES.

GENESIS xlix.

VER. 1, 2. Jacob having blessed Joseph's sons, and feeling that he drew near his end, sent for the rest of his children, that he might in the

* Chap. xxxiii. 18—20.   † John iv. 5.

same prophetic style declare to them what should befal them, and their posterity after them. The solemn manner in which he called them together, and bespoke their attention, shews, that being under a divine inspiration, he would deliver things of great importance; and such as, corresponding in many instances not only with the meaning of their names, but with their personal conduct, would furnish matter for reflection and encouragement.

Ver. 3, 4. "Reuben" being his first-born son, is first addressed. He is reminded of his superior advantages. He was the first effect of "his might," or "the beginning of his strength;" and to him as such naturally belonged "the excellency of dignity, and the excellency of power." But as Esau, and others, forfeited the birthright, so did Reuben. His character answered not to the dignity of his situation. He is charged with being "unstable as water." The word is used, I believe, in only three more places in the old testament,* and in them it is rendered light, or lightness; denoting not only a readiness to turn aside for want of solid principles, but that species of levity in particular which belongs to a lascivious mind, and which is ordinarily denominated *looseness*, or *lewdness*. Such

* Judges ix. 4. Jer. xxiii. 32. Zeph. iii. 4.

was the spirit of Reuben, or he could not have acted as he did towards Bilhah, his father's wife.* The manner in which the patriarch expatiates upon this crime, shews how heinous it was in his eyes. "Thou wentest up to thy father's bed: then defiledst thou it".... and to shew his abhorrence, he turns away from him, and addresses his other sons, as it were by way of appeal: "He went up to my couch!" For this lewd behaviour he is told, "he shall not excel." It is a brief mode of expression, alluding to the excellency of dignity and of power which pertained to him as the first-born; and denotes that all his advantages were reversed by his base conduct, and that which would otherwise have been a blessing, was turned into a curse. The double portion was taken from him, and given as we have seen, to Joseph,† the kingdom to Judah, and the priesthood to Levi; and thus the excellency of dignity, and the excellency of power, were separated from his tribe, which never sustained any conspicuous character in Israel.

From what is said of Reuben we may learn, the offensive, the debasing, and the dangerous nature of that light-mindedness which indulges in filthiness, and foolish talking, jesting, and lewd behaviour. Such appears to have been the

* Chap. xxxv. 22.   † Chap. xlviii. 5—7.

spirit of the false prophets in the times of Jeremiah, whose "lies and lightnes" caused God's people to err.* And such, alas, is the character of too many who sustain the name of christians, and even of christian ministers, at this day! Assuredly they shall not excel; and without repentance, wo unto them, when God shall call them to account!

Ver. 5—7. The next in order of years are "Simeon and Levi," who also in their posterity, shall reap the bitter fruits of their early sins: and having not only descended from the same parents, but been associates in iniquity, they, according to the meaning of the name of the latter, are joined together in receiving the reward of it. At the time when these young men, with equal treachery and cruelty, took each his sword and slew the Shechemites, Jacob expressed his disapprobation of the deed: but now he censures it in the strongest terms. "Instruments of cruelty are in their habitations;" which is saying that they were bloody men. Ainsworth renders it *sojourning habitations*, which heightens the sin, as being committed in a place where they had no residence, but by the courtesy of the country. "Oh my soul, come not thou into their secret; unto their assembly, mine honour, be not thou

* Jer. xxiii. 32.

united!" What we cannot prevent, we must be contented to disavow, having no fellowship with the unfruitful works of darkness. These young men took counsel together: they were very careful to conceal their design from Jacob their father, knowing beforehand that he would be certain to oppose their schemes; and now Jacob is no less careful to disavow all connexion with them in the horrid deed. Such a disavowal, though it must give the most acute pain to the sons, yet was worthy of the father. A great deal of evil had been wrought in his family: but be it known to all the world, by the dying testimony which he bears against it, that it was altogether contrary to his mind. And let young people hear and know, that the crimes of youth will sometime find them out. If they repent, and obtain mercy, as there is reason to believe these young men did, yet they shall reap the bitter fruits of their sin in the present life: and if they remain impenitent, tribulation and anguish will overtake them in the next.

The crime of these brethren is thus described: " In their anger they slew a man," even Hamor, king of the country, as well as Shechem his son; and that not in the open field of contest, but by assassination! Anger in general is outrageous; but in young men, whose immature judgment and slender experience afford but little check to it, it is commonly the most mischievous. " In their self-will they digged down a wall," or as some render it, " they houghed the oxen." The former would express their breaking into houses to murder the inhabitants, and the latter their cruelty, extending even to the dumb animals. Anger, when accompanied with " self-will," rages like fire before the wind. How important is the government of one's own spirit: and considering what human nature is, what a mercy it is that the wrath of man is under the divine controul! If Simeon and Levi had not repented of this sin, it is likely that the curse, like that of Noah on Canaan, would have fallen upon their persons; but as it was, it alights only upon their dispositions and actions—" Cursed be their anger, for it was fierce; and their wrath, for it was cruel!" God in mercy forgave them, but took vengeance of their inventions. And with respect to the tribes of which they were the heads, they were to be *divided and scattered in Israel.* " The Levites," says Mr. Henry, " were scattered throughout all the tribes, and Simeon's lot lay not together, and was so strait that many of that tribe were forced to disperse themselves in quest of settlements and subsistence. This curse was afterwards turned into a blessing to the Levites; but the Simeonites, for Zimri's sin, had it bound on. (Num. xxv.)

Shameful divisions are the just punishment of sinful unions and confederacies."

Ver. 8—12. From what was said of the three first sons, the rest might begin to tremble, lest the whole should be a succession of curses instead of blessings. But in what respects "Judah," we see a glorious reverse. The blessedness of this tribe principally consists in that blessing which was in it, the Lord Messiah. "Judah," saith the patriarch, " thou art he whom thy brethren shall *praise:* thy hand shall be in the neck of thine enemies, and thy father's children shall bow down before thee." In the first sentence, allusion is had to his name, which signifies *praise;* and the meaning of the whole is, that this tribe should be distinguished first by its victories over the Canaanites, and afterwards by its being the tribe which God would choose to bear *rule* in Israel. Hence also it is represented in verse 9, by a *lion,* the most majestic of animals, and the proper emblem of royalty. Much of this prophecy was doubtless fulfilled in David, and his successors: but all was prefigurative of the Messiah, who, in allusion to this passage, is called " the Lion of the tribe of Judah."* In him all that is said of Judah is eminently fulfilled. He is indeed the object of praise; his hand has been in the neck

* Rev. v. 5.

of his enemies, and before him his brethren have bowed down. Grappling with the powers of darkness, we see him as a lion tearing the prey: ascending above all heavens, as a lion going up from the prey: and seated at the right hand of God, as a lion couchant, or at rest after his toils, where it is at the peril of the greatest monarchs to rouse him up.*

That which before is represented under strong figures, is in ver. 10, declared plainly; viz. that Judah should be the governing tribe, and that its chief glory should consist in the Messiah, who should descend from it: yea, the very time of his coming is marked out. The sceptre, or government, should not depart from Judah, nor a lawgiver from between his feet, until Shiloh come. The government departed from ten tribes out of the twelve, during the reign of Hezekiah, and has never been restored: but Judah continued to rule with God. At length they also were carried into captivity; yet God's eye was upon them, and in seventy years they were restored. And notwithstanding the many overturnings of the diadem, by the successive monarchies of Persia, Greece, and Rome, yet it continued till the coming of Christ. The theocracy then being dissolved, and the power

* Psal. ii. 10—12.

given to him whose right it was, Judah in a few years ceased to be a body politic, or to have any government of its own. If there be such a thing as an irrefragable proof, surely this is one, that SHILOH, the *peaceable*, the *prosperous*, the *Saviour* is come; and it is a mark of judicial blindness and hardness of heart in the jews, that they continue to disbelieve it.

Of Shiloh it is added, "To him shall the gathering of the people be." As all the tribes of Israel gathered together, and anointed David king in Hebron; so all the tribes of man shall sooner or later submit to the kingdom of Christ. During his ministry, his enemies touched with fear and envy, were ready to say, Behold the world is gone after him! And no sooner was he lifted up upon the cross, than he began to draw all men unto him. Many myriads of his own countrymen, who had before seen no form nor comeliness in him, now believed in him. Now also began to be fulfilled all the prophecies which had gone before of the calling of the gentiles. For such was the value of his sacrifice and mediation, that it was considered as a light thing for him merely to raise up the tribes of Jacob: he must be a light to the gentiles, and God's salvation to the ends of the earth. Nor has this promise yet spent its force: probably the greater part of it is yet to be fulfilled. What is foretold to the church in the sixtieth of Isaiah, of multitudes of all nations gathering together unto her, will be the accomplishment of this promise concerning Christ; for those that are gathered to her are gathered first to him.

The 11th and 12th verses are expressive of the great plenty of wine and milk which the tribe of Judah should possess. Vines, even the most choice, were there so common, that you might have tied your beasts to them, as you would here tie them to an elm or ash; or so abundantly productive, that it should be the ordinary practice to bind a colt to the vine, and load it with its fruits. Wine with them should be so plentiful, that you might have washed your garments in it. The inhabitants, even the common people, might drink of it till their eyes were red; and such an abundance should there be of the milk of kine, that their teeth might be white with it. This *plenty* of milk and wine may have a farther reference however, to the plenty of evangelical blessings under the reign of the Messiah, in the same manner as the dominion ascribed to Judah has an ultimate reference to his dominion. The language used by Isaiah, "Come, buy wine and milk, without money and without price,"* certainly refers to the great

* Isai. lv.

plenty of those articles in the land of promise, and seems to allude to the very words of Jacob in this prophecy.

Ver. 13. The blessing of "Zebulun" predicts the situation of that tribe in the promised land. They should be a maritime people, bordering upon the sea of Galilee eastward, and upon the Mediterranean on the west. Its "border reaching unto Zidon," does not mean the city, but the country of that name, that is, Phenicia. If the future settlement of the tribes had been of *choice*, it might have been said that they contrived to fulfil these predictions; but being *by lot*, the hand of God is seen both in them and their accomplishment. There seems to be a distinction made between Zebulun being "*at* the haven of the sea," and his being "*for* a haven of ships." The first may denote his advantages; and the last the benevolent use he should make of them, opening his harbours for the reception of distressed mariners. We have all our situations and advantages according to the will of God, and should be concerned to employ them to a good purpose. This tribe had also its disadvantages: being far from the seat of divine instruction, its inhabitants are described as *sitting in darkness*. Upon them however, the light of the gospel, by the personal ministry of our Lord, sprung up.*

Ver. 14, 15. Next follows the blessing of "Issachar." The character given to this tribe intimates that it should be addicted to husbandry, as Zebulun was to the dangers and perils of the sea. He is compared to a "strong ass, couching down between two burdens;" not on account of any thing mean in him, but for his industrious, patient, and peaceable disposition. This situation would neither require the heroic qualities of Judah, nor the enterprising ones of Zebulun; and his disposition should coincide with it, preferring the fruits of peace and industry, though obliged to pay tribute for them, to the more splendid fortunes of commerce, or triumphs of war. Some men would pronounce Issachar, and those of his mind, mean spirits: but let not this part of the community be thought light of. If it be less brilliant, it is not less useful than the others. The king is served by the field. No condition of life has fewer temptations, nor is any more friendly to true religion. Though the people of this tribe were still and peaceable; yet there were amongst them *men who had understanding of the times, and who knew what Israel ought to do:* nor was it any dispa-

* Matt. iv. 15, 16.

ragement to their *brethren to be at their commandment.**

Ver. 16, 17. The blessing of "Dan" alludes to the meaning of his name, that is, *judging*, and signifies that he should maintain his authority; not only in respect of his rank amongst the tribes, but in the preservation of order in his own territory. His being compared to "a serpent by the way, that biteth the horse-heels so that his rider shall fall backward," would seem to intimate that the Danites would however be a subtil and mischievous people, carrying on their wars more by stratagem and artful surprise, than by conflict in the open field. Such were the wars of Sampson, who was of this tribe, against the Philistines.

Ver. 18. Here the man of God seems to have paused, perhaps on account of bodily weakness; and lifting up his eyes to heaven, said, "I have waited for thy salvation, O Lord." Had these words followed the blessing of Judah, we might have supposed that the salvation he referred to was the coming Messiah: but standing where it does, it appears to have been merely a sudden ejaculation, sent up at the close of his pilgrimage, in a view of being delivered from all its evils. It

* 1 Chron. xii. 32.

serves to shew the state of the patriarch's mind; and that while pronouncing blessings on his posterity in respect to their settlement in the earthly Canaan, he was himself going to a better country, even a heavenly one. When he thought that Joseph was dead, he talked of *going down into his grave mourning;* and afterwards, when he found him alive, he seems as if he could have descended into it rejoicing :* but it was not for him to determine the time of his departure, but to " wait" his appointed time. Old age is the time for the patience of hope to bear its richest fruits; and a pleasant thing it is to see this and other graces in full bloom, while the powers of nature are falling into decay.

Ver. 19. The patriarch resuming his subject, proceeds to bless the tribe of " Gad." His name signified a *troop,* and it is intimated that they should be a warlike people. Their situation was east of Jordan, where they were exposed to the incursions of the neighbouring nations; particularly those of the Moabites, the Ammonites, and the Syrians. But it is predicted, that however they might for a time be overcome, yet they should overcome at last; and this exactly accords with their history.† In this blessing we

* Chap. xxxvii. 35. xlvi. 30.   † Judges x, xi, xii,
1 Chron. v. 18—22.

see not only an example of the life of every believer, but the wisdom of God in so ordering it, as an antidote to presumption and despair. Present defeats have a tendency to preserve us from the one, and the promise of being finally victorious, from the other.

Ver. 20. Next follows "Asher," whose name signifies *the happy,* or *the blessed,* or *making happy;* and with his name corresponds his blessing. The meaning is, that his lot should be a rich one; yielding not only necessaries, but dainties, even royal dainties. Such is the lot of a few in this world, and it is well that it is but a few; for while men are what they are, great fulness would soon render them like Sodom and Gomorrha.

Ver. 21. "Napthali" is described by "a hind let loose," and is said to "give goodly words." The description would seem to hold up, not a warlike tribe, nor a tribe noted for its industry; but rather a people distinguished by their vivacity, timidity, and softness of manners. The diversity of natural dispositions contributes, upon the whole, to human happiness. Men have their partialities, some to this, and others to that; and if their wishes could be gratified, would commonly shape all others by their own favourite model: but after all, variety is the best. As the delicate could not subsist without the laborious and the resolute; so many a rugged spirit, both in the world and in the church, would be worse than useless, but for its union with others more gentle and affectionate.

Ver. 22—26. We next come to the blessing of "Joseph;" and on this the patriarch delights to dwell. His emblem, taken from the meaning of his name, is that of "a *fruitful bough*, situated by a well, by which its roots were watered, and its branches caused to run over the wall." The meaning is, that his posterity should be distinguished by their extraordinary encrease. But now the imagery is dropped, or rather changed, and his personal history reviewed. He was attacked at an early period, as by a band of archers, who "sorely grieved him, shot at him, and hated him." There is a delicacy in his speaking of the brethren, (who were standing by) in the third person rather than the second, and that under a figure: let him express it however in what form he will, they must feel it. He adds, "But his bow abode in strength, and the arms of his hands were made strong by the mighty God of Jacob: from thence is the shepherd, the stone of Israel." As his brethren were a band of archers, he is described under the same character, but as one only against many. Their arrows were those of "hatred;" but his of love, overcoming evil with good. They strengthened one another in an evil cause; but he was strengthened by "the mighty God of Jacob." In these particulars, surely, he was a type of Christ; and still more in being, by the blessing of the God of Jacob, "the shepherd and stone of Israel;" *providing* for their wants, and *supporting* their interests.

In blessing Joseph, Jacob feels his heart enlarged; pouring upon him the blessings of almighty God, the God of his father; blessings of heaven above, blessings of the deep that lieth under, blessings of the breasts, and of the womb; intimating also that his power of blessing when terminating on him exceeded that of his fathers, extending not only to the land in general, but to the very mountains, on which his children should reside. And that which drew upon his head all these blessings was the painful, but endearing circumstance, of his having been "separated from his brethren."

Joseph considered his separation as ordered of God for the good of others,* and he seems all along to have acted upon this principle: but a life so spent shall lose nothing by it in the end.

* Chap. xlv. 7, 8.

God will take care of that man, and pour the richest blessings upon his head, whose great concern it is to glorify him, and do good in his generation. Jacob felt much for Joseph's "separation." The spirit of his benediction was, By how much he was afflicted for the sake of others, by so much let him be blessed and honoured, and that to the latest posterity! And such is the mind of God, and all his true friends, concerning a greater than Joseph. *For the suffering of death, he is crowned with glory and honour—And I heard the voice of many angels round about the throne, and the living creatures, and the elders: and the number of them was ten thousand times ten thousand, and thousands of thousands; saying,* WORTHY IS THE LAMB THAT WAS SLAIN, *to receive power, and riches, and wisdom, and strength, and honour, and glory, and blessing!—Unto Him that loved us, and washed us from our sins in his own blood, and hath made us kings and priests unto God and his Father; to* HIM *be glory and dominion, for ever and ever. Amen.**

Ver. 27. The last blessing is that of "Benjamin." Of him it is said, "He shall ravin as a wolf: in the morning he shall devour the prey, and at night he shall divide the spoil." In this we see that it should be a warlike tribe; and

* Heb. ii. 9. Rev. v. 11, 12. i. v, 6.

this it was, or it could not have resisted all the tribes of Israel in the manner it did, as recorded in the last chapters of Judges. But this is saying no more than might have been said of many of the heathen nations. If Jacob had been influenced by natural affection, there had doubtless been something tender in the blessing of Benjamin, as well as in that of Joseph: but he was guided by a spirit of prophecy, and therefore foretold the thing as it was.

Ver. 28. Such were the tribes of Israel, and such "the blessings wherewith their father blessed them." But how blessed them? It might be thought that the first three at least were cursed, rather than blessed. No, they were rebuked, but not cursed, nor cast off like Esau: they still continued among the tribes of Israel. It must have been very affecting for these brethren thus to stand by and hear, as from the mouth of God, what would be the consequences of their early conduct on their distant posterity: and as their minds were now tender, it may be supposed to have wrought in them renewed repentance, or gratitude, as the subject required.

Ver. 29—33. The patriarch now gives directions concerning his burial. He desires to be interred, not in Egypt, but in the burying place at Mamre, where lay Abraham and Sarah, Isaac and Rebecca, and Leah. If he had been governed by natural affection, he might have chosen to lie by the side of his beloved Rachel: but he *died in faith,* and therefore requests to mingle dust with his fathers, who had been heirs with him of the same promise. Having said all he had to say, he chearfully resigned his soul into the hands of him that gave it, and was numbered with his departed ancestors.

Thus died Jacob; a man whose conduct on some occasions was censurable; whose life was filled up with numerous changes; but whose end was such that his worst enemies might envy.

DISCOURSE LVIII.

THE BURIAL OF JACOB, AND THE DEATH OF JOSEPH.

GENESIS l.

Ver. 1. We have seen the venerable patriarch yielding up the ghost; and now we see the expressions of affection towards him by the survivors. Let the memory of the just be blessed. It was revealed to Jacob in his life-time, that Joseph should "put his hand upon his eyes;" and Joseph not only did this, but in the fulness of his heart, "fell upon his face after he was dead, and wept upon him, and kissed him." This is all that we can do towards the most beloved objects, when death has performed his office. The mind is gone; the body only remains; and of this we must take a long farewell. Faith, however, looks forward to a joyful resurrection, and teaches us not to sorrow as those that have no hope.

Ver. 2. Joseph next proceeds to have his dead body embalmed with sweet spices. This was an art carried to great perfection in Egypt: the effects of it are not totally extinct even to this day. It was suitably applied in the present instance, not only as an honour done to a great and good man, but as a means of preserving the body from putrefaction, during its removal to Canaan.

Ver. 3. Nor was this the only honour that was paid to him. The family no doubt mourned very sincerely for him; and to express their respect for Joseph, the Egyptians, probably the court and the gentry, went into mourning; and not merely forty days, which was customary it seems for every one who had the honour of being embalmed, but in this instance, another month was added. The customs of polite nations, though often consisting of mere forms, yet serve in some instances to shew what should be. They express in this case a respect for departed worth, and a sympathy with afflicted survivors, weeping with them that weep.

Ver. 4—6. The days of formal mourning being ended, Joseph next proceeds to the burial of his father. But for this he must first obtain leave of absence from the king; and desirous of conducting the business with propriety, he applies to some of the royal household to make the request for him: not, as some have supposed, because it was improper for him to appear before the king in mourning apparel; for "the days of his mourning were past;" but with a view of honouring the sovereign, and cultivating the esteem of those about him. A modest behaviour is said to be rarely found in royal favourites: but by the grace of God it was found in Joseph. The plea he urged was nothing less than his being under a solemn oath, imposed upon him by the dying request of his father: a plea to which Pharaoh could make no objection, especially as it was accompanied with the promise of a return.

Ver. 7—11. We now behold the funeral procession. The whole family, (except their little ones, who with their cattle, were left behind) were, as we should say, the first followers; but all the elders of respectability, of the court, and of the country, with both chariots and horsemen, were in the train. It was "a very great company," not only in number, but in quality. For grandeur and magnificence it is said to be without a parallel in history. This great honour was not in consequence of any wish on the part of Jacob: all he desired was, to be carried by his sons, and buried in the land of promise. His desire was that of faith, not of ambition. But, as in the case of Solomon, seeing he asked for that which God approved, he should have his desire in that, and the other should be added to it. Thus God delights to honour those who honour him. And as it was principally *for Joseph's sake* that this great honour was conferred on his father, it shews in what high esteem he was held in Egypt, and serves to prove that whatever modern adversaries may say of his conduct, he was considered at the time as one of the greatest benefactors to the country.

Nothing remarkable occurred in the procession, till they came to the threshing-floor of Atad, which was within the land of Canaan, near to Jericho, and not many miles from the place of interment. Here they stopped, it would seem, for seven days, performing funeral obsequies, or "mourning with a great and sore lamentation." So great was it, that it drew the attention of the Canaanites, who, on seeing and hearing what passed, observed one to another, "This is a grievous mourning to the Egyptians;" (for such they considered them, seeing they came from Egypt) wherefore the name of the place was afterwards called, "Abel-Mizraim," *the mourning of the Egyptians.*

Ver. 12—21. Joseph and his brethren, having buried their father in the place where he requested to lie, return to Egypt, with the company which went with them. The pomp and hurry of the funeral, while it lasted, would occupy their attention; but this having subsided, the thoughts of the ten brethren were directed to other things. The death of great characters being often followed by great changes; conscious guilt being always alive to fear; and the chasm which succeeds a funeral, inviting a flood of foreboding apprehensions, they find out a new source of trouble: 'Peradventure, all the kindness hitherto shewn us has been only for our father's sake . . . . Peradventure, Joseph, after all, never forgave us in his heart . . . . and now our father is dead, so as not to be grieved by it, peradventure he will feel that hatred to us which we once felt to him; and if so, he will certainly requite the evil which we have done unto him.' Oh jealousy! Is it not rightly said of thee, Thou art cruel as the grave?

But how can they disclose their suspicions! To have done it personally, would have been too much for either him or them to bear, let him take it as he might. So they "sent messengers unto him," to sound him. We know not who they were; but if Benjamin were one of them, it was no more than might be expected. Mark the delicacy, and exquisite tenderness of the message. Nothing is said of their suspicions, only that the petition implies them: yet it is expressed in such a manner as cannot offend, but must needs melt the heart of Joseph, even though he had been possessed of less affection than he was.—(1.) They introduce themselves as acting under the direction of a mediator, and this mediator was none other than their deceased father. He commanded us, say they, before he died, that we should say thus and thus. And was it possible for Joseph to be offended with them for obeying *his* orders? But stop a moment. —May *we* not make a similar use of what our Saviour said to us before he died? He commanded us to say, *Our Father—forgive us our debts*. Can we not make the same use of this, as Jacob's sons did of their father's commandment?—(2.) They present the petition as *coming from their father:* " Forgive, I pray thee, the trespass of thy brethren, and their sin; for they did unto thee evil." And was it possible to refuse complying with his father's desire? The intercessor, it is to be observed, does not go about to extenuate the sin of the offenders; but frankly acknowledges it, and that if justice were to take its course, they must be punished. Neither does he plead their subsequent repentance as the ground of pardon; but requests that it may be done for *his* sake, or on account of the love which the offended bore to him.—(3.) They unite their own confession and petition to that of their father. It was certainly proper that they should do so: for though they no more plead their own repentance as the ground of forgiveness, than the mediator had done, yet it was fit they should repent, and acknowledge their transgressions, ere they obtained mercy. Moreover, though they must make no merit of any thing pertaining to themselves; yet if there be a character which the offended party is known to esteem above all others, and they be conscious of sustaining that character, it will be no presumption to make mention of it. And this is what they do, and that in a manner which must make a deep impression upon a heart like that of Joseph. "And now, we pray thee, forgive the

trespass of *the servants of the God of thy father!*"
It were sufficient to have gained their point, even though Joseph had been reluctant, to have pleaded their being children of the same father, and that father making it, as it were, his dying request: but the consideration of their being " the servants of his father's God," was overcoming. Were we to look back to some former periods of their history, we could not have considered them as entitled to this character: but since that time God had brought them through a series of trials, by means of which he had turned them to himself. And though they are far from considering their present state of mind as obliterating the guilt of their former crimes; yet knowing that Joseph was himself a servant of God, they knew that this consideration would make a deep impression upon him. It is no wonder, that at the close of this part of the story, it should be added, " And Joseph wept when they spake unto him !"

But this is not all: they go in person, and " fall before his face," and offer to be his " servants." This extreme abasement on their part seems to have given a kind of gentle indignancy to Joseph's feelings. His mind revolted at it. It seemed to him too much. " Fear not, saith he: for am I in the place of God?" As if he should say, It may belong to God to take vengeance: but for a sinful worm of the dust, who himself needs forgiveness, to do so, were highly presumptuous: you have therefore nothing to fear from me. What farther forgiveness you need, seek it of him.

Ver. 20, 21. There was a delicacy in the situation of the ten brethren in respect to this application to Joseph, as it would imply a doubt of his former sincerity. They were aware of this, and therefore in every thing they say, whether by messengers, or in personal interview, are careful to avoid touching upon that subject. Nor is there less delicacy in Joseph's answer. He does not complain of this implication, nor so much as mention it: but his answering them in nearly the same words as he had done seventeen years before, "Ye thought evil against me; but God meant it unto good, to bring to pass as it is this day, to save much people alive;" I say, his answering them in this language was saying in effect, 'Your suspicions are unfounded. What I told you seventeen years ago, I meant: and the considerations which then induced me to pass over it, induce me still to do the same. "Now therefore, fear ye not: I will nourish you, and your little ones." I will not be your *master*, but your brother, and as it were, your father.' In this manner did he "comfort them, and spake kindly unto them."

Ver. 22, 23. Joseph was about fifty six years old when his father died: he must therefore have lived fifty four years afterwards; during which period he saw Ephraim's children, of the third generation; and the grandsons of Manasseh were brought up, as it were, upon his knees.

Ver. 24—26. And now the time draws nigh that Joseph also must die; and like his worthy ancestors, he dies *in faith.*—(1.) He is persuaded of the truth of God to his covenant promises. "I die, saith he; and God shall surely visit you, and bring you out of this land, unto the land which he sware to Abraham, to Isaac, and to Jacob."—(2.) Under the influence of this persuasion he takes "an oath of the children of Israel;" that when they should depart from Egypt they would take his "bones with them." Such a desire might have arisen from merely a wish to mingle dust with his forefathers: but we are directed to attribute it to a higher motive. It is in reference to this exercise of faith, that his name is enrolled in the catalogue of believing worthies.* Having said all he wished

* Heb. xi. 22.

to say, "he died, being a hundred and ten years old; and they embalmed him, and he was put in a coffin in Egypt." As the burial of Jacob in Canaan would attract the minds of Israel to that country; so the depositing of Joseph in a moveable chest, together with his dying words, would serve as a memento, that Egypt was not their home.

CONCLUSION.

I HAVE endeavoured to intersperse reflections on the various subjects as they have occurred: but there are a few others which arise from a review of the whole, and with these I shall conclude.

First: *The truth of revelation, and its leading doctrines.* That which accounts for things as they are, or as they actually exist in the world, and that in such a manner as nothing else does, carries in it its own evidence. Look at things as they are, and look at this, and you will find that as face answereth to face in water, so doth the one answer to the other.

Look at the material creation around you; and ask the philosophers of all ages how it came into being. One ascribes it to a fortuitous assemblage of atoms; another conceives matter to have been eternal; another imagines God himself a material being. But Revelation, like the light shining upon chaos, dissipates in a few words all this darkness, informing us that, "In the beginning, God created the heavens and the earth."

Look at human nature as it now is; depraved, miserable, and subject to death. Ask philosophy to account for this. The task will be found to surpass its powers. None can deny the fact, that men are what they ought not to be: but how they came to be so, cannot be told. To say, as many do, that the stock is good, but that it gets corrupt in rearing, is to reason in a manner that no one would have the face to do in any other case. If a tree were found, which in every climate, every age, every soil, and under every kind of cultivation, brought forth the fruits of death, nobody would hesitate to pronounce it of a *poisonous nature*. Such is the account given us by revelation, and this book informs us how it became so. It is true, it does not answer curious questions on this awful subject. It traces the origin of evil as far as sobriety, and humility would wish to enquire. It states the fact, that God hath *made man upright*, and that he *hath sought out many inventions:* but there it leaves it. If men will object to the equity of the divine proceedings, and allege that what is in consequence of their first father's transgression, is on their part guiltless, they must go on to object. Every man's conscience tells him, he is accountable for all he does from choice, let that choice have been influenced by what it may; and no man thinks of excusing his neighbour in his ill conduct towards him, because he is a son of Adam. Out of their own mouth therefore will such objectors be judged.—But if the doctrine of the fall, as narrated in this book, be admitted, that of salvation by free grace through the atonement of Christ, will follow of course. I do not say that redemption by Christ could be inferred from the fall itself: but being revealed in the same sacred book, we cannot believe the one without feeling the necessity of the other.

Look at the page of history, and you will find yourselves in a world, of the existence of which you can find no traces till within about four thousand years. All beyond is darkness; and all pretensions to earlier records carry in them self-evident marks of fable. These things are accounted for in this book. If the world were destroyed by a flood, there could no nations have existed till a little before the times of Abraham. Nay, this book gives us the origin of all the nations, and calls many of them by the names which they sustain to this day.

Finally: Look at the antipathy which is every where to be seen between the righteous and the wicked, between them that fear God and them that fear him not. All the narratives which have passed under our review, as those of Cain and Abel, Enoch and his cotemporaries, Isaac and Ishmael, Jacob and Esau, are pictures of originals which the world continues in every age to exhibit. But this book traces this antipathy to its source; and gives us reason to expect its continuance till Satan and his cause shall be bruised under our feet.

Secondly: *The peculiar characters of sacred history.* It is the most *concise,* and yet *comprehensive* of any record that has ever yet appeared in the world. In the book of Genesis only, we have gone over the history of two thousand, three hundred, and sixty nine years. A common historian might have used more words in giving us an account of one of Nimrod's expeditions. Yet it is not like the abridged histories of human writers, which often contain a string of unconnected facts, which leave no impression, and are nearly void of useful information. You see human nature, as created, as depraved, and as renewed by the grace of God: you see the motives of men, and the reason of things, so as to enable you to draw from every story some important lesson, some warning, caution, counsel, encouragement, or instruction in righteousness.

CONCLUSION. 273

The reason of so much being included in so small a compass, is, it is *select*. It is not a history of the world, but of persons and things which the world overlooks. It keeps one great object always in view, namely, *the progress of the church of God*, and touches other societies and their concerns only incidentally, and as they are connected with it. The things which are here recorded are such as would have been mostly overlooked by common historians, just as things of the same kind are overlooked to this day. If you read many of even our Church Histories, you will perceive but little of the history of true religion in them. There is more of the genuine exercises of grace in a page of the life of Abraham, Isaac, or Jacob, than you will frequently find here in a volume. If the world overlooks God, and his cause, God in return overlooks them and theirs. His history holds up an Enoch, and preserves a Noah, while a world lying in wickedness is destroyed by an overwhelming flood. It follows an Abraham, an Isaac, a Jacob, and a Joseph, through all their vicissitudes, narrating the trials and triumphs of faith in these holy men; while the Ishmaels, the Esaus, and all who apostatised from the true God are given up, and lost in the great world. It traces the spiritual kingdom of God to its smallest beginnings, and follows it through its various obstructions; while the wars, conquests, and intrigues of the great nations of antiquity are passed over as unworthy of notice. In all this we see that the things which are highly esteemed amongst men, are but lightly accounted of by the Lord; and that He who hath heaven for his throne, and earth for his footstool, overlooks both in comparison of a poor and contrite spirit.

Lastly: *The slow, but certain progress, of the divine designs.* God promised Abraham a son when he was seventy five years old; but he was not born till he was a hundred. And when he is born, he lives forty years unmarried: and when married, under an expectation of great fruitfulness, it is twenty years more ere Rebecca bears children; and then it is not without earnest prayer. And now that he has two sons born, Jacob, in whom the promise is to be fulfilled, lives seventy five years single, and his life is a kind of blank: and when he goes to Padan-aram for a wife, he must wait seven years longer ere he obtains her: and when he has a family of children, they prove some of the worst of characters. The only one that is any way hopeful is taken away, he knows not how; and a long series of afflictions follow one upon another, ere any thing like hope makes its appearance. Yet all this while the Lord had promised, *I will surely do thee good;* and in the end the good is done. God's ways fetch an astonishing compass. His heart is large, and all his plans are great. He does not make haste to fulfil his counsels; but waits, and causes us to wait, the *due time.* But at that time they are all fulfilled.

We may observe a difference however, as to the time taken for the fulfilment of different promises. Those which were made to Abraham's other children, and which had no immediate relation to God's spiritual kingdom, as hath been remarked in the course of the work, were very soon accomplished, in comparison of that which was confined to Isaac. Small legacies are often received and spent before the heir comes to the full possession of his inheritance. And even those which are made to the church of God, and have respect to his spiritual kingdom, vary in some proportion to their magnitude. " God made promise of a son to Abraham : *five and twenty years* elapse ere this is accomplished. He also promised the land of Canaan for a possession to his posterity: there the performance required a period of *nearly five hundred years.* At the same time, Abraham was assured that the Messiah should descend from his loins, and that in him all the nations of the earth should be blessed: this promise was *nearly two thousand years* ere it came to pass. These events resemble the oval streaks in the trunk of a tree, which mark its annual growth: each describes a larger compass than that which precedes it, and all which precede are preparatory to that which follows. The establishment of Abraham's posterity in Canaan was a greater event than the birth of Isaac, and greater preparations were made for it. But it was less than the coming of Christ, and required less time and labour to precede it."

From this ordinary ratio, if I may so speak, in the divine administration, we are furnished with motives to patience, while waiting for the fulfilment of promises to the church in the latter days. The things promised are here so great and so glorious, that they may well be supposed to fetch a large compass, and to require a period of long and painful suspense ere they are accomplished. The night may be expected to bear some proportion to the day that succeeds it. It is a consolation however, that the night with us is far spent, and the day is at hand. The twelve hundred and sixty years of antichrist's dominion, and of the church's affliction, must needs be drawing towards a close: and a season so dark, and so long, augurs glorious times before us. We may have our seasons of despondency, like the patriarchs; but there will come a time, and that probably not very distant, when what is said of Israel in the times of Joshua, shall be fulfilled on a larger scale: *And the Lord gave them rest round about, according to all that he sware unto their fathers—There failed not aught of any good thing which* THE LORD *had spoken unto the house of Israel; all came to pass.*

ERRATA.

VOL I.

Page 4 line 1 *for* creations seem *read* creation seems
— 6 — 8 *for* the chaos *read* chaos
— 29 — 22 *for* impolite *read* unpolite
— 36 — 27 *for* its cause *read* the cause of them
— 53 — 12 *for* that was *read* that which was
— 64 — 25 *for* called after *read* called it after
— 141 — 8 *for* people *read* nations
— 171 — 9 *dele* for
— 199 — 2 *for* whorefore *read* wherefore
— 205 — 7 *read* laid it up
— 221 — 26 *dele* him
— 297 — 8 *for* Midiam *read* Midian

VOL. II.

Page 10 line 19 *for* running *read* union
— — 25 *for* without *read* with
— 22 — 6 *for* latter *read* ladder
— 63 — 2 *for* house *read* host
— — 5 *for* is truth *read* is a truth
— 64 — 14 *for* account *read* encouragement
— 85 — 8 *for* alleviate *read* extenuate
— 90 — 1 *for* acceeded *read* acceded
— 146 — 19 *for* yet will God *read* yet God will

www.ingramcontent.com/pod-product-compliance
Lightning Source LLC
Chambersburg PA
CBHW021713300426
44114CB00009B/119